Qian Qichen

Ten Ep

in Chin

Ten Episodes in China's Diplomacy

HarperCollins*Publishers*

HarperCollins books may be purchased for educational, business, or sales promotional
use. For information, please write: Special Markets Department, HarperCollins Publishers, 10 East 53rd Street, New York, NY 10022.

FIRST EDITION

Designed by Joy O'Meara

Printed on acid-free paper

Library of Congress Cataloging-in-Publication Data is available upon request.

ISBN-10: 0-06-085419-7
ISBN-13: 978-0-06-085419-5

05 06 07 08 09 ❖/RRD 10 9 8 7 6 5 4 3 2 1

CONTENTS

Foreword by Ezra F. Vogel   vii

Preface   xi

Introduction   xiii

1   Normalization of Sino-Soviet Relations   1

2   The Paris Conference on Cambodia   33

3   Flying to Baghdad   55

4   "Funeral Diplomacy" in Tokyo   83

5   The Road to Seoul   105

6   Withstanding International Pressure   127

7   From the Soviet Union to Russia   159

8   Fascinating Africa   191

9   Two Diplomatic Struggles over the Taiwan Question   231

10   The Return of Hong Kong and Macao   253

Appendixes: *Five Speeches at the School of International Studies, Peking University*   283

Index   339

FOREWORD

TEN EPISODES IN CHINA'S DIPLOMACY, by Qian Qichen, in which he describes his experiences as a diplomat, is the most detailed, informative, insightful account of recent Chinese foreign policy by any Chinese official or scholar.

Born in 1928, Qian Qichen has been the leading Chinese diplomat of his generation. He spent eight years in the Soviet Union, beginning in 1954, and served as ambassador to Guinea from 1974 to 1975. He held a number of important positions in the Ministry of Foreign Affairs before becoming vice minister (1982 to 1988) and foreign minister (1988 until 1997). He served as vice premier for ten years. He has served as a member of the Central Committee of the Communist Party and as a member of the Politburo.

For over two decades, beginning in the early 1980s, Minister Qian played a major role in China's foreign affairs on almost every continent. During this time he had contact with most of the world's leaders and senior diplomats. He played a major role in negotiations with Europe, the United States, the Middle East, and the Soviet Union (and later Russia).

The years when Qian Qichen served as vice minister and minister of foreign affairs, 1982 to 1997, were years when China greatly expanded its participation in world affairs, with the passing of Zhou

Enlai in 1976 and the end of the Cultural Revolution. Deng Xiaoping realized China's larger role when he launched a policy of reform and order to achieve the economic breakthrough that would raise the standard of living for the Chinese people. At the time, Deng could see that the Soviet Union's efforts to keep up with U.S. military advances were bleeding the country's resources, which could have been used to modernize the country. China, with its huge population and limited resources, needed to cooperate with other countries and with international organizations to proceed with modernization.

In 1977 Deng revived national entrance examinations for universities, which had an enormous impact on the selection and training of talented Chinese young people. Qian Qichen became vice minister just as members of the new, better-trained generation were entering the labor force. When Qian Qichen became vice minister, China had only a very small group of specialists on foreign affairs to draw from—almost no one who had studied in the West. However, after 1978, China paid more attention to the education of its young people, vastly expanding the teaching of English and other foreign languages, and sending vast numbers of students abroad for further training. By the mid-1980s, some of those who had studied abroad began to return to China, and took up positions in the government, in think-tanks and universities, as well as in the growing private sector. In a very short time, the large, well-educated population base and the revival of entrance examinations enabled China to develop specialists on all aspects of world affairs—the economy, law, finance, technology, the environment, international organizations, history, and the military. By the time Qian completed his term as foreign minister, he had vast numbers of talented, well-informed young people on whom he could draw. In his years of leadership in foreign affairs, Qian helped resolve border disputes with neighboring countries, thus providing a stable, peaceful environment.

One of the most difficult periods Qian faced was after the Tiananmen incident of 1989, when foreign countries imposed heavy sanctions on China. During this challenging time, Qian tried to implement Deng's efforts to keep a steady course that would gradually eliminate the sanctions. Qian had to deal with the Taiwan issue at a time when Taiwan's leaders pursued a policy of greater independence that was unacceptable to Beijing. In the early 1990s, as China prepared to resume sovereignty over Hong Kong, Qian had to respond to Governor Patten's efforts to change the agreements that had been reached previously to provide a smooth transfer of power in 1997.

Qian has served as honorary dean of the School of International Studies, Peking University. In this capacity, beginning in 2000, he has given annual lectures to students surveying the field of international relations, which are included in the appendixes to this volume.

In this book describing his experience in dealing with ten major issues, Qian Qichen provides a high level of concrete detail that sheds light on major issues in which he participated: the resumption of normal relations with the Soviet Union; Middle East crises; normalization of relations with Indonesia, South Korea, and South Africa; responding to Western sanctions after the Tiananmen incident of June 1989; the resumption of sovereignty over Hong Kong; and the Taiwan issue. The book also reveals how well informed Qian is on world matters and gives insight into how rapidly China has increased its understanding on global issues since it adopted its policies of openness. It gives perspective on how Chinese diplomats perceive the world. I know of no better volume for understanding how China views the world.

—EZRA F. VOGEL, HENRY FORD II RESEARCH PROFESSOR
OF THE SOCIAL SCIENCES, HARVARD UNIVERSITY

PREFACE

I AM VERY GLAD TO LEARN that the English edition of my book has gone to the press. An enormous number of people read English and may be found in almost every country. As the English edition is made available, the book will provide more people from different social, cultural, and ethnic backgrounds an opportunity to learn about China's diplomacy.

I must thank my old friend Mr. Brent Scowcroft, who encouraged me to produce an English version of the book, and offered valuable support. I would also like to thank the translators from the China Foreign Language Press for their excellent work. I must thank Professor Ezra F. Vogel, who did the careful proofreading of the English text in full. I am grateful to Mr. Rupert Murdoch for his support and to HarperCollins Publishers, particularly senior vice president Susan Weinberg and Mr. David Koral, for their willingness to help, without reservation. My thanks go as well to Ambassador Guo Jiading, who has made a final check on the full text of the translation. I also wish to thank Ambassador Yang Jiechi in the United States and his colleagues for their effective assistance in the related matters.

In this book, I have looked back on ten episodes during my diplomatic career, and included the transcripts of several speeches I made. It is not exactly a complete personal memoir, or a complete recounting of China's diplomatic experience during that period. In order to make each chapter complete, I have allowed some overlap between chapters. As for points of view, what I recorded in this book are major international events and how China saw them at the time. I fully understand that scholars, diplomats, and political figures of other countries may very well have their own perspectives.

As I noted in the foreword to the Chinese edition, I have made it a personal habit "not to leave a slip of paper, not a single word, in writing and to keep everything in mind." That is certainly true when I was doing underground Party work years ago. Later, when I became a diplomat, I did keep records of some documents and archives. These ten episodes are imprinted so deeply on my memory because I went through them personally. Yet, throughout the writing of the book, I did benefit from the able assistance of many who helped me check on the materials to make sure the facts and figures are correct and ensure the accuracy of my conclusions.

INTRODUCTION

ON MARCH 18, 2003, at the close of the Tenth National People's Congress, I officially retired. Replacing the old with the new is a law of nature. Moreover, it is a law beneficial to the development of my country and the progress of society. For leaders, stepping down can in a sense be regarded as a contribution to the revolutionary cause.

I was already seventy-five years old, well over retirement age. All I wanted of retirement was time—time to read books that I had always meant to read, and do things that I had always wanted to do. In fact, during the spring, I was inspired to write a poem about my feelings. It read in part: "In the mood of reminiscence of past events, I began reading a new book, free from the burden of official duties."

By "a new book" I did not necessarily mean a newly published book. To me, any book I have not read is new. So the new books I had in mind included the sages of the early Qin dynasty, "a hundred schools of thought contending," the wise men of ancient Greece and public debates; literature, history, philosophy, biography, memoirs—anything that is part of the wisdom of humankind. Some of these books, such as *A Brief History of Time* by Stephen W. Hawking, are difficult to understand, but they all give one food for thought. People often talk about taking a fresh worldview, and it seems to me that it is also necessary to take a fresh view of the universe. The universe is inconceivably vast, perhaps infinite. All things have their own laws. A man must, therefore, not be bound by his own experiences and thoughts.

As for "reminiscence of past events," I have never kept a diary. This abstention is a personal habit, a result of seven years of underground work for the Party in my young days. I do not rely on a single slip of paper; I do not put a single word in writing. Everything is in my mind.

From the 1980s to the early part of this new century, China's diplomacy withstood difficult tests and traveled along an uneven path. As a participant, I can see one picture after another when recalling those past events. Some scenes, which I experienced personally, flash back to me like close-ups in a film, unremittingly. Now I would like to write down in plain language my personal experiences of those events. I have no ambition to record them in a comprehensive way, but I have tried to be truthful and accurate. This book is neither a historical record nor a theoretical work. I call it simply *Ten Episodes in China's Diplomacy*.

JULY 30, 2003

Ten Episodes
in China's Diplomacy

1 NORMALIZATION OF SINO-SOVIET RELATIONS

An Important Decision

I ASSUMED THE POSITION OF VICE MINISTER of the Ministry of Foreign Affairs in May 1982 and took charge of affairs relating to the Soviet Union and Eastern Europe.

At that time, China and the Soviet Union were locked in a confrontation. The Soviet Union had deployed a million-strong force in the People's Republic of Mongolia and along the extensive border between itself and China. In the late 1970s, it had supported Vietnam's invasion of Cambodia and had invaded Afghanistan. These actions constituted a direct threat to the security of China.

There is a saying that "It takes more than one cold day to freeze the ice three feet thick." Thus despite the historical feud, from the 1950s to the 1980s Sino-Soviet relations can be categorized as ten years of debate from 1959 to 1969, ten years of confrontation from 1969 to 1979, and ten years of negotiation from 1979 to 1989. In this thirty-year period, there were both cold and hot wars.

But in early 1982, some subtle signs appeared, and certain changes began to brew between China and the Soviet Union.

It all started on March 24 of that year, when the Soviet leader Leonid Brezhnev gave a long speech in Tashkent, capital of the Soviet Republic of Uzbekistan. Though full of the usual attacks on China, his speech explicitly recognized China as a socialist country, stressed China's sovereignty over Taiwan, expressed a wish to improve relations with China, and proposed consultations between the two sides in order to adopt measures acceptable to both, so as to improve Sino-Soviet relations.

Comrade Deng Xiaoping immediately noted the content of Brezhnev's speech. At that time, negotiations between China and the United States on the issue of the latter's sales of weapons to Taiwan had made some progress, and the "August 17 Communiqué," which was the third of the three communiqués issued by China and the United States, was to be signed. A new framework of relations between China and the United States could be said to have been, by and large, established. The time was ripe to begin to improve relations between China and the Soviet Union.

Our analysis at the time was as follows. Since the Soviet Union had taken on a heavy burden by invading Afghanistan, and its global rivalry with the United States was growing more intense, its burdens were exceeding its capacity, and therefore it felt that it had to make a strategic adjustment. To thaw its frigid relationship with China would be a significant step in that direction. Objectively, this provided an opportunity for us to adjust our policy toward the Soviet Union.

Comrade Deng called the Foreign Ministry and instructed us to respond immediately to Brezhnev's speech. In those days, there was no formal system for press conferences. But I was director-general of the Information Department, and I had been considering appointing a spokesman. This was an opportunity for us to establish such a system, with a spokesman.

So the first press conference held at the Foreign Ministry took place on March 26, in the lobby of what was then the main building of the ministry. There was no special location for press conferences in the lobby; there were not even any seats. Some seventy to eighty foreign and domestic reporters had been invited. They all stood around me. My interpreter was Li Zhaoxing, who is the foreign minister as of this writing.

As the first spokesman for the foreign ministry, I made a brief statement consisting of only three sentences: "We have noted what Chairman Brezhnev of the Soviet Union said at Tashkent about the relations between China and the Soviet Union. We categorically refute the attacks on China in his speech. With regard to the relations between China and the Soviet Union and international affairs, we attach importance to the actual deeds of the Soviet Union."

After the statement, no questions were allowed, and we made it clear that if anyone tried to raise a question, no answer would be given. Thus ended the Foreign Ministry's first press conference.

Still, this unprecedented press conference and the short statement aroused great attention among domestic and foreign reporters. A reporter from the Soviet Union who was present gave me the thumbs-up sign and said, "Very good!" He had detected the unusual message in the statement.

The most important words in the statement were "noted" and "attach importance to." They implied that China was listening to what Brezhnev said and watching what he did. If Brezhnev's words were worth listening to, then obviously they included reasonable elements. In the past, China's attitude toward whatever the leaders of the Soviet Union said had been overall denunciation; we had simply turned a deaf ear. We had also turned a blind eye to what the Soviet leaders did—but now we wanted to watch what Brezhnev did; in other words, we wanted him to show us actual deeds.

The following day, the short statement was published in the middle of the front page of the *People's Daily*, indicating that despite its brevity, it was very important. It also—as mentioned above—drew wide international attention. Five major western news agencies and other foreign media covered the event and made profuse comments. One foreign news release said that this "prudent and subtle statement" was a sign of a possible change in the Sino-Soviet conflict after more than thirty years, and that such a change might alter the world situation.

That was not only the first time but also the last time I held a press conference in the capacity of spokesman for the Foreign Ministry. Since then, press conferences have become a regular practice of the ministry, held weekly. They are no longer events without seating. We eventually moved them to the International Club, where all the reporters could sit on chairs. Still later, the new Foreign Ministry building had a special hall for press conferences.

ONE HOT SUMMER DAY that same year, Comrade Deng invited a few top leading comrades and members of the Foreign Ministry to his home to discuss relations between China and the Soviet Union. They included Chen Yun and Li Xiannian. As a vice-foreign minister in charge of affairs concerning the Soviet Union and Eastern Europe in the Ministry, I too was present.

Deng said that we should take a large step by sending a message to the Soviet Union with the aim of making a significant change in Sino-Soviet relations. However, we needed to stick to our principles. The conditions were that the Soviet Union must take the initiative to remove the "three major barriers": it was to withdraw its troops from the Sino-Soviet border areas and the People's Republic of Mongolia, withdraw its troops from Afghanistan, and persuade Vietnam to withdraw Vietnamese troops from Cambodia. We all agreed with Comrade Deng's opinion.

China and the Soviet Union had been engaged in a protracted debate over who was right and who was wrong. We accused the Soviet Union of "revisionism," and the Soviet Union accused us of "dogmatism." This argument had been growing more and more acute. But now, Deng was putting forward conditions for an improvement of Sino-Soviet relations. He stressed three realistic issues, thus shifting from an ideological debate to a consideration of state interests, and indicating a trend toward adjustment of China's foreign policy in the future.

Comrade Chen Yun raised the question of how to send this message. The message needed to draw the recipient's attention without arousing any external guesses or suspicion. We could not call anyone from the Soviet embassy or send a visitor to the embassy, and we had no other means of contact with the Soviet Union at that time.

Comrade Deng proposed that in order to avoid speculation by outsiders, we should send Yu Hongliang, the director-general of the Soviet and European Affairs Department of the Foreign Ministry, to inspect the work of China's embassies in Moscow and Warsaw. On August 10, Yu set off for Moscow. Before his departure, we had prepared a memo of talking points based on Comrade Deng's instructions.

The Soviet authorities paid particular attention to Yu's unexpected appearance in Moscow, and to his request to see a vice minister of the Soviet Union's foreign affairs ministry. Vice Minister Leonid Ilyichev was invited to visit the Chinese embassy, and the first director general of the Far East department of the Soviet Union, Mikhail Kapitsa, interrupted his leave at his villa in the suburbs and hurried back to accompany Ilyichev. At the meeting, Comrade Yu recited to the visitors the 1,000-word memo, paragraph by paragraph, word by word, not missing a single word.

The memo pointed out that for many years relations between China and the Soviet Union had been abnormal, and that neither the Chinese people nor the Soviet people wanted to see this situation continue. It was time to do something to improve Sino-Soviet relations. Of course, the problems could not be solved overnight, but we held that as long as both China and the Soviet Union sincerely wished to improve their relations, these problems could surely be solved gradually in a fair and just manner through consultations. We proposed that a start could be made if, for example, the Soviet Union persuaded Vietnam to withdraw its troops from Cambodia, or if China and the Soviet Union both reduced their armed forces in their border areas. Also, both sides might consider an approach, which would be acceptable to all parties concerned, to withdraw Soviet troops from the People's Republic of Mongolia. We also said that we hoped a reasonable way could be found to solve the issue of

Afghanistan. All in all, as long as both sides were farsighted, were sincere about restoring friendly relations, and would start tackling one or two important issues, bilateral relations would change for the better. The actual form of exchanges of views was open to discussion.

Ilyichev narrowed his eyes, and listened attentively. A man with considerable seniority, he had served during Khrushchev's time as a member of the Secretariat, minister of the Propaganda Department of the Central Committee of the Communist Party of the Soviet Union, and editor of *Pravda* and *Izvestia*; and he had long been in charge of ideology and propaganda. After Khrushchev stepped down, Ilyichev retired from the central circle and became vice minister of foreign affairs. He was steady and prudent. When speaking, he measured each word carefully, often giving an impression of sternness and inflexibility. Having heard the memo, he made a normal diplomatic response: "Your ideas cannot help drawing our attention, both for their content and for the initiative with which they are presented." This standard response sounded as though he was not fully aware of the true meaning of our message. But Kapitsa was keen-minded and had discerned something new in the memo. He said that it might have a certain positive effect, but such important issues could not be solved by people at his level. This would have to be reported to the Politburo and the top Soviet leadership.

After that meeting, Yu Hongliang immediately went to Warsaw, so as to make it appear to the outside world that he had not made a special trip to Moscow—and to give the Soviet Union time to consider the memo and prepare a reply.

When Yu Hongliang returned to Moscow and met Ilyichev again, on August 18, Ilyichev's attitude was somewhat changed, and his tone became far more moderate. He said that he had reported the views of the Chinese side to the Central Committee, and the Soviet side would give a formal reply.

On August 20, Malcev, the first vice foreign minister of the Soviet Union, made an appointment to see Ma Xusheng, the interim chargé d'affaires of the Chinese embassy to the Soviet Union, and handed over a memorandum as a formal reply to the Chinese message. It indicated that the Soviet side was ready to discuss bilateral relations at any time, at any place, and at any level in order to "remove barriers to the normalization of the relationship." The term "remove barriers" was identical to the term used by the Chinese side, so we considered the response positive. Again, Comrade Deng invited me and Yu Hongliang to his home. He listened to our report on the details of our mission and made a decision on the spot to reopen Sino-Soviet negotiations.

Before the opening of the Twelfth National Conference of the Communist Party of the Soviet Union, China and the Soviet Union had decided internally that envoys at the vice ministerial level of both countries would begin political consultations on normalizing Sino-Soviet relations.

BEGINNING OF CONSULTATIONS

IN OCTOBER 1982, the Central Government appointed me special envoy to participate in the Sino-Soviet political consultations. This was an important and challenging mission. The special envoy of the Soviet Union, my counterpart, was Ilyichev. At their foreign ministry, he had been in charge of African affairs, not Chinese affairs. However, he had been engaged in negotiations on the Sino-Soviet border dispute and the state relations between China and the Soviet Union for ten years with four Chinese vice foreign ministers successively: Qiao Guanhua, Han Nianlong, Yu Zhan, and Wang Youping. He was regarded in Soviet diplomatic circles as a gifted negotiator.

The first round of consultations started in Beijing on October 5, 1982. We had prepared ourselves mentally from the start for a protracted tug-of-war. Deng Xiaoping instructed us not to make a sharp turn when dealing with the Soviet Union, and not to be too anxious to accomplish something. (If we were too anxious, the Soviet Union would take advantage of us.) He also instructed us to adhere to the principles and policies regarding the Soviet Union laid down in the report made at the Twelfth National Party Conference. We were determined to have a strategic picture in mind, adhere to our principles, and emphasize our earnest request that the Soviet Union stop sup-porting Vietnam's aggression in Cambodia and urge Vietnam to withdraw its troops from Cambodia. At the same time, tactically, we intended to hold high the banner of improving the relations between our two countries and safeguarding friendship between our peoples, so as to keep open the channel for consultations.

The first round of consultations lasted two weeks, ending on Oc-tober 21. There were six sessions in all. During the negotiations, I stuck to eliminating the "three major barriers," and pointed out that both sides needed to do some down-to-earth work in this regard. Once the barriers were removed, there would be no detour from the road toward normalizing relations. If we moved forward along this road, the good-neighborly friendly relationship between us would be gradually restored.

Ilyichev repeatedly expressed a wish to improve relations between our two countries, but he consistently tried hard to avoid discussing the "three major barriers." The Soviet stand could be summarized as three points: first, they criticized China for setting a "precondition" for the talks; second, they held that normalization of Sino-Soviet rela-tions must not "harm the interests of a third country"; third, they said that the Soviet Union "never threatens China." Ilyichev proposed re-peatedly that we jointly formulate a basic document for Sino-Soviet relations with the aim of reaching an agreement on improvement and development in economy and trade, science and technology, and cul-ture.

To counter the assertion that the removal of barriers was a "pre-condition," I pointed out that there were no preconditions. Certain is-sues had been raised for discussion, but these were not preconditions. If we had announced in advance that certain issues but not others could be discussed, that would have been a precondition. But in the course of our consultation, any and all issues could be discussed with no restriction. That constituted discussions with no preconditions.

I assured Ilyichev that the issues we had raised for discussion would not harm but benefit the interests of a "third country," as the Soviet Union called it. These issues would also improve relations between China and such a country. As the special envoy of the Soviet Union mentioned in the first round of talks, because China and the Soviet Union were two large countries and Sino-Soviet relations would affect the situation of Asia and the world as a whole, naturally our consultations would have to involve other countries. The point was whether the consultations would harm the interests of such countries or be detrimental to relations with such countries, or would they be in the interest of such countries and improve relations with these countries? I further pointed out that it would be insufficient to say that normalizing Sino-Soviet relations must not harm the interests of a third country. As a matter of principle, we were against harming the interests of all third countries.

To counter the claim that the Soviet Union did not threaten China, I pointed out that the Soviet Union had stationed a large number of troops with advanced weapons along the Sino-Soviet border, and in Mongolia and Afghanistan, adjacent to both China and the Soviet Union. So we did really feel threatened and were seriously uneasy.

I expounded primarily and especially on where to start to remove the "three major barriers." I said that the Chinese leaders had listed some barriers hampering the normalization of Sino-Soviet relations in the report made at the Twelfth National Conference of the Party. Those barriers could not be eliminated all at once. We held that it was necessary and possible to start by getting Vietnamese troops to withdraw from Cambodia. The military occupation of Cambodia by Vietnam, backed by the Soviet Union, had brought calamity to the Cambodian people and unnecessary suffering and sacrifices to the Vietnamese people. It had ruined the peaceful life of this region of southeast Asia, had increased China's insecurity, and had made the fragile Sino-Soviet relations even more tense, sharper, and more complicated. It was urgent to withdraw Vietnamese troops from Cambodia as soon as possible, to safeguard the peace and security of the region. This would also be a crucial step along the road to normalizing Sino-Soviet relations. Also, to start with this issue would be relatively realistic and practical. As was known to all, supporting

Vietnam's invasion of Cambodia was not the only action the Soviet Union was taking in Indochina. The Soviet Union should, therefore, realize that our demand was not excessive. We merely asked the Soviet Union to use its influence to get the Vietnamese troops out of Cambodia. We were not asking the Soviet Union to withdraw its own soldiers, or to be involved in anything else, though we could have made such demands. Our reasonable request should have drawn a positive response from the Soviet side. The Soviet Union obviously had the power and means to get Vietnam to withdraw its troops from Cambodia. If the Soviet Union calmly measured the pros and cons, was farsighted, made a political decision, and took the necessary measures, the problem would not be difficult to solve.

Regarding the insistence of the Soviet side on starting by preparing a statement of principles concerning Sino-Soviet relations, I told Ilyichev that the normalization of our relations could not be achieved by simply publishing such a statement. This, as a matter of fact, indicated that China was truly sincere about eventually signing a statement of principles. We held that when each side took actions to demonstrate its adherence to the principles, the time would be ripe for a statement. When a melon ripens, it falls off its stem. Where water flows, a channel is formed. That is to say, a statement of principles would be a natural result of the development of Sino-Soviet relations. It would summarize the practices of the two countries and guide their relations. Therefore, we held that the most pressing task facing both sides was to remove the barrier, so as to create conditions for a statement of principles at some future date.

The consultations were a tit-for-tat process. At times, the atmosphere was quite tense. Each side had prepared talking points against the other. Ilyichev had been in charge of ideology for a long time; he had a PhD and was compiling a dictionary of philosophy (later, he gave me a copy of the dictionary). When he spoke, his attitude was hard, and his terms were often abstract. He liked to make long-winded, rhetorical speeches. He talked in a roundabout way; his words were dogmatic but empty of meaning. Listening to him was extremely boring. The Chinese side showed no mercy in attacking his statements, and we often gave strongly worded responses. For instance, we often dismissed the ideas put forward by the Soviet side as "moonlight reflected in the water" or "a flower in a mirror." We stressed that unless the "three major barriers" were removed, improving our relations would remain just a fond dream.

During the period of the consultations, many outings and visits were arranged, so that the two sides could exchange views informally. In diplomacy, certain things must be said on formal occasions, but other things may be expressed in private. What is said at formal meetings is not necessarily important; what is said in private is not necessarily unimportant. In formal negotiations, one may utter tough words, but in private one can be more or less polite, and some message may be passed to the other side directly but without being recorded.

To create a relaxed atmosphere, I invited Ilyichev and his entourage to the Miyun Reservoir for an outing, and regaled them with tasty fresh fish. It was an opportunity to chat casually and have more personal contact. Ilyichev told me that he had been to this spot once before and had eaten some fish, but he had not done any fishing. He seemed to be on the alert, fearing that he might be hoodwinked. However, he was grateful, saying that this was a pleasant break and that it would give him more time to ponder the issues before giving us a reply.

It was a fine, crisp autumn day. Looking at the vast expanse of clear water at the reservoir, with fish diving and birds hovering, we felt relaxed and refreshed. While sipping tea, I said to Ilyichev that we hoped that the Soviet side would correctly understand our position, and realize that there was something new in it. For instance, to reduce forces along the border areas would be an obligation on both sides. On the issue of the withdrawal of troops from Mongolia, we wanted to find a resolution acceptable to all parties. We asked the Soviet Union only to urge Vietnam to pull its forces out of Cambodia, and this request did not involve the bilateral relations between Vietnam and the Soviet Union. The Soviet Union's support of the Vietnamese invasion of Cambodia was not only intensifying the situation in southeast Asia but also becoming a heavy burden on the Soviet Union. To solve that issue would be beneficial, not harmful, to the Soviet Union as well as to Vietnam. We could not see any difficulties for the Soviet side in this matter.

Ilyichev was all ears. Apparently he understood me. He understood our stand on the "three major barriers" and the possible approach to eliminating them. But he was adamant in reiterating the Soviet Union's own stand. Fearing a trap, he repeatedly insisted: "What we have said today is informal." He also insisted that in future consultations "both sides must not quote what we have said today."

The first round of political consultations between the special envoys of China and the Soviet Union provided an opportunity for us to sound each other out. It involved endless, repetitive arguments, but each side spoke its own mind. Although not much was achieved, this round initiated the process of normalization, marked the end of a stalemate with no dialogue, and symbolized the beginning of a long period of dialogue.

PROTRACTED WAR

THE SECOND ROUND of political consultations between China and the Soviet Union was held in Moscow in August 1983. At these meetings to seek a way to normalize Sino-Soviet relations, no consensus was achieved regarding essential issues.

During the consultations, I met the Soviet foreign minister, Andrey Gromyko, and crossed swords with him. Gromyko had been foreign minister for twenty-seven years, under five generations of Soviet leaders from Nikita Khrushchev to Konstantin Chernenko. He had what Westerners call a "poker face," expressionless when he was listening to others. In all circumstances, he appeared conceited and aggressive, and he was always ready for a diplomatic fight. No wonder Western reporters called him "Mr. No."

To my surprise, Gromyko accepted the Chinese position against hegemonism and for eliminating threats, saying that those principles should serve as the basis for normalizing Sino-Soviet relations. Then he disparaged the Americans, saying that they could not be trusted. He also said that the United States was preparing to launch a crusade against the Soviet Union, and that President Reagan intended to wipe out socialism worldwide. Gromyko said, as if giving a lecture, that since America had a policy of eliminating socialism from the world, China could easily conclude what kind of relations it should seek with the Soviet Union and the United States.

Gromyko was then seventy-four, and he stressed his seniority when speaking. I responded: "It is an objective fact that the international situation is tense. In my view, in such a situation, improving Sino-Soviet relations not only will be beneficial to the interests of the peoples of both China and the Soviet Union, it will also be in the interest of Asia and world peace. Talking of the United States, the People's Republic of China has been struggling with the United States for a long time, ever since the founding of New China. We are more qualified than anyone else to speak of this issue, and we know how to deal with the United States." For a moment, Gromyko was at a loss for words, looking somewhat embarrassed.

After that, special envoys from China and the Soviet Union held political consultations twice a year, in Beijing and Moscow. These were marathons, a contest of tenacity and willpower. We always stuck to our insistence that only when the barriers had been removed would it be possible to normalize Sino-Soviet relations. We countered the Soviet side by citing facts and logic; we undermined their illusions and did our best to make the Soviet Union do something about removing the barriers. At the end of the eighth round of consultations, in Moscow in April 1986, no substantial progress had been made on that issue. However, the consultations continued, and a channel of communication was maintained. Objectively, the consultations played a useful role in advancing Sino-Soviet relations.

In retrospect, there were also other reasons for the impasse. During that period, every one or two years another key leader died. Leonid Brezhnev, Yuri Andropov, and Konstantin Chernenko, respectively, died on November 10, 1982; February 9, 1984; and March 10,

1985. It was said that Brezhnev had been able to work only for an hour a day in his last years. All he could do was make a few telephone calls. It was impossible for him to handle state affairs. Brezhnev's successor, Andropov, a clever man, had served as ambassador to Hungary and knew the outside world well. He was ambitious and hated the bureaucracy of the Soviet government. Almost all those in the government loved alcohol and allowed it to hamper the performance of their duties. Andropov banned the production of alcoholic beverages, turned breweries into fruit juice producers, and penalized anyone who got drunk. But he achieved little success, because drinking alcohol was a "national habit." He suffered from serious illnesses, and headed the country for only a little over one year. Then Chernenko took over. His health was even worse, and his term in office was even shorter than Andropov's.

A country ruled successively by three ailing men was unable to do much in foreign affairs. Naturally, an issue as important as normalization of Sino-Soviet relations could not be solved during that period. However, contacts between China and the Soviet Union went to a higher level because of the three funerals.

When Deng Xiaoping received the news of Brezhnev's death, he immediately instructed the foreign minister, Huang Hua, to attend the funeral as a special envoy of the Chinese government. This was an extraordinary gesture after long years of no contact between senior leaders of China and the Soviet Union. Deng's aim was to seize the opportunity to get the Soviet Union to take steps toward normalization of relations, find out what the new Soviet leader's attitude toward China was, and spur the process of normalization. In addition, Deng gave instructions that a brief statement be published, not just criticizing Brezhnev or simply showering praise on him. Comrade Hu Qiaomu prepared a draft statement giving an account of the evolution of Sino-Soviet relations and pointing out that they had begun to deteriorate in the late 1950s and had worsened drastically in the late 1960s when Brezhnev was in power. The statement hinted that Brezhnev had been responsible for the setback, though without mentioning him by name. But it also expressed appreciation for a conciliatory speech that Brezhnev had recently made. This signaled that we hoped the new Soviet leader would make a new effort to improve Sino-Soviet relations. The statement was published as a written message to reporters from Huang Hua at the airport before he departed for Moscow; at the same time, the Foreign Ministry notified the Chinese embassy in Moscow of the statement. In fact, Huang Hua learned of the statement he was supposed to have made only when he arrived in Moscow.

On meeting the new leader of the Soviet Union, Yuri Andropov, and the foreign minister, Gromyko, Huang Hua emphasized that to improve Sino-Soviet relations, the Soviet Union must take measures to remove the barriers, commencing by doing one or two things. The Soviet side stressed that both parties should make efforts to promote exchanges in economy and trade, science and technology, and culture. It seemed that Andropov wanted to continue his predecessor's effort to improve Sino-Soviet relations but had not yet made up his mind to take any significant step.

At the formal meetings, the negotiations were rather like a discussion between two deaf men, each expressing his own view. However, this round did serve to help each side to get to know the other side's position better. Also, the contact prevented the relations between the two sides from becoming tenser. Those relations, as someone once described them, amounted to no more than "an embassy, an aircraft and a train," meaning that these were the only contacts remaining between the two countries. And actually the airplanes and trains shuttling between the two countries were mostly empty. But as the consultations continued, Sino-Soviet trade began to grow. Exchanges also increased in other fields. Students went to each other's country to study, and the number of official delegations increased.

At the end of 1984, significantly, Ivan Arhipov—who was the first vice chairman of the Council of Ministers of the Soviet Union and an old friend of the Chinese people—visited China at the invitation of vice premier Yao Yilin. This was the highest-level delegation sent by the Soviet Union since the deterioration of relations between the two countries in the late 1960s. In the 1950s, Arhipov had been the leader of a group of experts supporting China, and had contributed to China's first "five-year plan." He never said a nasty word about China, even in the most difficult period of bilateral relations. China welcomed his visit in 1984, and he was treated with great honor. Deng Xiaoping received him; Chen Yun, Peng Zhen, Bo Yibo, and many others who had worked with him in the past met him. These old friends met in a cheerful atmosphere, and the scenes of reunion were touching.

I remember that before he met Arhipov, Chen Yun invited Yao Yilin, Chen Chu, and me to his home to brief him about the visit. He was in a good mood. That night he wrote down this quotation in his own calligraphic style and sent it to me: "The hills and streams have no end, and there seems to be no road beyond. But, veiled by willows, bright with flowers, another village appears." With these famous lines of Lu You (1125–1210) of the southern Song dynasty, he expressed his feelings about the progress of the Sino-Soviet relations and his expectations for the future.

During Arhipov's stay in China, I accompanied him on a visit to the Yanshan Petrochemicals Company, the Wuhan Iron and Steel Works, the Yangtze River Bridge at Wuhan, and the Shenzhen Special Economic Zone. From time to time, I mentioned some projects built in China with the help of the Soviet Union. I also told him about the rapid development of the Shenzhen Special Economic Zone in the course of pursuing a reform and opening-up policy under the personal care of Deng Xiaoping. Arhipov was impressed by these achievements, and by the amazing speed of the related economic development. He could not help marveling at what the Chinese had attained, and often revealed his disappointment and dissatisfaction with the current situation in the Soviet Union.

During his visit, the two sides signed the Sino-Soviet Economic and Technological Cooperation Agreement and the Sino-Soviet Agreement on the Establishment of the Economic, Trade, and Science and Technology Cooperation Committee, which enabled the long-suspended cooperation in economics, science, and technology to be restored.

In July 1985, I accompanied vice premier Yao Yilin on a visit to the Soviet Union. Yao had a talk with Ivan B. Arhipov and met Tikhonov, chairman of the Council of Ministers of the Soviet Union. Negotiations concerning economic and trade cooperation went smoothly, and the two sides signed the Sino-Soviet Agreement on the Exchange of Goods and Payments from 1986 to 1990. The total volume of trade between China and the Soviet Union increased from 2.65 billion Swiss francs in 1984 to 4.6 billion Swiss francs in 1985. Both sides expressed satisfaction with the exchange of visits by high-ranking officials and the growth of bilateral trade. The Chinese side still urged the Soviet side to eliminate the "three major barriers," pointing out that otherwise the improvement of relations would be hampered.

BREAKTHROUGH

HOW COULD THE FROZEN NEGOTIATIONS on Sino-Soviet relations be thawed? The Chinese side continued to insist on eliminating the "three major barriers," but the three Soviet leaders—Brezhnev, Andropov, and Chernenko—had all avoided this important issue, dwelling on the trivial and trying to realize normalization simply by developing economic and trade cooperation and increasing visits. After Mikhail Gorbachev took over, he too initially showed no intention of moving forward on removing the barriers.

Deng Xiaoping pointed out—when he met with Nicolae Ceaușescu, leader of Romania, on the latter's visit to China on October 9, 1985—that the normalization between China and the Soviet Union depended on the removal of the three barriers, and that this should start with the withdrawal of Vietnamese troops from Cambodia. Once this issue was solved, the other disputes would be easier to settle. To break the stalemate in Sino-Soviet relations, Deng suggested a meeting at the highest level between China and the Soviet Union; and asked Ceaușescu to convey this in an oral message to Mikhail Gorbachev. Deng wanted to meet with Gorbachev if the Soviet side and the Chinese side reached an understanding on getting the Vietnamese troops to withdraw from Cambodia. Deng also said that although he had fulfilled the mission of making foreign visits as a leader, he would make an exception for this purpose.

On November 6, 1985, the Soviet side said that it had received the oral message. On November 23, the Soviet side said that the time was ripe for holding a Sino-Soviet meeting at the highest level and for normalizing relations. It proposed that leaders of the two countries meet in the Far East region of the Soviet Union or in China. On July 28, 1986, Gorbachev made a long speech in Vladivostok, a city in the Far East region of the Soviet Union, expressing a willingness to sincerely discuss with China "further measures" to establish neighborly, friendly relations, at any time and at any level. He announced that the Soviet Union would pull out six regiments of its army from Afghanistan, and that total withdrawal of the Soviet troops there would depend on whether or not external interference continued. He revealed that the Soviet Union was negotiating with Mongolia to withdraw "a substantial number of troops" from there. He also indicated that the Soviet Union would like to discuss with China troop reduction along the Sino-Soviet border. He mentioned Cambodia as well, saying that this issue was a matter between China and Vietnam and depended on the normalization of relations between them. All the Soviet Union could do was to hope that China and Vietnam would resume their dialogue and reach a peaceful settlement.

It is worth noting that Gorbachev accepted the Chinese argument regarding the Sino-Soviet border by agreeing to demarcate the Amur (Heilongjiang) River border along the central line of the main channel, and said that he hoped that the border area would be peaceful and friendly in the near future.

Compared with Gorbachev's past speeches, this one indicated that the Soviet stand had changed greatly.

As for the "three major barriers," Gorbachev did not use the hackneyed expressions such as "no preconditions," "not harm the interests of a third country," and "have never threatened China." He no longer avoided the issue of withdrawing troops from Afghanistan, Mongolia, and the Sino-Soviet border areas, and he showed a flexible attitude. He also used a moderate tone in talking about Vietnam and Cambodia, and said that it was the right time to address that issue.

For historical reasons, the Sino-Soviet border along the Heilongjiang (Amur) River had not so far been strictly demarcated. In the Qing dynasty, the river was simply regarded as the border. The Soviet Union had all along maintained the claim of the czars that the border was along the Chinese side of the river. This meant that all the islets in the river belonged to the Soviet Union, and that the Heilongjiang and Wusuli were inland rivers of the Soviet Union. Of course, China did not agree. We held that, according to international law and practice, the border of two countries along a river should be the central line of its main channel. The bloody Sino-Soviet conflict at Zhenbaodao in 1969 stemmed from this dispute. I must say that Gorbachev's attitude was more positive than the old one.

Additionally, Gorbachev was the first top leader of the Soviet Union to speak positively for the first time about China's modernization efforts. He said that he understood and respected such efforts. He also proposed detailed ideas for expanding and deepening the economic and technological cooperation between his country and China.

The central Chinese leadership decided to seize this opportunity and take corresponding measures. We expressed a prudently welcoming attitude toward Gorbachev's speech, but we would not loosen our insistence on removing the "three major barriers," and we continued to keep up the pressure. At the same time, we accepted the idea of regarding the central line of the main river channel as the border, and we agreed to resume the relevant border negotiations.

In this connection, Foreign Minister Wu Xueqian met Vladimir P. Fedotov, interim chargé d'affaires of the Soviet embassy in China, on August 13, 1985, and said to him:

We have given due attention to and made a sincere appraisal of the talk made by General Secretary Gorbachev at Vladivostok on July 28. The Chinese side has noted that there are words in that speech which have never been used before. For

*this, we would like to express our appreciation. The Soviet
Union is very clear about the principled stand and detailed
ideas of the Chinese side on eliminating the 'three major barriers' in order to realize the normalization of relations between the two countries, but Gorbachev's words were still far
from the elimination of the "three major barriers"; in particular, the withdrawal of Vietnamese troops from Cambodia was
not mentioned. We are not satisfied with this. To pull Vietnamese troops out of Cambodia and solve the issue of Cambodia in a fair and reasonable manner is China's greatest
concern. It is also the key message Comrade Deng Xiaoping
asked the Romanian President Ceauşescu to pass to the Soviet side last year. The Chinese side sincerely hopes to realize
the normalization of Sino-Soviet relations as soon as possible, and that the Soviet side will earnestly consider the Chinese stand. China welcomes what General Secretary
Gorbachev said about setting the border along the central
line of the main channel of the river in the eastern section of
the Sino-Soviet border. With this as the basis, the Chinese
side holds that the resumption of negotiations on the Sino-
Soviet border at an appropriate time is feasible.*

Comrade Deng talked about Sino-Soviet relations again when he
was interviewed on television by the American reporter Mike Wallace on September 2, 1986. Deng stressed that the key to improving
Sino-Soviet relations lay with the withdrawal of Vietnamese troops
from Cambodia. He also said that if Gorbachev would do something
specific on the issue of Vietnam and Cambodia, and remove this barrier, he himself would make an exception and meet Gorbachev anywhere in the Soviet Union. On September 7, we formally published
this interview, and made China's stand known to the world. As a matter of fact, this was an official response to Gorbachev's speech at
Vladivostok.

TOWARD NORMALIZATION

IN ORDER TO SPUR THE SOVIET UNION to go forward on the basis of Gorbachev's speech at Vladivostok, we did three things successively: we invited Nikolay Vladimirovich Talyzin, the first vice chairman of the Council of Ministers of the Soviet Union and chairman of the State Planning Committee, to visit China; we resumed the Sino-Soviet border negotiations; and we focused the negotiations on Vietnam and Cambodia in the subsequent twelfth round of Sino-Soviet political consultations.

Nikolai V. Talyzin visited China in September 1986. During his visit, the two sides discussed a loan from the Soviet government to China; the joint building of an aluminum plant in the Guangxi Zhuang Autonomous Region, expanding production of the Benxi Iron and Steel Works; and building a railway in the Xinjiang Uygur Autonomous Region. Also covered in the discussion were a number of economic and trade issues, such as equity joint-venture enterprises, compensation trade, the processing of materials supplied by Soviet clients, expanding border trade, and increasing the supply of traditional goods. Talyzin also probed our attitude toward Gorbachev's speech at Vladivostok. Chinese leaders told him that some aspects of Gorbachev's speech were welcome, but expressly pointed out that he had said nothing new about Vietnam and Cambodia—the issue that was China's greatest concern—and urged the Soviet side to make a political decision as soon as possible on it.

At the behest of the Chinese side, the foreign ministers of China and the Soviet Union agreed at a meeting in New York that the two countries' border negotiations would restart in February 1987 in Moscow. I was appointed head of the Chinese delegation. The head of the Soviet delegation was the vice foreign minister, Igor Rogachev. China and the Soviet Union had already held border negotiations, from February to July 1964 and from October 1969 to June 1978. In the first round of negotiations, the two sides exchanged maps and reached an oral consensus on the eastern section of the border, but no formal agreement was signed. In October 1964, following the resignation of Khrushchev, the border negotiations ceased. The second round of border negotiations lasted for nine years, and was eventually broken off following the Soviet invasion of Afghanistan in 1979. Now, the third round was held in a relatively amicable atmosphere, as Gorbachev had accepted the Chinese stand and thus provided common ground for the negotiations. I headed the Chinese delegation for two sessions of negotiations, in February and August 1987. Later, the vice foreign minister Tian Zengpei was in charge of the Chinese side of the talks. Before a scheduled summit meeting of the leaders of the two countries, the two sides had largely reached an agreement in principle on the eastern section of the border. As for the complicated western section, the two sides had reached unanimity on the principle of demarcation, and had agreed to establish working teams of experts to discuss the western section in detail, and a joint team to carry out aerial photography. The progress made in the third round of border negotiations was helpful for easing the confrontation along the border and became part of the effort to normalize Sino-Soviet relations.

The ninth political consultation was held after Gorbachev's speech at Vladivostok. Before the summit meeting, the two countries held as many as twelve rounds of political consultations, and I headed the Chinese side for eleven of them. When I was appointed foreign minister in April 1988, the vice foreign minister, Tian Zengpei, was appointed head of the Chinese delegation for the Sino-Soviet border negotiations and a special envoy of the Chinese government. In the final four rounds of the consultations, the Soviet side began to show a flexible attitude toward the key issues that had hampered the normalization of Sino-Soviet relations; it no longer avoided discussing Cambodia. However, the Soviet side said that this issue had to be solved politically. Later, it acknowledged that the withdrawal of the Vietnamese troops from Cambodia was a key factor. The Soviet side did not undertake to urge Vietnam to pull its troops out of Cambodia, but said that it would do what it could to promote the process of solving the issue of Cambodia. Judging by this, we became aware that the Soviet Union intended to pull its own troops out of Afghanistan, and then to solve the Cambodian issue as soon as possible, because of its own needs. Its new attitude was more positive than its old one.

In the twelfth round of political consultations, the Soviet side expressed its willingness to hold a special session on Cambodia and reach an understanding. In view of the existing situation, in order to get the Soviet side to put pressure on Vietnam we decided to accept its proposal. From August 27 to September 1, 1988, the two vice foreign ministers—Tian Zengpei and Rogachev—held several working meetings in Beijing especially on the issue of Cambodia. Finally, the two sides reached an internal understanding, having found some common ground and similar views. Of course, disputes still persisted, but the meetings indicated that the Soviet side was showing flexibility on the issue of Vietnamese troops in Cambodia. Owing to internal political pressure and the needs of external diplomacy, the Soviet Union was hoping to rid itself of the burden of this issue and thereby to improve Sino-Soviet relations and realize a summit meeting.

Following these consultations, I no longer had any contact with Ilyichev. Later, I heard that his wife had died and then that his only son had died too. Since there was no one else left at home, he donated his lifetime collection of books and oil paintings to museums in his hometown. When he died, in August 1990, I sent a telegram of condolence.

AN ICE-BREAKING JOURNEY

FROM DECEMBER 1 TO 3, 1988, I paid a formal visit to the Soviet Union in the capacity of foreign minister at the invitation of the Soviet foreign minister, Eduard Shevardnadze. That was the first time since 1957 that a Chinese foreign minister had paid a formal visit to the Soviet Union. The aim of the mission was to prepare for the meeting of the heads of state of China and the Soviet Union.

The two foreign ministers had had some contacts before this formal visit. But those meetings had all taken place at sessions of the United Nations in New York. As far as the length of separation and the degree of difficulty were concerned, the visit could be regarded as an icebreaker.

My entourage included Dai Bingguo, then director general of the Soviet Union and Eastern European Affairs Department of the Foreign Ministry; and Li Zhaoxing, then director general of the Information Department of the ministry. We took a CAAC flight and arrived in Moscow at noon on December 1. Shevardnadze came to the airport to meet us, and accompanied us to the hotel.

The ten people in our delegation were ushered into the hotel at Number 11 Kosygin Street, Lenin Hill. It was midwinter. Large snowflakes danced all over Moscow. The wind was biting cold. The Soviet side was very considerate about our accommodation. But as relations between the two countries were at a rather critical phase and the local environment was complicated, the key members of the delegation and I could not discuss anything important in our rooms. Early the next morning, in the teeth of a cold wind, we trudged in deep snow round and round the courtyard of the hotel, discussing our strategy.

The same day, I went to the Kremlin to meet Gorbachev, general secretary of the Central Committee of the Communist Party and chairman of the Presidium of the Supreme Soviet. At that time, he had just put forward his theory of "new thinking," and he gave the impression of being young and capable. Perhaps because of his enthusiasm for his new theory, he was particularly talkative. The meeting lasted one hour and forty minutes. He took the initiative to say that the Soviet Union had made errors in the past. When talking about the prospective Sino-Soviet summit, he volunteered to go to Beijing himself. I conveyed the Chinese leader's invitation for him to visit China in 1989; and said that as far as relations between our two countries were concerned, the Chinese side advocated emphasizing the future instead of remaining entangled in past issues. It was important, I said, to look forward, and explore ways to establish a new relationship.

During the visit, Shevardnadze and I had three negotiation sessions totaling about six and a half hours. The focus of the talks was the issue of Cambodia.

On this issue, both sides had a positive view of the meeting between the two vice foreign ministers in August 1988, and some consensus had been achieved when the two foreign ministers met in
September in New York. Now, both sides further expounded their respective views. I pointed out emphatically that the Vietnamese troops
must be completely withdrawn from Cambodia before the end of
June 1989. The Soviet Union and China should be of the same opinion on a time limit for the withdrawal and make it happen. In addition, after the Vietnamese troops had completely pulled out of
Cambodia, all foreign countries, including Vietnam, should stop military aid to all parties in Cambodia and not support any party in the
civil war there. As for the internal issues of Cambodia, I did not say
much, but briefly reiterated China's view: a four-party coalition government headed by Prince Norodom Sihanouk should be put in place;
the military forces of all parties to the civil war in Cambodia should
be frozen, reduced, and then dissolved; an international peacekeeping
force should be stationed in Cambodia; and strict international surveillance and an international guarantee should be instituted. The
Soviet side expressed its wish that the issue of Cambodia could be
solved as soon as possible, and agreed that Vietnam should completely withdraw its troops as soon as possible. However, it held that
the withdrawal of Vietnamese troops and the establishment of the international surveillance mechanism and the international guarantee
should be accompanied by a repudiation of the past policies of Cambodia, realization of dialogue between the various parties within
Cambodia, and a continuing dialogue between the countries of Indochina and the countries of the Association of Southeast Asian Nations (ASEAN). It advocated that after all parties in Cambodia had
reached a political settlement, all countries should immediately stop
military aid to all parties in Cambodia.

What the Soviet side did not want to promise was the time limit
for the withdrawal of the Vietnamese troops, saying that the Soviet
Union "had no way to give orders to Vietnam." But it conveyed the
wish of the Vietnamese to discuss the timetable of withdrawal directly with China, and said that it hoped that Vietnam and China

would engage in direct dialogue so as to accelerate the process of a political settlement in Cambodia. Seeing that the two sides were coming closer together, we proposed that the time limit for the withdrawal of the Vietnamese troops from Cambodia might be set in the period from June to December 1989. The two sides then reached an agreement on this issue.

The final result was that the working teams appointed by the foreign ministers of the two sides, after much discussion, reached an internal understanding in the form of a "joint record" on the issue of Cambodia, which was confirmed by Shevardnadze and me. Its core content was that China and the Soviet Union wanted a fair and reasonable settlement of this issue as soon as possible. Both sides said that they hoped the Vietnamese troops would be completely withdrawn from Cambodia in the shortest possible time: i.e., in the latter half of 1989 and no later than the end of 1989. China and the Soviet Union expressed a wish to help accelerate the realization of this goal.

Shevardnadze and I also discussed the reduction of the Soviet troops stationed in Mongolia and the border areas between China and the Soviet Union, as well as relevant negotiations, and made some progress on those issues.

On February 2, 1989, Shevardnadze paid a return visit to China to prepare for the summit meeting. I had two sessions with him. The focus was still Cambodia. I accepted the proposal made by the Soviet side, and agreed to continue the discussions on the basis of the two "joint records" reached previously. I also proposed to publicly announce a communiqué on Cambodia, outlining the unanimous stand of China and the Soviet Union on a political settlement. This communiqué and the time for the summit meeting were to be announced together as a package agreement.

After the two sides reached an agreement on the date for Gorbachev's visit to China, the Soviet side suddenly changed its mind and went back on its word. It refused to publish the communiqué, and agreed only to announce the date of Gorbachev's visit to China. On February 3, Shevardnadze arrived in Shanghai. Comrade Deng Xiaoping was scheduled to receive him the next day. But at midnight, the attitude of the Soviet side suddenly became stiff, and it did not agree to the publication of the joint communiqué on Cambodia.

We counterattacked right away. In the early morning of February 4, we notified the Soviet side that since the dispute was still rather serious, the joint communiqué on Cambodia would not be published for the time being, but the date of the summit meeting—which the two sides had agreed should be held in mid-May—was not to be announced either.

Before Deng Xiaoping met Shevardnadze, I reported to him that the Soviet side had retreated from its former stand on Cambodia, and I suggested that the date of the Sino-Soviet summit meeting should not be announced for the time being, and that both sides should continue their consultations. Deng said, "The date of the Sino-Soviet summit meeting must not be changed. But I will not mention the date of the visit. I'll leave it up to you to discuss it."

At the start of his meeting with Deng, Shevardnadze said: "President Gorbachev wants to visit China from May 15 to 18. I talked to Foreign Minister Qian Qichen about this yesterday." His intention was obviously to ask Deng to confirm the date of the summit meeting, and make it a fait accompli, so that he could avoid the issue of Cambodia and then force the Chinese side to make concessions later.

Deng reacted immediately, saying: "The discussions between the two foreign ministers have not ended yet, and I hope you will continue the discussions. It is up to you to decide the date. I'll listen to you." Then, Deng once again stressed the importance of an early settlement of the Cambodia issue.

Finding himself thwarted, Shevardnadze had to say that the issue of Cambodia could, of course, continue to be discussed.

At noon on the same day, on the plane back to Beijing, the vice foreign ministers of the two countries had another discussion, but both sides were adamant. Shevardnadze had planned to go to Pakistan right after landing in Beijing. But when the aircraft landed in Beijing, he went straight to the embassy of the Soviet Union, and postponed his departure time again and again. My approach was to stay at the airport waiting for him. I meant to insist on the announcement of the joint communiqué and the date of Gorbachev's visit to China by both sides. It was already dark when he returned to the airport, and in the lounge we had the final session. I said, "Your visit has been success-ful. The negotiations and your meeting with Chinese leaders have been fruitful. But it is inappropriate to go back on one's own words. You must be aware that the relations between the two countries have not yet been normalized. The announcement of the joint commu-niqué was the idea of the Soviet side, and the Chinese side accepted it. For this, the members of both working teams did a lot of work. That things would turn out like this is not what we expected."

As a matter of fact, Shevardnadze himself had been behind all this maneuvering. But now, realizing that it was a rather thorny is-sue, he seemed to put the blame on Rogachev, and he complained to me that it was really difficult for the Soviet side to settle the Cambo-dia issue, which was too complicated. Seeing that I had no sympathy for him, he decided finally to leave two directors general to continue the discussions with China, and he himself took the flight and left.

On February 5, the teams for the two sides worked late into the night, and finally reached an agreement. On February 6, both sides simultaneously announced the joint communiqué on Cambodia and the date of Gorbachev's visit to China. That day happened to be the first day of the first lunar month of that year.

Five years later, I was invited to visit Georgia, and I met with Shevardnadze, who was then the president of his country. I was re-ceived with great courtesy, and he personally held a banquet to wel-come me. After the visit, he saw me off to the airport. He was far more enthusiastic and warmer than he had been in Moscow.

The Summit Meeting

FROM MAY 15 TO 18, 1989, Mikhail Gorbachev paid a formal visit to China as scheduled.

For over forty years, Sino-Soviet relations had witnessed the ef-forts of several generations, stood the test of fire and blood, and un-dergone tortuous and dramatic changes. When I first visited the

Soviet Union, I was only twenty-six years old. I spent almost ten years all together as a diplomat in that country. Then, as a special envoy, I attended Sino-Soviet political consultations for seven years, with numerous sleepless nights. Now, the important moment—the summit meeting—long awaited by the peoples of both countries, had come at last. I could not help feeling excited.

The meeting of the leaders of China and the Soviet Union was an important event attracting the attention of the whole world. When discussing the protocol for meeting Gorbachev, Deng Xiaoping gave instructions that the reception arrangements must be appropriate, and when the two leaders met they should "shake hands, without hugging." Those concise words did not merely refer to a matter of etiquette, but precisely epitomized the nature of Sino-Soviet relations at that time, and graphically outlined the pattern for future relations.

As for the theme of the meeting, Deng said, "It should be 'end the past and open up a new future.'" Those words were explicit, and profound in meaning.

From ten A.M. to twelve-thirty P.M. on May 16, Deng and Gorbachev held a meeting of historic significance in the Eastern Chamber of the Great Hall of the People. I remember that Deng was looking exuberant and in good spirits that day. He had a surprisingly good memory, and did not need a script when talking. His words were clear, precise, and logical. He first recalled two aspects of China's history: first, China's sufferings had been inflicted by great powers for the past century; second, the source of the greatest threat to China over the past few decades. He summarized the ups and downs of Sino-Soviet relations, and stressed that the principal problem was that the Soviet Union had not treated China as an equal. He also said that nevertheless the Chinese side never forgot that the Soviet Union had assisted China in laying an industrial foundation in the early days of New China. As for the ideological debates, Deng said that he had been personally involved in them, and he recalled that the arguments of both sides had been empty words. "We do not believe that our views were always correct," he said. He particularly emphasized that the purpose of mentioning past affairs was to make progress and to end such pointless debates. The focus should be on the future, he stressed.

Gorbachev said that the Soviet side had its own views and opinions on certain issues with regard to how the relations between old Russia, the Soviet Union, and China had been formed. But in the not-too-distant past, in certain aspects of Sino-Soviet relations, the Soviet Union had made certain errors and was responsible for some friction. He agreed to put a full stop to the past disputes.

What Gorbachev said was quite appropriate. Obviously, he had done his homework. The former ambassador of the Soviet Union to China, Troyanovsky, said in his memoir, *Exceeding Time and Space*, that Gorbachev had told his entourage that he would like to talk to Deng Xiaoping as a man of the younger generation to a man of a senior generation. People may have all kinds of ideas about Gorbachev as a historical figure, but the great mission he accomplished during his visit to Beijing should occupy a prominent place in the history of Sino-Soviet relations.

The call by the two sides for "opening up a new future" referred to the relationship to be established between the two countries after the normalization of Sino-Soviet relations, with the specific connotations of the new relations between the two countries clarified, along with the rules to be followed. Deng profoundly summed up the historical lessons of the international communist movement, and stressed that alliances and confrontations were all unsuccessful in the end, and that Sino-Soviet relations should be established on the basis of the "Five Principles of Peaceful Coexistence." Gorbachev said at his press conference that he and Deng Xiaoping and other Chinese leaders all held that "the Sino-Soviet summit meeting signifies that the relations between the two countries have entered a new stage. The relations of the two countries will be built on the basis of universal rules of exchanges between countries and the principle of peaceful coexistence. Our starting point is that the normalization of Sino-Soviet relations is not aimed at any third country, or at harming the interests of any third country. It will organically combine with the current world development trend."

The joint communiqué published after the summit meeting formally confirmed the principles for Sino-Soviet relations. Hence, a new relationship emerged, different from that of the alliance of the 1950s, and different from the confrontations in the 1960s and 1970s. It was a relationship of nonalliance and nonconfrontation, and it was not aimed at any third country. It was a relationship between friendly neighboring countries. Later developments proved that this new type of state relations was beneficial to the peoples of the two countries, and also to safeguarding world peace and stability.

Through the summit meeting, China and the Soviet Union at last ended the abnormal situation that had lasted for decades, and once again established normal state-to-state relations.

Looking back, I must say that it was most significant to seize the historic opportunity at that time and to normalize Sino-Soviet relations. Later, the international situation changed dramatically, great changes took place in eastern Europe, the Soviet Union dissolved, and the world entered an unusual stage of instability and transformations. The framework established for the normalization of Sino-Soviet relations became the foundation for a friendly neighbor relationship free of ideology. This relationship further developed into a constructive partnership, and then a strategic relationship of coordination in the twenty-first century based on equality and trust. If we had missed the opportunity, the relations between the two countries would probably have developed in a different direction.

That day, as the summit meeting for the normalization of Sino-Soviet relations was going on inside the Great Hall of the People, outside the Great Hall some abnormal developments were taking pace, which finally led to a political turmoil.

China's diplomacy faced even more severe challenges and tests.

2 THE PARIS CONFERENCE ON CAMBODIA

AN EVENING BANQUET AT THE PALACE OF VERSAILLES

ABOUT SEVEN O'CLOCK IN THE EVENING, October 23, 1991, a grand ceremony for the conclusion of an agreement was held at the Centre International des Congrès on Avenue Kléber, Paris. Thirty people, including representatives of various factions in Cambodia and foreign ministers of eighteen countries, together with Secretary General Xavier Perez de Cuéllar of the United Nations, signed an agreement in five languages—English, Chinese, French, Russian, and Khmer. The representatives included twelve members of the Supreme National Council of Cambodia headed by Prince Norodom Sihanouk, its chairman; and the following foreign ministers and foreign secretaries: Gareth Evans of Australia, Mohamed Bolkiah of Brunei, Barbara McDougall of Canada, Roland Dumas of France, Madhavsinh Solanki of India, Alatas of Indonesia, Nakayama Taro of Japan, Phoune Sipraseuth of Laos, Badawi of Malaysia, Paul Manglapus of the Philippines, Wong Kan Sheng of Singapore, Arsa Sarasin of Thailand, Boris D. Pankin of the Soviet Union, Douglas Hurd of Britain, Nguyen Manh Cam of Vietnam, and Budimir Loncar of Yugoslavia. Secretary of State James Baker represented the United States. In my capacity as Chinese foreign minister, I also signed the agreement, on behalf of China.

What we solemnly signed that day was the Cambodian Peace Agreement* reached at an international conference in Paris.

In the 1980s, Cambodia was a hot issue that affected the international situation and had a considerable impact on China's diplomatic relations. The peace agreement was a historic event. As I pointed out at the press conference after the ceremony, the peace agreement marked the end of a thirteen-year war in Cambodia; it would restore Cambodia's independence and sovereignty; it would contribute to peace and stability in southeast Asia; and it would set a good example for the peaceful settlement of regional conflicts elsewhere.

At nine that evening the Palace of Versailles, southwest of Paris, was ablaze with light. The host country, France, held a grand banquet for all representatives attending the conference to celebrate the peace agreement. The palace, which had stood for more than 300 years, had witnessed the end of the First World War. Now it was witnessing joy over the end of another war. The most elated person present was Prince Norodom Sihanouk. He made a long off-the-cuff speech, expressing his gratitude to all the countries that had contributed to the settlement and acknowledging the resolve and earnestness of all factions in Cambodia, which had achieved unity and cooperation. Foreign ministers present at the banquet all made warm impromptu speeches expressing their satisfaction and offering their compliments at the peaceful settlement of a regional conflict by the efforts of the international community, and speaking highly of Prince Norodom

---

* The Cambodian Peace Agreement includes the Agreement on a Comprehensive Political Settlement of the Cambodia Conflict; the Agreement Concerning the Sovereignty, Independence, Territorial Integrity and Inviolability, Neutrality and National Unity of Cambodia; the Declaration on Rehabilitation and Reconstruction of Cambodia; and the Final Act of the Paris Conference on Cambodia.

Sihanouk for his contributions to realizing peace in Cambodia. When the banquet neared an end, people showed not the slightest sign of fatigue, and were reluctant to leave. They had photographs taken, talked animatedly, or walked from table to table signing their names on each other's menus as a souvenir. It was not until midnight that the banquet ended, amid the sounds of blessings and good-byes.

The Cambodian Peace Agreement has gone down in history as an example of a peaceful settlement of a regional conflict through international cooperation. But to China, it has a deeper significance.

THE CAMBODIAN ISSUE

THE CAMBODIAN ISSUE dates back to the 1970s. It had a direct effect on Sino-Soviet relations and was one of the "three major barriers" hindering the normalization of Sino-Soviet relations.

In 1975, after Vietnam won the war against the American invaders, its leaders, backed by the Soviet Union and disregarding Cambodian independence and sovereignty, made a series of demands on the Cambodian government that intensified the conflict between Vietnam and Cambodia. As a result, a large-scale armed clash broke out on the border. On December 25, 1978, Vietnam sent its troops into Cambodia; occupied Phnom Penh, the capital; and established the People's Republic of Cambodia, headed by Heng Samrin. After that, Vietnam kept troops stationed in Cambodia.

The Vietnamese act, in violation of international law, was naturally met with tenacious resistance by the Cambodian people, and by strong denunciations and opposition from the international community. Cambodia also became a factor in international political struggles. Within Cambodia, three factions—led respectively by the original Democratic Kampuchea party, Prince Norodom Sihanouk, and Son Sann—waged an armed struggle against Vietnam in the mountainous areas in the north and west of Cambodia; formed a united front; and established a coalition government headed by Norodom Sihanouk. Internationally, most countries, including ASEAN's members, China, the United States, Japan, and Western European nations, took the side of the coalition. Beginning with the thirty-fourth General Assembly of the United Nations in 1979, each assembly overwhelmingly passed a resolution demanding that Vietnam withdraw its armed forces unconditionally from Cambodia.

By the mid-1980s, the war in Cambodia was at a stalemate. Though Vietnam and the Phnom Penh regime were stronger, they were unable to defeat or wipe out the resistance forces. The two sides were contending on the battlefield but were also beginning to explore the possibility of a political settlement.

Vietnam was bogged in the mire of the war in Cambodia, which brought a heavy burden on the Vietnamese people and isolated Vietnam from the international community. The Vietnamese leaders, therefore, had no choice but to consider a political settlement. In 1985, Vietnam presented for the first time a plan to pull its troops out of Cambodia by 1990. In March 1986, the three factions of the Cambodian resistance forces held a cabinet meeting in Beijing and put forward "eight suggestions" for a political settlement and the establishment of a four-sided coalition government with Prince Norodom Sihanouk as the head. Phnom Penh responded quickly, and for the first time expressed its willingness to negotiate with the coalition government of Democratic Kampuchea. Subsequently, Vietnam also announced that if the three factions of Democratic Kampuchea held negotiations with the Phnom Penh regime and established a four-sided coalition government, it would be ready to negotiate with this government regarding the withdrawal of Vietnamese troops. Though this proposal was rejected by the coalition government and by the international community, both sides had begun to show signs that they were ready for negotiations.

By then, the Soviet Union, which had all along been backing Vietnam, had to make a strategic adjustment because of the heavy burden of the arms race, and seek to improve relations with the United States and China.

Deng Xiaoping seized this opportunity to make a strategic decision to adjust China's relations with the Soviet Union. He put forward the idea of normalizing Sino-Soviet relations, on the condition

that the "three major barriers" were resolved. Then the special envoys at the level of vice foreign minister of the two countries began
twelve rounds of consultations, which lasted for six years. One of the
most important themes of the consultations was the demand that the
Soviet Union urge Vietnam to withdraw its troops from Cambodia.

After Mikhail Gorbachev became the leader of the Soviet Union
in 1985, he adopted the slogan "new thinking" and began to adjust
the country's foreign and domestic policies in a comprehensive way.
In July 1986, he said at Vladivostok: "The settlement of the Cambodia
issue depends on the normalization of relations between China and
Vietnam. Now we have a good opportunity. The whole of Asia needs
this." The Soviet Union was sending a message that it would no
longer support Vietnam in the latter's confrontation with China.

The evolution of the international situation brought a ray of
hope for a political settlement of the Cambodian issue.

RELAXATION OF THE STAND OF THE SOVIET UNION AND VIETNAM

AFTER GORBACHEV'S SPEECH in Vladivostok, the special envoys of
China and the Soviet Union no longer avoided the topic of Cambodia
in their political consultations.

In April 1988, in Geneva, representatives of the Soviet Union, the
United States, Pakistan, and the Kabul government of Afghanistan
concluded an agreement on a political settlement of the Afghanistan
issue. The Soviet Union announced that it would withdraw all its
troops from Afghanistan before February 15, 1989. The Soviet side
publicly noted that this settlement was a good model for settling the
Cambodian issue, and that all foreign troops should be withdrawn
from Cambodia.

In June 1988, while I was in New York attending the Third Special Session of the General Assembly of the UN on Disarmament, I
met the Soviet foreign minister, Eduard Shevardnadze. He took the
initiative to talk to me about Cambodia. He said that the Geneva
agreement regarding Afghanistan was a breakthrough in efforts to

resolve regional conflicts, and implied that he hoped it could be applied to Cambodia. I said to him that the withdrawal of the Soviet Union from Afghanistan was a good thing, and therefore welcome. But China was more concerned about Cambodia. Previously, the Soviet Union had habitually said that China was wrong to raise the issue of Cambodia with it. Not until after four years of consultations did the Soviet side agree to discuss this issue. Settling the issue would be in the interests of Cambodia, Vietnam, the Soviet Union, China, and ASEAN. Shevardnadze said that a tendency toward national reconciliation had already appeared in Cambodia, but without China's participation there could be no political settlement. I replied that China had all along had a positive attitude toward the Cambodian issue. I also said that the Soviet Union could play an active role and exert significant influence. At that time, the twelfth round of the Sino-Soviet political consultations was about to begin, so I said that we hoped that the issue would make some progress at the consultations, and hoped that he would give instructions to the Soviet delegation to sincerely discuss Cambodia. He replied readily that the Soviet Union would not avoid this issue, but would actively participate in a political settlement.

When the twelfth round of the consultations was held, the Soviet side took the initiative to propose convening a special session on the Cambodia issue at the level of vice foreign ministers. At the end of August, a round of consultations devoted to Cambodia was held in Beijing between two vice foreign ministers: Rogachev of the Soviet Union and Tian Zengpei of China. Though there were still disagreements, both sides said that they hoped to see an early political settlement and agreed that all foreign troops must be withdrawn from Cambodia as soon as possible. The Soviet side promised to contribute its efforts within its capability.

On July 1, 1988, China published a Foreign Ministry statement, putting forward four points for the settlement of the Cambodian issue: (1) withdrawal of the Vietnamese troops from Cambodia as soon as possible; (2) establishment of a four-sided coalition government headed by Prince Norodom Sihanouk, after the withdrawal of the

Vietnamese troops; (3) a free general election in Cambodia, after the establishment of the coalition government; and (4) effective international supervision of the first three processes.

At about the same time, Vietnam began to change its attitude toward Cambodia. In July 1986, Le Duan, general secretary of the Central Committee of the Communist Party of Vietnam, died. In December, Nguyen Van Linh was elected the new general secretary. He summed up past experiences and lessons, began to adjust his country's foreign and domestic policies, and looked for a political settlement in Cambodia. In May 1988, one month after the signing of the Geneva Agreement on Afghanistan, Vietnam publicly undertook to withdraw 50,000 troops from Cambodia by 1989; withdraw all its troops before 1990; and agree to attend a "cocktail party" on the issue of Cambodia in Jakarta together with the three resistance factions and the Phnom Penh regime.

ASEAN was all for an early settlement of the Cambodian issue. So, headed by Indonesia, an informal conference was held in Jakarta. Those invited included the four sides in Cambodia; Vietnam; and some other relevant countries. Since this was an informal conference, the attendees could exchange views with no constraints. That is why it was called a "cocktail party."

In July 1988, the four resistance factions and Vietnam finally came to the "cocktail party" in Jakarta, but it achieved no substantial results. Vietnam refused to accept international supervision of the withdrawal of its troops, and insisted that in any case the withdrawal should be contingent on cessation of "external interference." Also, the Phnom Penh regime refused to dissolve simultaneously the powers of both Phnom Penh and Democratic Kampuchea, and resolutely rejected the participation of the Khmer Rouge.* Still, this was the first time that Vietnam, the Phnom Penh regime, and the three resistance factions had had the opportunity to discuss a political settlement.

---

* The term "Khmer Rouge" dates from the 1960s. It was a collective name for the Leftist factions in Cambodia at that time. Later, to the Western countries, it became a name referring to the Communist Party of Cambodia and Democratic Kampuchea.

After that, the position of the Khmer Rouge on the future power structure of Cambodia gradually became the focus of the international negotiations.

The Paris Conference Proposal

AFTER THE "COCKTAIL PARTY" had failed, Prince Norodom Sihanouk proposed to President François Mitterrand of France, who was attending the Forty-Third General Assembly of the UN, that France should convene an international conference on Cambodia in Paris.

The reasons for this proposal were both historical and practical. Historically, France had had close relations with the three countries of Indochina. In the late nineteenth century, France had established colonial rule over the Indochinese peninsula, and Vietnam, Laos, and Cambodia successively became part of French Indochina. Not until 1954 was France expelled from the Indochinese peninsula by the powerful resistance of the Indochinese peoples. Realistically, compared with other big powers, France was less involved in the Cambodian issue. To select France as the location for an international conference to discuss that issue was therefore acceptable to all parties.

Prince Sihanouk's proposal was to France's liking. The year 1989 happened to be the 200th anniversary of the French Revolution. President Mitterrand meant to do something to mark the occasion. If he could make a contribution to the settlement of the Cambodian issue, he would have the opportunity to play his role on the international stage, and his name would resound in French history.

As the possibility of a political settlement grew, the United States and some other countries began to make an issue of the Khmer Rouge. The Soviet Union and Vietnam were opposed to it, of course. The Western countries also tried to exclude the Khmer Rouge from the future power structure and keep it out of the process of the political settlement. But the United States and other Western countries were well aware that the Khmer Rouge was the strongest of all the resistance forces in Cambodia—and that to force Vietnam to leave Cambodia, the resistance forces were indispensable. Therefore, at first they were reticent regarding the Khmer Rouge. When the Paris conference was in the preparatory stage, however, keeping the Khmer Rouge out became their major consideration.

The United States now began its diplomatic efforts. In June 1988, when I attended the Special Session of the General Assembly of the UN on Disarmament, Michael Armacost, the U.S. undersecretary of state for political affairs, came to see me to discuss Cambodia. He said that the United States expected negotiations on Cambodia to speed up, probably in the following year. What the United States worried about was that if the withdrawal of the Vietnamese troops was too rapid, the Khmer Rouge might take power again. Therefore, he suggested, it was imperative to consider introducing international forces to disarm the Khmer Rouge. The United States wanted to discuss this issue frankly with China and Thailand. Nevertheless, Armacost had to admit that the Khmer Rouge would be the main force in the struggle against the Vietnamese troops. The United States knew that this was a sensitive issue, and that balance was needed in handling it.

I said to Armacost that China opposed rule by any single faction in Cambodia in the future, but that we also opposed the exclusion of any faction. This was what we could say in public. We supported rule by a coalition government truly headed by Sihanouk. As for how to reach this goal, I was sure that we would find a way.

When President George Bush of the United States visited China in February 1989, he raised the issue of the Khmer Rouge again with Deng Xiaoping. Deng suggested that the military force of each faction of Cambodia be reduced to 10,000, so that no faction would be powerful enough to make any trouble. He also expressly told Bush that China supported a four-sided coalition government headed by Prince Sihanouk, and that all international aid to Cambodia must be carried out through Sihanouk.

PROGRESS IN NEGOTIATION

I WAS INVITED TO VISIT the Soviet Union in early December 1988. Cambodia was one of the topics for discussion. At a session with

Shevardnadze, I focused on three points. First, China and the Soviet Union should see eye to eye on the timetable for the withdrawal of the Vietnamese troops, and the Soviet Union should urge Vietnam to withdraw. Second, after Vietnam had withdrawn its troops, all foreign countries must stop military aid to all the factions in Cambodia, must not support any faction that wanted to wage a civil war, and must establish a four-sided coalition government with Sihanouk as its leader. Third, the military forces of all factions should be disarmed, and international peacekeeping troops should be sent to Cambodia to exercise strict supervision over and provide an international guarantee for the withdrawal of the Vietnamese troops, and the process of national reconciliation in Cambodia.

Shevardnadze said that the Soviet side hoped to see an early settlement of the issue, but there should be certain conditions for the withdrawal of the Vietnamese troops.

After repeated discussions, we reached two points of internal understanding: (1) Both sides would endeavor to get Vietnam to withdraw all its troops quickly, for instance, in the latter half of 1989 or at the latest by the end of 1989. (2) Both sides agreed that as Vietnam withdrew its troops under international supervision, the relevant countries must gradually reduce to zero military aid to all factions in Cambodia. The Soviet side took the initiative and said that when Shevardnadze visited China the following year, the two foreign ministers would announce a joint communiqué on Cambodia.

During my visit, Gorbachev and Shevardnadze told me that the Soviet side hoped that China would negotiate directly with Vietnam. After the visit, the Chinese central leadership decided to negotiate directly with Vietnam regarding Cambodia, and laid down principles for the negotiations.

As a matter of fact, the foreign minister of Vietnam, Nguyen Co Thach, twice asked to visit China in 1988. Considering that Vietnam had not essentially changed its stand on the Cambodian issue, we refused his requests. At the end of that year, he wrote another letter expressing his wish to visit China: "The time is ripe for Vietnam and China to sit down together," he said; and he expressed the hope that the two sides would cooperate "to create conditions for an appropriate political settlement between the various Cambodian factions on the foundation of national reconciliation."

After studying his words, we decided that Vietnam was taking a new, flexible position, and so we could contact Vietnam regarding bilateral relations, and particularly regarding Cambodia. But considering that a meeting between the two foreign ministers would be a matter of great political importance, we concluded that the time was not yet ripe. So we told the Vietnamese authorities that it would take a great deal of preparatory work for the two foreign ministers to meet, and we suggested that Vietnam send a vice foreign minister to Beijing so that we could hold internal consultations on the political settlement of the Cambodian issue.

Vietnam accepted our proposal. In January 1989, its vice foreign minister, Dinh Nho Liem, visited Beijing. In consultations with China's vice foreign minister, Liu Shuqing, he said that Vietnam would withdraw all its troops from Cambodia. The two sides narrowed the gaps between them on various issues: halting foreign aid to all the Cambodian factions, guaranteeing a neutral nonallied position for Cambodia, and providing international supervision and an international guarantee. But Vietnam refused to take any responsibility for guaranteeing internal peace in Cambodia after withdrawing its troops, arguing that this was an internal Cambodian affair and should be resolved among the various Cambodian factions; it was not an issue to be discussed by Vietnam and China.

In view of this attitude, I particularly pointed out when meeting Dinh Nho Liem that the Cambodian issue was, basically, the responsibility of the four factions of Cambodia to settle without foreign interference. But Vietnam, as a party involved in the issue, as well as the Soviet Union, China, and Thailand, should have a clear-cut policy: after the foreign forces had been withdrawn, aid to various Cambodian factions must be halted; and Cambodia should achieve four-sided unity and national reconciliation, and put an end to civil war and instability. The relevant countries, Vietnam in particular, should shoulder their responsibilities for all these matters.

Dinh Nho Liem said that it was Vietnam's long-term strategy to settle the Cambodian issue as soon as possible, to normalize its relations with China, and to concentrate its efforts on economic construction. I told him that if the basic aspects of the Cambodian issue could be resolved, improvement and normalization of the relations between China and Vietnam would be a natural result.

UNEXPECTED COMPLICATIONS

THROUGH THE CONCERTED EFFORTS of China and other relevant countries, the international conditions for a political settlement of the Cambodian issue were gradually formulated. At the proposal of Prince Sihanouk, the Paris conference was set for the end of July 1989. As foreign minister of the host country, Roland Dumas wrote a letter to me in June 1989, inviting China to attend this international ministerial-level conference.

Just at that time, political turmoil took place in Beijing, and the governments of certain Western countries imposed sanctions against China. Soon a huge anti-China wave appeared in those Western countries, particularly in the media.

France played a nasty role in this anti-China wave. At that time, Chinese passengers at airports in France were arbitrarily discriminated against by the French police, and their movements were restricted. They were not allowed to call the Chinese embassy, not allowed to go to the toilet, and not even given drinking water. Dumas, who had just invited me to attend the Paris conference, said that he would halt all visits between France and China, and would not meet the Chinese foreign minister. As for inviting the Chinese delegation headed by me to attend the Paris conference on Cambodia, he said that it was an international conference, and meeting me could not be called a meeting between two foreign ministers.

Though the situation had changed drastically and was very complicated, we decided that China must attend the Paris Conference. There was speculation in the Western media that because of the turmoil in Beijing, China was too busy with its own troubles to play any role in international affairs. Our presence at the conference would be a good opportunity to make China's stand known to the international community. Besides, the conference would be the only place where China would have any public contact with the West at that time. We could make use of this opportunity to break through the diplomatic stalemate.

Though all the relevant parties of the international community favored an international conference to settle the Cambodian issue, each had its own ideas, requirements, and plan. In particular, there was great dispute over the internal problems of Cambodia. The focus of this dispute was the Khmer Rouge. Vietnam, the Phnom Penh regime, and some other countries advocated a union between Sihanouk and Hun Sen, but excluding the Khmer Rouge. The three resistance forces in Cambodia and the countries of ASEAN insisted on a provisional four-sided coalition government headed by Sihanouk. We knew that the struggle at the conference would be fierce, and without China's participation it would be almost impossible to reach any comprehensive settlement.

Before the Paris Conference, I had already arrived in Botswana, beginning a visit to six southern African countries. To attend the conference, I made a special trip from Botswana, going first to London and then arriving in Paris at noon on July 30.

That afternoon, I met Dumas. As soon as I saw him, I said gravely: "Didn't you announce that you would not see the Chinese foreign minister? I am the Chinese foreign minister, so you should not see me, should you?" Then I pointed out that in the anti-China wave, France had stirred up the waters and played an inglorious role, uncivilized and rude. This was exemplified by the inhumane treatment of Chinese passengers at French airports.

Rather embarrassed, Dumas had to apologize; he said that he had to use those words to deal with the French parliament and the media, and asked me not to take them to heart. Then he argued (lamely) that the recent actions of France were not aimed against China but were done out of "friendship" for China. Relations between France and China were very good, he said, and France had been one of the first countries to establish diplomatic relations with China. Therefore, his argument went, France had slightly overreacted. It was a case of "the more the love, the fiercer the reproach." Later, Dumas was involved in the scandal of selling weapons to Taiwan. I cannot imagine how he defended himself in that case.

Big-Country Diplomacy

on july 31, 1989, the international conference was convened in Paris, as scheduled. I made a speech on the first day. Its gist was as follows. Essentially, the Cambodian issue had been caused by the invasion of troops from another country and the protracted occupation. The key to settling the issue was, first, the complete withdrawal of foreign troops from Cambodia under international supervision; and second, after the withdrawal of the foreign troops, the maintenance of peace, prevention of further civil war, and realization of national reconciliation. These two basic issues were closely related, and neither was dispensable. China had no selfish interests to gain in this matter. If the international conference reached an agreement, China would, together with the other relevant countries, assume its obligations, stop military aid to any faction, and respect the results of Cambodia's free general election to be held in the future.

Before the conference, the United States had proposed that Secretary of State James Baker meet me during it to discuss bilateral relations and other relevant issues. At that time, the United States did all it could to impose sanctions on China. In fear of being criticized by the media for holding such a meeting, it requested that the meeting should be limited to a small group, and that the matters discussed should not be disclosed.

When I met Baker, we focused our discussion on Cambodia, separately from the bilateral relations between China and the United States. Baker said that the cooperation shown between our two countries at the conference indicated not only that they shared the same view on the Cambodian issue, but also that they had common political and strategic interests. He said that he hoped the two countries would together play a guiding role on the issue. He raised three questions: Would China grant asylum to Pol Pot and others? Would it consider stopping military aid to the Khmer Rouge? And would refugees have freedom of choice when being repatriated?

To those three questions, my reply was that no one from the Democratic Kampuchea side had asked China for asylum. After Vietnam had totally withdrawn its troops and the issue had been settled, China would, together with the other relevant countries, be willing to fulfill its obligation to stop military aid. The refugees were a matter between Cambodia and Thailand, I said, and had nothing to do with China.

During the conference, I met eleven foreign ministers, including Britain's foreign secretary, John Major, Japan's foreign minister Mitsuzuka Hiroshi, and Canada's foreign minister, Charles Clark. This was the first time since the political turmoil in Beijing that China had had high-level diplomatic contacts with Western countries. Shortly before the conference, participants in the meeting of the leaders of the European Union and the summit meeting of the Western G-7 group had declared that they would not hold any high-level meetings with Chinese officials at the ministerial level or above. But China could not be excluded from the political settlement of the Cambodian issue. When other countries discussed Cambodia at the international conference, they had to talk to China. So they had to say that it was an international conference—a multisided contact, not a bilateral contact. Thus the Paris Conference provided an opportunity for us to break the sanctions imposed by the West.

The Paris conference ended on August 1, without results. The following day, I flew to Lesotho to continue my southern African tour. The Chinese delegation headed by Liu Shuqing stayed behind in Paris to participate in discussions on matters of substance concerning Cambodia.

On the whole, most attending countries took the same stand on the political settlement of the Cambodian issue. During the conference, we did a lot of work with the three factions of Democratic Kampuchea. Their delegates, headed by Prince Sihanouk, often visited the

Chinese embassy in Paris to exchange information and discuss ways to cope with the situation. Sihanouk had deep feelings for and full trust in the Chinese leaders. They were all optimistic about the progress of the conference. We also had close consultations with the United States, Britain, Thailand, Singapore, Japan, and Canada. On the major issues, we synchronized our steps, and together guided the progress of the conference.

The dispute over the Khmer Rouge was so sharp that the conference was unable to reach any agreement. However, the conference did provide an opportunity for countries relevant to the Cambodia issue and the four sides in Cambodia to sit together for the first time to discuss the issue and lay a solid foundation for its final settlement.

Not long afterward, when I attended the General Assembly of the UN, I met Dumas again. He was disappointed by the failure of the Paris conference, and was in a pessimistic mood. I said to him that although the Paris Conference had not produced an agreement, it had been helpful, and most countries had reached a consensus. The stumbling block had been the stubborn attitude of Vietnam. France should expect a change in the Vietnamese attitude. I assured him that China supported the reopening of the Paris conference when the conditions were ripe.

A few days before my meeting with Dumas, I had met Secretary of State Baker again. Before I went to New York, Baker had told Han Xu, the Chinese ambassador in Washington, that he had had a very good talk with me and hoped to see me again during the UN General Assembly. During this period, it was almost always on multisided occasions that I met Western foreign ministers. But the channels for contact had all along been maintained.

I had a meeting with Baker on the evening of September 28. He said that the relations between our two countries had improved since the Paris conference. President George Bush and Baker himself were very concerned about the relations between the United States and China, he said, and he hoped that the two sides would continue a dialogue that would enable the relations between them to return to normality as soon as possible. On the Cambodian issue, Baker said that the United States was satisfied with the cooperation between the two countries at the Paris Conference. But he had significant reservations on the issue of the Khmer Rouge. The United States had originally wanted to exclude the Khmer Rouge, and had advocated a settlement between only the other three factions of Cambodia. But, as Prince Sihanouk held that it was necessary to include the Khmer Rouge in Cambodia's future power structure, the United States had to, though reluctantly, accept this. Baker said it was worrisome that the political settlement of the issue was turning into a settlement on the battlefield. He said that he hoped that China would play an active role, and force the Khmer Rouge to accept a political settlement. If the Khmer Rouge wanted to settle the issue on the battlefield, the United States and the countries of ASEAN would not allow them to play any role in Cambodia's future government.

I first told Baker that China was also satisfied with the cooperation between itself and the United States at the Paris conference. However, I reiterated China's principles on a peaceful settlement of the Cambodian issue. I said there was no possibility the Khmer Rouge would return to power, and China would not support such a solution. If the Soviet Union and Vietnam truly stopped supplying arms to Phnom Penh, China would stop supplying arms to the resistance forces of Democratic Kampuchea. The current problem was that there was no international supervision for the withdrawal of the Vietnamese troops, and people had reason to doubt Vietnam's sincerity. The international conference on Cambodia should expressly support a four-sided coalition government headed by Sihanouk. The detailed allocation of seats for each faction should be left to the four factions of Cambodia themselves, I emphasized.

Baker said that Shevardnadze had already expressed to him that if the relevant countries stopped supplying arms to the Cambodian factions, the Soviet Union would also stop supplying arms to the Phnom Penh regime. The United States held that the Soviet Union and Vietnam should exert pressure on Hun Sen to accept a certain division of power, while China should exert pressure on the Khmer Rouge and make them take a more realistic approach. It would never do to reach an agreement on the internal problems of Cambodia by relying on the four Cambodian factions alone. Therefore, China, the Soviet Union, the United States, and ASEAN should draft a plan for the settlement of those internal issues of Cambodia. Baker proposed that Sihanouk become head of state and Hun Sen prime minister, that each faction have two seats in the cabinet, and that the important positions such as ministers of foreign affairs, national defense, and internal affairs be filled by appointments by Sihanouk and Son Sann. In this way, Sihanouk would be guaranteed true power. If the big powers agreed with this arrangement and persuaded the four Cambodian factions to consent to it, Vietnam would probably give its consent, too.

I replied that this would depend on whether the four factions accepted his proposal, and it was particularly necessary to consult Sihanouk, who might object to the big powers' asking him to be head of state while imposing a prefabricated arrangement on him.

PEACE AGREEMENT

FOR SOME TIME AFTER the Paris Conference in August 1989, the tide of a political settlement of the Cambodian issue was at a low ebb. On the battlefields in Cambodia, fighting between the factions grew fiercer. Peace seemed remote.

To break through this stalemate, the five permanent members of the UN Security Council held six rounds of consultation at the level of vice foreign minister in Paris and New York from January to August 1990, and formulated a framework document for a comprehensive political settlement. This document basically satisfied each faction's minimum objectives and requirements, and was accepted by each of the relevant parties.

By then, the attitude of Vietnam had become more flexible, and China and Vietnam made a significant step toward the normalization of their relations. In early September 1990, General Secretary Nguyen Van Linh; Do Muoi, chairman of the Council of Ministers; and Pham Van Dong, adviser to the Central Committee of the Communist Party of Vietnam were invited to visit China. They held an internal meeting with General Secretary Jiang Zemin and Premier Li Peng in Chengdu, the capital of Sichuan Province in southwestern China. The Vietnamese leaders said that they were willing to accept the UN's supervision and inspection of the withdrawal of their troops. Both sides accepted the framework document prepared by the five permanent members of the Security Council, and agreed to make joint efforts to press the relevant factions of Cambodia to accept the document, so as to accelerate a comprehensive political settlement.

After this meeting, both China and Vietnam immediately sent representatives to Jakarta, to persuade the four Cambodian factions—which were having an informal conference there—to accept the document. Finally, the four sides announced their acceptance and decided to set up a twelve-person Supreme National Council consisting of members from the four sides.

In November, the working group of the Paris Conference completed the drafting of the framework document prepared by the five permanent members of the Security Council, together with its appendixes and relevant documents for a comprehensive political settlement. Then, suddenly, the Phnom Penh regime asked that the framework agreement be amended to increase the number of its members on the Supreme National Council of Cambodia or allow one of its representatives to be the vice chairman of the council.

So the final settlement of the Cambodian issue was delayed yet again.

To expedite the agreement, China once again played an important role. It and other relevant countries continuously held consultations with the four Cambodian factions on the power arrangements for the future Cambodian government. In July 1991, the Cambodian Supreme National Council held a working conference in Beijing, when the Phnom Penh side agreed that Sihanouk should become the chairman of the Supreme National Council, and no longer insisted that its own representative had to be the vice chairman or that the number of its members on the council had to be increased. In August, Vietnamese vice foreign minister, Nguyen Dy Nieu, visited China and held consultations with the Chinese vice foreign minister, Xu

Dunxin, on the Cambodian issue and on normalization of relations between China and Vietnam. I also met Nguyen Dy Nieu. Afterward, China and Vietnam issued a press communiqué unanimously agreeing that the framework document prepared by the five permanent members of the UN Security Council must not be changed, although the draft agreement prepared by the working group of the Paris conference could be amended, provided such changes were not in conflict with the contents of the framework document. In September, the Vietnamese foreign minister, Nguyen Manh Cam, visited China. This was the first time in more than ten years that the foreign ministers of China and Vietnam had met. We exchanged views on Cambodia, and both sides agreed to continue to exert active efforts for a final settlement.

On September 14, 1991, the Cambodia delegation, comprising representatives of the four factions, led by Sihanouk, arrived in New York for the first time in a dozen years to attend the UN General Assembly, indicating that a new Cambodian coalition government would soon be established.

During the General Assembly, the five permanent members of the UN Security Council, the two chairmen of the Paris Conference, the foreign ministers of all the countries attending the Paris Conference, the representative of the UN secretary general, and the members of the Supreme National Council of Cambodia reached the final framework agreement on the Cambodian issue, creating conditions for the reconvening of the international conference in Paris in October 1991.

On October 23, 1991, the Cambodian peace agreement was at last duly signed in Paris, finally realizing a political settlement of the Cambodian issue.

It was not easy to reach a peaceful settlement of the Cambodia issue at a time when the international situation was extremely complicated and unstable. For years, the UN and the international community had made unremitting efforts to solve all kinds of regional conflicts, but mostly to no avail. The reason the Cambodian issue could be solved was that the relevant countries, the big powers in particular, found common ground for settling this regional conflict. In a multipolar world, the common interests of the big powers are very often the key factor in maintaining regional stability and peace.

Interestingly, when the Cambodia peace agreement was formally signed, the "8.19 incident" set off political instability in the Soviet Union. Shevardnadze, who had all along been involved in the negotiations on Cambodia, left his post. The man who signed the document on behalf of the Soviet Union was the new foreign minister, Pankin, with whom none of us was familiar.

After the conclusion of the peace agreement, Sihanouk·returned to Phnom Penh, the capital of Cambodia, after an absence of thirteen years. Very soon, the UN also sent to Cambodia its provisional power agency and 22,000 UN peacekeeping troops. After concerted efforts by all parties for more than a year, a national general election was held for the first time in over twenty years in Cambodia, and Sihanouk was supported by all parties as head of state. On September 24, he resumed the throne. The Khmer Rouge was declared an illegal organization in 1994, since they had refused to take part in the general election.

3 FLYING TO BAGHDAD

A Sudden Storm

ON AUGUST 2, 1990, the Gulf crisis broke out when Iraqi forces stormed over the border into neighboring Kuwait. Soon afterward, Iraq formally declared that it had annexed Kuwait. This shocked the whole world.

Although the invasion was a surprise, there had in fact been signs that trouble was brewing in the region. In late July of that year, I happened to be in Saudi Arabia, preparing to sign the communiqué for the establishment of diplomatic relations between China and Saudi Arabia. Prince Faisal, the Saudi foreign minister, and I held a meeting on the first day of my visit, and everything went smoothly. Both sides decided to formally sign the communiqué the next day. But to my surprise, Faisal did not show up. We wondered if the Saudis had changed their minds; then we were informed that an urgent matter had come up, and the prince did not have time to sign the communiqué. When he came back, in the evening, he told me that he had been trying to mediate between Iraq and Kuwait at the request of King Fahd, as conflict was imminent.

The problem between Iraq and Kuwait dated back to 1921, when Iraq won independence from Britain. Both Iraq and Kuwait had been part of the Turkish Ottoman Empire, and Kuwait was part of the Iraqi province of Basrah. Britain occupied the area after the Ottoman Empire was dissolved following the First World War, but not until 1961 did it grant independence to Kuwait. Border disputes were frequent between Iraq and Kuwait. Kuwait is a small country with a small population, but it is rich in oil resources. Iraq became heavily indebted, particularly to Kuwait, during its eight years of war with Iran in the 1980s. In 1990, the dispute grew acute and many Arab countries tried to mediate, but without success. Now, as many Kuwaitis were on vacation in Europe, Iraq took the opportunity and crossed the border.

Both Iraq and Kuwait are developing countries, and both had good relations with China. But the invasion and occupation of Kuwait by Iraq was a gross violation of the rules of international relations. The spokesman for China's Ministry of Foreign Affairs issued a statement on the day of the invasion, announcing the stand of the Chinese government and calling for a settlement of the dispute through peaceful negotiations. On August 8, the vice foreign minister, Yang Fuchang, urgently summoned the ambassadors of the two countries, calling on Iraq to withdraw its troops as soon as possible, and expressing China's hope that the two Arab countries would solve their dispute through negotiations. On August 22, I met Prince Al-Sabah, the deputy prime minister and concurrent foreign minister of Kuwait, who was visiting China. I stressed that China resolutely opposed the invasion and annexation of Kuwait by Iraq. We demanded that Iraq unconditionally withdraw from Kuwait, and that Kuwait's independence, sovereignty, and territorial integrity be restored and respected.

At the time of the invasion, there were almost 5,000 Chinese workers and overseas Chinese, including more than 100 compatriots from Hong Kong and Taiwan, in Kuwait. By August 29, we had evacuated all of them to safety. Taiwan had a commercial representative office in Kuwait, but after the invasion, the person in charge of it fled, so that the Taiwanese compatriots had to turn to us for help.

The Gulf is a place of strategic importance. Any crisis there affects the strategic balance of the whole world.

The UN made a quick response. On August 2, the Security Council held an emergency meeting and adopted Resolution 660, condemning Iraq's aggression against Kuwait and demanding an unconditional withdrawal of Iraqi troops. China voted for the resolution. Later, the Security Council imposed sanctions, including an air and sea blockade, on Iraq. It also established a special committee—the 661 Committee—to monitor the implementation of the resolution and sanctions. China voted in favor of all these measures.

The Arab countries were most anxious about this crisis. They hated to see conflicts between brother states. The Gulf countries were busy with diplomatic mediation, and put forward many proposals for ending the impasse. But the interests and positions of the Arab countries differed, and there were many fruitless disputes over how to settle the crisis.

Meanwhile, the Soviet Union was facing growing domestic political and economic difficulties, and was too busy with its own troubles to take any meaningful stand on the Gulf crisis.

The response of the United States at that time was most forceful. On August 7, President George Bush signed an action program to send troops to the Gulf, and immediately afterward a massive U.S. military force began to move to the region.

A Visit to the Middle East

AS A LARGE COUNTRY, and particularly as one of the five permanent members of the UN Security Council, China is important in safeguarding world peace and regional stability—a fact that now became apparent to all. Many Arab countries sent special envoys to China. The foreign ministers of Kuwait, Jordan, and Saudi Arabia made working visits to Beijing. Iraq also sent its first deputy prime minister, Ramaddan, to China to state Iraq's view of the affair.

The most important diplomatic activities, however, took place at the UN.

From late September to early October 1990, I was in New York to attend the Forty-fifth General Assembly of the UN. At a meeting of the Security Council on September 25, I stated China's stand on the Gulf issue, and called on Iraq to heed the demands of the international community, take a cooperative attitude toward the Security Council, and immediately withdraw its troops from Kuwait. I pointed out that the Chinese government was in a favor of settling the Gulf crisis through peaceful means, supported the role played by the Security Council, welcomed the continuous mediation of the Secretary General of the UN, and supported the efforts of the Arab countries on the basis of relevant resolutions adopted by the Security Council. I also pointed out that China, in principle, did not agree with any military involvement by big powers in the Gulf region, because it would make the situation more complicated, and called upon the relevant countries to exercise maximum restraint. Concerning Resolution 670—the air embargo on Iraq—which had just been passed, I stressed that in implementing this resolution the relevant provisions of international law should be observed, to avert any act endangering civil aircraft or air passengers.

During the General Assembly session, the Chinese delegation borrowed from countries of the Non-Aligned Movement a room of less than thirty square meters to be used as a conference room. It became a center of multilateral diplomatic consultations and dialogues on the Gulf crisis. In that small room I met, one after another, the foreign ministers and leaders of some sixty countries.

I met a dozen foreign ministers of Middle Eastern countries, and found that all of them were worried about a possible war and were opposed to Iraq's invasion of Kuwait. But they disagreed on how to resolve the crisis. They praised China's stand and expressed the hope that China would play a greater role in dealing with the issue, now that diplomacy within the Middle East had proved insufficient.

The Secretary General of the UN, Xavier Perez de Cuéllar, said to me that a war—whether it would be fought in the name of the UN or in the name of the United States—must be avoided. If the United States insisted on a fight of its own, that would be especially dangerous. He said that the earlier Korean War was a bad example. He did not believe that the United States would let the UN command American troops.

The Soviet Union's Foreign Minister, Eduard Shevardnadze, told me that his country had sent Yevgeny Primakov, who was very familiar with Middle Eastern affairs, to Iraq twice as a special envoy. But nothing had been achieved as far as mediation was concerned. Primakov had managed only to secure the return of the 5,000 or so Soviet oil specialists and other experts. He said that the Soviet Union could do little, as the Arab countries were too divided.

At that time, the United States was eager to get authorization from the UN to take military action against Iraq. Together with some other Western countries, the United States, while praising China's stand, tried to get China onto its side.

When I meet the French foreign minister, Roland Dumas, I proposed that France should use its influence to get Iraq to withdraw from Kuwait. But he only shrugged and said that sometimes a friend might not listen to you. I emphasized to the foreign ministers of the West that the Security Council had already passed a number of resolutions, and we should give a bit more time to the UN, the Arab countries, and other parties concerned to pursue mediation. It was not easy for China to vote for the sanctions against Iraq, as three of the five permanent members of the Security Council were imposing sanctions on China.

On October 15, King Hussein Ibn Talal of Jordan proposed to the Chinese ambassador there that China send a senior special envoy to Iraq and other countries in the Gulf region. Earlier, Oman and Palestine had made similar proposals.

In light of the world situation and for the sake of peace in the Gulf, the Chinese central leadership decided to send me to Egypt, Saudi Arabia, Jordan, and Iraq from November 6 to 12 in the capacity of special envoy.

Since the 1980s, China has advocated and maintained a foreign policy of independence stressing improvement of bilateral relations with neighboring countries from the standpoint of its own security and interests; and, on the basis of its vital interests, establishing normal relations with countries throughout the world, including the Western nations.

In the Middle East, China had few direct interests, nor did it seek any private gains. Therefore, it was greatly trusted and respected by the Arab countries. At the same time, as a large developing country, China was gaining more and more say and influence concerning major international affairs. My visit to the Middle East to seek the possibility of a peaceful settlement to the Gulf crisis would strengthen China's international position and expand our influence in that region. It was of profound significance. To maintain world peace is China's consistent aim for its diplomacy. The effort to avoid war is China's contribution to the cause of world peace, no matter what the final consequences might be.

I was the only foreign minister of the five permanent member countries of the UN Security Council to visit Iraq during the Gulf crisis.

My brief was not to offer a prefabricated solution, or to act as a mediator, but to listen to the opinions of the various sides, try to persuade Iraq to withdraw from Kuwait, and strive to win a peaceful settlement to the Gulf crisis.

At the preparatory meeting before the visit, I stressed that we should have different foci when talking to different countries. Iraq was the major target of my visit, and we must express to Iraq that the armed invasion and occupation of another country on any pretext was unacceptable. The situation was very grave, and it was in Iraq's highest interest to avoid war. We should fully understand and sympathize with the plight of Kuwait and Saudi Arabia, and make clear China's opposition to aggression and its upholding of justice. At the same time, we must stress that a military settlement might not be the best choice for them. The crisis should be settled in accordance with the relevant resolutions of the UN. As for Jordan and Egypt, primarily we would like to find out their attitudes, and discuss with them the possibility of a peaceful settlement in the Gulf.

On learning of my mission, the United States asked that I meet Secretary of State Baker in Cairo. It was agreed that the meeting would take place on November 6. The United States was well aware that it needed an affirmative vote from China, a permanent member of the UN Security Council, if the council was to authorize military action.

MEETING SECRETARY BAKER IN CAIRO "BY CHANCE"

ON THE MORNING OF OCTOBER 31, Washington sent us a message saying that Baker was scheduled to visit Middle East countries beginning on November 3 and asking me to meet him in Cairo on the afternoon of November 6. We agreed. Shortly afterward, the United States sent a non-paper* stating that the meeting of two foreign ministers would help to synchronize the steps of the five permanent members of the Security Council regarding the Gulf crisis. It also stated that to reach a peaceful settlement, Iraq must withdraw from Kuwait and the sovereignty of Kuwait must be restored.

Later, Saudi Arabia suggested that I meet King Fahd in Jidda, a port city on the western coast of Saudi Arabia, after my visit to Iraq. So my itinerary was: Beijing—Cairo—At Taif—Riyadh—Amman—Baghdad—Jidda—Beijing.

Because of the UN sanctions on Iraq, no international airlines were flying to Baghdad, so I had to charter an airplane, after getting special approval from the UN. At first, we planned to fly to Iraq via Turkey. But Turkey for some reason refused us permission. We had to change our route: we entered Iraq via Jordan and left via Saudi Arabia.

We left Beijing at nine A.M. November 6, and, after a flight of twelve hours, landed at Cairo at three-thirty P.M. local time. James Baker had arrived that morning and was scheduled to leave that af-

---

* Non-paper is a form of diplomatic document, used primarily by one party to express its preliminary view, stand, or proposal on a specific issue for bilateral or multilateral discussion, but with no formal binding effect.

ternoon. So the visiting Chinese foreign minister encountered the secretary of state of the United States "by chance," as the United State's sanctions against China were still in place, and meetings of senior officials of the two countries were supposed to be banned. However, during the Gulf crisis, the United States needed China's cooperation, so contacts and exchanges between the two sides increased quickly. In fact, the meeting in Cairo was the fourth contact between China and the United States since the summer of 1989.

On the day Iraq invaded Kuwait, the American ambassador to China, James Roderick Lilley, briefed us on the position of the United States, and asked us about our attitude. From August 4 to 5, the assistant secretary of state, Richard Solomon, visited Beijing to exchange views with China on the situation in the Gulf. President Bush wrote several letters to China's president, Yang Shangkun, seeking cooperation on the matter. Baker also wrote letters or sent messages to me for the same purpose. I met him at the Paris Conference on Cambodia in July 1989, and then at the Forty-fourth General Assembly of the UN in New York in September 1989. I also met him during the Forty-fifth General Assembly of the UN in September 1990. At that meeting, the main topic of discussion was the Gulf crisis. The United States wanted China to issue a joint communiqué with it on this issue. In view of the relations between our two countries at that time, we thought it unwise to make an announcement on this single issue, so we did not agree. Baker once told me that if the sanctions against Iraq did not work after a few months, armed force would have to be considered. The United States would request authorization from the UN to take multilateral military action, but if the UN refused to grant such authorization, the United States would take unilateral action in accordance with Article 51 of the UN Charter. At the meeting in Cairo, the American side was anxious to learn our attitude on the issue of armed intervention with authorization by the UN Security Council.

With the assistance of the Egyptian authorities, I met Baker in the VIP room at Cairo Airport. Our talks lasted an hour and a half. Baker expressed appreciation for China's assistance toward a settlement of the Gulf crisis. He said the United States had no intention of permanently stationing its forces in the Gulf region; once the crisis was over, it would pull its troops out immediately, except for a naval force that it had kept stationed in the region since 1949. Baker said that if, when I visited Iraq, I could convince President Saddam Hussein that China would support a UN resolution authorizing the use of all appropriate means to end the crisis, this would increase the possibility of a peaceful settlement. He also said that the United States would continue the sanctions, which had already been in force for three months, and be ready to increase its troops to keep further political, economic, and military pressure on Iraq. If the sanctions did not work, he added, he hoped that China would not hinder the authorization to take all necessary actions, including military action.

I told him that the principal purpose of my visit was to discuss with leaders of the Arab countries the possibility of a peaceful solution to the Gulf crisis. There was no "plan," nor was there any authorization to mediate. All we wanted to do was to persuade the Iraqi leaders to comply with the resolutions of the Security Council. I would tell them candidly that they must either withdraw from Kuwait unconditionally or face a tremendous disaster. I said that the present situation in the Gulf region was extremely dangerous and the danger of a war was growing. At the same time, there was a growing demand from the international community for a peaceful resolution. The Chinese government was deeply worried about the situation in the Gulf region.

Regarding the relations between China and the United States, I said that, despite some disputes, the cooperation between the two sides on the Gulf issue was quite good. We held that it was the key to a peaceful settlement. I stressed to Baker that as long as there was a hope of peace, even a slim hope, the international community should strive to settle the issue by peaceful means.

We also discussed other possibilities. I told him that China, like many Arab countries, held that it would be unrealistic and unhelpful to try to solve many other Middle Eastern issues together with the issue of Iraq's invasion and occupation of Kuwait. But if the United

States could emphasize that it did concern itself with other issues of the Middle East, that would help to remove doubts felt by the Arab countries and would play a tremendous role in reassuring the Arab people—without distracting attention from solving the present crisis. As for a "partial settlement"—an idea that had been raised by some countries, Baker explained that it referred to an offer to allow Iraq to maintain control of Kuwait's Rumailah oil field or Bubiyan Island in return for a withdrawal of its troops from Kuwait. He said that the United States opposed such a proposal because it would be seen as a reward for Iraq's aggression. He also said that Egypt and some other countries opposed another proposal, for the convening of an international conference on settling other issues in the Middle East immediately after the withdrawal of Iraq's troops, believing that it would make Saddam a "hero." The United States kept its commitment to the security of Israel, but also sided with Egypt, Saudi Arabia, and Morocco in pushing forward the Middle East peace process, Baker said.

Baker held that the sanctions imposed on Iraq were the most stringent in history, but he was not sure whether they would force Iraq to withdraw its troops. He asked me how long, in China's view, the sanctions should be continued. If the sanctions did not work, should other means be considered? My reply was that it was very difficult to make an accurate estimate of the time needed for the sanctions to take effect. I pointed out that when the U.S. military entered Saudi Arabia, the purpose, as the United States claimed, was to protect the security of that country. Now, the emir of Kuwait had asked the army to liberate Kuwait. If the United States took military action to do so, would it limit its operations to the territory of Kuwait? Baker replied that the liberation of Kuwait would inevitably involve military action within the territory of Iraq.

Baker and I also spent some time discussing bilateral relations, and we reached an understanding on exchanges of visits by the foreign ministers of our two countries. But Baker did not want this made public, and I had no intention to press him to publicize it. The news released later was that the two sides had a consultation on the Gulf issue only.

SHUTTLING AROUND THE MIDDLE EAST

AFTER MEETING BAKER, I formally began my Middle Eastern journey.

Exchanges between China and Arab countries may date back to remote antiquity. As early as the Eastern Han dynasty (25–220), a certain Gan Ying, on an abortive mission to Rome, reached Tiao Zhi, which was the region of present-day Iraq and Syria.

I had visited the Middle East many times. But this trip was rather different from the previous ones, for a war was imminent. All those who have experienced war know how cruel it is and treasure peace. As long as there was a slim hope, we must not let it slip.

On the morning of November 7, I met President Mohammed Hosni Mubarak of Egypt, and then Esmat Abdul Megid, the deputy prime minister and concurrent foreign minister. China and Egypt had good relations, and the leaders of the two countries had long been acquainted. So our talks were frank and open. Egypt held that Iraq's invasion of Kuwait had been plotted long before, and Iraq had resorted to fraudulent means. On July 24, President Mubarak had visited Iraq, Kuwait, and Saudi Arabia. At his meeting with Saddam Hussein, he was told that Iraq would not take any military action against Kuwait. Mubarak had conveyed this message to the emir of Kuwait, and, together with King Fahd of Saudi Arabia, had arranged a meeting of the leaders of Iraq and Kuwait in Jidda. On the very next day, Iraq invaded Kuwait. All Egypt's efforts to persuade Iraq to withdraw from Kuwait had proved futile. Now the situation was critical; if the United States attacked Iraq, Saddam Hussein and his country faced disaster. Moreover, such a war would affect the entire Middle East. So Mubarak hoped that I would make Saddam realize the gravity of the situation, and adopt a flexible attitude.

I promised to point out the danger to Saddam Hussein. I also hoped that Egypt would use its own influence in the region and efforts toward a peaceful solution. I asked Mubarak if there was any possibility of solving the issue without bloodshed. His reply was that the present problem was not that no consideration had been given to saving Iraq's face, but that Saddam Hussein simply refused to accept any reasonable suggestion. If Iraq made no positive response to the demands of the international community, Iraq would be given a telling blow. In that way, the issue of occupation of Kuwait would be solved.

That evening, I left Cairo and flew to a small town called At Taif in western Saudi Arabia. This is a mountainous summer resort with a mild climate and a tranquil environment, and it had been chosen as a place of temporary exile by Kuwait's elite families and government leaders following the invasion. The whole Kuwaiti government had moved here. Each minister had a suite of rooms in a luxury hotel, which also served as a government department.

That evening, I met the Kuwaiti emir, Jaber al-Ahmad al-Sabah, and Crown Prince Saad Al-Abdulla al-Salem al-Sabah, who was also the prime minister.

The emir looked rather feeble and spoke slowly in a low voice. He condemned the Iraqi leaders for treachery and flagrant occupation of Kuwait in defiance of the UN resolutions. He said that the whole world would reject Iraq's invasion and occupation of Kuwait. Iraq's attempt to wipe Kuwait from the map would never succeed, he said. Saddam Hussein claimed to be acting in the interest of the Arab countries, and therefore proposals to settle the crisis put forward by Arab countries were useless. Saddam was slaughtering the Kuwaiti people. If that went on, the Kuwaiti people would soon be annihilated. No more chances should be given to Iraq. He stressed that it was imperative to exert more pressure and force Iraq to implement the UN resolutions.

I reiterated to him that China firmly supported the lawful government of Kuwait, and sympathized with Kuwait over the calamity it had suffered. Iraq, whose action had been condemned by the international community, was totally isolated. Tricks on the part of Iraq, such as the release of a few hostages, would by no means ease its situation. The only way out for Iraq was to remove its troops. If Iraq obstinately stuck to a road of self-extinction, that outcome would be its own choice.

Perhaps because of his poor health, the emir did not speak much, and our meeting lasted only thirty-five minutes.

Then I talked to Crown Prince Saad. Robust and vigorous, he spoke in a resonant and excited voice, full of indignation and resolve. He expounded the views of the government of Kuwait, and expressed the hope that the UN Security Council would take strong steps to force Iraq to withdraw its troops. He gave his opinion that the Security Council's economic sanctions were not working as expected, and could even be considered a failure. Kuwait, as a small country, was unable to withstand the worsening situation. The Security Council ought to take new measures to force Iraq to withdraw its troops from Kuwait. He said he hoped that China would join with Kuwait's other friends to rescue the Kuwaiti people "by all means."

I told him that China had voted for the ten Security Council resolutions on Iraq. I assured him that the sanctions would begin to bite on Iraq as time passed.

Failing to get my response to his request "by all means," Prince Saad proposed that the UN draw up a timetable for the sanctions to take effect, or discuss a new resolution on further measures to force Iraq to withdraw its troops. He asked me if China would support a time limit for the sanctions to take effect. Just then, Sabah al-Ahmad al-Jaber said that they did not want to see China in the capacity of a mediator, but China should make Saddam Hussein understand that Iraq must abide by the Security Council resolutions or it would face disaster.

I expressed my agreement, and told them that I and James Baker had reached a consensus on this issue—not to give Iraq any room for manipulation.

The crown prince seemed not to catch the foreign minister's meaning, and asked again: If Saddam refused to observe the resolutions, would the Security Council discuss measures to force Iraq to abide by them? I smiled, and said, "I believe so." The crown prince was satisfied with that reply. On this note, our talks ended.

After meeting the Kuwaiti leaders, I flew to Riyadh, the capital of Saudi Arabia. When I arrived, it was already midnight.

The next afternoon, I met the foreign minister, Faisal. He explained that Saudi Arabia did not want to see a war break out and was striving to win peace. Now the outcome—war or peace—was up to

Iraq. But it seemed that Iraq was unwilling to withdraw its troops. Saudi Arabia hoped that China would support all necessary measures, including military action, to force Iraq to withdraw. He also strongly criticized the position of Jordan, Palestine, and Yemen regarding the Gulf crisis. I briefed him on my talks with Baker and with the leaders of Egypt and Kuwait. I made it clear that China would, as always, uphold justice and continue making efforts in this respect.

On the evening of November 9, I flew to Jordan. I had a talk with the deputy prime minister and concurrently foreign minister, Marwan Qasem, the following morning, and then a talk with King Hussein Ibn Talal at noon.

Jordan's attitude toward the issue was not entirely the same as that of Egypt, Saudi Arabia, and Kuwait. The Jordanian leader stated that Jordan had all along called on Iraq to pull out of Kuwait and release the hostages at once, and urged that the crisis should be solved within an international framework and within the scope of the Arab nations. However, he pointed out, great pressure exerted by certain parties had interrupted the peace efforts. The intention of a certain country which was pushing the Arab countries to take action was to gain control of the region's resources.

King Hussein also complained that all the international community had done was to impose an embargo on Iraq, while refusing to communicate with it. Then he expressed his appreciation for China's stand, and said that he hoped that I would talk directly to the Iraqi leader in a way easier for Iraq to accept.

I pointed out that China had nothing to gain from the Gulf crisis, and hoped only that the crisis would be settled peacefully, so as to pave the way for settling other issues in the Middle East. I also stressed that if a war broke out it would mean self-destruction for Iraq. And neighboring countries would be involved too. At present, I said, the international community had reached consensus on the settlement of the Gulf crisis; and if Iraq showed flexibility, particularly if it could give a clear response on the issue of withdrawal from Kuwait, that would benefit the efforts of the international community toward a peaceful settlement.

MEETING SADDAM HUSSEIN

I ARRIVED IN BAGHDAD at noon on November 11. Because of the sanctions, the airport was empty. There was not a single aircraft in sight. This was completely different from what I had seen when I had visited Iraq half a year earlier. At that time, planes took off and landed constantly, and people thronged the airport building.

At noon and in the evening that day, respectively, I held two rounds of talks with Tareq Aziz, the deputy prime minister and concurrently foreign minister. Aziz was a Christian, had been Iraq's foreign minister for many years, and was regarded as a faithful follower of Saddam Hussein.

I gave him an account of my Middle Eastern tour, including my meetings with the Kuwaiti leaders and with James Baker. I told him that the occupation of Kuwait was not acceptable. Now the situation was so serious that war might break out at any minute. A war would be a calamity for Iraq, which was facing a choice of life or death. The international community hoped to settle the Gulf crisis in a peaceful way. Therefore, Iraq should show flexibility concerning the withdrawal of its troops from Kuwait.

Aziz gave a good number of reasons for the invasion of Kuwait. He said that Kuwait had deliberately lowered the price of its oil, an action tantamount to an economic war against Iraq. He also said that the most dangerous issue in the Middle East was not Iraq's occupation of Kuwait, but Palestine. During our talks he was most concerned about whether the United States would truly take military action, and what China's attitude was toward possible authorization for military action granted by the UN Security Council.

I reiterated China's stand on the settlement of the Gulf crisis, and told him that we supported the convening of a UN conference on the Middle East. But it was very difficult to link the Gulf crisis to the other Middle Eastern issues. I also told him that the United States might take military action without the authorization of the Security Council—as Baker had already dropped such a hint.

While I was talking to Aziz, two stenographers were working in turns. When one worked, the other left. I guessed that they were printing out their notes and reporting to their superiors. Obviously, Saddam was not unaware of the situation; in fact, he was closely watching what was going on every minute to make sure that everything was under his control.

On the morning of November 12, I went to see Saddam. Two unmarked cars were sent to pick us up. They raced through the streets and pulled up before a building that looked like barracks. We were escorted into the building and asked to take a short rest. Then another two cars were sent for us and the drivers were changed too. Again they drove extremely fast and finally took us to the meeting place.

About eleven o'clock, I met the Iraqi leader. I had met him in early March that year, when I visited Iraq. But this time, he was in uniform with a pistol at his side, giving the impression that he was prepared for war.

I first explained the Chinese government's concern about the tense situation in the Gulf region, and its hope for a peaceful settlement of the crisis. I said that the danger of war was growing daily. I asked for his opinion.

Saddam Hussein was direct, without diplomatic niceties. But it seemed to me that his arguments were forced and he had an arbitrary air about him.

He said that Kuwait had been part of Iraq since ancient times, just as Hong Kong was part of China. Then he gave a detailed account of the historical relations between Iraq and Kuwait. Iraq, he said, had never legally and formally recognized the border between it and Kuwait. He made all sorts of criticisms of the Kuwaiti government, charging that the United States and other Western countries had conspired against Iraq before the invasion, and that Kuwait had been in collaboration with the United States and Israel. He also said that although Kuwait had a small population and was militarily weak, it had enough resources to bring Iraq down through economic warfare. Therefore, the invasion of August 2 was an act of self-defense by Iraq.

Saddam stressed that Palestine was the fundamental issue in the Middle East. To solve the problems of the Middle East, we would have to adopt the same standard, not a double standard. The present stand-off, he said, could not be solved without the withdrawal of American troops from the region and the lifting of UN sanctions. Iraq had all along been ready to make sacrifices for the sake of peace. In an atmosphere of equality and mutual respect, Iraq was willing to talk openly and generously with various parties. Without a prior guarantee, any flexibility on Iraq's part might lead to serious consequences, he stressed.

Regarding his comparison of Kuwait to Hong Kong, I pointed out that Hong Kong was completely different from Kuwait. Hong Kong had all along been a part of the territory of China. It had been occupied by Britain by force for more than a century after the Opium Wars of the 1840s. Even so, China had adopted peaceful means to negotiate with Britain, and had finally reached an agreement on the question of Hong Kong. But Iraq and Kuwait recognized each other as sovereign states, and each had an embassy in the other's capital. Both nations were members of the UN as well as of the League of Arab States. In any event, military occupation of Kuwait by Iraq was not acceptable.

From the long-term point of view, I said, all the issues of the Middle East should be settled, but the occupation of Kuwait by Iraq was the most pressing issue because the danger of war was intensifying.

Then, Saddam changed the subject by asking me if the United States would truly resort to force. Apparently, like Aziz, he was most concerned about this.

I replied that a big power that has mobilized a huge army would not retreat without achieving its aim. I told him that China had no intention of making any proposal or of acting as a mediator. In order to avoid war, Iraq should make a proposal regarding a settlement.

During the whole discussion, Saddam showed no intention of withdrawing from Kuwait. Aziz, who was present at the talks, told me later that Saddam's attitude had been more flexible this time than at any other time. As for Saddam's claim that he was "willing to talk to various parties," Aziz explained to me in private that this might start on a small scale, among three or four Arab nations including Iraq and

Saudi Arabia, and that Iraq was also willing to talk to the United States.

In hindsight, I can see that a number of strategic mistakes Saddam made were all based on his mistaken assumption that as long as Iraq gave some signs of flexibility, the United States would not really go to war.

On the same day, November 12, I also met President Yasir Arafat of the Palestine Liberation Organization, at his request. He stressed that the Gulf crisis should be settled peacefully within the scope of the Arab nations and the international organizations. An attack on Iraq by the United States, he said, would be a severe blow to the economy and military forces of the Arab region. He accused the United States of wanting to control the oil resources of the Gulf region so as to bring pressure to bear on Europe, Japan, the Soviet Union, and China. For that purpose, the United States would station its troops in the Gulf region for a long time. He said that he believed the dispute between Iraq and Kuwait could be solved in the spirit of mutual accommodation. He also said that he did not demand settling all the Middle East issues in one package, but that there must be an agreement that talks on Kuwait should be followed by an international conference on Palestinian and other Middle Eastern issues. I understood his sense of urgency in reaching an early settlement of the Palestinian issue, but it was unrealistic to link the Palestinian question with the Gulf crisis.

I returned to Saudi Arabia, and met King Fahd and Foreign Minister Faisal.

I met Faisal first, and gave him an account of my visits to Jordan and Iraq, focusing on Saddam's attitude. Faisal rebutted Saddam's opinions one by one. The only thing he did not criticize was the double standard of the United States regarding the Arabs and Israel. He reiterated that the Gulf crisis could not be resolved within the Arab world; it could be resolved only in accordance with international law.

When I met King Fahd, it was already ten-thirty at night. He talked about the relations between Saudi Arabia and China, as well as Saudi Arabia's foreign policy, before getting to the topic of the Gulf crisis. Apparently he was already informed about my meeting with Foreign Minister Faisal and focused directly on key issues.

Regarding Iraq's wish for a dialogue with Saudi Arabia, he said that before Iraq had invaded Kuwait, he had tried many times to get in touch with Saddam, in the hope of stopping the invasion. Later, he had several times urged Iraq to withdraw from Kuwait. But Saddam always refused to see him. He emphasized that Iraq's invasion and occupation of Kuwait were a serious matter of principle. Nobody in the Arab community or the international community would accept that outcome. He also criticized Saddam for deliberately confusing two different issues: Kuwait and Palestine. He held that the issue of Palestine was a matter of national independence, whereas the issue of Kuwait was a matter of aggression by one Arab brother nation against another. He also cited Saddam's relations with Iran as an example to indicate that it would not be embarrassing for Iraq to withdraw from Kuwait. If Saddam wanted to find a way out, he should bear in mind the interests of his state and people, and unconditionally leave Kuwait.

I told Fahd that Saddam had said that if he could get some guarantees, Iraq could take a flexible attitude. But he had not mentioned what kind of guarantees he wanted. At this, Fahd said pensively that if Saddam wanted guarantees to avoid bringing a calamity on the Iraqi people, that would be what everybody hoped for. In addition, if Saddam was a responsible person he should make a personal sacrifice and hide in a certain part of the world. The problem had been started by him, so he was the only one who could put it right.

After the meeting, I was escorted to the airport by Faisal. When my special plane took off, it was already early on the morning of November 13. My Middle Eastern journey had come to an end.

This journey had made me realize that the Arab nations' positions on the Gulf issue were not identical, and so it was difficult for them to take any unanimous action at the time to defuse the crisis. My impression of Saddam was that he was only an ambitious adventurer claiming to be safeguarding the interests of the Arab nations and supporting a settlement of the Palestine issue. When chaos erupted in Iran in the 1980s, he took advantage of it to fight an eight-year war against that country. The invasion of Kuwait was a wanton betrayal of justice, an act of the strong bullying the weak. But his estimate of the situation was totally incorrect.

It seemed that war could not be prevented.

Through diplomatic channels, we briefed the relevant countries on my visit. Their reactions were positive, they considered the visit a reflection of the serious, responsible attitude of China as a large country, and another demonstration of China's willingness to make efforts for peace.

After my visit to Iraq, Saddam made a gesture of flexibility in a speech in which he called for dialogue and expressed his willingness to release his Western hostages group by group. His claim to be prepared to make sacrifices caused some speculation throughout the world. But, in the end, he did nothing substantial at all.

American "Deal"

SHORTLY AFTER I RETURNED to Beijing, I received a letter from James Baker, expressing his satisfaction with our talks in Cairo, and saying that President Bush had been pleased with his report. He added that the United States was considering the next step, and he would like to see me again shortly.

On the afternoon of November 20, Baker telephoned me from Paris, to discuss two interconnected matters: first, the United States was going to ask for the UN Security Council's authorization to use force; second, he hoped that I would personally attend the ministerial meeting of the Security Council to be held on November 28. He later invited me to pay a formal visit to Washington.

Baker had been a businessman for a long time, and had once served as secretary of the treasury. He tended to treat everything as if it were a business transaction. He was fond of "doing business." Linking the two matters mentioned above was obviously another of his "deals."

Baker said that in the United States' proposal there would be no words like "use of force," but the meaning would be the same. By then, he had rounded up nine other members of the Security Council to support the resolution. They were Britain, France, the Soviet Union, and six nonpermanent members of the council. He said that the United States hoped that China would vote for, or at least not veto, the resolution.

He said he understood that it would take time for the Chinese government to carefully consider the issue. However, he hoped that I would give him a hint that the Chinese government would handle the matter in a positive and active manner. If China intended to veto the resolution, then the United States would not put it forward, because its rejection would be a blow to the prestige of the United States.

I said that, given the gravity of the situation in the Gulf and the strong demand for a peaceful political settlement, the international community should continue and even strengthen its political, diplomatic, and economic pressures on Iraq. We must be most discreet in raising an issue as serious as waging a war on another nation. As for the United States' resolution, China would not give any official reply before seeing it.

At this, Baker read the draft to me over the telephone. There was a choice of wording in parentheses in the first paragraph of the operative part of the draft: (all necessary means) and (all necessary means, including force).

Baker also said over the telephone that he hoped that I would personally go to New York to attend the ministerial meeting of the member countries of the Security Council to be held November 28–29, and then invited me to pay a formal visit to Washington after the meeting. He said that if China would vote for, or at least not veto, the United States' draft, an appropriate opportunity would be created for a visit by me. He further said that my formal visit to Washington would be a good beginning for the resumption of the exchange of visits by senior officials of both countries. President Bush was to visit Latin America beginning December 1, and would probably meet me on November 30. Baker also said that he himself was looking forward to visiting China the following year.

We reckoned that the United States would table its draft resolution on the use of force against Iraq in November, when it would be the chairman of the Security Council. The invitation for me to pay a formal visit to the United States in order to secure China's support for, or at least refraining to veto, the U.S. draft, meant that the United States was linking China's support in the Gulf crisis to normalization of Sino-American relations.

China has all along adhered to principles in handling foreign affairs. Moreover, it has been gaining more and more influence in international affairs. During the Gulf crisis, China upheld justice, and strove to settle the crisis in a peaceful way. However, China's opposition to war did not mean that it supported Iraq's aggression. The central leadership decided to abstain from voting on the United States' resolution. At the same time, this was a good opportunity to promote the normalization of relations between China and the United States. Therefore, on November 24, we replied to the United States that I would attend the ministerial meeting of the Security Council and make a formal visit, at its invitation, after the meeting.

Since James Baker was fond of "doing business," naturally he was good at bargaining too. On learning that I had accepted the invitation, the United States changed its mind at once. On the afternoon of November 25, B. Lynn Pascoe, the American interim chargé d'affaires in China, hurried to the Foreign Ministry to pass a letter from Baker to me. In the letter, apart from stressing again the importance of my presence at the ministerial meeting of the Security Council, Baker said that since the United States had not invited the foreign ministers of the member countries, or the five permanent ones, of the Security Council to visit Washington, he hoped to announce my visit there after a bilateral meeting in New York. Pascoe added that the United States hoped China would cast an affirmative vote on its resolution. If China vetoed the draft or abstained from voting, that would have an adverse impact on my visit to the United States.

The United States had gone back on its word and was trying to force a bargain by linking my visit to our affirmative vote. This was not acceptable.

In diplomatic negotiations it is imperative for both sides to have a mutual understanding and reach a mutual accommodation. An agreement can be reached only by give and take. It will never do to go back on one's own word or resort to tricks.

I replied at once that the United States had violated the agreement reached on November 20 by the two foreign ministers, and demanded that the United States check and confirm the records of the talks between Baker and me. At the same time, I said that if the United States changed its attitude, I would not attend the meeting.

On November 26, the United States softened its attitude. Pascoe conveyed a message from Baker to the effect that China's understanding of the telephone conversation of November 20 was correct. But the United States hoped very much that China would vote for the resolution. Pascoe also explained that the junior official at the State Department knew little about the situation and that the message sent to him was a mistake.

On November 27, President Bush wrote letters to General Secretary Jiang Zemin, President Yang Shangkun, and Premier Li Peng. The gist of the letters was that the United States hoped China would support its proposal at the UN Security Council, and that my visit to the United States would provide a decisive opportunity for material progress in normalizing bilateral relations.

ABSTAINING FROM THE VOTE

ON NOVEMBER 28, I led a team of ten people to attend the Security Council. They included three of my colleagues at the Foreign Ministry: Zhang Yijun, director general of the Department of North American and Oceanian Affairs; Wang Changyi, director general of the Department of West Asian and North African Affairs; and Qin Huasun, director general of the Department of International Organizations and Conferences.

It was foggy in Beijing that day, and our flight was postponed again and again, foreshadowing a difficult journey. When we finally got to New York, it was midnight. We were told that James Baker and other officials were still waiting for us at the Waldorf Hotel, ready to begin talks. When we got to the hotel, we saw a whole roomful of American officials, including Baker.

During our discussions, the American side kept trying to persuade us to vote for their resolution. I told Baker that the use of force was a grave matter, and we must be cautious. Military action might seem to be a quick solution, but the damage to property and the loss of life had to be taken into account. Again, there would be serious aftereffects. Then, I said that the war the Americans had waged against China in Korea under the flag of the UN was still fresh in Chinese minds, and the United States was still applying sanctions to China, so our relations were not normal. Considering all this, it would be a great favor on China's part if it did not veto the draft.

On the afternoon of the day when the votes were to be cast, I was busy meeting other foreign ministers. Baker called me several times on behalf of President Bush, trying to get China to vote yes for the United States' resolution.

But China had already made up its mind about the vote, and the decision could not be changed. I refused Baker's request.

At three-forty in the afternoon, the ministerial meeting of the Security Council began. The agenda was to discuss and vote on Resolution 678, sponsored by the United States. The key point of the draft was that unless Iraq had completely abided by all the relevant resolutions of the Security Council on or before January 15, 1991, authorization would be granted to all member countries of the UN, in cooperation with the Kuwaiti government, to use all necessary means to uphold and carry out the relevant resolutions of the Security Council.

The atmosphere in the meeting hall was electric. Not only were the guest seats full; even the aisles on both sides were crowded. The focus of attention was China's vote. If we vetoed the resolution, it would be killed.

At five-thirty, I explained China's position on the vote. First, I stated that as a matter of principle China was opposed to Iraq's aggression against Kuwait. China stood for a peaceful settlement, and against any settlement by force. Then I pointed out that China had no interests in the Gulf region, nor did it seek any. The only issue China was concerned with was how to maintain peace and stability there. Accordingly, China advocated a peaceful solution to the Gulf crisis. It might take longer, but there would be less damage and fewer aftereffects. If a war broke out, all those involved would suffer tremendously. That would have a most adverse impact on the Gulf countries and on world peace and stability, as well as on the world economy. I said that the words "use of all necessary means" in the draft in fact meant allowing the use of force. This went against the Chinese government's constant advocacy of a peaceful settlement. Therefore, China found it impossible to vote for the proposal. On the other hand, the crisis had been caused by Iraq's invasion and annexation of Kuwait, and Iraq had done nothing substantial on the key issue of withdrawal from Kuwait. The United States' proposal demanded that Iraq fully observe Resolution 660 and other relevant resolutions of the UN Security Council, which urged Iraq to remove its troops from Kuwait at once. China was in favor of this, and therefore would not veto the draft.

The draft was finally adopted by twelve affirmative votes, two negative votes, and one abstention.

China had abstained from voting, and Cuba and Yemen had cast the negative notes.

MEETING PRESIDENT BUSH

THAT EVENING, BAKER HELD a banquet for all the foreign ministers of the permanent members of the Security Council. He appeared cheerful, but he informed us through a staff member that President Bush was busy handling the Gulf crisis and would not have time to see me when I went to Washington. That night, the State Department notified the Chinese embassy in Washington of this decision. Obviously, Baker, who was "good at business deals," felt that he had lost this "deal," and was disappointed.

If we refused to visit Washington, we would appear peevish and narrow-minded. Yet it was inappropriate for us to go to Washington if the president would not see us. After discussing the matter among ourselves, we decided to go to Washington and demand to see the president.

The Chinese ambassador to the United States, Zhu Qizhen, drove from New York to Washington that very night. He called Brent Scowcroft, the president's national security adviser, at three o'clock in the morning. At six o'clock in the morning, Scowcroft replied that I was welcome to visit Washington as scheduled, and that President Bush was looking forward to seeing me.

I took a flight from New York to Washington at nine-thirty on November 30, and at eleven I and Baker held talks, during which he told me that President Bush would announce later that day an invitation to Foreign Minister Aziz of Iraq to visit the United States. Also, Bush was prepared to send Baker to Iraq to meet Saddam Hussein. I said that such steps were important and positive, and we would support them. When I visited Baghdad, the Iraqi side had informally expressed a wish to have a direct dialogue with the United States. I had also suggested the previous day that the most important thing to do was to talk with Saddam himself. Baker said that he had conveyed my opinion to President Bush, and it was one of the reasons why Bush had made these decisions.

Baker also explained to me the arrangement of my meeting with Bush. He tried to explain away his embarrassment by saying that since China had not voted yes, he had personally felt it would be inappropriate to arrange a meeting with the president. But now all that was over, and President Bush himself had made the decision to see me. I just smiled and changed the subject by saying that in order to secure the adoption of the United States, resolution at the UN Security Council; Baker had visited twelve countries and had held discussions with their foreign ministers. The United States stressed that China had played an important role as a permanent member of the Security Council; so, "Why didn't you visit China?" I asked. I had sent a letter of invitation, but all I had received in reply was a telephone call. "Discussing issues over the phone can sometimes be misleading," I said, "but I still invite you to visit China."

At one-forty on the afternoon of November 30, I went to the White House to see President Bush. The meeting with the president lasted forty-five minutes. Bush said that he paid special attention to the relations between the United States and China, and hoped that our relations would gradually improve, up to the resumption of visits between our leaders. He said he was grateful for China's cooperation with the United States on the Gulf issue. The most important thing was that China's abstention from voting on the U.S. resolution in the Security Council had not prevented its adoption.

I said that China and the United States had cooperated very well on the Gulf issue. China had voted yes on ten relevant resolutions of the Security Council. It had not been easy for China to abstain from that one vote. The Chinese leaders had repeatedly discussed the issue, I told him.

I also told him about my visit to Iraq. I said that there was no difference between China and the United States on the demand for Iraq to withdraw from Kuwait. In the future, many aspects of international affairs would require cooperation between us. Though the two countries were in different circumstances and had different views on and different approaches to various issues, we could find common ground in safeguarding world peace.

Before the end of the visit, I held a press conference. The questions raised by the reporters mostly focused on Sino-American relations, and they were rather surprised to learn about the meeting between President Bush and myself.

In October 2002, I escorted President Jiang Zemin on a visit to the United States. In the Bush Presidential Library, I saw many acquaintances. One of them was Scowcroft. When we talked about the Gulf crisis, both of us remembered details that had happened twelve years before. I said to him, "Sorry we had to wake you up from your dream that night." This sent everyone into laughter.

Although Resolution 678 was adopted by the Security Council, the majority of nations still wanted to avoid the use of force if possible. After the proposal for exchange of visits by the foreign ministers of the United States and Iraq came to nothing, the Secretary General of the UN, Perez de Cuéllar, wanted to meet Saddam Hussein in a final effort to obtain a peaceful settlement. In this, he hoped for China's assistance. When I heard the news I was on a business trip in Hainan Province. I instructed the Foreign Ministry at once to ask our ambassador to Iraq, Zheng Dayong, to inform the foreign minister of Iraq, Tareq Aziz, of de Cuéllar's wish. Iraq gave its consent to the visit, but this final effort did not succeed.

It has been twelve years since the Gulf War. Saddam Hussein misjudged the situation at that time, and turned a deaf ear to the advice of various parties. He made an unwise decision at a critical moment for his country, refusing to abide by the UN resolutions calling for Iraq's withdrawal from Kuwait. Consequently, the Iraqi people suffered greatly in the ensuing war. But this was not the end of the tragedy. Even as I write, war has again come to the ancient land of Mesopotamia, to the reaches of the Tigris and Euphrates rivers, and the regime of Saddam Hussein has fallen.

4 "FUNERAL DIPLOMACY" IN TOKYO

From February 23 to 25, 1989, I was in Tokyo for Emperor Hirohito's funeral as a special envoy of the president of China. Besides attending the funeral activities and meeting Japanese government leaders, I conferred with President Suharto of Indonesia, who was also attending the funeral, about normalization of Sino-Indonesian relations, and we reached an "agreement on three points," opening the door to the resumption of diplomatic relations between our two countries, which had been severed for twenty-three years. This made front-page news in the Japanese press and attracted widespread attention. China was said to have carried out successful "funeral diplomacy" in Tokyo.

FUNERAL RITES

THE FUNERAL FOR EMPEROR HIROHITO was held on the morning of February 24, 1989, in Tokyo, at Shinjuku Imperial Park, a large national park located between Shinjuku and Shibuyaku. In the Edo era, it belonged to the Naito family, feudal lords in Shinshu (today's Nagano-ken). At that time, the Tamagawa water passed the park, so it was called the Tamagawa Garden. In 1872, it was expropriated by the state to be used as an agricultural experimental field. In 1879, it became the Shinjuku Imperial Botanical Garden under the administration of the Imperial Household Agency. In 1906, part of it became a landscape garden designed by a Frenchman in the French style, with a total area of 580,000 square meters. It also had a Western-style garden, a Japanese-style garden, a children's amusement park, and a greenhouse. In 1949, it was made a national park and opened to the public.

When Hirohito died, the Committee for Emperor Hirohito's Funeral Rites set up a black-and-white tent in the Shinjuku Imperial Park as the main assembly hall. The funeral began at seven-thirty A.M. and ended thirteen hours and twenty minutes later, at eight-fifty P.M.

The rites were divided into two parts. First was the religious ritual,* which only the royal family could attend. The scene was hidden from public view by a large curtain. Then came the funeral rites, at which Emperor Akihito, Prime Minister Takeshita Noboru, and other dignitaries delivered eulogies, and the foreign guests expressed their condolences.

To ensure that the funeral would proceed smoothly and that the guests would be safe, some 32,000 policemen had been mobilized, and unprecedented precautions were taken. The streets of Tokyo, especially around the imperial palace, and the main assembly hall at the funeral were heavily guarded. I remember that the sky was gray and it was drizzling. The day was chilly, and the diplomatic attendees all wore heavy overcoats with turned-up collars. Each guest was given a paper hand-warming bag.

At nine-thirty in the morning, the hearse started from the imperial palace; passed the National Diet building (the Diet is Japan's parliament), the Akasaka Imperial Residence, etc.; and drove to Shinjuku National Park, arriving at ten-ten. The religious ritual was held first, for the royal family. Emperor Akihito and other family members offered sacrifices and paid their last respects to Hirohito.

Then the funeral rites began. Emperor Akihito, Prime Minister Takeshita Noboru, the speaker of the House of Representatives, and

---

* The rites are of the Japanese state religion, Shinto. Only members of the imperial family and Shinto priests may be present at these rites.

the speaker of House of Councilors, the president of the Supreme Court, and others delivered the memorial speeches. Then the foreign dignitaries paid their last respects to the deceased in front of the coffin, each in turn as his or her name was announced. When the funeral was over, at least ten pallbearers carried the coffin, walking slowly to the gate of the park and then putting it into the hearse, which next drove directly to the royal cemetery of Tokyo.

That evening, Takeshita held a reception for the foreign guests at the Akasaka Hotel to thank them for their attendance.

One thing worth mentioning is that before the funeral there had been a spate of arguments denying the aggressive nature of the Sino-Japanese War and absolving Hirohito from responsibility for it. In addition, the Japanese media gave much publicity to his life and career, and stressed how he had shared "happiness and adversity" with his people and had devoted himself to the peace and prosperity of Japan. On February 14, Takeshita had said, in response to questions addressed to him in the Diet, that whether or not the last war had been aggressive could be left to the historians of later generations to decide. On the same day, Kanmi Muranaoru, director of the Cabinet Legislation Bureau, claimed that Hirohito could not be held responsible for the last war by either civil or international law. This was the first time that the Japanese government had denied that Hirohito had held any responsibility for the war.

A spokesman for China's Ministry of Foreign Affairs responded immediately, stating strongly that the aggressive war launched by Japanese militarism in the past had brought untold disaster to the Chinese people and other peoples of Asia. He demanded that the Japanese authorities respect historical facts. Any attempt by Japan to deny the nature of the war and shrug off responsibility violated the principles and spirit of the Sino-Japanese Joint Declaration and the Sino-Japanese Peace and Friendship Treaty and affronted the people of China and other Asian countries who had suffered from the war. All in all, it was unfavorable to Japan itself. Liu Danian, a member of the Standing Committee of China's National People's Congress and a leading historian, also criticized such claims by Japan.

Hirohito had been brought up since childhood according to the code Bushido. He was a regent beginning in November 1921 and acceded to the throne in November 1926. As the supreme authority in Japan and commander in chief of its armed forces, he was the prime culprit in Japan's seizure of China's three northeastern provinces in 1931 and instigating the eight-year war of aggression against China from 1937. His responsibility for this aggression can never be denied.

China was the largest victim of the invasions launched by Japanese militarists, and many Chinese people, some overseas, had urged the Chinese government not to send a high official to Hirohito's funeral. After much deliberation, our central leadership decided to send me as a special envoy of the head of state. Both external and internal responses were positive, and this act of the Chinese government was generally acceptable. It conformed to normal diplomatic protocol while also taking the feelings of many Chinese people into consideration. Japan indicated that it attached great importance to its relations with China and was grateful that China had decided to send an envoy to the funeral. In fact, the protests from China and other countries prompted Takeshita to consult with other cabinet members on November 21 as to how to quiet down the controversy.

On the next day, the Japanese ambassador to China, Nakajima Toshijiro, explained what Takeshita had said in the debate at the Diet. According to Nakajima, Takeshita had always taken a consistent stand. Takeshita's understanding was as follows. First, Japan had caused great damage to neighboring countries during the war. The international community regarded the war as aggressive and condemned it. Second, the Japanese government had clearly stated its position on its past conduct in the Sino-Japanese Joint Declaration of 1972, this position remained unchanged, and the fact of Japanese aggression could not be denied. Third, as a peaceful nation, Japan was determined to contribute to the world's peace and stability to ensure that such aggression would never happen again.

On February 24, when I met the Japanese foreign minister, Uno Sosuke, in Tokyo, he expressed regret on behalf of the Japanese government at his prime minister's remarks, and emphasized that Japan's position as laid down in the Joint Declaration of 1972 had not changed at all. I said that only by facing history correctly could we build our future relations and avoid insulting the peoples who had suffered from the war.

That afternoon, Takeshita met me at his official residence. He said that he was adamant about developing Sino-Japanese friendship on the basis of the Sino-Japanese Joint Declaration and the Sino-Japanese Treaty of Peace and Friendship. I told him that only if Japan had a correct attitude toward history could friendly Sino-Japanese relations continue. That night, a senior Japanese statesman, Ito Masayoshi, came to the Chinese embassy for a one-on-one meeting with me. He expressed his appreciation for my attendance at the funeral, and said that he too was eager to contribute to Sino-Japanese relations.

The following day, all the leading newspapers in Japan reported in detail my meetings with the Japanese prime minister and foreign minister. Some reported that the exceptional meeting—during a period of national mourning—between Takeshita and myself showed that the Japanese government had realized how seriously the rest of the world was taking the prime minister's remarks denying responsibility for the war, and that it wanted to seek China's understanding. Some reports warned that Japan must not stress national differences when dealing with historical issues concerning neighboring countries and should take a down-to-earth attitude.

Then, at a debate in the Diet on February 27, Takeshita revised his former speech; he confirmed that the war had brought heavy losses to Japan's neighbors, and that the fact of aggression could not be denied.

This episode proved that China's decision to send someone of appropriate rank to Hirohito's funeral was appropriate. It had taken protocol into consideration and had also benefited the relations between China and Japan; moreover, it had encouraged Japan to take an appropriate attitude toward the nature of the war.

But though I focused mainly on Sino-Japanese relations during my attendance of Hirohito's funeral, the real breakthrough I made there was in bilateral relations between China and Indonesia.

BREAKTHROUGH WITH INDONESIA

AT THE FUNERAL, I met President Suharto of Indonesia; as a result, the relations between our two countries, which had been suspended for twenty-three years, were quickly restored. It was a successful negotiation through which I made a diplomatic breakthrough on a special occasion.

Possibly, the significance of this "funeral diplomacy" can be seen only from the standpoint of the up-and-down relations between China and Indonesia and their complicated evolution.

China and Indonesia are neighboring countries and had a long period of friendly relations. The two countries have similar histories, in modern times, of struggles against colonialism and imperialism. Indonesia was one of the first countries to establish diplomatic relations with China. In April 1955, Premier Zhou Enlai attended the Asia-Africa Conference in the Indonesian resort city of Bandung, and elaborated the famous Five Principles of Peaceful Coexistence to which China adheres in its foreign relations. Then Zhou paid a formal visit to Indonesia, and both sides signed the Treaty on Dual Nationality, which set an example for solving the problem of dual nationality between China and other countries. China had always supported Indonesia's struggle to recover West Irian, and Indonesia had supported China's bid to restore its lawful seat in the UN Security Council.

However, in September 1965, turmoil in Indonesia led to drastic changes in the domestic situation and the eventual suspension of diplomatic relations between China and Indonesia.

The "September 30 incident" took place in 1965. According to reports from Indonesia, a group of officers—led by Lieutenant Colonel Sutopo Untung, commander of the Third Battalion of the Armed Police Forces of the Indonesian president—arrested and killed six other commanders. One of those arrested and killed was Ahmad Yani of the armed forces, the rationale being that the "generals committee" of the armed forces was plotting to stage a coup. Several generals of the Indonesian armed forces immediately took countermeasures against Untung. Soon Indonesia began a widespread persecution of the so-called Indonesian communists and the pro-Sukarno political forces.

China had no knowledge whatsoever about the "September 30 incident" before it took place, and made no statement about the political situation in Indonesia for a long time after the incident. But the Indonesian military authorities accused China of having been behind the incident. Indonesian troops even searched the Commercial Section of the Chinese embassy in Jakarta. On October 30, 1967, diplomatic relations between the two countries were suspended.

But in the 1970s the international situation changed. China recovered its lawful seat at the UN, becoming one of the five permanent members of the Security Council. In 1972, President Richard Nixon of the United States visited China, and the two countries published a joint communiqué smoothing relations between them. In addition, China established formal diplomatic ties with Japan and many countries in Western Europe, Latin America, and Africa. In 1973, after the Paris Treaty on Peace in Vietnam was signed, the United States ended its aggressive war in Indochina, and began to reduce its military presence in Southeast Asia. In consequence, the Association of Southeast Asian Nations (ASEAN) made significant adjustments in its foreign policies. The relationship between ASEAN and China changed from mutual hostility to friendly cooperation. Three of the six ASEAN countries—Malaysia, the Philippines, and Thailand—quickly established diplomatic relations with China.

At that time, then, the peace and stability of Southeast Asia depended on how relations between Indonesia, the leader of ASEAN, and China developed.

By the end of 1978, Comrade Deng Xiaoping paid formal visits to Thailand, Malaysia, and Singapore. This was the first time that the highest Chinese leader had visited members of ASEAN. The two sides exchanged sincere opinions about safeguarding peace and stability in Southeast Asia, about relations between China and the ASEAN member states, about increasing mutual understanding, and about assuaging the doubts of Southeast Asian countries concerning China. From then on, the relations between China and the ASEAN

members continued to develop. The two sides reached a consensus
on and closely cooperated in opposing the Vietnamese invasion of
Cambodia, peacefully solving the problem of Cambodia, and safeguarding peace in Southeast Asia. At the same time, economic and
commercial contacts between China and all the member states of
ASEAN increased rapidly. Cultural exchanges, too, became more frequent.

In November 1988, during a visit to Thailand, Premier Li Peng
announced the four principles for establishing, recovering, and developing China's relations with all the ASEAN member countries: (1)
Strict adherence to the Five Principles of Peaceful Coexistence in the
relations between countries, (2) Persistence in opposing hegemonism
in all circumstances, (3) Upholding equality, mutual benefit, and
common development in economic relations, and (4) Following the
line of independence, mutual respect, close cooperation, and mutual
support in international affairs.

In this context, Sino-Indonesian relations improved, and contacts
between China and Indonesia increased. In 1975, Suharto said that
Indonesia was ready to improve its relations with China since
Malaysia, the Philippines, and Thailand respectively had established
diplomatic relations with China. In November 1977, for the first
time, Indonesia sent a delegation from its Industrial and Commercial
Organization to participate in the Guangzhou Trade Fair. In April
1985, at the invitation of the Indonesian government, Wu Xueqian—
who was state councillor and foreign minister—led a Chinese delegation to Indonesia to attend celebrations for the thirtieth anniversary
of the Bandung Conference.

Indonesia, as the largest country in ASEAN, plays a leading role in
that organization. Regarding the problem of Cambodia, Indonesia and
the other members of ASEAN took a common stand. Indonesia held
two informal conferences—called "cocktail parties"—in July 1988 and
February 1989 to solve the problem. However, no breakthrough was
made. As one of the co-chairs of the Paris Conference on Cambodia,
Indonesia felt it necessary to maintain close consultations and good
cooperation with China in order to solve the problem of Cambodia.

Many farsighted Indonesians believed that in reality China would remain a strong power in the region and that Indonesia must therefore not ignore China anymore.

Thus the changes in the international situation and common strategic interests made Indonesia alter its attitude toward China.

In March 1988, Suharto rescinded the demand that China should offer a public apology for what Indonesia claimed was China's involvement in the "September 30 incident." He spoke of a reconciliation between the two countries. In early 1989, the Indonesian foreign minister, Ali Alatas, informed Ambassador Li Luye, China's permanent representative to the UN, that Indonesia would try to promote the process of restoring relations. Alatas also asked to meet the Chinese foreign minister. Li Luye replied that China was willing to restore diplomatic relations as soon as possible, basing these relations on the Five Principles of Peaceful Coexistence. Meanwhile, the Chinese foreign minister expressed a hope of meeting Alatas as soon as possible.

We knew that Alatas would not accompany Suharto to Tokyo for Hirohito's funeral, so a meeting between the two foreign ministers would be hard to arrange. We therefore notified Indonesia that the Chinese foreign minister would go to Japan to attend Hirohito's funeral as a special envoy and that this was a good chance for both sides to meet. If convenient, the Chinese foreign minister hoped to meet with President Suharto. On February 13, Indonesia's permanent mission to the UN informed China that the minister of state, Murdiono, would accompany Suharto to Tokyo and wanted to confer with the Chinese foreign minister. Detailed arrangements could be made by the embassies of the two countries in Tokyo. Indonesia also said that Murdiono, as the minister of state, was very familiar with bilateral relations between China and Indonesia.

Murdiono was a major general and had been a subordinate of Suharto when the latter was in the military. After Suharto became president, Murdiono served as secretary to the cabinet, deputy minister, minister of state, and director of the Indonesian Coordinating Committee on Relations with China. Obviously he was a right-hand man of the president. His role was to draft speeches for the president, promulgate government orders and regulations, and coordinate relationships between the president and all the governmental departments. He was also the public spokesman for the cabinet. Aptly, he was known as the "junior president." Indonesia's decision to put him in charge of normalizing Sino-Indonesian relations was well thought out.

"AGREEMENT ON THREE POINTS"

THE TALKS BETWEEN CHINA and Indonesia in Tokyo were the result of years of efforts by both sides. According to our analysis at that time, the talks might lead to two possibilities. One, Indonesia would take a more active attitude toward resumption of the relations between the two countries. Two, given its different internal options, Indonesia might propose a plan for step-by-step normalization of relations. We had worked out solutions to all possible problems, in order to make full use of this opportunity to encourage normalization.

On the afternoon of February 23, I had my first meeting with Murdiono, at the Tokyo Imperial Hotel, where the Indonesian mission was staying. I found him easygoing, frank, intelligent, and humorous.

At our meeting, I first reviewed the direct trade carried out by both sides in recent years and our smooth cooperation in international affairs, including the problem of Cambodia, and expounded China's views on the current situation in Asia and internationally. I said that China and Indonesia were two of Asia's large countries, with populations of 1.1 billion and 170 million, respectively. We were both facing the task of building our own countries and improving our people's living standards, and for this we needed a peaceful international environment. Our two countries could play an important role in promoting regional peace and stability, I said.

I explained the Five Principles of Peaceful Coexistence followed by China in foreign relations. I said that the most important of the five principles was mutual respect for sovereignty and noninterference in each other's internal affairs. We abided by the principles not only in our relations with foreign countries but also in our relations with political parties. We firmly maintained that the affairs of a political party were part of the internal affairs of its country, and every country had the right to deal with such affairs by itself. China would never use relations with political parties to interfere in other countries' internal affairs.

Regarding the normalization of the relations between our two countries, I said that the time was ripe for resumption of diplomatic relations, and that China had all along felt positively about this. I said that I would like to take the opportunity to hear his opinion.

Murdiono agreed with my analysis of the international situation. Then he referred to the serious effects of two incidents* in Indonesia. He said that Indonesia also had five principles, in its case for dealing with internal problems. These were called Five Basics for the Establishment of the Country: (1) belief in Allah, (2) just and civilized morality, (3) unification of the country, (4) democracy, and (5) social justice and prosperity. He said that while Indonesia's national philosophy and ideology might be different from those of other countries, Indonesia was willing to develop relations with other countries on the basis of respect for their ideologies. At the same time, Indonesia hoped that other countries would respect its ideology, its worldview, and the "five basics." In addition, he emphasized that Indonesia consistently adhered to the "one China" policy. He did not mention the accusation that China had been involved in the "September 30 incident."

I stressed that we respected Indonesia's "five basics," and at the same time that we hoped both sides would follow the Five Principles of Peaceful Coexistence in international relations. We had noticed that Indonesia was particularly concerned about noninterference in the internal affairs of other countries. I stressed that China had no

---

* One of these was the "September 30 incident" in 1965. The other was the "Madiun incident" of September 1948.

connection with the Indonesian Communist Party—we did not even know whether there was such a party today. There had once been some Indonesians living in China, but most of them had left and probably only a few dozen remained. Some of these had retired; others were employed. We did not allow Indonesians living in China to engage in political activities. I suggested that discussions on the normalization of relations be continued through both sides' representative missions to the UN, possibly in preparation for a conference between our foreign ministers.

Murdiono agreed to this, and then he looked at his watch and suggested we take a break. He gave us no reason for this, but in fact he went to the next room to brief Suharto about our talk. Five minutes later, he came back, saying with a smile: "His Excellency President Suharto would like to meet you alone."

Suharto gave me the impression of a white-haired senior professor who spoke gently and courteously and treated people politely. Actually, though, he had had a military career. As a boy, he had gone to a school attached to a mosque. At the age of nineteen, he had joined the army. Step by step, he rose to the rank of general. After the "September 30 incident," he succeeded President Sukarno. From 1968 to 1998, he was reelected president seven times. According to the media, under Suharto the political and social order in Indonesia had remained basically stable, and the Indonesian Communist Party was a thing of the past. At that time, he had decided to restore relations with China. However, when Suharto was in power there were severe restrictions on the lives and activities of ethnic Chinese living in Indonesia, and this situation lasted until he left office. Not until Sukarno's daughter Megawati Sukarnoputri succeeded him as president did the lives of the Indonesian Chinese improve.

Still, when I met him alone, Suharto had a very friendly attitude and was in a good mood. I first conveyed greetings from China's leaders, and then briefed him on my meeting with Murdiono. I complimented him on the achievements Indonesia had made in its national economy under his leadership.

Suharto thanked me and asked me to send his greetings to

China's leaders. He stated that Indonesia always abided by the ten principles approved at the Bandung Conference, and that the most essential of these were mutual respect for sovereignty, mutual noninterference in internal affairs, and the development of equal relations. He said that after the "September 30 incident," Indonesia had outlawed indigenous Communists, but that did not imply hostility or hostile politics toward communist countries. If the governments, people, and parties of China and Indonesia followed the principles of peaceful coexistence, respect for sovereignty, and noninterference in each other's internal affairs, the road to substantive relations and cooperation between them would be smooth. Suharto also said that Indonesia had always recognized the People's Republic of China as the sovereign power over all Chinese territory. In the future, political negotiations should be carried on between our two countries alone; there was no need to get help from any third country. To start with, each side should remove doubts about the other. He agreed that our permanent representatives to the UN should continue to be in contact, and that our foreign ministers could meet directly if necessary.

I said to him that relations between China and Indonesia, established on the basis of the Five Principles of Peaceful Coexistence, not only accorded with the interests of the two countries but also would conduce to peace in Asia and the world as a whole, and would set an example for other countries in our region.

After I met with Suharto, Murdiono said seriously that we needed to solve the most urgent problem right away. Everyone was puzzled at first, then we all laughed because what he meant was that we needed to use the toilet before continuing our meeting. Perhaps because the talk and the meeting with the president had been very smooth, he was in a good mood and felt able to crack a joke.

The next topic we discussed was how to announce to the media that representatives of China and Indonesia had met. Indonesia suggested that both sides meet the journalists, and make a joint declaration. Our side agreed. The announcement contained three points: (1) Both sides agreed to take further steps to normalize relations, (2) Relations between our two countries should be established on the basis of the Five Principles of Peaceful Coexistence and the ten principles of the Bandung Conference, (3) Both sides had agreed to discuss the details of normalizing relations through their missions to the UN. The foreign ministers of the two countries could meet if necessary.

Murdiono asked me what we should say if we were asked at the press conference how our meeting in Tokyo had come about. I said we could say that it had been discussed and decided through UN channels. If we were asked who had taken the initiative in suggesting the meeting, I said, we could say that both sides had expressed the hope of meeting.

We decided to meet the journalists. He would make the opening speech and announce the agreement. Then I would give a supplementary explanation that we were satisfied with this meeting and that the normalization of relations had already begun.

Because the joint news conference was impromptu, there was no time to inform all the media organizations, including the Chinese ones. Nevertheless, the news conference made headlines in all the major Japanese dailies and was featured by the television stations the next day. The prospect of normalizing relations between China and Indonesia, the leading nation in ASEAN, was hailed as "another victory for Chinese diplomacy" and "an epoch-making event" that would have a great impact on peace and stability in the Asia-Pacific region.

The Japanese prime minister, Takeshita, expressed his pleasure to me personally over the outcome of my talks with the Indonesian leaders. Takeshita, who liked to use numbers to explain things, said that there were six countries with a population of more than 100 million in Asia—China, India, Indonesia, Japan, Bangladesh, and Pakistan. So when all the Asian countries with a population of more than 100 million had established relations with China, that would be something worth celebrating. The Tokyo conference between China and Indonesia turned out to be successful "funeral diplomacy" for China.

Negotiations for Reconciliation

After the Tokyo conference, in order to speed up the process of normalization, further discussions were held through UN channels, focusing on what steps we should take to realize reconciliation. We suggested to Indonesia that both sides publish a communiqué on reconciliation. As for the content, who was going to sign the communiqué, and when it should be published, we would like to hear the opinion of Indonesia. We could further discuss the specific problems in our relations after the reestablishment of diplomatic relations.

However, an anti-Chinese wave spread through the United States and other Western countries after the turmoil in Beijing in June 1989. The U.S. government announced sanctions against China that included halting high-level contacts and preventing international organizations from extending loans to China. The two international "clubs for rich countries"—the European Economic Community (EEC) and the Seven-Nation Economic Summit—also halted high-level contacts with China and froze ongoing cooperative projects. In this situation, Indonesia took a wait-and-see attitude toward normalization of its relations with China.

Given the complicated, grim international environment, China insisted on diplomatic principles, sought pragmatism and flexibility, and dealt with matters calmly, with the result that it quickly overcame the sanctions and gained understanding from more and more countries. This led many countries to change their stance and restore friendly relations.

Indonesia too soon reactivated its interest in the reestablishment of diplomatic relations. Besides keeping in contact through UN channels, the two sides used the sidelines of international meetings to exchange opinions on how to complete the procedures for reestablishing diplomatic relations as soon as possible.

In August 1989, I met the Indonesian foreign minister, Alatas, at the Paris Conference on Cambodia. This was the first high-level contact between China and Indonesia since the meeting in Tokyo in February. Alatas told me that the leaders of his country had decided to normalize diplomatic relations, and all that remained was to solve technical problems. This could be done by our permanent representative missions to the UN, and during the UN Assembly our foreign ministers could confer with each other again.

I said that since the time was ripe, we should work hard to complete the procedures for reconciliation. I suggested that both sides dispatch teams to negotiate directly in Beijing or Jakarta while the representatives to the UN kept in contact, because the Chinese permanent representatives to the UN were not very familiar with the technical problems.

In early October, I again met Alatas in New York. We decided that the bureau-level officials of our ministries of foreign affairs should lead delegations of seven or eight people each to meet in Jakarta in November or December to discuss and solve the technical problems involved in resuming diplomatic relations. If necessary, a second conference could be held in Beijing. After an agreement was reached and authorized by our governments the communiqué on the resumption of diplomatic relations would be signed formally. At the same time, both sides agreed to exchange lists of problems that needed to be discussed via each other's representatives to the UN by the end of October.

From December 4 to 8, Xu Dunxin, assistant foreign minister and director general of the Department of Asian Affairs at the Ministry of Foreign Affairs, and Johan Louhanapessy, the director general for Political Affairs at the Indonesian Ministry of Foreign Affairs, held talks in Jakarta on the technical problems. These included providing facilities for each other while both sides reestablished their embassies, the size of buildings and staff of their embassies, the issue of dual nationality and overseas Chinese, and the debt owed by Indonesia to China. Admittedly, numerous complicated technical problems needed to be discussed, and it would take a fairly long time to solve them one by one.

China considered Indonesia the leader of ASEAN, and believed that our resumption of diplomatic relations with Indonesia would lead the only ASEAN countries which did not have diplomatic ties with China—Singapore and Brunei—to establish relations quickly, thus improving our overall relations with ASEAN. Also, these moves would impede the "flexible diplomacy" advocated by the Taiwan authorities and weaken the sanctions against China imposed by Western countries. Therefore, we were prepared to be flexible regarding the technical problems. As for complicated issues, we discussed principles only and left details to be discussed after the resumption of diplomatic relations.

This stand of ours paid off. The technical problems were all solved satisfactorily, including Indonesia's debt to China, which was settled during negotiations between teams of experts of both sides in Beijing and Hong Kong in March and May 1990.

THE CLOUDS DISPERSE, AND THE SUN SHINES

ON JULY 1, 1990, Foreign Minister Alatas visited China at my invitation. This was the first time an Indonesian foreign minister had visited China since the suspension of diplomatic relations in October 1967. General Secretary Jiang Zemin told Alatas that the black clouds which had hovered over our two countries for twenty-three years were dispersing, and a bright day was coming.

During the visit, Alatas and I held two rounds of talks. On the afternoon when the delegation arrived, at Indonesia's suggestion, Alatas and I held an "exclusive meeting" on the problem of resuming diplomatic relations. Alatas started by saying that all problems between our two countries had been solved after several rounds of talks on technical problems since the meeting in Tokyo in February the previous year. He told me that Suharto had instructed him to strive to complete normalization within that year. Moreover, it was not an establishment but a resumption of diplomatic relations—that is, a reopening of our embassies. All that was needed, therefore, was a simple exchange of notes. Of course, the ceremony could be a grand one to show its importance. Alatas also said that Suharto intended to invite Premier Li Peng to visit Indonesia, and our resumption of diplomatic relations could be announced during that visit. The visit could take place before August 17, Indonesia's independence day, or at another convenient time for both sides within the year.

Alatas said that it was necessary for both sides to sign a communiqué, as the outside world was paying considerable attention to his visit to China. The communiqué should include the date of normalization of diplomatic relations, the ambassadors to be exchanged, and the news of Li Peng's visit to Indonesia. At the same time, both sides could publish a press communiqué. Alatas showed me drafts of the reconciliation communiqué and the press communiqué for our consideration. I agreed to the resumption of diplomatic relations by way of an exchange of notes immediately, and expressed appreciation for Suharto's suggestion of combining the resumption of diplomatic relations with a high-level visit.

Next, both sides held the first round of formal negotiations focusing on the problem of Cambodia. Alatas said that both Indonesia and China had made important efforts toward a political settlement of the Cambodian issue. Several informal conferences on Cambodia were being held in Jakarta to seek a rough framework for solving the problem. These efforts broke down over disputes about how to obtain a cease-fire, who would make up the international supervisory organization and the transitional government, how to deal with Vietnamese immigrants, and so on. But the conferences in Jakarta led to the international meeting in Paris. Alatas said that the basic spirit of the conference held in Paris the previous year was an all-around settlement of the Cambodian issue. But now too many cooks were spoiling the broth. Relevant parties made new proposals. The result was that the peaceful settlement of the Cambodian issue had lost momentum and direction. He emphasized that a cease-fire must be linked to an overall solution, and that we should be alert to the danger of coming up with only a partial solution. He expressed the hope that China would continue to persuade Prince Norodom Sihanouk, Son Sann, and Khieu Samphan to face the core problem and accept a just and reasonable compromise.

I said that we appreciated the efforts Indonesia had made to solve the problem of Cambodia. China and Indonesia had a common understanding in seeking a political solution. We agreed with Indonesia's stand on solving the problem comprehensively. No partial solution would work; on the contrary, such a solution would leave many after-effects. I stated that China would do its best to persuade the three forces in Cambodia to work together, and I hoped that the problem would be solved completely within the framework of the Paris Conference.

The following day, we held the second round of formal negotiations. This time, we discussed the resumption of diplomatic relations and reached a consensus on several points: (1) Both sides decided to restore diplomatic relations on August 8, 1990, and agreed to send ambassadors to each other and would provide facilities for the re-opening of the embassies. (2) Premier Li Peng would pay a formal visit to Indonesia from August 6 to 9, 1990. (3) China appreciated Indonesia's adherence to its "one China" policy. As this was a sensitive problem for China, it was necessary to reach a confidential understanding. If there was a need to discuss it further, China would send a negotiation team to Indonesia before July to reach a confidential memorandum of understanding which would be signed when Li Peng visited Indonesia. (4) Because Alatas wanted both sides to sign a trade treaty when Li Peng visited Indonesia, China would present a draft treaty for Indonesia to study. (5) Both sides decided to sign the communiqué on the resumption of diplomatic relations on July 3, and hold a joint news conference.

Alatas said that Indonesia understood the importance of the Taiwan question to China, and that he believed China and Indonesia could find an appropriate way of stating their position on this. China agreed to send a team to negotiate a confidential memorandum of understanding in this regard. During our meetings, Alatas kept in touch with Murdiono in Jakarta by telephone. This showed that the negotiations for the resumption of relations were proceeding under the direct control of Suharto.

At six P.M. on July 3, a ceremony was held at the Fang Fei Garden of the Diaoyutai State Guesthouse in Beijing for the signing of the communiqué on the resumption of diplomatic relations between

China and Indonesia and for the agreement on settling the debt owed by Indonesia to China. More than 100 journalists covered this important event. The ceremony lasted less than twenty minutes, but it was the fruit of years of hard work by both sides. A new chapter in the relations between China and Indonesia thus began.

After the ceremony, Alatas and I held a joint news conference. First I announced that the diplomatic relations established between China and Indonesia in 1950 and then later suspended for twenty-three years would be restored on August 8, 1990. The common wish of the people of the two countries had finally been realized. I emphasized that the normalization of relations between the two countries with the biggest populations in the Asia-Pacific region would have a far-reaching effect on the peace, stability, and development of this region. It had been possible to restore normal relations because of the foresight of the leaders of the two countries. I added that I believed Premier Li Peng's forthcoming visit to Indonesia would do much to revitalize the relations between the two countries after the resumption of diplomatic relations.

Alatas said that the important progress we had made foretold the opening of a new page in the history of relations between our two countries. The resumption of diplomatic relations not only accorded with the interests of the people of the two nations, but also would make a great contribution to the peace and stability of Asia. He also said that Li Peng's visit to Indonesia would be a historic event and would raise our relations to a new level.

Next, we answered journalists' questions. One journalist remarked that Singapore had once indicated that it would establish diplomatic relations with China only when China had restored diplomatic relations with Indonesia. He asked if, since China and Indonesia had restored diplomatic relations, China was preparing to establish diplomatic relations with Singapore. I answered that both China and Singapore were making preparations to do so.

Answering a question on economic cooperation between Indonesia and China following the resumption of diplomatic relations, Alatas said that Indonesia and China had resumed direct trade contacts in 1985. Since then, there had been striking developments in the trade relationship between the two countries. He explained that the first thing the two sides would do following the resumption of normal relations was to prepare a new trade treaty. He noted that Indonesia and China, as two important countries in the Asia-Pacific region, would cooperate not only in trade but in many other fields as well.

Another journalist asked about Indonesia's trade and investment relations with Taiwan. Alatas said that, unlike the other ASEAN countries, Indonesia had established diplomatic relations with China in 1950, on the basis of the "one China" policy. This policy had not changed even when relations between our two countries were suspended. After Indonesia established diplomatic relations with China and during the period when the relations were suspended, Indonesia had kept economic and trade relations with Taiwan, but it always persisted in its "one China" policy. Indonesia recognized only one China, he emphasized—the People's Republic of China.

The restoration of relations between China and Indonesia received favorable responses internationally, especially in the ASEAN countries. On July 4 the Singaporean Ministry of Foreign Affairs welcomed the normalization of relations between China and Indonesia, and reiterated Singapore's readiness to establish formal diplomatic relations with China. The Thai Ministry of Foreign Affairs stated that the resumption of diplomatic relations between China and Indonesia would develop all-round the relationship between ASEAN and China and would promote a consensus on the problem of Cambodia. The Philippines and other countries in the region also published statements or remarks welcoming the restoration of diplomatic relations between China and Indonesia.

Following the resumption of diplomatic relations with Indonesia, China established diplomatic relations with Singapore and Brunei in October 1990 and September 1991, respectively. China then had full diplomatic relations with all six members of ASEAN. In July 1991, ASEAN sent me an unprecedented invitation to attend the opening ceremony of the twenty-fourth ASEAN Ministerial Conference, to be held in Malaysia. This was an opportunity for me to consult the foreign ministers of the ASEAN countries. In July 1994, ASEAN admitted China to the ASEAN Regional Forum; in July 1996, China became a formal dialogue partner of ASEAN; at the end of 1997, we established the "Good-Neighborly Partnership of Mutual Trust in the Twenty-first Century" with ASEAN; in November 2002, China and the leaders of the ASEAN countries—by then grown to ten—signed a Framework Agreement on China-ASEAN Comprehensive Economic Cooperation, and decided to establish a China-ASEAN free trade area in 2010. Both sides also signed the Declaration on the Conduct of Parties in the South China Sea and the Declaration on China-ASEAN Nontraditional Security Cooperation, and other documents. Thus relations between China and the ASEAN countries entered a new phase of development.

5 THE ROAD TO SEOUL

First Time in the ROK (Republic of Korea)

THE FIRST TIME I VISITED SEOUL was in November 1991, when I attended the third Asia-Pacific Economic Cooperation (APEC) ministerial-level conference there. China had just completed the procedures for joining APEC and was represented at the conference for the first time. The usual practice is to hold such a conference annually. The delegations of all member countries are headed by both the minister of foreign affairs and the minister of economy and trade. Li Lanqing, then minister of Foreign Trade and Economic Cooperation, and I led the Chinese delegation to Seoul.

It was a surprise for China's minister of foreign affairs to show up in Seoul. There had been no official relations between China and the Republic of Korea since 1945 at the end of World War II. Indeed, China and the ROK had been on opposite sides during the fierce fighting in the Korean War several years later. Today, tourists from the ROK can be seen everywhere in China, and Chinese citizens are free to go to the ROK for sightseeing; but in the early 1990s ROK was still off-limits to China, and not many Chinese had been there.

On November 12, a CAAC airplane carrying the Chinese delegation landed at Kimpo Airport, near Seoul. At that time, there were no regular flights between our two countries, as China had not yet established diplomatic relations with the ROK. Our airplane did not stay in the airport but flew back to Beijing right away. It came back to pick us when the conference ended.

Our Korean hosts gave us a warm welcome at the airport and then, to avoid our being harassed by reporters, they ushered us onto a special bus to take us downtown. But a large number of reporters were waiting for the Chinese delegation at the Shilla Hotel, the biggest hotel in Seoul, all eager for any information or for signs of a diplomatic breakthrough. As soon as we walked into the lobby, we were surrounded by the media. They were not interested in the recent admission of China to APEC. Cameras flashed and zoomed in, microphones were shoved under my nose, and people were all shouting questions at the same time. I remember that a few women reporters from Taiwan butted in from time to time in their high-pitched voices. The hubbub made it impossible for me to hear the questions clearly, let alone answer them. So I thanked the reporters, telling them that we would have opportunities to meet again, and then we followed our Korean hosts hurriedly into the elevators. Unexpectedly, the reporters followed us to our floor and crowded in front of our hotel rooms so that we could neither get in nor get out. Seeing this, our Korean hosts decided to seal off the entire floor, placing guards there around the clock to keep order and prevent any incidents.

The APEC conference was a great success. In their speeches, the ROK's foreign minister Lee Sang Ock and the foreign ministers of the other member countries extended a warm welcome to the three new members (People's Republic of China, Chinese Taipei, and Hong Kong). I, in my turn, thanked all the member countries for their support. I said that it was a major step in the economic cooperation of the countries in the Asia-Pacific region to have China, Chinese Taipei, and Hong Kong in APEC. I also expressed our appreciation to the ROK for its efforts to bring all the countries together.

During the conference, the ROK kept its promise. It did not invite the Taiwan "ambassador" to the ROK to take part in any activities concerning the conference, including the welcoming banquet given by the ROK president.

ASIA-PACIFIC ECONOMIC COOPERATION

There were twists and turns about China's participation in APEC.

The idea of creating APEC was first put forward by Robert Hawke, prime minister of Australia, when he visited Seoul in early 1989. Its main purpose is to strengthen economic contacts and cooperation between countries such as the United States, Canada, Australia, and New Zealand, and the east Asian region. At first, Australia hoped China would support the plan, and it sent a special envoy to China to obtain that support. But it soon changed its attitude, along with the United States and some other Western countries, after the political turmoil of 1989 in Beijing. China did not attend the first ministerial conference, which was held in Australia; or the second, which was held in Singapore. But any economic cooperation in the Asia-Pacific region without the involvement of China is unthinkable. China is a large country with a huge market. It has wide economic connections with countries in the Asia-Pacific region. Its economy has been growing continuously, rapidly, and with strong momentum. All the member countries of APEC realized that it was important for China to join. One passage in a joint declaration passed at the second ministerial meeting reads as follows:

> The ministers acknowledge that the three economic entities of the People's Republic of China, Taiwan, and Hong Kong are of special and important significance to the Asia-Pacific region, whether considering their current economic activities or their role in the future prosperity of the region. It is appropriate that the three economic entities attend APEC

meetings in future. The ministers agree that talks with the three parties should continue until an arrangement can be made which is satisfactory to the three parties as well as all current members of APEC, to have them join APEC as soon as possible, preferably at the Seoul Conference.

Indonesia, a member of APEC, was talking with China about resuming diplomatic relations and was the first to give us this information. Soon afterward, the ROK, which was to host the third ministerial meeting, began secret discussions with China about the matter.

The complexity of China's joining APEC lay mainly in what name and status Taiwan and Hong Kong were to assume if they were admitted to APEC at the same time. Unlike the UN or other international organizations, whose members are sovereign states, APEC is a forum for discussing economic issues, and its members are called economies. National flags and emblems are not seen at its meetings. Therefore, it was possible for Hong Kong and Taiwan to join APEC as economies.

China presented its basic principle regarding this issue: With the precondition that there was only one China, the People's Republic of China would join APEC as a sovereign country, while Taiwan and Hong Kong would join as regional economies.

The ROK displayed particular enthusiasm for getting China into APEC before the meeting in Seoul. Although the ROK had diplomatic relations with Taiwan at the time, it had realized that establishing diplomatic relations with China would be in its best interest given the prospects for future economic development and changes in political structures in east Asia. By taking advantage of its status as the host country of the next ministerial meeting of APEC, the ROK did all it could to help China become a member, and thereby to promote contacts with China at the same time. This had become an important objective of the ROK's foreign policy.

At that time, diplomats from the ROK could not pay official visits to China, but we bent the rules to invite Lee See Young, the assistant foreign minister of the ROK, to Beijing many times to negotiate a solution to the issue. Lee came to Beijing in his capacity as chairman of APEC's meetings of senior officials, and through him the discussion was passed to other members for their comments and suggestions. Lee also went to Taiwan and Hong Kong frequently to discuss the matter.

The negotiations were extremely difficult, but not because the ROK and other APEC members had different views regarding the principles of sovereign states and the regional economy. The difficulty came mainly from Taiwan. Taiwan insisted that it should have "equal status" within this regional organization. It had repeatedly refused to join APEC under the name of "Taiwan, China." Nor would it accept the arrangement that its "foreign minister" would not attend APEC meetings. Moreover, it refused to discuss these issues directly with China. As a result, the negotiations reached an impasse.

It can be imagined how hard all this was for Lee See Young, who had made frequent trips to China, Taiwan, and Hong Kong, passing on information and at the same time trying to work out a compromise acceptable to all three sides. For some time, there was hardly any progress. Reportedly, only after Lee threatened Taiwan—saying that if it still refused to compromise, APEC would admit China and Hong Kong first—did Taiwan reluctantly give in.

After six rounds of talks over a period of nine months, we finally found a solution which was acceptable to Taiwan and Hong Kong and to which all the APEC members agreed.

On October 2, 1991, in New York, Lee and Qin Huasun, head of the Department of International Organizations and Conferences of the Ministry of Foreign Affairs, signed a memorandum of understanding regarding the simultaneous entry of the three parties. Included in the memorandum were the basic principles we had always stressed and specific provisions on the name Taiwan was to use and the rank of officials participating in APEC activities. It required Taiwan to use the name "Chinese Taipei," and only the minister responsible for economic affairs could attend APEC meetings. Its "minister" and "vice minister of foreign affairs" would not be allowed to attend the meetings.

APEC also signed the same memorandum of understanding with Taiwan and Hong Kong. Meanwhile, China reached an agreement with the ROK stipulating that Taiwan's "ambassador" in Seoul would not be allowed to participate in any activities related to the third APEC ministerial meeting. This cleared the way for the Chinese delegation to attend the meeting in Seoul.

MEETING WITH PRESIDENT ROH TAE WOO

ACCORDING TO THE SCHEDULE, President Roh Tae Woo of the ROK was to meet the ministers of all the APEC members the afternoon we arrived in Seoul. We arrived at Cheong Wa Dae, the presidential residence, on time. In the meeting hall, all the guests lined up in protocol order. Then the protocol officer of the presidential office told me that the president wished to have a private meeting with me after the group meeting.

Although Roh Tae Woo had been in the army for many years, he was a gentle man. He was strongly in favor of establishing diplomatic relations with China. He had assumed the post of president in February 1988. On the basis of the changing international situation and the situation on the Korean peninsula, he put forward his "northern policy," with the objective of establishing diplomatic relations with China, the Soviet Union, and other socialist countries in eastern Europe during his tenure, in order to guarantee peace and stability on the Korean peninsula.

The successful Olympic Games in Seoul in October 1988 increased the ROK's international influence. Since China, the Soviet Union, and many eastern European countries had sent delegations to the Seoul Olympics, tension between the ROK and these countries had eased.

In early 1989, Hungary became the first socialist country to establish diplomatic relations with the ROK. By September 1990, when the Soviet Union established diplomatic relations with ROK, the vast majority of eastern European countries had normalized their relations with the ROK.

Roh Tae Woo had made several attempts to improve relations with China, but with scant progress. As there was only a little more than one year left before his term expired, Roh would certainly not pass up the chance of meeting the Chinese foreign minister in Seoul.

After the group meeting, Lee Sang Ock led me into a meeting room that had traditional Korean decor. Then President Roh, who was wearing a dark blue suit, came in and shook hands with everyone.

Roh first welcomed the Chinese delegation and congratulated China on joining APEC. Then he talked about the relations between the ROK and China. He said that geographically China and the ROK were separated by only a narrow strip of sea, and that there was a long history of contacts between China and Korea. The western coast of the ROK and the eastern part of China's Shandong peninsula were so close that, according to an old saying, "one could hear roosters crow and dogs bark from the other side." It was only in the past few decades that the two countries had become isolated from each other. This was regrettable and unnatural, he said. Fortunately, in recent years relations between the two countries had improved. Chinese athletic delegations had participated in the Asian Games and Olympic Games held in the ROK in 1986 and 1988, respectively, and after that trade between the two countries had resumed. The Korean side was happy and satisfied with such progress. The ROK had already established diplomatic relations with the Soviet Union and eastern European countries, but it should have a closer relationship with China. For the sake of peace and stability on the Korean peninsula, and peace and development in the Asia-Pacific region, the ROK hoped to improve its ties with China, to the extent of establishing diplomatic relations as soon as possible.

Graceful in manner, Roh smiled constantly as he talked. He particularly mentioned the Shandong peninsula, he said, because he had always believed that he was descended from people who had emigrated from Shandong, whose Chinese surname was Lu (the Chinese equivalent of Roh). Later, on an official visit to China, he went to Shandong in search of his roots.

I thanked President Roh for the audience, and praised the Korean side for its preparatory work for the APEC ministerial meeting. I agreed that historically China and Korea had had frequent contacts with each other, and that geographically the two countries were close neighbors. Since each side could hear roosters crow and dogs bark from the other side, it was strange not to visit each other. I noted that the present abnormal situation was a direct result of World War II. I added that we hoped that the north and south sides of the Korean peninsula could coexist in peace and have more contacts with each other. Trade between China and the ROK had developed considerably in recent years, and we hoped both sides would work together to achieve greater development. It was also my wish that the United States and Japan would improve relations with the Democratic People's Republic of Korea (DPRK). I said all I wanted to say, but I did not give an answer to Roh's inquiry about establishing diplomatic relations with China.

News of our meeting was reported on local television stations one hour after the meeting was over. Large pictures showing President Roh shaking hands with me also appeared on the front pages of major newspapers in Seoul the following day. The media did not give specific details about our conversation but generally referred to it as a "turning point" in relations between China and the ROK.

The next day I had breakfast with Lee Sang Ock. This breakfast had been arranged before we came to Seoul, and the South Koreans were very pleased. This was the first time we had sat down together to have breakfast and exchange views. Before that, whenever I attended the annual UN meetings, the ROK foreign minister would ask to meet me, but China had never consented. Not until September 1991, after the DPRK and South Korea had been admitted to the UN simultaneously, did I have a courtesy meeting with Lee during a UN General Assembly session.

Now, Lee and I first discussed the routine affairs of the session. Then Lee switched the topic to relations between our two countries. He said that the previous year the trade volume between us had been worth US$3.8 billion, and this year it would probably exceed US$5 billion. If more time was needed to establish diplomatic relations, he suggested that each side upgrade the unofficial trade office already established in the other country to an official one, to meet the needs of the rapidly developing trade. I said that in the long term our relations would move in that direction, but for the time being it was better to maintain the status quo. I suggested that people from both sides, including diplomats, keep in touch and exchange views. Lee said that his side understood that China needed time to prepare for the establishment of diplomatic relations with the ROK. They wanted only to realize the objective as early as possible. In reply, I quoted a Chinese adage: "Where water flows, a channel takes shape."

Something amusing happened that night. Park Chul Un, the ROK's minister of teenage sport, who had often asked to see me, called again. I was at first unwilling to see him, but on the telephone he said that he had been to China many times and had many friends in China. One of them was my younger brother Qian Qi'ao, then vice mayor of Tianjin in charge of culture and sports. They had met during an international sports competition hosted by Tianjin. At around eleven P.M., Park and his assistant came to my room. After exchanging a few words of greeting, Park said he was willing to establish a secret liaison channel and work together toward establishing diplomatic relations between the ROK and China. He said he had obtained approval from President Roh before coming to see me. He would soon resign from his current post to participate in the campaign for the general election of president, and one of his main political goals was to normalize relations between our two countries. Then he took out two gold keys, telling me that the large one was for me and the small one was for my brother. With these keys, he wished to open the door to our relations.

For several years at that time, quite a few high-level officials of the ROK were able to obtain visas on separate pieces of paper* to visit

---

* This is a special type of visa. It is issued to people when—for whatever reason—a visa cannot be stamped on their passports or other traveling documents, or when their passports or traveling documents are not officially acknowledged.

Beijing privately. They would invariably tell their host—irrespective of the nature of the organization—that they wanted to contribute to the establishment of diplomatic relations between the two countries. But since these emissaries were of different sorts, it was hard to distinguish those with good intentions and those with not-so-good intentions.

I listened carefully to what Park said. Then I told him that although diplomatic relations did not exist between our two countries, there had been official contact between the two sides, so there was no need for any secret channel. Upon returning to China, I had the two keys examined by the People's Bank of China, and found that they were made of real gold. Now kept in the Ministry of Foreign Affairs, the two keys serve as a footnote to the development of relations between China and the ROK.

BREAKING THE ICE

NOTHING IN ITS BILATERAL relations would hinder China from establishing diplomatic relations with the ROK. The difficulties came from our relationship with the DPRK. China had to make the DPRK—a close ally for decades—understand and accept the shift in its foreign policy.

The cold relationship between China and the ROK had historical roots. During the 1930s and 1940s, Kim Il Sung and other Korean revolutionaries joined the Anti-Japanese United Force in northeastern China to fight against Japanese aggression, together with the Chinese people. The friendship between China and the DPRK was forged at that time. At the end of World War II, with the Thirty-eighth Parallel as the demarcation line, the United States and the Soviet Union respectively occupied the southern and northern parts of the Korean peninsula. In August 1948, the ROK was founded, and one month later the DPRK came into being.

On October 1, 1949, the People's Republic of China was founded. Six days later, it established diplomatic relations with the DPRK.

The Korean War broke out in June 1950. China and the Soviet

Union supported the DPRK, while the United States and Japan supported the ROK. Three years later, an armistice was signed, with a demilitarized zone separating the two sides roughly following the Thirty-eighth Parallel. The military face-off on the Korean peninsula has continued until the present day.

Starting in the mid-1970s, with new developments and changes in the international situation, many countries, out of pragmatic considerations, recognized both Koreas and established diplomatic relations with both. Although the Soviet Union and eastern European countries did not recognize the ROK, they began to have contact with it in multilateral events such as international sports competitions and conferences. By the early 1980s, nearly 100 countries had established diplomatic relations with both Koreas. Meanwhile, noticeable changes took place on the Korean peninsula. The antagonistic north and south, until then, not only began to have contacts, but held high-level talks as well. In 1972, they issued a joint declaration stating that they would eliminate all outside interference to promote the reunification of Korea.

After the Third Plenary Session of the Eleventh Party Congress, in 1978, China shifted its priority to economic development, and a policy of reform and opening-up was initiated. Under these circumstances, a pressing issue of our diplomacy was how to expand the scope of China's international exchanges to create a favorable outside environment for our modernization drive.

With this background, the further easing of the tension on the Korean peninsula, the promotion of peaceful negotiations between the two Koreas, and improvement of relations with our close neighbor—the ROK—were placed on our agenda.

We decided on a new principle in accordance with the changed situation. China would participate in all international events hosted by the ROK that had been entrusted to it by an international organization, so long as China was a member of that organization. By the same token, China would allow the ROK to participate in international events held in China. This meant that instead of refusing to have any contact with the ROK, China now followed the common international practice and the principle of reciprocity in all multilateral events. This provided the conditions for normal exchanges between the two countries later.

At that time, China was considering bidding for the next Asian Games. As the level of sports in China improved, China had for years wanted to host the Asian Games. Many other Asian countries had the same intention, and one barrier China needed to overcome when bidding for the games was whether it would admit athletes from the ROK. If a country refused to admit athletes of a member country of the Asian Olympic Council for the purpose of participating in international competition, then that country would not be eligible to bid for the Asian Games. In August 1983, Beijing submitted its application to the Asian Olympic Council to host the Eleventh Asian Games in 1990. The application was accompanied by a letter from China's minister of foreign affairs, in which he promised to welcome all member countries of the Asian Olympic Council to participate in the games in Beijing.

In consideration of its relationship with the DPRK, China promptly informed that country of its decision. We said that if China was awarded the right to host the Asian Games, it would welcome the DPRK's participation. It would also abide by the regulations of the Asian Olympic Council and welcome all athletes from all member countries, including the ROK.

Deng Xiaoping had always shown concern for the relationship between China and the ROK. In April 1985, talking about Sino-ROK relations, he said that improvement of this relationship would bring economic benefits to China and lead the ROK to sever its ties with Taiwan.

During the period from May to September 1988, Deng mentioned Sino-ROK relations several times when he met foreign dignitaries. He said that promoting relations with the ROK would only benefit China. Economically, it would be beneficial to both sides; politically, it would help China's reunification.

He also said that the time was right for China to quicken its steps and widen the scope of its economic and cultural exchanges with the

ROK. Promoting unofficial relations between China and the ROK was an important strategic move which would be of great significance in maintaining peace and stability on the Korean peninsula, as well as for China's relations with Taiwan, Japan, the United States, and Southeast Asia.

Deng also cautioned that since this was a delicate issue, we should handle it with care. Especially, we should first obtain the understanding of the DPRK.

Following Deng's instructions, we eased many restrictions concerning our relationship with the ROK in multilateral international events. Visits between the two countries accelerated. In 1986 and 1988, China sent squads comprising several hundred people each to Seoul to participate in the Asian Games and the Olympic Games held there. When the Eleventh Asian Games were held in Beijing in 1990, both Koreas participated. Vice President Lee Jong Ock of the DPRK was present at the opening ceremony. The national flags of the DPRK and the ROK were raised simultaneously, and for the first time ever, in Beijing.

Trade with the ROK developed rapidly following the easing of China's policy toward the ROK. The trade volume between the two countries already exceeded US$1 billion in 1988. As the volume of trade increased, the former way of trading—via Hong Kong—could no longer meet the demand. The two countries began to consider establishing unofficial trade offices in each other's territory to help conduct direct nongovernmental trade between the two sides. Unexpectedly, this issue drew special attention from the DPRK, even involving the top leaders of the DPRK and China.

TALKS WITH THE DPRK

IN NOVEMBER 1988, when the foreign minister of the DPRK, Kim Yong Nam, visited China, I held special talks with him about China's trade relations with the ROK. I told him that China and the ROK were considering setting up unofficial trade offices in each other's country. Later, leaders of China and the DPRK exchanged views on this issue several times. In the second half of 1989, when Kim Il Sung came to Beijing for a visit, Jiang Zemin talked with him about the issue. The next year, when Kim Il Sung visited Shenyang, Jiang talked with him about the matter again. By then, Kim Il Sung was fully aware of China's stand, and gave his assent.

In October 1990, the China International Chamber of Commerce and the Korea Trade and Investment Promotion Agency (KOTRA) reached an agreement regarding the establishment of trade offices in each other's capital, and the offices were in place in early 1991.

Soon after that, a new problem arose. This time it was about the two Koreas joining the UN. As the largest organization of governments in the world, the UN admits only sovereign states. The DPRK had always opposed admitting both North and South Korea to the UN, lest it should effectively perpetuate the split between them. At that time, both the DPRK and the ROK had UN observer status. But the ROK had made efforts all along to join the UN as a full member, and more and more UN member countries were prepared to support it.

In May 1991, when the Chinese premier, Li Peng, visited the DPRK, he brought up the topic with his counterpart there. He said that if the ROK again proposed joining the UN during the Assembly that year, China would find it difficult to oppose this. Moreover, once the ROK became a member, it would be difficult for the DPRK to join the UN. The prime minister of the DPRK made no reply. But before Li Peng ended his visit, President Kim Il Sung met him and talked about this issue. Kim said that the DPRK would cooperate with China on the issue. Later, an editorial was published in newspapers in the DPRK, saying that the DPRK would not oppose the simultaneous admission of North and South Korea to the UN.

I visited the DPRK from June 17 to 20 that year, and met Kim Yong Nam and President Kim Il Sung. Kim Yong Nam told me that to prevent the situation at the UN from becoming unfavorable to the DPRK, it had decided to take the initiative and apply for membership. He maintained that both Koreas should join the UN at the same time. If the United States insisted on discussing the applications of North and South Korea separately, the DPRK hoped that

China would raise an objection. And if the United States vetoed the DPRK's application, the DPRK hoped China would veto South Korea's application.

What most worried the DPRK was the possibility that the ROK's application would be approved and the DPRK's application rejected. In our talks, I explained in detail the UN procedure for reviewing applications for membership. I said that China would consult the relevant countries, and try to persuade them to be cooperative on this issue. This remark finally removed all the worries of the DPRK side.

When Kim Il Sung met me at Mount Myohyang, a scenic spot, he particularly mentioned the UN issue. He said that all efforts should be made to ensure that the DPRK and the ROK join the UN simultaneously. If their applications were discussed separately, the United States might use its veto power, demanding to inspect the DPRK's nuclear facilities. In that case, the DPRK would be placed in a difficult position. On issues related to the UN, he said, the DPRK would not make things difficult for China. So he hoped that China would not make things difficult for the DPRK.

I told Kim Il Sung that all the relevant countries had a common understanding that the northern and southern sides of the Korea peninsula would join the UN simultaneously. The issue would be discussed in one resolution, and so the situation the DPRK worried about would not happen.

On September 17, 1991, a resolution was adopted at the General Assembly of the UN, admitting the DPRK and the ROK to membership simultaneously.

STARTING NEGOTIATIONS FOR ESTABLISHING DIPLOMATIC RELATIONS WITH THE ROK

AFTER WE RETURNED TO CHINA from the APEC meeting, we began to ponder the issue of establishing diplomatic relations with the ROK.

Roh Tae Woo was in his last year as president. He was eager to establish diplomatic relations with China so that he could realize the objectives of his "northern policy," put forward at the beginning of his term. Both Koreas had already joined the UN, and they often attended international conferences together and participated in the same sporting events. More than 100 countries had established diplomatic relations with both of them. The conditions for China to establish diplomatic relations with the ROK were, basically, ripe.

In March 1992, during a session of the National People's Congress, I held a news conference, as was usual on such an occasion. At previous news conferences, some foreign journalists would ask whether there would be any changes in the Sino-ROK relationship, and my reply would always be as follows: China's stand has not changed, and we will not have official relations with the ROK. But that year my reply was different. I said there was no timetable for China to establish diplomatic relations with the ROK. This was a clue for sensitive foreign journalists.

In April that year, the forty-eighth annual session of the UN Economic and Social Commission for Asia and the Pacific (ESCAP) was held in Beijing, with the ROK's foreign minister, Lee Sang Ock, attending. He had been the chairman of the forty-seventh session, so following common international practice, I met him at the Diaoyutai State Guesthouse and gave a banquet in his honor.

Lee and I exchanged views on issues of interest to both sides, and then I talked alone with him about Sino-ROK relations. I said that although the time was not yet ripe for formal negotiations to establish diplomatic relations, we could establish liaison channels first so that we could have regular contacts with each other. Lee agreed to my suggestion. After the discussion, we decided on the appointment by each side of a chief representative who would be at the vice-ministerial level, and a deputy chief representative who would be at the ambassadorial level. The deputy chief representative would lead a working group to start talks in Beijing and Seoul as soon as possible. Before this meeting, the ROK side had tried hard to find out what our stand was. They wanted to make a breakthrough at this meeting, but they also worried that their actions might backfire if they pushed too hard. So they felt relieved.

After the foreign ministers' meeting, China and the ROK appointed their chief and deputy chief representatives. The Chinese chief representative was Vice Foreign Minister Xu Dunxin, and the ROK's chief representative was Vice Foreign Minister Roe Ching Hee. The working group was headed by the Chinese ambassador to the ROK, Zhang Ruijie, and the ROK's ambassador to China, Kwon Byong Hyon, and it included six or seven people from each side. Talks began in May. To ensure the secrecy of the talks, the ROK side suggested that we hold them first in Beijing, because it would be almost impossible to keep such talks secret in Seoul.

Our first round of talks was held in Building 14 of the Diaoyutai State Guesthouse. The building was isolated and quiet, and would not be discovered by the media. The personnel from the ROK side came to Beijing individually via a third place. Once they settled in, they did not leave the building. In the first round, our intention was to focus on general topics, and sound out the intentions of the other side. But they were anxious. After exchanging a few pleasantries, they immediately wanted to talk about establishing diplomatic relations with China.

In reply, we put forward our principle on establishing diplomatic relations. We demanded that the ROK side sever diplomatic relations with Taiwan, abrogating all their treaties with it and withdrawing their embassy. For a while, the ROK side stalled, proposing to demote their embassy in Taiwan to a "liaison office." We rejected the suggestion, and that ended our first round of talks.

The second round of talks was also held in Beijing. We reiterated our principle on establishing diplomatic relations. This time the ROK side made some concessions. But they still said that since the relationship between Taiwan and the ROK had lasted for a long time, they wanted China to agree that the ROK could maintain special relations with Taiwan after establishing diplomatic relations with China. We sensed that this was the last card of the ROK side. We were sure that so long as we adhered to our guideline, it was possible to make a breakthrough in the talks. Then we suggested that a third round of talks be held in Seoul, and the ROK side agreed.

In the third round of talks, the ROK side accepted our principle on establishing diplomatic relations, and we reached an agreement on the matter. It included a confidential memorandum, among other things.

All three rounds of talks took less than two months. At the end of June, all the work had been completed. All that was left was for the chief representatives to meet, initial the communiqué for the establishment of diplomatic relations, and decide on the date for the foreign ministers to officially sign the communiqué and release it.

TRIP TO PYONGYANG

CHINA'S ESTABLISHMENT of diplomatic relations with the ROK contributed to easing tension on the Korean peninsula and safeguarding the stability of the Asia-Pacific region. We kept the DPRK informed of the progress of the talks in order to help it better understand China's position on the issue.

In April 1992, before the start of the talks with the ROK, President Yang Shangkun of China went to Pyongyang to take part in activities celebrating the eightieth birthday of Kim Il Sung. Entrusted by the Central Committee of the Communist Party of China, Yang analyzed the international situation and explained China's foreign relations. He told Kim that China was considering establishing diplomatic relations with the ROK. He also stressed that China would continue to support the DPRK's cause of reunification, as it had always done. Kim said that the situation on the Korean peninsula was precarious. He said that he hoped China would coordinate the relations between China, the ROK, the DPRK, and the United States. After returning to China, Yang briefed the top leaders on Kim's views.

In June-July of that year, I accompanied Yang on a visit to Africa. We returned to Beijing on July 12, and General Secretary Jiang Zemin welcomed us at the Great Hall of the People.

After the welcoming ceremony, Jiang, Yang, and I discussed establishing diplomatic relations with the ROK. Jiang told me that, in order to show China's respect for the DPRK, after much consideration the Central Party Committee had decided to send me to Pyongyang to convey a message from Jiang to Kim, telling him of China's decision to establish diplomatic relations with the ROK.

The matter brooked no delay. After we obtained permission from the DPRK, I boarded a special air force plane, and flew to Pyongyang three days later.

It was not an ordinary foreign visit. I felt a little uneasy on the plane to Pyongyang. I was not certain whether the DPRK side would fully understand China's position. Although Kim Il Sung had agreed to meet me, I was not sure whether what we were going to tell him would be a shock. What would his reply be? Beijing is not very far from Pyongyang. Before I had much time to think, the plane landed at Sunan Airport near Pyongyang.

On my previous visits to the DPRK, there would have been many people lined up at the airport to give a warm welcome. This time the plane landed at a quiet area of the airport, and the foreign minister, Kim Yong Nam, was the only person there to welcome us. We shook hands and said a few words of greeting. Kim told me that we were to go to another city, by helicopter.

There was a small table in the cabin. Kim and I sat face to face while the others sat on two sides. It was a hot summer day, and the cabin was like a big steamer. Before long, the helicopter landed near a lake. Someone in the Chinese delegation told me that President Kim had villas at this lake and usually spent the summer there. We alighted from the helicopter and were taken to a villa to rest.

At around eleven A.M., President Kim met us in another villa. He stood at the door of the meeting room to greet and shake hands with everyone. Then we took our seats on each side of a large table.

I first expressed gratitude to President Kim for meeting us despite his tight schedule, and passed on to him Jiang Zemin's regards. Then I conveyed Jiang's message. I said that Jiang, on behalf of Deng Xiaoping and other comrades of the Central Party Committee, sent his high respect and best wishes to President Kim. Jiang pointed out that the relations between the two parties and the two countries had progressed in a sound way, and that this made the Chinese side very happy and satisfied. The current international situation was volatile, and dramatic changes might take place at any moment. Under such circumstances, we should seize the opportunity to create an international environment in which we could develop and increase our national strength. It was of great significance for the two parties and the two countries—China and the DPRK—which respected and understood each other, to continually improve their friendly cooperation. As for the relationship between China and the ROK, after pondering the recent changes that had taken place in the world and on the Korean peninsula, we believed that the time was ripe for China to begin negotiations with the ROK about establishing diplomatic relations. We were sure that President Kim would understand and support our decision. We would, as always, make every effort to strengthen the traditional friendship between the two parties and the two countries forged in the struggle we had waged side by side for decades. We would continue to support the DPRK's socialist construction and policy of independent and peaceful reunification, help ease tension on the Korean peninsula, and help improve the DPRK's relations with the United States and Japan.

President Kim thought for a moment before he said that he had caught every word of my message. "We understand China's independent foreign policy," he said. "We will continue with our efforts to promote our friendly relations with China. We can overcome all difficulties and persevere in maintaining and building socialism." He then asked me to give his regards to Deng Xiaoping and other Chinese leaders when I returned to Beijing.

President Kim then had a look at the gift we had brought for him—a jade carving of nine dragons playing with a ball and some fresh lychees—and saw off his guests.

In my memory, this meeting was the shortest of all the meetings President Kim Il Sung had had with a Chinese delegation. After the meeting, the DPRK did not give a banquet in our honor, contrary to what it had always done in the past.

At this critical moment in history, President Kim, by taking into account the overall interest of DPRK's relations with China and the situation on the Korean peninsula, made a positive and wise decision. He demonstrated the breadth of vision of an old revolutionary, which impressed me very much.

We had a simple lunch together with Kim Yong Nam. Then we got into the helicopter and flew to Pyongyang. We were supposed to return on the same day, and our plane was waiting for us at the airport. After saying good-bye to our host, we flew back to Beijing.

It was almost five P.M. when we arrived in Beijing. We got into a car and went directly to Jiang Zemin's office in Zhongnanhai. I reported to him in detail about our visit to the DPRK. After hearing my report, Jiang asked me a few questions and said that he was very satisfied.

By then, the mission entrusted to me by the central leadership was completed.

China Establishes Diplomatic Relations with the ROK

AT NINE A.M. on August 24, 1992, Lee Sang Ock and I officially signed the communiqué for the establishment of diplomatic relations between China and the ROK. We were in the Fangfeiyuan compound of the Diaoyutai State Guesthouse in Beijing. Television stations of both countries broadcast the ceremony live to the rest of the world. Many countries soon reported the news, and expressed their congratulations.

The establishment of diplomatic relations between China and the ROK was widely welcomed by the international community, except Taiwan. Infuriated, Taiwan accused the ROK of "being ungrateful," and it withdrew its "embassy" from Seoul one day before China and the ROK established diplomatic relations.

In late September, or one month after the big occasion, President Roh Tae Woo of the ROK paid an official visit to China at the invitation of President Yang Shangkun. Lee Sang Ock was a key member of

Roh's delegation. I went all the way back to Beijing from the UN to welcome the ROK's delegation. In May 1993, I paid an official visit to the ROK and held talks with its new foreign minister, Han Sung Joo. I also met with the new president, Kim Young Sam.

It has been over a decade since our two countries established diplomatic relations, and in that time bilateral relations have developed beyond our expectations. As close neighbors, the leaders of China and the ROK have made frequent visits to each other and effectively promoted understanding, exchanges, and cooperation between the two countries in all fields. By 2002, the trade volume between us had exceeded US $40 billion. China had become the third largest trading partner of the ROK, which was the fifth largest trading partner of China. In addition, the ROK's investment in China exceeded US $10 billion, and it has continued to increase. Both sides have been strengthening their cooperation in international organizations such as the UN, and in international affairs. China and the ROK have the same objective in safeguarding the peace and stability of the Korean peninsula and in making it a region without nuclear weapons.

In late February 2003, I paid an official visit to Seoul again, to attend the inaugural ceremony of the new president of the ROK. I met the outgoing president, Kim Dae Jung; and the incoming president, Roh Moo Hyun.

From the establishment of diplomatic relations to this day, although the government of the ROK has changed several times, relations between China and the ROK have been developing smoothly, thanks to the solid foundation we laid at the very beginning.

6 WITHSTANDING INTERNATIONAL PRESSURE

During the ten years that I served as China's foreign minister, the most difficult time for Chinese diplomacy was the late 1980s and the early 1990s. All of a sudden, the international situation changed. The governments of Western countries announced one after another that they would impose sanctions against China. Various political powers, for different motives, set off an anti-China campaign. In a little more than one month—from June 5 to July 15, 1989—the United States, Japan, the European Community, and the G7 Economic Summit announced one after another that they would stop all bilateral high-level visits, stop exporting arms for military or commercial purposes, and defer new loans to China provided by international financial organs. For a while, the pressure of isolation was extremely great. China fought back courageously and wisely, and it did not take long before we triumphed over the sanctions and survived the crisis.

History has proved that the Great Wall of China is impregnable.

THE GATHERING POLITICAL STORM

IN THE WARM SPRING of late April and early May 1989, when flowers were in full bloom everywhere in Beijing, it seemed that the air was filled with restlessness. Many people felt a bit uneasy, as if something unexpected was about to happen.

China's diplomatic work proceeded as usual. In late May, after seeing off Mikhail Gorbachev, the president of the Soviet Union, I set out on a planned official visit to Latin America. Ecuador was my first destination. Then I would make a stopover in Mexico before I continued on to Cuba, and finally the United States.

Since there was no direct flight from China to Latin America, I boarded a CAAC flight in Beijing on May 31, and flew to Ecuador via the United States on June 2. When I was passing through the United States, the Americans were gracious to me. The security guards knew me very well, as I attended the UN General Assembly there every year. I was under their protection around the clock from the time I entered U.S. territory till I left it. When they bade farewell to me, they said they hoped to see me again in a few days' time. Unexpectedly, however, I had to cancel my visit to the United States.

On the afternoon of June 3 (the morning of June 4, Beijing time)—the second day after my arrival in Quito, the capital of Ecuador—footage of the "Tiananmen Square incident" from CNN and the BBC was broadcast repeatedly on local television. At that time we were not able to get news from inside China. The usually friendly overseas Chinese in Ecuador were all grave-faced when they asked us what had happened in China. The atmosphere turned tense and grim.

It was extremely difficult to get in touch with people in China at that time. After many efforts, we finally contacted the vice foreign minister, Zhou Nan, who briefed us on what had happened in China. Only a day later did we receive a related report from Beijing.

On June 4, at the harbor city of Guayaquil, I held first a provisional press conference and then a symposium for overseas Chinese, at which I answered many questions. I stressed that China's policies of reform and opening-up had not changed, and would not change in the future. The local press, as well as some big international news agencies, reported the press conference. They said that China's foreign minister did not evade questions but gave specific answers, and made clear the position of the Chinese government.

As the situation was becoming more and more serious, I decided to proceed with my visit to Cuba but I canceled my scheduled trip to the United States.

From Ecuador to Cuba, we chose to fly via Mexico. When we arrived at the international airport at Mexico City on the evening of June 6, to make the transfer, I could sense an unusual atmosphere. The foreign ministry of Mexico issued an announcement saying that the Mexican government had canceled the Chinese foreign minister's visit to the country. The airport lounge was full of reporters who had gotten news of my arrival. For reasons of safety, the Mexican government had made arrangements for us to board a car as soon as we had disembarked from the plane, leaving Gao Shumao, a member of our delegation, responsible for going through the formalities and claiming the luggage. The reporters took him to be the Chinese foreign minister. They rushed up to him and bombarded him with questions. Remaining calm and smiling all the time, Gao did not say a word. Inadvertently, he became the man in the spotlight that night.

Around ten o'clock that evening, some Chinese students who were studying in Mexico came to the Chinese embassy and asked to see me. From the way they banged on the door of the embassy, they seemed to be agitated. I asked the embassy people to let them come into the lobby, where I would meet them. They became quiet after they entered the embassy. I asked what schools they originally came from in China, and what their majors were. I told them honestly what had happened in China. One student said that he hoped I could represent the people. I said that, as foreign minister, I should of course represent my country and people. Then I told them to obtain more news about what had really happened, and advised them not to be credulous. Finally, they all calmed down and left the embassy quietly.

On June 7, we arrived in Havana. As the first Chinese foreign minister to visit Cuba since Fidel Castro's revolution of 1960, my primary task was to improve relations between China and Cuba, and strengthen mutual understanding.

For years China and Cuba had taken different attitudes toward the Soviet Union. Cuba was closer to the Soviet Union than to China. It was wary of China, having formed many misunderstandings about our country. When the Cuban foreign minister had visited China at the beginning of 1989, he expressed a wish to improve bilateral relations. My trip was a return visit.

The Cuban leader, Fidel Castro, valued my visit. On the following evening, he gave a welcoming banquet in my honor in the Palace of the Revolution. We talked for a long time after the banquet. When the other guests had left, he invited me to his office upstairs, and we continued talking till midnight.

Energetic, enthusiastic, voluble, and inquisitive, Castro displayed a strong interest in everything about China. I briefed him on Gorbachev's recent visit to China and on the normalization of relations between China and the Soviet Union. Castro was pleased, saying that the socialist countries and Third World countries were all in favor of China's normalizing relations with the Soviet Union, which he said was an event of historic significance. He said that the Cuban government fully supported the Chinese government over the Tiananmen Square incident, and would provide a venue or other conditions for me to make any announcement. Castro said China needed solidarity; it should not fall into a state of anarchy, as Western countries hoped it would—that would be a global tragedy.

Castro said that he believed I had made the right decision when I canceled my visit to the United States, as I would have been confronted with numerous provocative questions by the reporters there. I agreed, adding that on such an occasion, no matter what you said, and even if you remained silent, some reporters would distort the facts. When you tried to correct the mistakes, nobody would pay any attention to you. Castro smiled. Obviously, he was one of the people who were constantly vilified by the Western media.

I was impressed by Castro's strong interest in everything having to do with China. He asked me one question after another. He asked about the difference between the southern and northern parts of China, how Hong Kong would be managed after it was returned to the motherland, what route one had to take to travel from China to Cuba, what type of plane one would take, and so on. He listened to me attentively. When our conversation ended at midnight, he did not show any sign of fatigue. Later, when some curious people asked the interpreter what we had talked about, he replied in a humorous way, "Ten thousand whys."*

THE UNITED STATES SENDS A SPECIAL ENVOY TO CHINA

JUST AT THE TIME WHEN the call for sanctions against China by Western countries, headed by the United States, was at its most vehement, the United States secretly sent an envoy to China.

As a matter of fact, imposing sanctions against China did not accord with the United States' global strategy or its long-term interest. In the triangle of China, United States, and the Soviet Union, China and the United States had cooperated effectively to restrain the Soviet Union's expansion. To isolate China would not serve the interest of the United States, and this was clear to the U.S. government.

During that period, President George Bush had several times sent messages to China, saying that he valued Sino-American relations highly. He explained that the sanctions against China were imposed because of pressure from Congress and the general public. He expressed the wish that the Chinese leadership would understand this.

On June 21, 1989, President Bush wrote a secret letter to Deng Xiaoping asking to send a special envoy to China to have a frank talk with Deng. Deng replied to Bush the next day. He pointed out that our relations, which had been cultivated by both sides over many years, were facing a severe challenge. To prevent them from declining

---

* *Ten Thousand Whys* is a very popular Chinese children's book (note by translator).

further, Deng agreed to let Bush send a special envoy in top secrecy, with whom, he said, he was willing to hold frank and sincere talks. Bush decided to send the national security adviser, Brent Scowcroft, accompanied only by a deputy secretary of state, Lawrence Eagleburger; and a secretary.

The U.S. government had spent much time pondering the selection of the special envoy. Officials revealed in private that they had considered sending the former president Richard Nixon or the former secretary of state Henry Kissinger, but because both were so famous it would be difficult to keep the visit a secret. Scowcroft held an important post in the Bush administration, and so sending him to China indicated that the U.S. government valued Sino-American relations, but at the same time would not attract much attention.

In his book *The Politics of Diplomacy*, the former U.S. secretary of state James Baker said that President Bush originally wanted to send only Scowcroft to China, but Baker objected. He told Bush that if the United States sent only an official from the National Security Committee with no one from the State Department accompanying him, it would be difficult for the U.S. diplomatic mechanism to work. In fact, Baker himself wanted to be the special envoy, as he says in his book, but this proved difficult, so his deputy, Eagleburger, accompanied Scowcroft.

After Scowcroft arrived in China, he was not to have any contact with the U.S. embassy, which would not be informed of his activities in Beijing. James R. Lilley, U.S. ambassador to China, had already left Beijing on orders from the U.S. government. In the United States, only President Bush and Secretary of State James Baker knew of the secret visit.

The United States also deliberately chose July 1 as the day of the visit. Since it was near the Fourth of July, Scowcroft's leaving Washington on that day would not attract much attention. The plane was a C-141 military transport disguised as a commercial carrier. It would refuel in midair, and it carried special communications equipment so that Scowcroft would not have to use the equipment in the U.S. embassy in Beijing. In fact, the United States took more stringent measures to keep Scowcroft's visit to China secret than it had done when Kissinger flew from Pakistan to China on his secret diplomatic mission in the early 1970s. At least the U.S. ambassador to Pakistan had been informed of Kissinger's secret trip to China. The present case was a demonstration of how complicated and sensitive Sino-American relations were at the end of the 1980s.

Interestingly, in his book *A World Transformed,* co-written with President Bush, Scowcroft says that when the C-141 was entering China, none of the few people in China who knew of the secret visit had thought of informing the military. So the air defense troops telephoned President Yang Shangkun to report an unidentified airplane entering Chinese territory near Shanghai and asked if they should shoot it down. Scowcroft says that he was lucky, because the call was put through to the office of President Yang, who told the military that it was a plane with a most important mission.

However, I am dubious about the perilous experience described by Scowcroft. As far as I know, the Chinese and American sides had fully exchanged views about the route of Scowcroft's plane and the time when it would enter Chinese territory, and the Chinese government had made careful arrangements. The Americans had asked if their plane could avoid the route over Shanghai in order to save time. But we thought that would be more complicated as far as formalities were concerned and it would not save much time, so we did not accept the request. We did agree that the American plane would carry no national identification. Still, the plane entered Chinese territory along a route and at a time designated by China.

In any case, Scowcroft arrived in Beijing on the afternoon of July 1, at the Capital Airport. No national flags were displayed at the venues for meetings, talks, or banquets, or on the car Scowcroft used or at the hotel where he was staying. No news reports were released about his arrival or when he left Beijing. All photographs were taken with the prior consent of Scowcroft, and they were sealed as historical materials.

Scowcroft had a tight schedule in China. He was to stay only for twenty hours. Deng Xiaoping would meet him first, and then Li Peng and I would have talks with him. This was a very important visit because it would decide in which direction Sino-American relations would move.

Deng himself set the keynote for his meeting with Scowcroft. Before the meeting, on the morning of July 2, Deng said to Li Peng and me, "We will talk only about principles today. We shall not talk about specifics. We don't care about the sanctions. We are not scared by them."

I told Deng that the G7 Economic Summit would soon be convened, and might then impose new sanctions on China.

Deng said in a firm tone, "Not even seventy nations can daunt us, let alone seven!" He said that we wanted to improve Sino-American relations, but we were not afraid of the Americans. Fear would not help us. The Chinese people should have backbone and aspirations. Have we ever feared anybody? After liberation, we fought a war with the United States, which had an overwhelming advantage over us, with air supremacy. But we were not afraid of them. China, as a nation, feared no evil spirits nor any blusters. Deng stressed that all diplomats should keep this in mind.

Deng then went into the Fujian Room in the Great Hall of the People, where he said to Scowcroft, "I know you have long been concerned about the development of Sino-American relations. You were involved in the historic visit to China of President Nixon and Dr. Kissinger in 1972. We have many friends like you in the United States." Then Deng pointed out that current Sino-American relations were in a delicate, or one could even say perilous, state. Actions on the part of the United States that would lead our relations to a dangerous situation, or even to a final rupture, were continuing, he said. There was no sign of cessation. On the contrary, the pace was stepping up. Three days earlier, the U.S. House of Representatives had passed a measure imposing further sanctions on China. Still, he said, there were cool-headed high-level leaders on both sides. In the United States there was President Bush; in China there was himself as well as other Chinese leaders. But the issue could not be solved by a few friends only. What President Bush said would serve the interests of the United States. What Deng and other Chinese leaders said, and the decisions they made, would serve the interests of the Chinese nation and the Chinese people, he stressed.

Deng blamed the United States for the current situation. China had not offended the United States. It was the United States that had directly infringed on the interests and prestige of China in many regions. There was a Chinese saying, "It is up to the person who tied the knot to untie it." He said that we hoped the Americans would do something concrete to win back the trust of the Chinese people and stop adding fuel to the fire.

Deng also objected to the United States' interference in the Chinese legal system. He told Scowcroft clearly that China would allow no outside interference in its internal affairs. China would not make concessions no matter what the consequences. The Chinese leaders would not take rash actions or make thoughtless remarks in regard to Sino-American relations then or in the future. But China would remain steadfast when it came to safeguarding its independence, sovereignty, and national dignity.

Scowcroft said that President Bush was a real friend of Deng and the Chinese people. He had had direct and close contacts with China and the Chinese. This experience of his made him unique among the presidents of the United States.

Hearing this, Deng remarked that Bush had explored the streets of Beijing on a bicycle. Everyone laughed and the atmosphere became more relaxed.

Scowcroft said, "Yes, it is precisely because of the above reason that President Bush recently wrote a letter in person to you and sent me to China to convey his message."

He defended the United States' decision to impose sanctions on China. He said he had not come to China to negotiate specific plans for solving the difficulties in current Sino-American relations. Rather, he was in China to explain to us the difficulties faced by President Bush, and Bush's determination to safeguard, restore, and improve Sino-American relations. Because of domestic circumstances in each country, our relationship was now facing its greatest disturbance since Nixon's first visit to China. President Bush was uneasy about this, so he had chosen Scowcroft for this secret trip to make contact with the Chinese leaders and safeguard Sino-American relations.

Scowcroft said that Congress had asked the Bush administration to adopt harsher measures. President Bush had opposed the bill and would oppose it in the future. But if Congress passed the bill unanimously, Bush would be in a very difficult position if he tried to veto it. The president did not always have enough power to influence in which direction a situation would turn.

Deng told Scowcroft sternly that he hoped American politicians and ordinary Americans understood one fact. The Communist Party of China had led the Chinese people in fighting wars for twenty-two years (it would be twenty-five years if the Korean War was included). In these wars more than 20 million people had died, before the Party achieved a final victory and established the People's Republic. China was an independent country. It implemented a foreign policy of independence and peace. China would not tolerate interference in its internal affairs, nor would it dance to any other country's tune. China would be able to withstand all difficulties no matter what they were. No political power in China could replace the leadership of the Communist Party. This was not empty talk, he stressed: our experience over the past few decades was proof of it. When dealing with China, all countries must abide by the Five Principles of Peaceful Coexistence, among which were equality and mutual benefit, mutual respect, and noninterference in each other's internal affairs. We hoped that Sino-American relations would develop on the basis of the Five Principles of Peaceful Coexistence, and that existing problems could be solved properly. Otherwise, China would not be to blame if bilateral relations worsened.

Finally, Deng said, "We agree with some of your comments. But we have different opinions about most of what you said. Anyway, whether this unpleasant situation will be brought to an end depends on what the Americans will say and do in the future."

Deng then excused himself, and asked Li Peng to continue the talks with Scowcroft. Before Deng left, Scowcroft said to him,

"Chairman Deng, you seem to be in good health." Deng said, whimsically, "I am an old man now. Eight-five years old. The Voice of America first said I was critically ill, and then it said I was dead. Don't trust rumors." He thus not only replied to Scowcroft's polite remark but also criticized the untruthful reports of the U.S. media. Moreover, he hinted to the American government that it was unwise to impose sanctions on China because the decision had been based not on facts but on rumors.

In his talks with Li Peng and me, Scowcroft admitted that actions of the Chinese government were China's internal affair, but he stressed that some Chinese affairs had an impact on the United States and could develop into political problems there. That was what mattered in the current situation.

Li said that all government leaders, no matter of what country, must base their policies on facts. They should not base their principles, policies, or actions on inaccurate information or rumors. There was a saying in China that emotion should not take the place of policies. For a period of time, the policy makers in the United States, including Congress and government leaders, had not had a clear or accurate understanding of what had recently happened in China. Their sentiments had been whipped up by inaccurate information and rumors.

After Scowcroft returned to the United States, he reported to President Bush on his visit to China, particularly his meeting with Deng. On July 28, Bush wrote a secret letter to Deng. In the letter, Bush first thanked Deng for meeting Scowcroft, and then told him that the United States and Japan had deleted some strong wording offensive to China from the final communiqué released by the G7 Economic Summit. Bush also defended the United States' policy regarding China and attempted to shift the responsibility for the tension in Sino-American relations onto China.

In his letter, Bush said: "Brent Scowcroft told me of your reference to the Chinese proverb: 'It is up to the person who tied the knot to untie it.' Herein lies our major dilemma. You feel we 'tied the knot' by our actions. But we believe it is what happened next that 'tied the knot.' I have great respect for China's long-standing position about nonintervention in its internal affairs. Because of that, I also understand that I risk straining our friendship when I make suggestions as to what might be done now. But the U.S.-China relationship, which we have both worked so hard to strengthen, demands the candor with which only a friend can speak. In spite of a U.S. Congress that continues to try to compel me to cut off economic ties with China, I will do my best to keep the boat from rocking too much."

President Bush continued: "Please understand that this letter has been personally written, and is coming to you from one who wants to see us go forward together. Please do not be angry with me if I have crossed the invisible threshold lying between constructive suggestion and 'internal interference.' When we last met, you told me you had turned more and more day-to-day matters over to others; but I turn to you now out of respect, a feeling of closeness and, yes, friendship. You have seen it all—you have been up and down. Now I ask you to look with me into the future. This future is one of dramatic change. The United States and China each have much to contribute to this exciting future. We can both do more for world peace and for the welfare of our own people if we can get our relationship back on track."

On August 11, Deng wrote a reply to Bush. He first expressed his appreciation for Bush's efforts in maintaining and developing Sino-American relations. Then he gave an explanation of the meaning of "tied the knot."

Deng said, "It's true that I talked about 'tying the knot and untying the knot.' What I meant was that the United States has become deeply embroiled in China's internal affairs. It has taken the lead in imposing sanctions on China, and has greatly infringed on China's interests and dignity. The difficulties thus created in Sino-American relations were caused solely by the Americans, who should take actions to solve the difficulties. The sanctions imposed on China by the United States are still in place, and interference in China's internal affairs still occurs. I hope this situation can be changed as soon as possible. I believe President Bush can do something in this respect."

The argument about the meaning of "tying and untying the knot" was not an ordinary argument about the meaning of words. It was the crux of bilateral relations.

From China's standpoint, it was U.S. interference in China's internal affairs that had tied a knot in Sino-American relations. Only if the Americans took the initiative could Sino-American relations move forward again. But the Americans did not acknowledge their responsibility. Rather, they put the blame on China. Both sides argued fiercely over this crucial point for the process of lifting the sanctions imposed on China by the United States.

To Tie or Untie the Knot

SCOWCROFT'S VISIT TO CHINA was the first contact between Chinese and American leaders after the United States announced sanctions against China. His visit did something to keep bilateral relations from worsening. But because the United States did not lift its sanctions, the knot in our relations remained tied.

Meanwhile, though, relations between the United States and the Soviet Union improved somewhat. Leaders of the two countries were to meet at Malta in early December. Concerned that China might become closer to the Soviet Union again, the United States sent another special envoy to China.

On November 6, Bush wrote a letter to Deng, telling him that the forthcoming U.S.-Soviet summit would not impair China's interests. He said that the geopolitical reason that had led to President Nixon's first visit to China still applied, and China and the United States had similar interests in many important areas. Bush also said that after he met with the Soviet leader Gorbachev at the summit, he wanted to send a special envoy to China to inform Deng of their talks and discuss ways to normalize Sino-American relations.

At the time when Deng received Bush's letter, he too was pondering how to resolve the key issue of the impasse. It so happened that Henry Kissinger was visiting China at this time. Kissinger was a longtime friend of the Chinese people and had made great contributions to the development of Sino-American relations. Deng asked Kissinger to convey a "package solution" of the impasse to Bush.

Deng's proposals were as follows: (1) China would permit Fang Lizhi and his wife to leave the U.S. embassy in Beijing to go to the United States or a third country, (2) The United States, in ways that suited itself, should make an explicit announcement that it would lift the sanctions on China, (3) Both sides should make efforts to conclude deals on one or two major economic cooperation projects, (4) The United States should extend an invitation to Jiang Zemin to pay an official visit the following year.

The purpose of the proposal was to crack the hard nut that was troubling relations between China and the United States and bring the Sino-American relations back to the normal track.

Upon returning to the United States, Kissinger reported to Bush on his China visit. On November 15, Deng replied to Bush's letter of November 6, saying, "I always consider you a friend of China. It is my hope that during your term as president Sino-American relations will improve rather than go backward. I hope to change the ever-worsening situation between China and the United States by the time I retire. Since reading your letter, I have had some ideas about how the two sides can work together to restore and improve our bilateral relationship. I have entrusted Dr. Kissinger to pass on my proposals to you. I hope and believe that I will get a positive response from you. Both I myself and China would welcome a special envoy from you."

The American side responded quickly. On December 1, Bush wrote to Deng, telling him that within a week after the Malta summit between the United States and Soviet leaders Bush would send Brent Scowcroft as his special envoy on an official visit to China to brief the Chinese leaders on the Malta talks. He also asked the Chinese side to further elaborate on the package solution proposed by Deng. Bush said he hoped and believed we could find a way to bring Sino-American relations back to normal.

In his letter, Bush also said he was making efforts to "untie the knot." He asked China to be cooperative and make the same efforts.

On December 9, Scowcroft visited Beijing again. Accompanying him again were the deputy secretary of state, Lawrence Eagleburger, and others. Unlike his previous visit to China, this two-day visit was an open one. Deng Xiaoping, Jiang Zemin, and Li Peng met with him individually. I also held rounds of talks with him. The first round was scheduled, but the second one was added at his request.

After briefing us about the Malta summit talks, Scowcroft changed the topic to the package solution proposed by China.

I told Scowcroft about our intention when Deng proposed the package solution. First, to serve the best interests of China and the United States, we should end the current dispute as soon as possible, and turn to the future; second, any solutions reached between China and the United States should be effected simultaneously or almost simultaneously; third, if new disputes arose between the two countries later, both sides should exercise great restraint, and keep in close contact to solve the problems.

I said the package solution was a demonstration of China's good faith. It also took into consideration the United States' reaction and Bush's ideas, as mentioned in his previous letter. China also considered follow-up actions: (1) Both sides should make efforts to conclude deals on some major economic cooperation projects, (2) The United States should invite Jiang Zemin for an official visit in the following year. By that time, Sino-American relations should be in relatively good condition.

I stressed that the United States and China should refrain from doing things that would harm the other side. China has never done anything harmful to the United States, I said, and we hoped that the United States would never do anything harmful to China. The United States and China should treat each other properly, and support each other. Only such a situation would contribute to regional and world peace and stability.

I said that I hoped the Americans would give our suggestions serious consideration before giving us their response. If they needed more time, they could give us the reply later. If the United States wanted to have more discussions about the issue with China, I was willing to go to the United States in late January the following year (sometime around China's Spring Festival).

Scowcroft said that China's suggestions were very important, and he would take them back to the United States for further study. Then he told us his initial reaction to our proposals. He attributed the U.S. government's position on China to the complex political situation in his country, and said that he hoped China would understand. Bush, he said, was not a man who would act on these matters without any restraint. The sanctions on China announced in June were intended to satisfy the demands of the American people. Under the current circumstances, if Bush tried to lift the sanctions, Congress would very probably pass, by an overwhelming majority, a bill that the president could not veto. As for Fang Lizhi, said Scowcroft, he thought that detailed negotiations were needed. He preferred to hold the negotiations in Beijing, but they could also be held in the United States if sensitive topics were to be touched on.

I told him that since the issue was quite complicated, I hoped the United States could study it carefully and work out a plan. A solution to the problem required efforts from both sides, I stressed.

Scowcroft's official visit to China actually nullified America's ban on high-level visits. During our talks, both sides agreed to end the dispute as soon as possible, and to move toward the future. Some progress was made in Sino-American relations.

Several days later, the U.S. deputy secretary of state, Lawrence Eagleburger, put forward a counterproposal. He said the United States would, in principle, accept China's package proposal, but he wanted to make the following statements. First, in order to satisfy the common interests of all parties concerned, the U.S. ambassador to China, James R. Lilley, would talk with a Chinese representative about the issue of Fang Lizhi. Second, other aspects of Sino-American relations would be discussed in Washington between the Chinese ambassador there and American representatives. Third, the United States agreed in principle to make serious efforts to reach agreements on cooperative projects, and would welcome China's suggestions for these projects. Fourth, the United States agreed in principle to invite Jiang Zemin to visit the United States sometime in the following year, so as to complete the process of bringing bilateral relations back on track. Fifth, the United States was willing to make a proposal about an action plan to be adopted by both sides to resume normal relations.

While Scowcroft's visit to China helped improve bilateral relations, it caused trouble for him at home. At the welcoming banquet held in his honor, we proposed toasts to each other. This scene was captured by the media, and when the pictures were printed in newspapers and were shown on televised news programs, they caused a great stir in the U.S. mass media. In his book *A World Transformed*, Scowcroft said that picture of him and his Chinese host toasting each other caused him great embarrassment in the United States. When I visited the United States in 2002, Scowcroft mentioned the incident, complaining to me in a joking tone, "You really made me suffer."

It was routine diplomatic protocol for the Chinese host to give a welcoming banquet to Scowcroft, a special envoy of the U.S. on an official visit to China. His was a diplomatic mission aimed at safeguarding the interests of the United States. The reason some media and individuals in the United States made a fuss about the visit was that they wanted to exert pressure on the Bush administration, which stood for maintaining relations with China.

Twists and Turns

AFTER SCOWCROFT RETURNED to the United States, there were signs of improvement in Sino-American relations, but just at this moment dramatic changes took place in eastern Europe.

The Romanian government was rocked by domestic unrest. The ruling Romanian Communist Party was overthrown overnight, and its leader, Nicolae Ceaușescu, was executed on December 25.

The political changes in eastern Europe brought about changes in the international situation. The United States began to assess the general situation of the world, and was no longer so eager to improve relations with China. Thus Sino-American relations backpedaled to where they had been before China's package solution was proposed. The package solution was put aside.

In *A World Transformed*, Scowcroft gives his explanation of how the United States saw the situation. He believed that the downfall of Ceaușescu caused China to backpedal in regard to Sino-American relations. The truth was just the opposite: China did not backpedal; it was the United States that backpedaled, because it did not know whether China could withstand the storm following the changes in eastern Europe.

In April 1990, China suggested sending a special envoy to the United States to inform it of Li Peng's recent visit to the Soviet Union, and to exchange views on existing problems in bilateral relations. The United States rejected the suggestion, saying that the domestic atmosphere was not suitable for such a visit. Soon afterward, the United States suggested that officials from both sides meet in a third country. China believed that exchanging the latest information was something between China and the United States, and that this should not be done in a third country, so it rejected the United States' suggestion. Because of the United States' negative attitude, no special envoy was sent to the United States.

On May 14, Deng Xiaoping asked Hosni Mubarak of Egypt, who was in China on an official visit, to convey a message to President Bush. In the message, Deng cautioned Bush not to get too excited over what had happened in eastern Europe, and not to treat China in the same manner as it treated the eastern European countries. Otherwise, new disputes or even conflicts would arise, and these would serve the interests of neither country.

The historic changes in eastern Europe, plus the political turmoil in the Soviet Union, dramatically altered the strategic foundation for Sino-American cooperation. Believing that they no longer needed China's cooperation, some people in the United States began to talk about how to "restrain China."

With this background, the United States turned a deaf ear to Deng Xiaoping's advice, and Sino-American relations again reached an impasse.

In the summer of 1990, Iraq's invasion of Kuwait set off the Gulf crisis. This had a direct effect on the interests of the United States. The Gulf region had oil reserves accounting for two-thirds of the total in the world, and so it was a lifeline for the economies of the United States and other western countries. The United States knew that if it did not stop Iraq's military expansion immediately, its own interests and the interests of the other Western countries would suffer seriously.

When the United States began to deal with the Gulf crisis, it realized that it needed China's cooperation more than at any time before. The United States needed China's support if it wanted to get authorization from the UN Security Council to use force to expel the Iraqi troops from Kuwait. As two of the five permanent members of the Security Council, China and the United States shouldered important tasks in solving major international problems and easing regional conflicts. Consultation between the two countries was required to deal with unexpected incidents around the world. The existing deadlock would not serve the interests of either side, nor would it be conducive to world peace and stability.

The United States had to reassess its relations with China, and it began to try to improve bilateral relations. From then on, Sino-American relations took a turn for the better.

On the afternoon of August 31, the American embassy in China passed a letter from President Bush to Deng Xiaoping. In the letter, Bush said that the United States would not lower the level of Sino-American relations, which he considered to be of strategic importance. The United States appreciated China's position regarding the occupation of Kuwait by Iraq.

I was to pay an official visit to Iraq in November that year. When James Baker, the U.S. secretary of state, heard about this, he said he would be on a tour of the Middle East at the same time and hoped to meet me in Cairo to exchange views about the invasion.

On the afternoon of November 6, I met Baker in a waiting room at Cairo International Airport. Baker said he hoped that China would not obstruct the passage of any resolution by the UN Security Council authorizing the use of all necessary means, including military action, against Iraq. In exchange for China's support, he promised that the United States would find an appropriate time to lift the sanctions against China, and would not oppose a World Bank plan to provide loans worth US$110 million to be used for projects under China's Spark Program.

I told him that the United States was already lagging behind in economic cooperation. Improvements had been made between China and Japan and between China and the European Community in economic cooperation. China did not link the Gulf crisis to Sino-American relations. No matter in which direction these relations eventually went, China, as always, would stick to the position that all conflicts should be resolved through peaceful means.

As the situation in the Gulf region got more and more tense, the United States was determined to use military force against Iraq. Whether it could get authorization for this from the UN Security Council became a pressing task for its diplomacy. How China would vote in the Security Council would be vital as to whether or not the United States could legitimately send troops to the Gulf region.

Baker handled foreign affairs as if he were doing business. At the negotiating table, he liked to say, "Let's make a deal." This time was no exception. From the meeting at Cairo International Airport to another one in New York at midnight on November 28 to the voting in the Security Council on November 29, he always used meetings with President Bush as his bargaining counters in "making deals."

I have described the development of this matter in detail in chapter 3, "Flying to Baghdad," so I shall not repeat it here.

BAKER'S VISIT TO CHINA

ON OCTOBER 10, 1991, Bush told Zhu Qizhen, the Chinese ambassador to the United States, that he had decided to send Baker on a visit to China—and without attaching any conditions. Bush said this was his own decision.

Bush told Zhu that it was extremely important for both sides to restore Sino-American relations to normal, for this would best serve the interests of both countries. He said that he hoped Baker's visit to China would be a turning point in bilateral relations. Bush stressed that, given the political climate in the United States, both sides must ensure that Baker's visit was a success. A general election was to be held in the United States the following year, and the political climate there would have an impact on Sino-American relations. Therefore, both sides must take action quickly; otherwise, he would be powerless to maintain bilateral relations.

On November 15, 1991, Baker arrived in Beijing for an official visit. This was the first visit to China by the secretary of state since the United States had severed all contacts and halted visits with Chinese leaders in 1989.

Although the tension between China and the United States had eased slightly, making contact was still a sensitive topic, and the situation in the United States had become even more delicate.

Probably having learned some lessons from Scowcroft's visit, Baker told the Chinese side several times that he had come to discuss and solve problems. He said that he hoped the press would publish photos of his meetings with Chinese leaders rather than photos showing them clinking glasses at banquets.

I held several rounds of talks with Baker. He said that the visit itself indicated that the ban on top-level contacts between China and the United States had been lifted. This was politically unpopular in the United States, and many Americans found it very difficult to understand. The U.S. Congress was anxious to take over the decision-making power concerning policy toward China. If it succeeded, that would be a disaster for Sino-American relations. If Baker's visit to China was unfruitful, it would be more difficult to maintain the bilateral relationship, he explained. So his visit itself was tantamount to "having filled up the Chinese basket." Now he hoped he had a full basket when he returned to the United States.

I asked him what he wanted to put into his basket. His answer was straightforward. He said that he actually had three empty baskets: (1) arms proliferation prevention; (2) promoting economic cooperation; (3) promoting human rights.

During their meeting, Premier Li Peng told Baker that China did not object to holding discussions about the three topics, and that it hoped to put something into each one. China, however, had its own empty baskets, and it hoped the United States would support its bid to restore its status as a founding country of the General Agreement on Tariffs and Trade.

The two countries now began arduous negotiations regarding how to fill up each other's "baskets."

During the evening banquet on November 15, Baker requested a private meeting with me. At our meeting, he said repeatedly that the most important thing was what we were going to tell the press about this visit to show that we had made achievements. I said that if China did not get anything out of the negotiations, there would also be strong repercussions in China. When Scowcroft visited China two years previously, both sides had come to some agreement, and China had taken some actions. But the United States did not honor some of its commitments. The changing situation in eastern Europe had probably caused the United States to adopt a "wait and see" attitude. So, if both sides had reached agreement on some issues, they must carry out the agreement. If they could not reach an agreement, they should tell the public why.

Baker said that if China asked Bush to do more than what China was able to do in return, it would increase dissatisfaction in the United States. It was crucial to show that his visit had led to achievements, so that the people at home would recognize the importance of his visit.

At noon on November 17, the last round of talks between Baker and me was held. The negotiations, which went on until five-thirty P.M., were extremely difficult, and the departure of the American delegation had to be delayed seven times. There were heated arguments, but all the people on both sides, including both foreign ministers, worked continuously, with no one leaving the site of the talks.

Finally, the negotiations achieved some progress. The American side promised to support China's bid to join GATT, and the difficulty surrounding the time for Taiwan's entry into GATT would be solved in the same way as Taiwan's admittance to APEC. The United States agreed to cancel the three punitive measures, including banning the export of satellites to China, announced on June 16 of that year. It also promised to nullify Special Article 301 imposed on China. The United States would give serious consideration to establishing three joint committees on trade, economy, and science and technology. And it agreed to resume the ministerial conference at an appropriate time the following year.

China promised to adhere to the MTCR Guidelines and Annex, on condition that the United States lifted the ban on the export of satellites to China. It also promised to do more to protect intellectual property rights, on condition that the United States nullify Special Article 301 imposed on China.

China insisted on the principle that its internal affairs should not be interfered with by other countries when the issue of human rights was discussed. Still, it briefed the United States on matters the latter was concerned about. The United States produced a long list of detained Chinese "dissidents," which was full of mistakes. Some names were written only in Roman letters, without Chinese characters, so it was hard to identify who was meant. There was a Wu Jianmin on the list. I told Baker that the director of the Information Department of the Ministry of Foreign Affairs was called Wu Jianmin, and he was right here in the room. And Wu Jianmin said, "Yes, I am here." Baker joked, "Oh, you've been released." Everyone burst out laughing.

Baker was satisfied with his visit, and Bush also considered Baker's visit fruitful and of positive significance for Sino-American relations. Media around the world also responded positively. The visit was generally considered a success for China's diplomacy. It marked the beginning of the lifting of sanctions that had been imposed on China by the United States and other Western countries for two years and more.

DIVIDE AND DEMORALIZE THE
ANTI-CHINA FORCES

JAPAN WAS A RELUCTANT member of the Western bloc of countries that imposed sanctions against China. It endorsed the resolution of the G7 Economic Summit imposing sanctions simply because it wanted to take the same position as the other six countries.

On August 1, 1989, I met the Japanese foreign minister, Mitsuzuka Hiroshi, in Paris, where I was attending the international conference on Cambodia. He told me that Japan had explained China's position at the G7 Economic Summit held fifteen days earlier. It had advised the Western world not to escalate sanctions against China. As stability resumed in China, in 1990 Japan ratified the granting of the third batch of loans to China that had been put on hold after the Tiananmen incident.

Of course, Japan did this for its own interests, and China regarded Japan as a weak link in the united front of Western countries that had imposed sanctions against China—and therefore the best target for attacking such sanctions. In addition, China had other strategic considerations when it chose Japan as the first country to be persuaded to lift the sanctions. Through high-level contacts between the two countries, China invited the Japanese emperor to pay his first visit to China, and bring the bilateral relationship to a new stage. In the 2,000-year history of exchanges between Japan and China, no Japanese emperor had ever visited China. If the Japanese emperor paid a visit to China, that would not only break Western countries' ban on high-level visits with China but it would also be of profound significance for Sino-Japanese relations. It would also prompt more ordinary Japanese to support the policy of friendship toward China.

To realize such a visit entailed a great deal of careful work. First, we needed to increase contacts between the foreign ministers of the two countries.

The Japanese foreign minister, Nakayama Taro, paid an official visit to China from April 5 to 7, 1991. During our talks, I told him that although there had been difficulties and setbacks, bilateral relations had improved since the latter part of the previous year, thanks to efforts made by both sides. That year, the minister of finance, Hashimoto Ryutaro, and the construction minister, Nakao Eiichi, had already visited China, and Nakayama was on his first visit to China. I expressed appreciation to Japan for its efforts, and for being the first country in the Western bloc to resume and improve relations with

China. Nakayama said that he hoped I could pay an official visit to Japan before the Japanese prime minister, Kaifu Toshiki, visited China. We could decide on the schedule of Kaifu's visit during my visit to Japan.

Since the following year was the twentieth anniversary of the establishment of diplomatic relations between China and Japan, Nakayama suggested that both countries undertake various activities, including visits by their leaders. I said I totally agreed with his suggestion. I also said that if the Japanese emperor could pay an official visit to China the following year, it would be the most important event in Sino-Japanese relations. The Chinese people would give the emperor a warm welcome, taking the friendly relationship between our two countries to a new stage. Nakayama said that the Japanese government would study China's suggestion.

About two months later, from June 25 to 28, I paid a return visit to Japan, meeting Nakayama again. We continued our discussions about the programs to celebrate the twentieth anniversary of the establishment of diplomatic relations.

I said that twenty years was but a short moment in the history of bilateral relations. The anniversary provided us with an opportunity to review the past and open up the future, and to discuss conscientiously how to promote Sino-Japanese relations in the third decade following normalization. I suggested that we hold one more round of high-level visits the following year, and then told Nakayama again that China would welcome a visit by the Japanese emperor.

Nakayama agreed with what I said. Then we decided on the date of Kaifu Toshiki's visit to China in August. As to the Japanese emperor's visit, Nakayama said that his government was still pondering the matter.

On August 10, 1991, Prime Minister Kaifu Toshiki arrived in Beijing, becoming the first head of government from a Western-bloc country to pay an official visit to China since the West had imposed sanctions against China. His visit indicated that Japan had lifted the sanctions and that bilateral relations had been resumed.

Since Japan was the only country that had suffered atomic bombing, China understood the Japanese people's concern about nuclear proliferation. So while Kaifu Toshiki was in Beijing, China announced that it would join the Nuclear Nonproliferation Treaty. Kaifu officially informed China that the Japanese government had decided to provide it with the third batch of loans, worth 129.6 billion Japanese yen, to be used in twenty-two projects in 1991.

General Secretary Jiang Zemin paid an official visit to Japan from April 6 to 10, 1992. He met people from all walks of life, and stressed the importance of Sino-Japanese friendship and the significance of an official visit to China by the Japanese emperor. This further dispelled doubts on the Japanese side.

From October 22 to 27 Emperor Akihito and his wife, Michiko, paid an official visit to China. In a speech at the welcoming banquet given by President Yang Shangkun, Akihito said, "During the long history of Sino-Japanese relations, there was a short period when Japan caused the Chinese people to live in dire misery, about which I feel deep regret. Since the end of the war, on the basis of a soul-searching decision that we should never start a war again, our citizens are determined to take the road of peace." Compared with previous statements made by Japanese leaders about their country's invasion of China during the Second World War, this statement by Akihito moved one step further by including deep remorse, although it fell short of an apology.

Akihito's visit to China not only raised Sino-Japanese relations to a new level, but also played an active role in breaking the sanctions imposed on China by Western countries. And, as Sino-Japanese relations returned to normal, the European Community (EC) began to change its attitude toward China.

As an organization of European integration, the European Community plays an important role not only in the economic integration of Europe but also in its policies to the outside. Its major representatives are the three countries which serve as its previous, current, and next chair. The chairperson is elected every six months.

During the UN General Assembly every September, the EC foreign ministers would meet with the Chinese foreign minister to exchange views on the international situation and bilateral relations. But after the Western countries imposed sanctions against China in 1989, they halted contacts with China. Later, Europe found that although the United States was most active in imposing sanctions against China, it had frequent contacts with China in private, and Japan was also improving its relations with China. Europe was lagging behind in this respect. Fearing that they might lose their market share in China, the EC countries decided to catch up and resume contacts with China.

On June 28, 1990, the Italian foreign ministry informed the Chinese embassy in Rome of a decision of the EC summit meeting at Dublin that the foreign ministers of the three EC chairperson states would like to meet with the Chinese foreign minister during the UN General Assembly that year. I considered this a positive gesture, and so on the morning of September 28 that year, I met in New York with the three foreign ministers: Gianni De Michelis of Italy, Gerard Collins of Ireland, and Jacques Poos of Luxembourg.

Since De Michelis was the current EC chairperson, the meeting was primarily between him and me. The atmosphere was cordial. De Michelis said that although past events had caused some problems for bilateral relations, the world had undergone great changes. Europe and China had similar views on many international issues. Without the participation of China, it would be difficult to establish a new international order following the cold war. He assured me that the EC hoped to normalize relations with China as soon as possible.

De Michelis said the West once thought that it could influence China's system. But now it was realized that the system that suited Europe might not suit China as well and that countries with different systems could still cooperate. He also told me that, as chairman of the EC Council, he would officially propose, at the EC Council meeting to be held in October, the "complete normalization" of Sino-European relations.

I briefed De Michelis and the others on China's position on international issues. I told them that China would not change its policies of reform and opening up. I said I appreciated De Michelis's view that the situation in one country could be different from that in another country, stressing that human rights should be embodied in the laws of each country and protected by its laws. This meeting marked the end of the ban on high-level contacts between Europe and China.

It is worth mentioning that when China's diplomacy was undergoing its most difficult time, many Western countries still maintained friendly relations with China. One of them was Spain, which said it could understand what had happened in China. After the Tiananmen incident of 1989, Spain had kept implementing a loan agreement signed with China, and other economic cooperation projects. It also made efforts to restore political contacts with China.

On October 1, 1990, the Spanish foreign minister, Francisco F. Ordonez, made an appointment to meet with me in New York. During our meeting, he said that Spain had all along supported maintaining friendly relations with China. Spain was pleased at the good atmosphere in which the talks between the Chinese foreign minister and the three EC foreign ministers had been held. He told me that those EC countries which had favored tough measures against China had somewhat changed their attitude. The foreign ministers of the EC would hold a meeting the following week, at which they would make the decision to resume relations with China as soon as possible.

During that meeting, we reached an agreement that our two countries would exchange official visits soon. In November 1990, Ordonez paid an official visit to China, becoming the first foreign minister from the West to do so after the EC lifted its sanctions against China. Three months later, I paid an official visit to Spain.

Ordonez, who had been diagnosed with cancer, bought some royal jelly in China, and found that it gave him strength. When I heard about this, I particularly asked someone to take more royal jelly to him, in the hope that this Chinese medicine would build up his resistance and help him return to health eventually.

Given the fact that more and more countries were violating the ban on contacts with China, the EC foreign ministers finally announced after the Luxembourg conference on October 23, 1990, that except for contacts at the level of head of government, military exchanges and cooperation, and the arms trade, the EC would lift all the restrictive measures against China that had been adopted since June 1989. Moreover, it would normalize relations with China immediately.

Spain and Italy played a positive role in prompting the EC to make the announcement. This was a step taken by the EC in its attempt to improve relations with China, and another major victory for China in its fight against the sanctions imposed by the West.

A Friend in Need Is a Friend Indeed

IN THOSE DIFFICULT YEARS when Western countries were imposing sanctions against China, we felt grateful to the developing countries, who took our side and gave us much-needed support.

Though they could not make up for the economic losses caused by the sanctions, the developing countries had given us much support politically. At the UN General Assembly, in particular, leaders and foreign ministers from Asia, Africa, and Latin America were as friendly to China as ever. Frequent contacts with them became a principal part of my activities outside conferences.

The UN General Assembly sessions were normally held every September in New York. The daily agenda was usually tight. Still, I would find time to meet leaders or foreign ministers from Asia, Africa, and Latin America. I normally met with thirty to forty such leaders every year when I was in New York to attend the General Assembly. I made it a point to meet the foreign ministers of ASEAN, the Gulf countries, and the Rio Group every year.

Foreign ministers from African countries often praised China for its foreign policy. They expressed their hope of strengthening solidarity with China, and of making concerted efforts for economic development and world peace. Thanking them, I would say that the most important thing was to develop the economy and increase a country's strength. Only then could a country have its say in international affairs, and play a greater and more critical role in safeguarding world peace.

The Gulf countries showed great concern about what China thought of Iraq's invasion of Kuwait in 1990. When I met the foreign ministers of the Gulf countries, I told them that China had always opposed the invasion, and had asked Iraq to withdraw its troops from Kuwait. At that time the situation in the Gulf was tense. It was a hot topic at and outside the UN. My statement helped give the Gulf countries a good understanding of China's position. Everyone was serious at the start of the meetings, but the atmosphere lightened up after the talks had been under way for a while.

The foreign ministers of the Latin American countries showed great interest in China's economic growth, and in its policies regarding reform and opening-up. I gave them brief accounts.

Relations between China and the ASEAN countries had improved greatly by this time. After Indonesia resumed diplomatic relations with China, Singapore and Brunei established diplomatic relations with China. The communiqués for establishing diplomatic relations were signed by me and the foreign ministers of the two countries in New York during the UN General Assembly session.

A relationship between countries, just like a friendship between people, needs to be tested in adversity. The relations between China and the developing countries had withstood the trials and tribulations. The support of these old friends greatly eased the difficulties faced by China, and gave it more strength to break the sanctions imposed on it.

The Sky Did Not Clear Up after the Rain

AS A LARGE COUNTRY, China has an important strategic status on the international stage. It is a huge market, with great potential. In this time of global economic integration, countries have to become ever more interdependent if they want to develop. With this background, China needs the rest of the world, and the rest of the world also needs China.

The sanctions imposed on China by the Western countries went against the tide of history and against the principles guiding international relations. While they harmed China, the Western countries suffered as well. So it was only two years before they were lifted.

But the diplomatic struggles continued. Sino-American relations, for instance, did not remain stable for long. One incident after another cropped up to trouble the relationship.

Some people probably still remember the "*Yinhe* incident." On the basis of its intelligence, the United States insisted that the Chinese cargo vessel *Yinhe* was heading for a certain country with materials to be used for making chemical weapons. After careful investigation, China found that the accusation was not based on facts, and informed the United States of the result of its investigation. Chinese leaders also issued a statement making clear the government's position on the matter. Believing their intelligence was reliable, the United States persisted with its own investigation. When the *Yinhe* docked, the United States had all the containers moved ashore, and U.S. specialists searched them thoroughly. To their disappointment, they did not find the materials which they claimed were being carried. The event became a farce.

In 1997, Jiang Zemin paid an official visit to the United States, and in 1998 President Bill Clinton visited China. Sino-American relations were advancing smoothly, but then in May 1999 the Chinese embassy in Yugoslavia was hit by five U.S. missiles. The attack killed three Chinese journalists and injured more than twenty others. The news infuriated the Chinese people and shocked the world. The American airplanes involved took off from the U.S. mainland, followed the route, and struck a target worked out by a control center. All five missiles hit the intended target. How could anyone say that the attack was a "mistake"?

In 2001, shortly after the Republicans won the presidential election, I was sent on a visit to Washington, where I met President George W. Bush, Vice President Dick Cheney, Secretary of State Colin Powell, Defense Secretary Donald Rumsfeld, and National Security Adviser Condoleezza Rice. We talked about bilateral relations and international issues. The talks were satisfactory, and both sides expressed the hope that Sino-American relations would advance smoothly. Unexpectedly, only a week later, an aircraft collision happened over the South China Sea. It might have seemed to be an accidental occurrence. But U.S. spy planes frequently had been flying close to Chinese territory in the South China Sea area. Given these circumstances, the midair collision seemed anything but accidental.

7 FROM THE SOVIET UNION TO RUSSIA

FIRST VISIT TO THE SOVIET UNION

MY FIRST TRIP ABROAD was to the Soviet Union. That was more than fifty years ago, when I was sent to study at the Central Communist Youth League School in Moscow in August 1954. I was twenty-six years old at the time, and my daughter, who was my first child, was only twenty days old.

The Central Committee of the Communist Youth League of China sent a number of Youth League officers to the Central Communist Youth League School of the Soviet Union for one-year courses every year from 1951 on. I attended the fourth session, led by Comrade Xu Jingwu, who was then doing youth work in northeastern China. The assistant leader was Zhang Xueshu of Peking University.

Our group of twenty-one—nineteen students and two interpreters—left Beijing for Moscow in a Soviet plane. After two stops, we reached Irkutsk, where we spent the night. The next day, after several stops, we finally arrived in Moscow. It seemed to have just rained there, because I kept stepping into puddles as I walked out of the airport.

The Central Communist Youth League School was situated in the town of Vishnyaky, on the outskirts of Moscow. Nearby were a wood of white birch trees, a sizable lake, and the mansion of a government official in the reign of Czar Peter the Great, which had been turned into a museum.

The Youth League School offered three major courses: the history of the Communist Party of the Soviet Union (Bolsheviks), philosophy, and political economics; and several minor courses, such as Russian language, Youth League work, and physical education, which included skiing in winter. The school took the approach of combining lectures in class and independent study after class. Every day, the teachers gave lectures for three to four hours. The Soviet professors had a profound grounding in theory and recited Marxism by chapter and verse. They could point out the exact source of any particular view or sentence, to the page. After class, we had to spend a lot of time reading the assigned theoretical books—the Marxist classics in Russian. In addition, the teachers organized seminars based on the content of the courses. Teachers and students, who could raise questions with each other, established an interactive relationship in the seminars.

Before we went to the Soviet Union, we had studied Russian for only two weeks, so at first we needed an interpreter for lectures and for communication between the teachers and the students. Therefore, learning Russian became our primary task.

We were divided into four small classes according to our proficiency in Russian. First we took a test, in which we were required to point out on the map some cities of the Soviet Union and answer a few questions such as, "How did you come here?" in Russian. I was in the same class as several students who had previously studied Russian by themselves in China. The other students jokingly called us the "advanced class." Early in the morning after we got up, we would try to memorize new words by heart and read some text aloud. When the course ended, several students including me were able to answer questions in Russian.

Besides in-class learning, the Central Communist Youth League School organized visits to sites related to Russian revolutionary history, memorials, factories, and collective farms, as well as some recreational activities. We visited the former residence of Tolstoy, the memorial to Gorky, and the Tretyakov Gallery. We also watched the classic ballet *Swan Lake* and some famous operas at the Moscow State Theater.

During the winter vacation of 1955, we toured Leningrad. We visited the Winter Palace, the Smolny Cathedral, and the cruiser *Aurora*, which was famous for having fired the shot which signaled the storming of the Winter Palace in the October Revolution. We had a group photo taken in front of a small thatched cottage on the bank of Lake Razlive, on the border between the Soviet Union and Finland, where Lenin wrote his famous work *The State and Revolution* in 1917. During the summer vacation, we toured Ukraine and took a cruise on the Black Sea and around the Crimea.

The mid-1950s witnessed a blossoming of Sino-Soviet relations. The teaching staff, students, interpreters, and even service personnel of the Central Communist Youth League School were very warm-hearted toward the Chinese students, and took good care of our studies and daily life. On learning that the Chinese students liked peanuts, our language teacher said in the class that she would get us some. After a long time, she did bring us some peanuts, which she had spared no pains to find in Moscow. When she gave those peanuts to us, her face was wreathed in smiles. Valia, the class interpreter, was entrusted by the school authorities to arrange various activities and visits for the students during the vacations. She did all she could to help the Chinese students with their problems. Her patience, warmheartedness, and consideration left a deep impression on us.

At that time, the Chinese students regarded the Soviet Union, the homeland of Lenin, as the "revolutionary sacred place" and a model for other socialist countries. Great economic achievements had been made by the Soviet Union, which had won a splendid victory in the antifascist war. There seemed to be no doubt that a splendid future lay ahead for Soviet social development. The People's Republic of China had been founded only a few years previously, and lagged behind the Soviet Union in many respects. In particular, China was eager to learn from the Soviet experience in economic construction. We were very excited about being in the Soviet Union. We led a happy life there, and were determined to study hard and model ourselves on the Soviet people.

However, as I stayed longer and my contacts with Soviet teachers and students increased, I discovered that there were also some unsatisfactory social phenomena in the Soviet Union. I heard them voice dissatisfaction with their lives. I was surprised, and wondered why so many problems still existed in the Soviet Union after decades of socialist construction. Could socialism be so imperfect?

Working in the Soviet Union after Graduation

IN THE SUMMER OF 1955, before I had finished my studies at the Central Communist Youth League School in the Soviet Union, the local Chinese Communist Party organization informed me that I was to work at the Chinese embassy in Moscow after graduation.

Comrade Zhang Wentian was the Chinese ambassador to the Soviet Union when we arrived there, but he was replaced in early 1955 by Comrade Liu Xiao. Chen Chu and Zhang Dequn served successively as minister counselor at the embassy.

My first post was in the Chinese students affairs department at the embassy. At that time, about 4,000 Chinese students went to study in the Soviet Union every year, among whom 2,000 were in Moscow, and the rest were scattered in Leningrad, Kiev, Sverdlovsk, Odessa, and other cities. The students affairs department of the embassy helped them contact schools and choose subjects to study, and extended ideological education. It even helped them with problems in their daily lives. Li Tao, a counselor sent by the Chinese Ministry of Education, held the post of department director. While I was working there, I visited almost every Soviet school where there were Chinese students. At one time, I lived in Leningrad for a year, in charge of the affairs of the 1,000 Chinese students studying there.

In 1960, I was transferred to the Research Office of the Chinese embassy, where I worked till I was summoned back to China in 1962.

During the eight years I studied and worked in the Soviet Union, many significant changes took place both within it and in Sino-Soviet relations. In particular, Khrushchev's "secret report" on Stalin at the Twentieth Congress of the Communist Party of the Soviet Union in 1956 caused a furor both in the Soviet Union and in the West. Before long, China published articles such as "The Historical Experience of the Dictatorship of the Proletariat" and the two Parties began to split. The year 1959 marked the beginning of the Sino-Soviet "cold war," which lasted thirty years. When I returned to China in early 1962, the communist parties of China and the Soviet Union were at the peak of a "ten-year war of words," and Sino-Soviet relations were degenerating into a serious confrontation.

Return to Moscow

TEN YEARS LATER, in early 1972, when I was working at the cadre school in Anhui Province, I was appointed political counselor at the Chinese embassy in the Soviet Union. China was going through the hardships of the ten-year "cultural revolution" at that time. New knowledge of socialism was dawning after a period of social unrest.

It took a full week to travel from Beijing to Moscow by train, so I was able to get a good view of the Soviet Union along the way. All the time, I was eager to find out how that country had changed while I had been away. Outside the train window was a vast expanse of open country, with forests of towering white birches and boundless grassland. The landscape remained splendid, but few tall buildings, new factories, or new cities were in sight. The dowdy clothing and luggage of the hurrying passengers at the stations and the scenes of people rushing to stalls to buy food—and especially the fact that many people were carrying bread in their hands—indicated that few changes had taken place in the Soviet Union, and that its development was at a standstill. The "magnificent program" of achieving communism within twenty years that Khrushchev had boasted of some years previously seemed to have melted into thin air.

The only apparent change was the small number of passengers on the Trans-Siberian train between Beijing and Moscow—a dramatic contrast with the situation ten years earlier. Now we had almost a whole carriage to ourselves, and the conductor was the only person to chat with. In 1972, China and the Soviet Union had few contacts, but the transnational trains between the two countries still ran.

With an area of twelve hectares and a grand main office building, the Chinese embassy in the Soviet Union was located on Lenin Hill in Moscow. The number of staff members in the embassy had been sharply reduced. Owing to the tension in Sino-Soviet relations, the Soviet government had posted several police sentries around the embassy to bring it under full "protection." This actually meant that they were keeping a close watch on us.

From some upstairs rooms at the embassy, we had a clear view of the large shining red star on the pinnacle of the Moscow State University building. In November 1957, in the auditorium of this very university, Chairman Mao Zedong had told the Chinese studying in the Soviet Union: "You young people . . . are like the sun at eight or nine o'clock in the morning. Our hopes are placed in you." Thereupon, the Chinese students shouted at the top of their voices the slogan, "Strive for the construction of our motherland for fifty years." It was a very moving scene.

As circumstances changed with the passage of time, the warmth and vitality had vanished. The Chinese embassy in the Soviet Union had little work to do. Our diplomatic contacts with the Soviet Union had shrunk to almost zero, apart from routine protests or rebuttals, as well as some courtesy calls.

In the early 1970s, Comrade Liu Xinquan was the Chinese ambassador to the Soviet Union. I was one of three political counselors in the Chinese embassy. The others were Ma Lie and Wang Jinqing. As Moscow was a hub of communications, many Chinese delegations still passed through there. One task of the embassy staff was to give them an introduction to the Soviet Union and instructions to assist them during their stay.

We also took every possible opportunity to travel in the Soviet Union, and to learn about the situation in various places. I visited Transcaucasia and the Baltic coast. The Soviet government paid particular attention to our travels, and adopted rigorous monitoring measures. It was, for instance, a daily occurrence for us to be tailed. The tails were very easy to detect. We either threw them off or played jokes on them. Once, while traveling, I said directly to the tail: "It must be hard for you to trudge behind us. It happens that we do not know the way. Please come to the front, and lead the way for us." The tail was greatly embarrassed.

In the summer of 1974, I left the Soviet Union for a new post in Africa.

I spent ten years in the Soviet Union, off and on, from 1954. I witnessed both the climax and the deterioration of Sino-Soviet relations, which underwent the most difficult times and greatest tension during the last two years of my stay.

The "August 19 Incident" (1991)

I paid many visits to the Soviet Union after I left in 1974. In 1982, I began to take charge of the negotiations with the Soviet Union over the normalization of Sino-Soviet relations.

It was completely unexpected that the Soviet Union would collapse virtually overnight in the 1990s, succumbing to increasingly severe political and economic conflicts within Soviet society.

In the late 1980s, the three states on the Baltic coast—Estonia, Latvia, and Lithuania—made the first calls for independence, and demanded control of their own state property. Then Georgia in Transcaucasia declared independence. Like falling dominoes, all fifteen constituent republics of the Soviet Union had claimed sovereignty by the end of 1990, and four of them had explicitly announced their withdrawal from the Soviet Union.

In this process, Russia's declaration of independence exerted the decisive influence. On June 12, 1990, Russia stated clearly that it was a sovereign state. The union constitution and laws had supreme power within the boundaries of the Russian Federation. When Soviet laws contradicted the sovereignty of the Russian Federation, Russia would terminate the validity of Soviet laws on the territory of Russia. Russia also declared its right to dispose of all its state property, settle its social problems, and withdraw from the Soviet Union. Afterward, that day was called Independence Day and the National Day of the Russian Federation.

The Soviet Union was first composed of Russia, Ukraine, Byelorussia, and the Transcaucasian republics in 1922. In August 1940, it became the world's largest country, with fifteen constituent republics spanning eleven time zones. Russia had the largest area and population of the fifteen republics, and its GNP accounted for over half of the Soviet GNP. In fact, Russia's day-to-day business was directly administered by the organizations of the Soviet government. Its independence caused the sudden collapse of the Soviet Union.

President Mikhail Gorbachev proposed a new union treaty in 1990, to redefine the relationship between the union and its constituent republics. The draft treaty was published in November. Its core content was that the central government of the Union had the power to pass the constitution and take charge of national defense, security, and foreign affairs. All republics should follow the principles of respect for each other's sovereignty and territorial integrity, non-interference in each other's internal affairs, and peaceful settlement of disputes. Every republic could make its own decision on its state system. The leaders of each republic joined the Union Committee, and participated in making the basic policies of the Union in domestic and foreign affairs.

After the draft treaty was published, the three Baltic states refused to sign it. Georgia stated, "Georgia will never join any treaty in any form before it obtains real sovereignty." Russia and Kazakhstan set the central government's recognition of their declaration of sov-

ereignty and clear division of powers as preconditions for their joining the treaty.

In the spring of 1991, the Soviet political and economic situation
worsened. To overcome the crisis, Gorbachev consulted with the leaders of nine other republics, including the Russian Federation, and decided to take emergency measures to stabilize the situation in the
Union and get the new union treaty signed as soon as possible. This
was called the "nine-plus-one" agreement or the "Novo-Ogaryovo
process." George A. Arbatov, the director of the Institute for U.S. and
Canadian Studies of the Soviet Academy of Sciences, said, "The
'Novo-Ogaryovo process' rekindled people's hope." It was commonly
considered that the pressing problems facing the Soviet Union could
be solved on the basis of *a federation* instead of a union, even without the Baltic states.

In mid-May 1991, when General Secretary Jiang Zemin visited
the Soviet Union, Gorbachev emphasized in talks with him that the
settlement of many Soviet problems depended on upgrading the
Union. The chief task was to work out a new union treaty which
would define the terms of reference and territories of the Union and
its constituent republics. Any constituent republic that signed the
treaty could enjoy all kinds of special treatment within the common
economic space of the Soviet Union. Otherwise, the republic would be
considered a foreign country. Gorbachev also said, "Representatives
from all the fifteen constituent republics have arrived in Moscow, and
are discussing this issue. In the election of the pope, no one can leave
the Vatican until a result is achieved. The participants may leave only
when the smoke rises from the Vatican chimney and the result of the
election is made public. Like that election, we are also going to hold
the Federation Committee conference. No one is permitted to leave
Moscow until the smoke rises from the chimney."

In early August, Gorbachev announced that the new union treaty
was to be signed officially on August 20. After that, he went to
Crimea on vacation.

In mid-August, an unsigned draft treaty was published. It clearly
stipulated that the Soviet Union would adopt a federal system, and

changed the name of the state from the Union of Soviet Socialist Republics to the Union of Soviet Sovereign Republics. The draft treaty recognized the sovereignty of all the republics, their ownership of all the natural resources within their territory, and the supremacy of each republic's laws within its own territory. The Union would be empowered by all the signatories to defend itself and its overall sovereignty and territorial integrity, conclude treaties, declare war, approve the Union budget, and issue currency.

The "August 19 incident" took place just one day before the treaty was to be signed. Even today, exactly what happened around August 19, 1991, is still something of a mystery.

Jack Matlock, the U.S. ambassador to the Soviet Union, recalling the event, said, "In June 1991, the mayor of Moscow, Gavriil Popov, told me that some people were plotting a coup to overthrow the government. I reported this to Gorbachev upon U.S. President Bush's order. Gorbachev said, 'The situation is fully under my control.'"

Anatoly Chernyaev, assistant to President Gorbachev, gave the same account in his memoirs. He also mentioned that he and Gorbachev talked about similar warnings each of them had received.

Vladimir Kryuchkov was the head of the Soviet security services (KGB) at that time. His account goes like this: "On August 4, 1991, Gorbachev went on vacation in the Crimea. Just before he went, he asked me, Internal Affairs Minister Boris Pugo, and Defense Minister Dmitriy Yazov to prepare for a state of emergency. On August 5, the three of us met in Moscow. We were all clearly aware that after a short period of time the USSR would no longer exist. So we decided to do something. On August 18, I, Pugo, and Yazov went to see Gorbachev, in the hope of bringing him back to Moscow to address the problems. Gorbachev said that we could do whatever we liked. He would neither approve nor disapprove."

In the small hours of August 19, TASS and the central Soviet television station announced a presidential decree to the effect that Gorbachev could no longer carry out his presidential duties, owing to health problems, and that Vice President Gennadi Yanayev had been named acting president. This was followed by a statement signed by the acting president, prime minister, defense minister, and KGB chairman, announcing the establishment of a "State Committee for National Emergency," which was composed of eight members, including the above four. The committee immediately declared a state of emergency in some Soviet regions for six months, in an open letter to the people of the Soviet Union.

This move aroused strong repercussions throughout the Soviet Union, with Russia, Ukraine, and some other republics voicing their opposition to the state of emergency. This strong opposition stunned the committee that had declared the takeover of the state power.

On the afternoon of August 20, the committee held a press conference, at which it appealed for the early return of Gorbachev. On August 21, some members of the committee went to see Gorbachev in the Crimea, together with a few leaders of the Soviet Communist Party and government, such as the prime minister of the Russian Federation, Ivan Silayev; Anatoly Lukyanov; and Vladimir Ivashchenko. Later, Gorbachev issued a statement through the central Soviet television station that he had taken full control of the situation and would resume his presidential duties. Early the next morning, Gorbachev returned to Moscow.

The "August 19 incident" had collapsed.

On August 22, I met the Soviet ambassador to China, Nikolai Solovyev, at his invitation. Solovyev first conveyed a message from Gorbachev to the Chinese leaders. Gorbachev said in this message that he was in normal health, and the Soviet Union's constitutional order would be fully restored in a few days. The Soviet guidelines for democratic reform, and its adherence to international treaties, pacts, and other obligations would remain unchanged. The Soviet cabinet would ensure the restoration of the national legal system and the revival of the economy. I reassured the ambassador that the Chinese government always held that the internal affairs of the Soviet Union should be handled by the Soviet people themselves. I said that we believed that the good-neighborliness and friendship between the peoples of

China and the Soviet Union would continue to develop on the principles stipulated in the two Sino-Soviet joint communiqués issued in
1989 and 1991.

The Collapse of the Soviet Union

THE NEXT DEVELOPMENTS showed that things would not turn out as
Gorbachev wished. On the contrary, the Soviet Union quickened its
pace toward collapse.

On August 24, 1991, Gorbachev dismissed the Soviet cabinet. On
August 25, he resigned as general secretary of the Communist Party
of the Soviet Union. Meanwhile, he commanded, in his capacity as
president, that local Soviets freeze the property of the Communist
Party and stop the activities of all political parties in Soviet military,
judicial, and state organizations. In early September, the Soviet Congress of People's Deputies—the highest organ of state power in the
Soviet Union—was dissolved.

On September 6, the Soviet State Council, consisting of the Soviet president and leaders of the constituent republics, decided to recognize the independence of the three Baltic states—Estonia, Latvia,
and Lithuania.

On September 7, I telegraphed the foreign ministers of the three
states, informing them of the Chinese government's recognition of
their independence. China's vice foreign minister, Tian Zengpei, went
to the three states to negotiate the establishment of diplomatic relations. In mid-September, China established official diplomatic relations with all three.

The events of December 1991 dealt a fatal blow to the Soviet
Union.

On December 7 and 8, the Russian president, Boris Yeltsin, and
the Ukrainian president, Leonid Kravchuk, held talks in a hunting
lodge in a forest in Byelorussia with Stanislav Shushkevich, chairman of the Byelorussian Supreme Soviet. Their meeting lasted two
whole days in top secrecy.

On December 8, the three leaders issued a declaration that the

Soviet Union, as a subject of international law, was "no longer in existence," as the negotiations over the union treaty had "come to a dead end," and all constituent republics had withdrawn from the Soviet Union and established themselves as independent states.

In addition, Russia, Ukraine, and Byelorussia had decided to set up the Commonwealth of Independent States (CIS), which was open to the other republics to join. Its Coordinating-Consultative Committee was to be located in Minsk, the capital of Byelorussia.

This agreement was soon approved by the Supreme Soviets of the three states. Then the leaders of the five states of Central Asia declared their willingness to join the Commonwealth as founding states.

On December 17, the Russian parliament announced that it was the owner of the property of the Supreme Soviet of the USSR. On December 18, the Russian government took over the Kremlin.

In Alma-Ata, Kazakhstan, eleven republics signed the Declaration and Protocol on the Agreement for the Establishment of the Commonwealth of Independent States on December 21. The Russian newspaper *Izvestia* ran the headline "Soviet History Ends in Kazakhstan."

The Soviet Union had become a country without a government or territory, and Gorbachev was a president with nothing to preside over.

On December 25, 1991, five days before the sixty-ninth anniversary of the founding of the Soviet Union, Gorbachev read out on television, in an open letter to the people of the Soviet Union, his resignation as president. Less than half an hour after his speech ended, the national flag of the Soviet Union was lowered at the Kremlin, and the tricolor of the Russian Federation was raised.

On the next day, the Supreme Soviet of the USSR held its last meeting, to announce the dissolution of the Soviet Union.

On December 27, the Russian Federation officially took the Soviet Union's seat at the UN.

DIVIDED OPINIONS ON THE COLLAPSE
OF THE SOVIET UNION

THE COLLAPSE OF THE SOVIET UNION can be regarded as one of the most astonishing and thought-provoking events of the twentieth century.

The collapse did seem to happen almost overnight, but the various factors behind it had been accumulating for a long time. The observations made of the Soviet Union in the 1930s by two famous French writers should be mentioned here.

In their published diaries, Romain Rolland and André Gide, while admiring the "mighty waves of overwhelming vitality and the spirit of youth of the Soviet people, striving for the best future for mankind," nevertheless noted that a kind of privileged elite was emerging in the Soviet Union. Both Rolland and Gide frequently contrasted the towering memorial buildings and the spacious villas of the leaders with the poky, shabby, crowded houses of the common people. Gide wrote, regarding consumer goods: "There were already over two to three hundred people lining up at the department store before it opened. There were only about 500 mattresses for sale that day, but customers were as many as eight hundred to a thousand. Before it was dark, everything had gone. The demand was so great that it would not be met even a long time later."

Rolland noted his concern about the state of mind of the Soviet people: "I was convinced that they underestimated the vitality of other peoples. Even if the capitalist government and system are their enemies, they should not underestimate their vitality. Soviet working people firmly believed that they possessed and created all the best things with their hands, and the rest of the world had lost these good things, such as schools and sanitary facilities. The young Soviet people could not compare their intellectual achievements and thoughts with those of their Western counterparts freely. I was deeply worried that a sudden comparison someday would lead to turbulence."

Gide obviously shared this opinion. He wrote: "The Soviet people show astounding ignorance of the situation outside their country.

Furthermore, they are convinced that everything in the Soviet Union is better than what it is in foreign countries." A young Russian once said to Gide: "A few years ago, we could draw on experience in some aspects from Germany and the United States. Now we no longer have any need to learn from foreigners."

The Russian scholar Arbatov's account of the Soviet Union in the 1970s went like this: "Economists had realized that the Soviet economy had been experiencing extensive growth for which the resources were becoming exhausted. Therefore, the transition from extensive development to intensive development and from relying on administrative orders to using economic levers to control the economy, emphasis on the ongoing new scientific and technological reforms, etc., must be put on the agenda. When these issues were brought up at the Congress of the Communist Party of the Soviet Union, there were only some discussions, and everything remained as before."

In the late 1980s, Anatoly Chernyaev, assistant to President Gorbachev, said that when Gorbachev was advocating "loyalty to socialist values and to the pure ideals of the October Revolution" and similar slogans, "we were completely at a loss as to what kind of society we lived in."

One former leader of the Central Committee of the Communist Party of the Soviet Union, Yegor Ligachev, said: "We were astonished at the huge gap in science and technology between the Soviet Union and the West. We were also worried about the stagnation of the social democratization process in the Soviet Union. All these aspects influenced our living standards and social ideology. After some social problems, such as housing, were solved in the first few years of the reform period, the following years were full of difficulties, especially the phenomenon of economic disorganization. The anxiety about reversing the economic downslide coupled with ignorance of the laws of economics led to the hasty decision to effect a quick transition to a market economy. Many problems, especially the severe shortage of consumer goods, thus followed, resulting in strident complaints from the general public."

In his analysis of the reasons for the collapse of the Soviet Union,

Ligachev stressed the following factors. First, many leaders of the Communist Party had degenerated morally under various influences from both at home and abroad. Second, the Soviet Union wasted large amounts of capital on strengthening national defense, and assigned its best brains with the best equipment and materials to this unproductive sector.

Chernyaev added that Moscow was vulnerable to arms threats of Western countries and had spiraled into an arms race, which bankrupted the Soviet Union.

The former chairman of the Council of Ministers of the Soviet Union, Nikolai Ryzhkov, held that the Russian parliament's declaration of sovereignty in June 1990 was the decisive factor in the collapse, which was irreversible from then on. The other republics had no choice but to become sovereign states themselves.

President Nursultan Nazarbayev of Kazakhstan listed two significant events in the collapse of the Soviet Union. One was Russia's declaration of sovereignty in 1990, when no other constituent republic except Estonia had declared independence. The second was the withdrawal of the Communist Party of the Russian Federation from the Communist Party of the Soviet Union. The main pillar of the Soviet Union—Russia—had collapsed, and the discipline and ideology needed to maintain and ensure national unity no longer existed.

It is now apparent that Russia is responsible for both the success and failure of the Soviet Union.

China Recognizes Russia and the Commonwealth of Independent States

ON DECEMBER 25, 1991, I gave a report on the international situation and diplomatic work to the Twenty-third Meeting of the Standing Committee of the Seventh National People's Congress of China. I said in the report: "The collapse of the Soviet Union marked the end of the Soviet-U.S. confrontation, the east-west cold war and polarization that had lasted nearly half a century after World War II. The people of China and all the republics of the former Soviet Union have a long tradition of friendship and contacts. Following the collapse of the Soviet Union, the Chinese government will continue to develop friendly relations and cooperation with these republics on the principle of noninterference in each other's internal affairs and respect for the choice of the people of every state."

On December 27, I sent a telegram to the Russian foreign minister, Andrei Kozyrev, and officially informed him of the Chinese government's decision to recognize the government of the Russian Federation and appoint the former Chinese ambassador to the Soviet Union, Wang Jinqing, the new ambassador to the Russian Federation. I also expressed the Chinese government's willingness to maintain and develop friendly relations and cooperation with Russia on the basis of the Five Principles of Peaceful Coexistence.

Wang Jinqing had arrived in Moscow as ambassador of China to the Soviet Union at the end of November 1991. But before he could present his credentials, the Soviet Union ceased to exist, so the Chinese government had to send him new credentials. It was not until early February 1992 that Wang finally presented his credentials to the Russian president, Boris Yeltsin.

On December 27, 1991, I telegraphed the foreign ministers of Ukraine, Byelorussia, Kazakhstan, Uzbekistan, Tajikistan, Kyrgyzstan, Turkmenistan, Georgia, Armenia, Azerbaijan, and Moldova to inform them that the Chinese government had decided to recognize their independence, and was prepared for negotiations over the establishment of diplomatic relations with them.

At that time, a delegation led by the minister of Foreign Trade and Economic Cooperation, Li Lanqing, and the vice foreign minister, Tian Zengpei, was on a visit to Ukraine, Russia, and other former Soviet republics. They happened to be in Moscow when China's telegram of recognition arrived. During Li Lanqing's meeting with the Russian deputy prime minister, Aleksandr Shokhin, Li conveyed messages to Yeltsin from President Yang Shangkun and Premier Li Peng. Tian Zengpei held talks with his Russian counterpart Georgi Kunaze on

Sino-Russian relations. On the evening of December 29, the two sides signed a summary of talks that confirmed the Five Principles of Peaceful Coexistence as the basis of Sino-Russian relations, and the basic principles stipulated in the two Sino-Soviet joint communiqués of 1989 and 1991, respectively, as the guidelines for Sino-Russian relations. The two sides agreed to continue to fulfill the obligations prescribed in all the treaties and agreements signed between China and the Soviet Union, and increase contacts at all levels. Moreover, the two countries would approve the Agreement on the Eastern Section of the Sino-Soviet Boundary as soon as possible. This summary of talks was the first guiding document for developing Sino-Russian relations in the new context.

While the Chinese and Russian vice foreign ministers were holding talks, Li Lanqing led the Chinese delegation on a visit to Byelorussia. The delegation had been scheduled to visit the former Soviet countries in central Asia, but all the chief leaders and foreign ministers of those countries went to attend a CIS summit in Minsk on December 30. Therefore, the delegation decided to fly to Urumchi, capital of China's Xinjiang Uygur Autonomous Region; and then visit Uzbekistan, Kazakhstan, Tajikistan, Kyrgyzstan, and Turkmenistan from January 1, 1992, on. The Chinese delegation conducted negotiations over the establishment of diplomatic relations and signed communiqués in each country. As there was no time for printing out the communiqués on the establishment of diplomatic relations, many of the originals were handwritten copies, which were unprecedented in the diplomatic history of the People's Republic of China.

Meanwhile, Ambassador Wang Jinqing, who was a member of the Chinese delegation, arrived in Ukraine to discuss the establishment of diplomatic relations. China and Ukraine signed the Communiqué on the Establishment of Sino-Ukrainian Diplomatic Relations on January 4, 1992.

During the visits, the Chinese delegation also signed economic and trade agreements with five countries, including Ukraine and Uzbekistan. All the leaders of the countries in the former Soviet central Asia met the Chinese delegation and expressed their willingness to develop all-round relations with China. Some suggested that they exchange visits with China's leaders as soon as possible; some asked when China would send its ambassadors to their countries; others said that they had made a preliminary decision on the site of the Chinese embassy.

In mid-January 1992, Wang Jinqing was engaged in negotiations with Armenia, Azerbaijan, Georgia, and Moldova over the establishment of diplomatic relations. Then he visited these countries one after another, and signed communiqués on the establishment of diplomatic relations. The Sino-Byelorussian communiqué was signed in Beijing on January 20, 1992. By then, China had set up diplomatic relations with all the former constituent republics of the Soviet Union.

New Sino-Russian Relations

THE COLLAPSE OF THE SOVIET UNION, the consequent abrupt changes in the international situation, and the setback to the world socialist movement, coupled with political and economic pressure from the Western powers on China since 1989, had complicated and worsened the international situation facing China.

Under these circumstances, Comrade Deng Xiaoping said, "Socialism seems to have been weakened by severe setbacks in some countries. But the people have been tempered, and have drawn a lesson from these setbacks." He told us not to panic and not to think that Marxism had failed, became obsolescent, or had disappeared. Deng pointed out that China would not waver in its determination to build socialism: we were building socialism with Chinese characteristics that continually enhanced social productivity and advocated peace.

In the spring of 1992, Deng delivered a famous speech during his tour of south China, saying that further reform and opening-up would give more vitality to China's socialist cause.

At that time, what type of relationship China should establish with Russia and the other CIS countries became an urgent question for China's diplomacy.

Before the political and economic systems of the Soviet Union showed obvious changes, Deng had clearly pointed out that China's attitude to state relations did not depend on social systems. No matter how the Soviet Union changed, we should remain composed and develop relations, including political relations with it, on the basis of the Five Principles of Peaceful Coexistence without any ideological disputes.

Accordingly, China's diplomacy developed a policy of contacting Russia and the other CIS countries regarding politics, the economy, and other aspects on the basis of equality and noninterference in each other's internal affairs, beyond differences in ideology and social systems. This policy brought China's relations with these countries to a new period of development.

In early 1992, the Russian foreign minister, Kozyrev, expressed in a letter to me Russia's willingness to develop its relations with China at the same level and on the same scale as previous Sino-Soviet relations.

At the end of January 1992, the first Summit Meeting of the UN Security Council was convened in New York. Premier Li Peng of China and President Boris Yeltsin of Russia attended the meeting. This was also the first time since Russia replaced the Soviet Union at the UN that a Russian leader had participated in UN activities. Li and Yeltsin met at the UN headquarters and exchanged views on Sino-Russian relations.

Yeltsin first promised that Russia would faithfully abide by the two Sino-Soviet joint communiqués, and would approve the agreement on the eastern section of the China-Russia boundary as soon as possible, saying that he hoped to raise Russo-Chinese relations to a new level. Li said that China did not handle its relations with other countries on the basis of ideology or social system. The people of China and Russia had a tradition of friendship, and the 4,000-kilometer Sino-Russian border should be a border of peace and friendship. Moreover, the economies of China and Russia were, to a large extent, complementary. Yeltsin emphasized that Russia attached great importance to the development of economic cooperation between Siberia and the

Russian Far East, and their neighboring provinces in China.

This was the first contact between the Chinese and the new Russian leaders. Both sides felt satisfied with the meeting, and regarded it a good start.

From then on, Sino-Russian contacts in various aspects began to increase, and a new dimension gradually unfolded for Sino-Russian relations.

In February 1992, the Standing Committee of the National People's Congress of China and the Russian Parliament ratified the Agreement on the Eastern Section of the China-Russia Boundary.

In March the foreign minister, Kozyrev, paid an official visit to China. Before he came, he wrote me a letter to inform me that his entourage would include five leaders of border regions and provinces and some individuals in industrial and business circles in the Russian Far East. This showed that Russia laid great stress on the development of economic and trade ties between the Russian Far East and its bordering Chinese provinces.

During the meeting with Kozyrev, I said, "The summary of talks signed by the two sides at the end of last year when the Chinese delegation was visiting Russia laid a foundation for the development of Sino-Russian relations. During the successful meeting of the leaders of the two countries in January this year, China and Russia achieved a greater common understanding on developing the Sino-Russian partnership of good-neighborliness and friendship. We believe that the increasing contacts between the Chinese and Russian leaders through various channels are beneficial, and we are willing to continue these contacts."

Kozyrev commented, "Russo-Chinese relations did not start from nothing. They have a foundation. In the past, the Russian Federation supported the normalization of Soviet-Chinese relations. Russia's foreign policies are aimed at balancing Russia's foreign relations by developing friendly relations with the Western countries and Russia's neighboring countries, especially China. As for its relations with China, Russia values the past and stresses the future. Russia is more than willing to further develop economic and trade relations with China."

I assured him: "The development of economic and trade relations between China and Russia has bright prospects. Recently, China decided to open four cities—Suifenhe, Heihe, Manzhouli, and Huichun—along the Sino-Russian border for better communication between the two countries."

Kozyrev confirmed the significant role of the meeting between the Russian and Chinese leaders during the UN Security Council Summit in New York and expressed his hope that this kind of contact would continue. Kozyrev told me that President Yeltsin had mentioned, while in New York, that he would like to pay a visit to China.

I told him that China would welcome Yeltsin at a time convenient to both sides. The first Russian president's visit to China was thus put on the agenda, and in preparation for it, China and Russia carried out a series of vigorous diplomatic activities.

In April 1992, the new Russian ambassador to China, Rogachev, took up his post. Both he and his father were sinologists. Rogachev had worked in China twice previously, in the 1950s and 1970s. Premier Zhou Enlai had awarded him the Medal of Sino-Soviet Friendship. In the 1980s, when he held the post of Soviet vice foreign minister, I discussed with him the normalization of Sino-Soviet relations. I also participated in two rounds of talks on the border issue with the Soviet delegation headed by him. Therefore, we knew each other very well.

During the talks with Rogachev, I first reviewed the contacts between the Chinese and Russian leaders since the normalization of Sino-Soviet relations, and noted that Yeltsin's forthcoming visit to China was a logical continuation of the high-level contacts between the Chinese and Russian leaders. I indicated that China was willing to develop economic and political relations with Russia on a new basis and said that the two sides should continue their negotiations over the Sino-Russian border and disarmament in the border regions. Sino-Russian economic and trade relations had made some progress, which China and Russia should actively promote, consulting with each other on possible problems. Rogachev fully agreed with me on these points.

In late August, Russia formally proposed the date of Yeltsin's visit to China.

During the UN General Assembly in September, I consulted Kozyrev about the specific schedule of the visit and the documents to be signed during it.

In October, the Russian vice foreign minister, Kunaze, came to China and negotiated with the Chinese government over the political documents and joint communiqué related to Yeltsin's visit. The western boundary between China and the former Soviet Union had become the border between China and four other countries, including Russia. Kunaze therefore led delegations from Kazakhstan, Kyrgyzstan, and Tajikistan, as well as Russia, to hold talks with China on the issue of the borders.

On October 24, China and the four countries signed a summary of their border talks, which confirmed the principles that had been agreed on in the Sino-Soviet negotiations and recorded in the two Sino-Soviet joint communiqués for the settlement of these issues. The summary also stated that the agreement on the border alignment achieved in the Sino-Soviet negotiations remained valid in principle. The signatories consented to setting up a working group to draft border agreements and pledged to continue to hold talks on border issues that had not yet been agreed on.

I said to Kunaze: "After the collapse of the Soviet Union, China and Russia carried over the achievements made by China and the Soviet Union since the normalization of Sino-Soviet relations, and discarded the negative elements. Therefore Sino-Russian relations keep progressing on the basis of complete equality, peaceful coexistence, and mutual benefit. We believe that Sino-Russian relations will be healthier and more normal than Sino-Soviet relations. We are delighted that our border areas are full of vitality. China is opening its border cities as well as those along the coast and rivers. Our land opening is mainly oriented toward Russia and the other CIS countries. As a result, our borders will become open and available for contacts and friendly cooperation, instead of being in a state of closure and military confrontation. Therefore, we must adjust to the new situation and apply new approaches to the settlement of disputes in our border negotiations."

The border negotiations between China and Russia, Kazakhstan, Kyrgyzstan, and Tajikistan gradually developed into the "Shanghai Five" mechanism. The leaders of these five countries met annually, and the topics of their discussion extended to confidence-building measures in border regions, regional security, the strengthening of economic and trade cooperation, and so on. Later, Uzbekistan joined the mechanism, which was the predecessor of the Shanghai Cooperation Organization (SCO).*

Visit to the New Russia

In november 1992, I paid a visit to Russia, Uzbekistan, Kyrgyzstan, and Kazakhstan. This was the first visit of a Chinese foreign minister to these countries since the collapse of the Soviet Union and the independence of these new countries.

On November 24, I flew from Alma-Ata to Moscow, where I met President Yeltsin in the Kremlin two hours after my arrival.

Boris Yeltsin was born in 1931 into a peasant family in Sverdlovsk. After graduating from Ural Kirov Technical College as an architecture major in 1955, Yeltsin was engaged in construction work. Later, he became the first party secretary of Sverdlovsk and then of Moscow, and was elected as the Russian president in June 1991. A sports lover, he looked strong and energetic. When he was young, he played on a volleyball team; later he took up tennis.

After everyone was seated, Yeltsin came straight to the point, saying that a new dimension marking a historic phase in Russo-Chinese relations had opened up. He continued, "Russo-Chinese relations will be given priority in Russia's foreign policies related to

---

* In April 1996, China, Russia, Kazakhstan, Kyrgyzstan, and Tajikistan held a summit in Shanghai and signed the Treaty on Deepening Military Trust in Border Regions. The "Shanghai Five" structure was thus established. In June 2001, the heads of state of China, Russia, Kazakhstan, Kyrgyzstan, Tajikistan, and Uzbekistan signed the Declaration on the Establishment of the Shanghai Cooperation Organization at a summit in Shanghai, announcing the establishment of a new multilateral organization—the Shanghai Cooperation Organization (SCO)—based on the "Shanghai Five" structure.

Asian or international politics." Yeltsin spoke highly of China's achievements in reform and opening-up, and commented, "Russo-Chinese cooperation has taken a significant step forward. Instead of a sharp decrease, the trade volume between Russia and China has increased by a large margin and is expected to reach US$4.5 billion this year." At this point, the Russian foreign minister, Kozyrev, interposed, "The figure may well reach to US$5 billion this year."

At this meeting, Yeltsin confirmed the date of his visit to China. He said that he believed the two sides could seek common ground on many issues during his visit, and he hoped that the visit would be substantial and deal with concrete matters. Yeltsin instructed a Russian official at his side that the old Soviet clichés should be avoided in the documents to be signed during his visit to China. Many Soviet documents were alike in wording, since, often, one document was simply copied from another, or from this or that Five-Year Plan.

Yeltsin said that he had never been to China, which had a lot of things to teach Russia. Then he began to talk about his busy schedule after December.

I told him that I had come to Russia to make further preparations for his visit to China. Before I left China, Jiang Zemin and other Chinese leaders had asked me, in particular, to tell Yeltsin that they were looking forward to meeting him in Beijing. Yeltsin's visit would achieve positive results and open up a new phase in Sino-Russian relations, they said. Russia was China's largest neighbor, and the Russians were a great people. We believed that the Russian people could overcome their present difficulties and move toward prosperity. The Chinese government attached great importance to the development of relations with Russia and valued the tradition of friendship between the Chinese and Russian people. It was hoped that the friendly relations of mutual benefit and cooperation would be consolidated and continue to develop.

Then I reviewed the experiences—the hardships and successes—of Sino-Soviet relations over the past decades. We held that the key to maintaining the healthy and sustained development of state relations was noninterference in each other's internal affairs, respect for each other's choices, and cooperation based on mutual benefit and equality. I also told Yeltsin about the resolution on establishing a socialist market economy passed by the Fourteenth National Congress of the Communist Party of China, which had closed only one month before. I emphasized that a market economy was also conducive to the development of Sino-Russian economic cooperation. In addition, I proposed that China and Russia strengthen their transportation links, and build the Sino-Russian border into an open, vibrant area that promoted contacts, peace, and friendship between the two countries.

Yeltsin was in high spirits throughout our talk, which lasted one hour. He obviously had a great interest in everything going on in China. He would have raised more questions if there had not been a government meeting five minutes later.

On the next day, Kozyrev and I held talks to discuss the two sides' preparations for the high-level Sino-Russian meeting, and we initialed the Joint Statement on the Basis of Mutual Relations between the People's Republic of China and the Russian Federation.

Before returning to China, I gave a press conference at which I answered reporters' questions about China's principle of developing relations with Russia and the other CIS countries, the influence of China's relations with these countries on the international situation, and other relevant topics. I emphasized that China had always held that differences in ideology, social system, values, and cultural tradition should not become obstacles to the development of state-to-state relations, which should be based on the following principles: in politics, peaceful coexistence, mutual respect, noninterference in each other's internal affairs, good-neighborliness, and friendliness; in economic cooperation, equality and mutual benefit. If we arrived at such a common understanding, Sino-Russian relations would certainly develop smoothly.

I continued, "The world is full of diversity, and all countries differ greatly from each other in ideology, religion, national culture, social system, and path to development. In a world of such diversity, recognition and respect for such a reality are a prerequisite to peaceful coexistence and common development."

Referring to China's relations with Russia and the other CIS countries, I pointed out that Sino-Soviet relations have experienced alignment as well as a long period of confrontation. Since then, China's principle for its relations with Russia and the other CIS countries has been nonalignment and nonconfrontation, which are characteristics of normal state relations. It is unnecessary and impossible to return to alignment or confrontation, which always provoked international tension. Only the establishment of normal state relations could contribute to regional and world stability and play a constructive role in the international situation.

Yeltsin's Visit to China

ON THE MORNING OF DECEMBER 17, 1992, Yeltsin and his wife arrived in Beijing. Yeltsin's entourage numbered nearly 100, including the president of the Russian Republic of Sakha, the chairman of the Supreme Soviet of the Russian Republic of Bashkortostan, the Russian foreign minister, the chairman of the Russian Supreme Soviet, and the Russian deputy prime minister. The figure would top 250 if the correspondents and others were counted.

The Chinese president, Yang Shangkun, presided over the welcoming ceremony in the Great Hall of the People, and then had talks with Yeltsin. Yang said that the Sino-Russian high-level meeting was of great significance and had attracted wide public attention. He also said that he believed Yeltsin's visit would promote the development of Sino-Russian relations. Yeltsin said that he was satisfied with the arrangements made by the Chinese government for his visit, and that his scheduled visit to the Imperial Palace was of great interest to him as an architect. He remarked that all the members of the delegation wanted to become "real men" for once—Chairman Mao Zedong having said that he who had not mounted the Great Wall was not a real man.

Yeltsin added that the Russian people's friendship with the Chinese people had propelled the Russian leaders to take measures to develop all-round friendly relations with China.

Yang stated, "We have every reason to promote friendly relations. Since both China and Russia are now facing the task of developing their national economies, establishing stable relations of good-neighborliness, friendly cooperation, and mutual benefit seems all the more imperative. The present trade volume between China and Russia has already surpassed the Sino-Soviet record, and this is a good beginning. There is ample room for cooperation between China and Russia, each having its own strengths in the economy, trade, and other areas. Apart from high-level meetings, the two countries should increase their contacts at all levels, such as cooperation between business enterprises."

On the following day, Premier Li Peng had talks with Yeltsin. Li emphasized that the Chinese and Russian people had a tradition of friendship, and future Sino-Russian relations should develop on the basis of "equality, mutual benefit, good-neighborliness, and friendliness." Yeltsin indicated that developing Russo-Chinese relations was being given priority in Russia's diplomacy, and the unique place of Russia's relations with the East could not be replaced by its relations with the West. He added that Russia respected China's domestic and foreign policies.

At noon, Jiang Zemin, general secretary of the Communist Party of China, treated Yeltsin to a banquet at the Diaoyutai State Guesthouse.

Jiang mentioned that he had been very familiar with the names of the Russian scientists Lomonosov and Mendeleyev since his childhood. In China, many people were fond of the works of Russian writers such as Tolstoy and Pushkin. Sino-Russian relations had experienced both happy times and deadlocks, but had shown some progress in recent years. Yeltsin's visit would promote the healthy, smooth development of Sino-Russian relations, he said.

Yeltsin noted that there was huge potential, and a wide scope, for the development of Russo-Chinese relations, and that he had come to China with sincere hopes. During this visit, the two sides would sign twenty-five documents—a number that could be registered in the Guinness Book of World Records. Yeltsin added, "China has made great achievements in social welfare, reform, and opening-up. Frankly, for Russia, some particular approaches adopted in China's reform and opening-up are worth learning."

Jiang told Yeltsin that the Fourteenth National Congress of the Communist Party of China had systematically elaborated on Deng Xiaoping's theory of building socialism with Chinese characteristics and had set up the socialist market economic pattern. Jiang said that China would make unswerving efforts in economic construction toward the goal set by the congress. During this process, China hoped to engage in all-round cooperation with Russia.

On the evening of December 17 and the afternoon of December 18, signing ceremonies were held for the Joint Statement on the Basis of Mutual Relations Between the People's Republic of China and the Russian Federation and twenty-four agreements on intergovernmental and interdepartmental cooperation and related documents. Yang and Yeltsin signed the Joint Statement. Kozyrev, Deputy Prime Minister Shokhin, and I signed the agreements on intergovernmental cooperation in culture, science, and technology; mutual exemption of visas for tourist parties; the peaceful utilization and research of outer space; and other matters.

The presidents declared in the joint statement that the two countries regarded each other as friendly. This marked a step forward in Sino-Russian relations and was based on a legacy of all the achievements since the normalization of Sino-Soviet relations.

During his visit to China, Yeltsin was received not only by the leaders of ministries and commissions but also by local leaders from several Chinese provinces and regions, including Heilongjiang, Jilin, and Inner Mongolia. These leaders, in turn, had contacts with leaders of Russian republics, border regions, and provinces.

Yeltsin was scheduled to visit Shenzhen on December 19. However, early that morning, the director of the Office of the President of Russia informed the Chinese assistant foreign minister, Dai Bingguo, that some important issues in Russia called for the president's personal attention. After careful consideration, Yeltsin decided to return to Russia that very morning.

Kozyrev accompanied Yeltsin and his wife back to Russia, while the other members of the delegation visited Shenzhen.

This early return, according to Yeltsin himself, was due to certain troubles that had developed in the forming of the cabinet. They resulted from "dividing the portfolios" and compelled him to go back and straighten out the problems personally.

In September 1994, Jiang Zemin paid an official visit to Russia. This was the first visit to Russia by a Chinese president since the collapse of the Soviet Union. Following their talks, Jiang and Yeltsin signed a Sino-Russian Joint Statement, which declared: "China and Russia have established a new constructive partnership based on the principles of peaceful coexistence—complete equality, good-neighborliness, friendly cooperation, mutual benefit, nonalignment, and avoidance of targeting any third country."

In April 1996, Yeltsin paid a second visit to China. An important achievement during this visit was a joint statement of the development of a strategic partnership of cooperation between China and Russia.

Before this visit, China and Russia had agreed upon the essential text of the joint statement. On the evening of April 23, the Russian embassy in Beijing informed the Chinese Foreign Ministry that Yeltsin believed the text the two sides had agreed on did not precisely reflect the trend of Russian-Chinese relations in the years ahead. He suggested that the relations between China and Russia be defined as "a strategic cooperative partnership of equality and mutual trust for the twenty-first century." Our Foreign Ministry immediately reported this to Jiang, who accepted Yeltsin's suggestion.

In December 1999, Yeltsin made his last presidential visit to China. After he returned to Russia, he suddenly appeared on television—at midnight on December 31, the eve of the new millennium—to announce his retirement. He said, "Russia must enter the new millennium with new politicians; new faces; and new, intelligent, strong, energetic people." He immediately signed a decree entrusting the duties of president to Prime Minister Vladimir Putin and handed over the nuclear safety code to Putin. Putin signed a decree on the same day providing a legal guarantee for the safety of the persons and property of Yeltsin and his family.

In March 2000, Putin was formally elected president. In July, he visited China at the invitation of Jiang Zemin, and they signed the Beijing Declaration, which stressed that the development of a cooperative partnership of equality and mutual confidence for the twenty-first century was in the fundamental interest of both the Chinese and the Russian people. In addition, the two presidents held three successive meetings on other occasions during the year 2000, including one at the UN Millennium Summit.

At President Putin's invitation, Jiang Zemin paid his fifth visit to Russia since taking office as the president in July 2001. I accompanied Jiang on this important visit. On July 16, in the Kremlin, Jiang and Putin signed the Treaty of Good-Neighborliness and Friendship Between the People's Republic of China and the Russian Federation. Then they issued a joint statement, pointing out that the treaty summed up the main principles, spirit, and achievements of Sino-Russian relations based on historical experience, and prescribed in legal form the peaceful aim of being "forever friends, never enemies." The treaty clearly stipulated that these friendly relations were based on a new type of state relations characterized by nonalignment, nonconfrontation, and not being directed against any third country.

The treaty laid a solid foundation for future Sino-Russian relations.

8 FASCINATING AFRICA

MY FIRST TRIP TO AFRICA

I FIRST CAME INTO CONTACT with Africa in 1964, when I was working for the Chinese Ministry of Education and accompanied the minister, Yang Xiufeng, on a visit to Egypt, Algeria, Mali, and Guinea. We spent six weeks in Africa, from April 1 to May 14. The other two members of the delegation were Ji Xianlin, a professor at Peking University; and Hu Sha, a director general in the Ministry of Education. I was then thirty-six years old, about the same age as Hu Sha. The eldest of the four of us was Yang at age sixty-six, followed by Ji, who was seventeen years older than I. So the delegation was a combination of the old, the middle-aged, and the young.

After the trip, Ji published his travel notes, and I also published some short articles about the dramatic differences in customs and cultures between North Africa and sub-Saharan Africa (Africa south of the Sahara Desert), as well as African peoples' brotherly friendship toward the Chinese.

Our journey to Africa highlighted the hardships of travel at that time; it took us a week to reach Cairo. We first left Beijing for Kunming, the capital of Yunnan Province in southwestern China; and flew to Rangoon, the capital of Myanmar, the next day. On the third day, we arrived in Dacca, the capital of what was then East Pakistan. We left for Karachi, in what was then West Pakistan, at midnight. After a day's rest in Karachi, we headed for Cairo—our first stop in Africa.

In Egypt, we at once felt the remoteness of African civilization. At that time, there was a show called "Sound and Light" performed at night at the foot of one of the pyramids. It made one feel as though one had returned to the age of the pharaohs. This show is, I believe, still being performed today, though it has been improved many times.

From Egypt, we headed west along the North African coast, and then turned south to the hinterland of the African continent.

During the 1960s, national liberation movements flourished in Africa. One by one, the African countries threw off the shackles of colonialism and obtained their independence. Algeria, Ghana, Guinea, and Mali were pioneers of these national liberation movements, with China as their staunchest supporter.

Not long before our trip, Premier Zhou Enlai had visited Africa. We noticed, now, that African policemen stood at attention and saluted our motorcade, holding the Chinese national flag. People along the road waved to us, and children shouted "Zhou Enlai! Zhou Enlai!" Every African country gave us a warm welcome, and we were overwhelmed by the deep friendship shown to us by our African hosts.

At that time, Algeria, Mali, and Guinea had just achieved independence, and they were paying particular attention to education. They were anxious to eliminate the influence of colonialism and produce their own cadres of talented people. President Modibo Keite of Mali told us that his country planned to have universal primary education for school-age children in ten to twenty years. Guinea reestablished state control of education and nationalized private schools as soon as it became independent. Its president, Sekou Toure, personally promoted educational reform. Mali and Guinea each devoted 20 percent of the state budget to education, including accommodation for all middle-school students and clothes for some. Algeria's educational fund accounted for up to 30 percent of the state budget, and all college students were subsidized. In some girls' schools, each student was lodged in her own room, and the food provided was excellent.

During our visit to Mali, the Chinese government suddenly ordered Yang Xiufeng to attend the May Day holiday celebration in Zanzibar, which had just joined the Republic of Tanganyika to form the United Republic of Tanzania.

Yang needed an English interpreter, since the Zanzibaris spoke English, but there was only a French interpreter in our delegation. After much discussion, I was chosen to accompany Yang as his secretary, interpreter, and bodyguard, since I was the youngest person in the delegation and could speak English.

Transportation between African countries was very inconvenient then. To get to Zanzibar Yang and I first had to fly to Paris. At that time, China and France had just established diplomatic relations, and the Chinese embassy in France had not yet been set up—there were only a few Chinese doing preparatory work. So the two of us had to cook our supper on our own. Next, we flew to Rome, where we had to turn to the Algerian embassy for help, since China and Italy had no diplomatic relations. Then we left Rome for Tanganyika and Zanzibar, via Kenya. After the celebrations in Zanzibar, we flew back to Guinea via Sudan, Nigeria, and Ghana, to continue our African tour. All this traveling back and forth was very hard for Yang, at his age; but fortunately everything went well, and my special task came to a successful conclusion.

My African trip of 1964, which was my second foreign trip following my visit to the Soviet Union, brought me face-to-face with the colorful cultures of a splendid land. I never thought that ten years later I would be appointed ambassador to an African country.

Ambassador in Africa

IN JULY 1974, I WAS APPOINTED Chinese ambassador to Guinea and Guinea-Bissau.

I arrived in Conakry, the capital of Guinea, in August 1974. On my way from the airport to the Chinese embassy, the scenes outside the car window reminded me of my visit there ten years previously. The beautiful landscape of Conakry, on the Atlantic Ocean, was the same, but the buildings by the roadside looked shabby. The passion inspired by the national liberation movement seemed to have vanished in the current economic recession.

The Guinean Ministry of Foreign Affairs soon made arrangements for me to present my credentials, as is customarily the first task of a new ambassador. On August 20, I presented my credentials to President Sekou Toure of Guinea, and delivered greetings and respects from Chairman Mao Zedong and Premier Zhou Enlai. Toure praised the friendly and cooperative Sino-Guinean relations and said that the Guinean people would never forget China's aid to them. The ceremony was very grand and was attended by the prime minister and a dozen other ministers.

Concurrently, I was the first Chinese ambassador to Guinea-Bissau, which had just gained its independence after a guerrilla war. In this capacity, I was invited to attend its celebrations for the first anniversary of independence in Boe, the provisional capital—a former guerrilla base. At the same time, I was to present my credentials to President Luis Cabral.

President Toure of Guinea sent airplanes and a motorcade to take about twenty people to the ceremony, including ambassadors and foreign guests. We first flew to the capital of Boke Province, bordering Guinea-Bissau, and then went to Boe by car.

As we crossed into Guinea-Bissau, we found ourselves in a desolate and sparsely populated land. There was no real road, and our car was guided by local people along what was said to have been a guerrilla track. In Boe the "hotel" we stayed at was just a thatched hut furnished with only two bamboo beds. The wind blew through holes in the walls. A bucket of cold water in the morning was all we had to wash with, and the latrine was a hole in the ground behind the hut. Although the Ministry of Foreign Affairs of Guinea-Bissau did its best to see that we were well fed, we were glad that we had brought some canned food and biscuits with us.

On September 25, I presented my credentials to Cabral in a nearby thatched hut only a little bigger than ours. Cabral, known as Cabral Jr., was a younger brother of the late Amilcar Cabral, a former secretary of the African Party for the Independence of Guinea and Cape Verde (PAIGC), who had been assassinated in 1973. Both of them had visited China and had friendly feelings for China. In the 1960s, China had supported PAIGC in its struggle for independence, and had trained more than twenty cadres for PAIGC, all of whom later assumed key positions in the party branches, government departments, and military divisions.

Luis Cabral expressed his gratitude for China's support, saying, "Our first cadres were trained in China. We defeated the enemy by drawing on China's experience in our struggle for liberation. Now that the war is over, we will draw strength from our own people as well as China's experience to revive the economy."

Less than one month after I presented my credentials, the government of Guinea-Bissau moved its capital to Bissau, which had been the capital of Portuguese Guinea. On December 16, I went to Bissau, and discussed with the Guinea-Bissau government matters concerning the establishment of the Chinese embassy and China's technical aid to Guinea-Bissau in paddy rice growing. Cabral, Prime Minister Francisco Mendes, and General Secretary Aristides Pereira all welcomed the establishment of the Chinese embassy, and promised to do all they could to help us choose the site of the embassy and complete its establishment as soon as possible.

Bissau was a small city, Westernized and consumption-oriented. The buildings were all in a neat Portuguese style. Although half an hour's driving was enough to see the whole city, large companies of many countries had local agents there. The market was full of goods from Portugal, Western Europe, and Japan. Still, Bissau's economy was backward, and its cultural facilities were scanty. In the whole city, there were only two hospitals, one Portuguese-owned beer brewery, one middle school, one cinema, and a couple of stationery stores which also sold a few books. With independence, Portuguese investment flowed out, and local businesses were hard pressed to survive. It occurred to me that economic rejuvenation would be the major task of the Guinea-Bissau government for a long time to come.

Later, Guinea-Bissau and Cape Verde became two independent countries. The population of Guinea-Bissau is mainly composed of Africans, while Cape Verde is chiefly inhabited by people of Portuguese descent or of mixed African and Portuguese blood.

The Ministry of Foreign Affairs of Guinea-Bissau chose a two-story house on Domingo Street in Bissau for the Chinese embassy, and we accepted. The street was named after Domingo Lamos, an outstanding PAIGC warrior, who was once the commander of the Gabú military region in eastern Guinea-Bissau and died in battle.

TWO MEETINGS WITH GUINEAN PRESIDENT TOURE

AS CHINA'S AMBASSADOR TO GUINEA, I was mainly in charge of economic cooperation between our two countries. China had been aiding Guinea's economic construction in dozens of projects, including the People's Palace, a radio station, a theater, the Martyrs' Cemetery, a hydroelectric power station, an oil mill, and factories making tea, sugar, cigarettes, and farm machinery. China had also sent a medical team to Guinea. All these projects helped to meet the urgent need to develop Guinea's economy and raise its people's standard of living. The Chinese embassy kept a close eye on these projects while they were under construction and when they went into operation.

Sino-Guinean relations were then very good. The two countries had always been under clear skies, as President Toure often said. But of course this did not mean that there were no problems at all. African affairs had various complications.

On November 16, 1975, Toure suddenly called me in to talk about the Angolan issue. The president did most of the talking, for almost one hour. Prime Minister Edouard Beavogui and nine other ministers were also present—an indication that Toure attached great importance to the meeting.

After all the participants had shaken hands and were seated, Toure said, "I called in the Chinese ambassador today because the Democratic Party of Guinea and the Guinean government want the Chinese ambassador to send an important message to the Communist Party of China and the leaders of the Chinese government. China and Guinea have always trusted and cooperated with each other. The Chinese and Guinean peoples have the same ideology and adopt the same strategy. The two countries have common goals, and take actions and positions in unison—as harmonious and uniform as the two hands of a single person." He paused and then went on: "In international affairs, especially Asian affairs, we declare our position in step with Beijing. But the Guinean people are in the vanguard of understanding African affairs." Then, with a severe look, he said, "I am afraid that the grave situation in Angola at present is beyond China's understanding."

At that time, the Angolan people had just achieved independence after a long struggle, putting an end to 500 years of colonial rule. There had been three groups fighting colonialism: the National Front for the Liberation of Angola (FNLA), the National Union for the Total Independence of Angola (UNITA), and the Popular Movement for the Liberation of Angola (MPLA). The Chinese government had been supporting the Angolan people's just struggle against colonialism and all three groups, without taking sides among the three.

Toure explained, "The FNLA was founded by the Democratic Party of Guinea. Holden Roberto, president of the FNLA, went to make speeches at the UN with a Guinean passport, and obtained recognition and financial aid from the Organization of African Unity (OAU) in response to Guinea's proposal. But Roberto later became a client of the U.S. Central Intelligence Agency (CIA). Guinea disclosed his treachery, and urged the dismissal of the FNLA from the OAU, which is the leading agency in African affairs. Jonas Savimbi, president of UNITA, openly admitted that UNITA had gotten support from the racist regime of South Africa. So UNITA is also an agent of imperialism. Now the Guinean people find it humiliating to hear that China stands on the side of the followers of imperialism."

He went on, in a milder tone, "In fact, only the MPLA has kept fighting Portuguese colonialism on behalf of the Angolan people since February 4, 1961. The FNLA is based in Zaire, and has simply made a few statements, without any real struggle. Mobutu Sese Seko, the leader of Zaire, is a traitor. He was responsible for the death of Zaire's first leader, Patrice Lumumba. Guinea welcomes China's presence in Zaire and in any other reactionary African country. But China should not help the counter-revolutionary forces of Mobutu."

Toure concluded, "Guinea would like the Communist Party of China and the Chinese government to give careful consideration to the real situation of the revolutionary and counter-revolutionary forces so as not to harm the African anti-imperialist cause."

I immediately realized that this was an African response to the Sino-Soviet confrontation. I told Toure, "The Chinese Ministry of Foreign Affairs has just made a statement on the Angolan issue. The Chinese people are pleased to congratulate the Angolan people on their overthrow of the 500-year colonial domination and achievement of independence after a long struggle. The Chinese government always supports the just struggle of the Angolan people, and has provided aid to the three Angolan resistance groups. Since January 1975, we have stopped giving military aid to any of the three groups in order to prevent an Angolan civil war. The present harrowing situation in Angola is completely a result of the superpowers' scramble for domination there. Despite the complex situation in Africa, we firmly believe that the Angolan people can settle their own affairs appropriately if all external interference is removed."

On December 2, I presented China's stand on the Angolan issue to the Guinean government, as outlined by our Ministry of Foreign Affairs. The Guinean foreign minister, Fily Sissoko, perceiving the importance of my words, sent for someone to take down what I said. He made no comment except, "I will report this to the president in thirty minutes."

From then on, the Angolan issue was laid aside. It was never mentioned again until October 28, 1976, when I met Toure at the farewell reception before I left my ambassadorial post. He said, "Guinea has a deep trust in China, despite some puzzling things. China is striving for the benefit of proletarians all over the world. Therefore, the Guinean people always hold China in high regard. Guinea is determined to maintain, develop, and strengthen Sino-Guinean relations. Guinea was once worried about the Sino-Soviet dispute, and some Guineans once suspected that Guinea was simply a radical flank of the Communist Party of China. Meanwhile, China might have thought that Guinea had assumed a direct or indirect anti-China position. Guinea has faced threats not only from imperialist powers but also from some socialist powers. It is hoped that China and Guinea can cooperate intimately in African affairs and stick together through all difficulties. Divergence of views should be kept within Guinea and China and from our common enemies."

I expressed my gratitude for his friendliness toward China and my understanding of his worries about the Sino-Soviet dispute. I assured him, "Sino-Guinean friendly cooperation will never change. It is understandable that China and Guinea have different views about the Soviet Union. China will not ask Guinea to keep step with China in its relations with the Soviet Union."

Toure had experience leading labor union movements, and was famous for his eloquence. A collection of his rousing speeches to the public had reached over sixty volumes by that time. He had received warm and wide support and finally achieved success in Guinea's struggle for independence from France. In times of surging African national liberation movements, Toure was always full of enthusiasm for the cause. However, he was not able to lead Guinea out of its economic recession. In March 1984, he died of a heart attack at age sixty-two.

TRAVELING THROUGH AFRICA

AS DEVELOPING REGIONS that had once suffered the oppression and exploitation of imperialism and colonialism, China and the African countries could easily understand each other's pursuit of independence and freedom, and could have a natural feeling of intimacy. Since the founding of the People's Republic of China, we have been supporting the unremitting struggle of the African people for independence, and actively aiding African countries in developing their national economies. Therefore, the African people and their leaders always see China as their most reliable friend. African countries also give China a great deal of valuable support and help. At the Twenty-sixth Session of the UN General Assembly in 1971, twenty-six of the seventy-six votes for restoring all the lawful rights of the People's Republic of China in the UN came from African countries, leaving an indelible impression on the Chinese people. The United States and other Western countries put pressure on China by making use of human rights issues at the UN Human Rights Conference. Most African countries' firm support of China has contributed significantly to China's ten consecutive successes in foiling the draft resolution against China in the protracted international battle over human rights as well as China's victory in the diplomatic struggles related to Taiwan. Although the Taiwan authorities adopt "money diplomacy" to poverty-stricken African countries, those countries still stand by our side, adhering to the "one China" principle and opposing Taiwan's "independence," "two Chinas," "one China, one Taiwan," and Taiwan's admission to the United Nations or any other international organization that can be joined only by a sovereign state.

In 1989, it was again our African friends who stood by us and extended a helping hand in the difficult times following the political turmoil in Beijing, when Western countries imposed sanctions on China.

In mid-July 1989, the Seventh Conference of Chinese Diplomatic Envoys was held to discuss ways of coping with the sanctions and open up a new road for our diplomacy. In my report "On the International Situation and Foreign Policy," I emphasized that China should focus on its central task of economic construction and continue to pursue its independent foreign policy of peace.

An important task at that time was to break the diplomatic blockade of the Western countries and show the world that China's guiding principles and foreign policies remained unchanged.

Internationally, there was a strong movement to isolate China. It became the vogue to impose sanctions on China. But the African countries' attitude toward China remained unchanged. They were still very friendly to us. Therefore, I decided to pay a visit to Africa.

I first went to six countries in southern Africa: Lesotho, Botswana, Zimbabwe, Angola, Zambia, and Mozambique. Then I visited Egypt and Tunisia in North Africa, in September.

I explained China's domestic situation to the leaders of the countries I visited, and told them that China would never yield to any external pressures, as other countries did not have the right to interfere in China's internal affairs and impose their own social systems, ideologies, or values on us. Our African friends fully agreed with me because many African countries were subject to the same pressures.

President Robert Mugabe of Zimbabwe mentioned his past worries about China's situation. The foreign minister of Angola, Pedro de Castro van Dunem, said that if the Communist Party of China and the Chinese government had lost control of the situation, it would have dreadful consequences and bad effects on the Third World. Many other leaders promised that at the forthcoming Inter-Parliamentary Union (IPU) Conference, they would vote against any resolutions which would interfere in China's internal affairs.

The first head of state, the first head of government, and the first foreign minister to visit China after the political turmoil of 1989 all came from Africa. They wanted to show the whole world Africa's unwavering friendship with China in its most difficult times. China had helped them in the past, and now they would show their utmost support for China when China needed it most.

All this formed a sharp contrast with the Western countries' groundless censure of China and their unreasonable canceling, delaying, or suspending high-level exchanges with China.

The situation in Africa grew grim in the 1990s. The West made use of the drastic changes in eastern Europe to increase its political pressure on African countries, and used its so-called aid program to incite fear and seek concessions. The attempt of the West to apply its overall political and economic patterns and values to Africa sharpened various conflicts in Africa, and destabilized the political situation of many African countries. The world economic recession, the drop in the prices of raw materials and agricultural products, and the decrease in the flow of capital into Africa dragged the African countries deeper into debt and economic crisis. Some pro-Soviet African countries felt lost when the Soviet Union tightened up its strategies toward Africa—as did some pro-Western African countries when the United States pressed its presumed democracy on them.

In these circumstances, the African countries turned to China. Seeing the correctness of China's adherence to the policies of independence, reform, and opening-up, they tried to defend their sovereignty and develop their national economies with Chinese support. This brought new meaning and significance to China's relations with Africa.

Jiang Zemin, general secretary of the Communist Party of China, attached great importance to our diplomatic work in Africa. He often called on Chinese leaders to visit Africa, and he set a good example by leading the Chinese delegation, in his capacity as president, on visits to a dozen countries all over Africa.

In the latter half of 1990, I went to Africa again, visiting Morocco, Algeria, and Egypt.

At the beginning of 1991, I set out on another African trip, during which I visited Ethiopia, Uganda, Kenya, and Tanzania.

In January 1992, I visited Mali, Guinea, Senegal, Côte d'Ivoire, Ghana, and Namibia, and passed through South Africa.

From then on, it seemed to become the usual practice for me to visit Africa at the beginning of every year. After being appointed foreign minister, I made, all together, twelve visits to Africa, and I came to know almost every African leader and foreign minister. I visited all the African countries, some more than once, except for the few that had not established diplomatic relations with China.

During my visits to Africa, I received the deep impression that the African countries were indignant at the political conditions attached to the financial assistance provided by Western countries.

In 1992, President Felix Houphouët-Boigny of Côte d'Ivoire told me that the democratization of Africa in the past two years was a kind of fanaticism, and that starving people had no freedom since poverty and freedom were incompatible.

President Paul Biya of Cameroon, recalling his visit to China in 1987, told me that China's achievements had left a deep impression on him. He also told me that the emergence of more than seventy political parties in Cameroon (with a population of only 12 million), coupled with external interference, had affected the stability of the country as it began its democratization process. He was very worried that some power was making use of the lofty ideal of democracy to interfere in other countries' internal affairs, although Cameroon valued the principles of human rights and democracy.

President Gnassingbe Eyadema of Togo, who had been in power for thirty-six years, was an old-timer among African leaders. He had survived many dangerous situations, despite the hostility of the West. When I visited Togo in 1995, Eyadema held a stately parade and pageant with over 20,000 people to welcome me. Referring to human rights, he said indignantly: "The Western countries never said a word about human rights in the time of colonialism, nor did they say anything about it when seizing African resources. Now they have been brazenly talking about human rights. They know no shame!" He pointed out that Africa, consisting of fifty-three countries, had a crucial position in the international arena. There could be no world peace without stability in Africa, so the prosperity of the world economy should not be achieved at the cost of Africa's economic development.

China has always defended Africa's interests in the international arena. China gives full respect to the African countries' struggle to defend their independence and sovereignty and their efforts to maintain national unity and economic development and raise their people's standard of living. China has also supported a series of their reasonable proposals, such as debt reduction or exemption, protection of African economic interests, and promotion of "South-South cooperation" and

"North-South" dialogue. China took a clear stand on choice of a secretary general of the UN and stood up for the reappointment of the African candidate. All these actions showed China's support for Africa.

Coming into Contact with South Africa

SOUTH AFRICA—THE LARGEST and perhaps the most important country in Africa—was the last country there to establish diplomatic relations with China.

As the international situation and the domestic situation in South Africa changed, the racist government of South Africa set about improving its relations with China. In April 1989, the South African government unofficially asked Liang Zhaoli, president of the Chinese Association of South Africa, to convey to the Chinese government its wish to develop bilateral relations leading to the establishment of formal diplomatic relations with China. In May, the Chinese government sent back a message through Liang to express its appreciation of the position assumed by the South African government and its hope that South Africa could conform to the trend of the times and adopt enlightened policies. China indicated that it would give careful consideration to developing bilateral relations with South Africa when the conditions were ripe.

In 1990, the South African government kept notifying the Chinese government of its wish to establish relations with China and of its gratitude for China's efforts in developing Sino-South African relations and China's support for the political settlement of the domestic problems of South Africa. The South African government even indicated that it could, tacitly, coordinate its diplomacy with China's. Obviously, South Africa was eager to establish normal, direct relations with China. Of course, we were also willing to do so. However, the following key points had to be made clear: (1) South Africa must abolish its apartheid system, which violated human rights. (2) South Africa must sever its so-called diplomatic relations with Taiwan.

In 1991, the abolition of the three pillars of the apartheid system—the Group Areas Act, the Land Act, and Population Registration Act—marked a turning point in South Africa. This forebode the end of apartheid. All the major political powers in South Africa wanted to seek political compromise. Political settlement had become an irreversible trend of the times.

At the same time, other African countries softened their attitude toward South Africa, and the international community greatly relaxed its sanctions against South Africa.

One of the two obstacles to normalizing relations between China and South Africa was about to be removed, but the other obstacle— the Taiwan question—remained.

In October 1991, the foreign minister of South Africa, Pik Botha, paid a secret visit to China accompanied by Leo Henry Evans, deputy director general of the Ministry of Foreign Affairs; and P. J. Botha, the South African consul-general in Hong Kong. I met Pik Botha in a lounge at the Beijing International Airport, and he returned to South Africa as soon as the meeting ended.

Botha, regarded as the spiritual leader of the liberals who advocated reforming apartheid in the Democratic Party of South Africa, was appointed foreign minister at age forty-five, in 1977. He was once reprimanded by the conservatives in the Democratic Party for saying in a speech that a black person might be elected president in the new constitutional structure if the rights and security of the white racial group were guaranteed.

At our meeting, Botha first explained to me, "White people, mainly the Dutch, arrived in South Africa long ago. They should be considered Africans just as British people were called Americans when they emigrated to North America. At the end of the eighteenth century, the British conquered the Boers, who were the descendants of the original Dutch white settlers. South Africa then became a British crown colony. Therefore, white South Africans should not all be lumped together, since the British were invaders and the Dutchmen resisted the external invasions."

Next, he explained to me the development of the political settlement of South Africa's problems and the related policies of the South African government.

I said, "In your presentation of South African history you completely ignored the crucial position of the black people as the main
body of South Africa's population. The apartheid system pursued by
the white South African authorities is inhumane. China hopes that
South Africa will continue the process of political settlement of its
problems."

Referring to bilateral relations, I told him, "South Africa is an
important country in Africa, as China is in Asia. Taiwan is part of
China. Sino-South African relations should continue to develop.
Diplomats of the two countries have come into contact. China pro-
poses that we set up offices in each other's territory and thus build
channels for direct contact. Also, China's Xinhua News Agency plans
to dispatch resident correspondents to South Africa. In short, both
sides may have some contacts first. Then we may proceed with discussions on the possibility of further development of the relations
between our two countries."

Botha responded, "Building reliable channels for contact is very
important for establishing relations. China is welcome to set up resident offices in South Africa. Influenced by the Western media, South
Africa has formed many misconceptions about China over the years.
Now China is undergoing changes, quietly and according to its own
cultural tradition. China will be among the greatest powers in the
world in the next century if it continues its reform and opening-up."

On the subject of Taiwan, Botha made a long speech, which had
obviously been prepared in advance. He said, "The relations between
South Africa and Taiwan were established long ago, when South
Africa was isolated. Therefore, the problem cannot be solved
overnight. However, the situation is changing. South Africa will adhere to the 'one China' principle, and not interfere in China's internal affairs. We hope that China can overcome division and accomplish
reunification."

After Botha returned to South Africa, he wrote me a letter, expressing his gratitude to me for giving him and his country a special
and courteous reception during his significant visit. He said, "Our
talks were the first historic meeting between the governments of our

two countries. The People's Republic of China has an extraordinary history. China will certainly play an important role in Africa and the world as a whole. We can benefit greatly from good relations. We attach great importance to our relations with the Chinese in Taiwan, Hong Kong, and Macao. Our relations with the People's Republic of China will develop at an appropriate time. It is to be noted that channels permitted by the present circumstances have been opened up by our meeting."

The South African press acclaimed this meeting as an inspiring diplomatic breakthrough that paved the way for future official contacts between China and South Africa. The press also predicted that China and South Africa would set up "indirect agencies," such as scientific, cultural, and other research institutes, in each other's territory.

During the same year—1991—China and South Africa reached an agreement through a series of secret discussions on setting up nongovernmental agencies in each other's territory.

In February 1992, China's Institute for International Studies set up its Center for South African Studies in Pretoria. In the following month, a South African Center for Chinese Studies was established in Beijing.

Passing through Johannesburg

IN JANUARY 1992, I was to visit five West African countries. In the trip plan submitted by the Foreign Ministry, I suggested adding Namibia in southern Africa. I thought that this would be a good opportunity to develop diplomatic relations with Namibia, which had been independent for just over one year.

For historical reasons, there were usually convenient air links between African countries and their previous suzerains, but few existed between African countries themselves. My last stop in West Africa was Ghana, from which there was no direct flight to Namibia. I had to fly first to Lagos, the capital of Nigeria; and then to Johannesburg in South Africa, where I changed flights for Namibia. This route afforded me an opportunity to pass through South Africa, when I had to stop at the Johannesburg airport to change planes.

South Africa soon approved China's application for entry, and offered a special plane to carry our delegation from Johannesburg to Cape Town, the legislative capital of South Africa, so that we could meet Foreign Minister Botha there. Then the plane would carry us directly to Windhoek, the capital of Namibia. Since we were only passing through South Africa, reciprocating Botha's visit to Beijing International Airport instead of making an official visit, I declined the warm invitation with thanks, and agreed to meet Botha at the Johannesburg airport.

During the meeting, we exchanged views on the South African situation, wider African issues, and bilateral relations. Botha explained his country's latest developments, and showed appreciation for the concept of "one country, two systems" proposed by Deng Xiaoping. He said that he believed South Africa and China shared many interests and that relations between the two countries would continue to progress. He also said that he would never give up his efforts to develop relations with China. He expressed his gratitude for my warm reception the year before and his hope that we would have more opportunities to meet each other.

I said, "Sino-South African relations have developed considerably since our last meeting. Although we are still some distance away from normalizing our relations, our objective is clear, and we should keep in contact with each other to foster trust." Then I reiterated China's stand on the Taiwan question.

After the meeting, Botha treated us to a banquet at the airport, where we dined in a harmonious atmosphere. After the banquet, Botha suggested that we visit Pretoria, which is only forty kilometers from the Johannesburg airport. We accepted the invitation and agreed to have a look around the city by car, since we still had some time. On our way to Pretoria, we got out of our cars and stood on the top of a hill to get a panorama of the city. We were impressed by the modern European-style city, but we reminded ourselves that it was enjoyed only by white people, since South Africa still practiced apartheid. Black people

Meeting Kofi Annan, secretary general of the United Nations.

Meeting Mikhail Gorbachev in the Kremlin in December 1988.

At the headquarters of the United Nations in New York on
September 28, 1988. *Left to right:* Edvard Shevardnadze, the
author, U.S. Secretary of State George Shultz, UN Secretary
General Perez de Cuéllar, French Foreign Minister Roland Dumas,
and Foreign Secretary Geoffrey Howe of the United Kingdom.

On November 29, 1990, the UN Security Council passed a resolution authorizing member states to use all necessary means to execute UN resolutions and restore peace and security in the Gulf region. The photograph shows the author, head of the Chinese delegation, holding up a hand to indicate abstention from the vote.

Meeting President George W. Bush on March 22, 2001,
while visiting the United States.

With President George Bush *(right)* and National Security Adviser
Brent Scowcroft at the Bush Library in Texas in October 2002.

Meeting President Bill Clinton at the White House on April 29, 1997.

Talking to Fidel Castro during a visit to Cuba in June 1989.

June 1955, by the small lake near the
Central Communist Youth League School.

Meeting President Nelson Mandela of South Africa at his
official residence in Cape Town, December 1997.

could only work in the city in the daytime and each evening had to return to the black people's communities outside the city.

The meeting between Botha and me in Johannesburg marked a
step forward in China's adjustment of its policy toward South Africa.
At the same time, it dealt a blow to the Taiwan authorities. The staff
members of the Taiwan "embassy" in South Africa were extremely
nervous, and in great fear that this would undermine their beachhead
in Africa. So they made a strong protest to the South African Ministry of Foreign Affairs.

Besides Botha, I also met Walter Sisulu, vice president of the
African National Congress (ANC) of South Africa; and Dikgang
Moseneke, vice president of the Pan-Africanist Congress of Azania. I
reported the situation to them, and won the understanding and support of the various liberation movements in South Africa for the adjustment in our policy toward their country. When I met Sisulu, I
asked him to send President Nelson Mandela an invitation from the
Chinese government and President Yang Shangkun to visit China at
his convenience. The same invitation was also given to Sisulu. He
said that President Mandela was eager to visit China, and would do so
when conditions were ripe.

Mandela's Visit to China

MANDELA WAS, OF COURSE, a world-famous African political leader.
He waged a prolonged and arduous struggle in leading the South
African people to abolish apartheid. From June 1964 on, he spent
twenty-seven years in prison. Staunch in his political beliefs and supported by thousands of people in South Africa and the international
community, Mandela was released by the South African government
on February 11, 1990, when he was seventy-three years old.

China's leaders sent Mandela congratulations on his release. On
March 28, at the press conference of the Third Session of the Seventh
National People's Congress of China, I expressed our joy at Man-
dela's release.

As soon as he was released, Mandela began a series of visits to

African countries. When he was visiting Zambia and Uganda, the Chinese ambassador—or chargé d'affaires—to the two countries met him and invited him, on behalf of the Communist Party of China, to visit China in October. Mandela said, "I have long desired to see the great country and people of China. But my schedule in October is too tight for a visit to the Far East. A Chinese tour should not be too hasty since China is a big country. Next May it will be more convenient for me to have a good look at China."

We were wondering why Mandela was slow to take up this offer, although he had often expressed his desire to visit China as soon as possible. Later, someone near to him revealed to us that Mandela hoped to receive a formal invitation from the Chinese government. Therefore, I specially asked President Sisulu to transmit to him a formal invitation from the Chinese government and from Yang Shangkun.

Six months later, Mandela finally visited China, from October 4 to 10. Yang Shangkun held a welcoming ceremony and banquet for him. Jiang Zemin also met him and gave him a banquet. Prime Minister Li Peng held talks with him. The Chinese government donated money and materials worth a total of US$10 million to the ANC. Peking University conferred an honorary doctorate on Mandela. The high level of the reception was almost equal to that for a head of state. At a press conference in Beijing, Mandela said that he had been deeply moved by all this.

In the previous three years, we had developed a wide range of communication through many channels. Both the South African government and the leaders of the ANC had acquired a clearer understanding of China's stand on the political settlement of South Africa's problems and the essence of the Taiwan question. This laid a good foundation for the establishment of formal diplomatic relations between China and South Africa.

The Taiwan authorities were extremely nervous about our diplomatic overtures to South Africa, and kept a close watch on our actions, doing everything possible to create obstacles and undermine our efforts. It used every means to win over the South African government and the ANC, which was about to come to power. Mandela said candidly that he had received an invitation to visit Taiwan when he was about to visit the mainland of China. He explained, "The ANC and I are grateful for China's long-term support, and we value our friendship with China. South Africa will establish diplomatic relations only with the People's Republic of China and get rid of Taiwan's office." He also promised to be frank with China about how the ANC would handle the invitation from Taiwan.

BEFORE AND AFTER THE SOUTH AFRICAN GENERAL ELECTION

THE YEARS 1993 AND 1994 were a turning point in South Africa's domestic situation. Its political parties agreed that the first democratic election in South Africa regardless of race was to be held in April 1994.

Soon after Mandela's visit to China, Taiwan promised US$25 million to the ANC, which was in urgent need of money for the election. Moreover, the ANC was a national movement consisting of people from all walks of life with different political beliefs, including a pro-Taiwan group. Under these circumstances, the ANC made the decision that Mandela should go to Taiwan to receive financial aid.

The ANC sent Thabo Mbeki, who was then head of the ANC's Department of International Affairs (and as of this writing is the president of South Africa), to China to give an explanation, lest Mandela's visit to Taiwan affect the ANC's relations with China.

When I met Mbeki, he stated, "Taiwan has agreed to provide a large amount of aid to the ANC, and invited Nelson Mandela to accept it. The ANC considers the aid vital, and decided that Mandela would go to Taiwan to receive it in July 1993. This does not mean a change in the ANC's policy toward China. The ANC recognizes the People's Republic of China as the sole legitimate government of the whole of China, and will never betray its old friend. The ANC will make great efforts to establish diplomatic relations between China and South Africa. We believe that this goal will be achieved in the near future."

I replied, "The ANC should be alert to this kind of activity on Taiwan's part. It is understandable that you accept the aid, but you should by no means accept any attached political conditions. We believe that the ANC can handle its relations with Taiwan properly."

In that period, we found that the government of South Africa attached more importance to economic and trade relations and personnel exchanges with China than to political relations. The ANC's idea was neither to abandon Taiwan nor ignore China's international status and influence.

We were on high alert, and well prepared for this situation. They wanted to resort to "dual recognition."

In October 1993, I met Gerrit Viljoen, counselor to the president of South Africa, when he visited China. Viljoen said, "For South Africa, the establishment of diplomatic relations between our two countries largely depends on the results of the democratic reform and presidential election in South Africa, scheduled for next year. Mandela's victory will be conducive to the establishment of diplomatic relations between China and South Africa. But if Fredrick Willem de Klerk wins, South Africa will keep its diplomatic relations with Taiwan at the ambassadorial level, and be slow to establish diplomatic relations with the People's Republic of China. If China can provide adequate aid to the economic development of South Africa, establishing diplomatic relations will be easier. But in any case, South Africa will maintain its relations with Taiwan."

The general election was to be held from April 27 to 29, 1994. This election was very important to South Africa as well as China. It was most likely a good opportunity for normalization of the relations between the two countries.

Early in 1994, I suggested to the Ministry of Foreign Affairs that we make preparations and develop specific plans and strategies well in advance for the establishment of diplomatic relations between South Africa and China after the South African general election.

China's vice foreign minister, Tian Zengpei, visited South Africa as a guest of our Center for South African Studies. He made wide contacts not only with high-level figures but with people from all walks of life in South Africa. We were hoping to persuade the ANC to start negotiations with us as soon as possible and to invite our representatives, and not those of Taiwan, to the presidential inaugural ceremony.

On February 20, Tian Zengpei met Mandela, Mbeki, and other South African leaders and delivered a letter to Mandela from Jiang Zemin. Jiang said in the letter that he wished Mandela and the ANC success in the general election, and that he anticipated the birth of a united and democratic new South Africa with racial equality. He also wrote that as a new South Africa was born, the issue of normalizing Sino-South African relations would become part of the agenda, and that China was glad that Mandela had stated repeatedly that the ANC would take the same stand as the UN on establishing diplomatic relations with the People's Republic of China.

During the talks, Tian stressed that it was a logical historical development for the new South Africa to establish diplomatic relations with China without inviting official representatives of Taiwan to the celebration ceremony after the general election. China wished to reach an understanding on the establishment of diplomatic relations between China and South Africa before the general election and hoped that the two countries would sign the documents and declare the establishment of diplomatic relations immediately after the new South African government was set up.

Mandela said, "The ANC is very grateful for China's constant support to the ANC over the years. The establishment of diplomatic relations between the People's Republic of China and South Africa, which will be beneficial to both countries, should have been accomplished earlier. South Africa will seriously study China's proposal and reconsider the diplomatic relations existing between the current South African government and Taiwan in order to solve the problems completely."

Tian Zengpei submitted the draft Joint Communiqué on the Establishment of Diplomatic Relations between the People's Republic of China and the Republic of South Africa and the memorandum of understanding prepared by the Chinese government to Mbeki for

ANC's study in preparation for reaching an agreement on principles before the general election. At the same time, the Chinese side restated its principled position on the Taiwan question.

Mbeki said, "The ANC has repeatedly stated that it adheres to the 'one China' principle, and regards its relations with China as very important. No problems stand in the way of establishing diplomatic relations. But we are now busy with the election campaign. I am afraid we have no time to spare for the negotiation over the establishment of diplomatic relations, since we have to deal with many complicated political struggles and make all kinds of plans and personnel arrangements that are to be adopted after the general election. Furthermore, the new South African government will be a government of national unity, including some officials in the current South African government. The ANC needs some time to work on those whose attitude toward China is dramatically different from that of the ANC."

Mbeki did not make any clear commitment in the matter of inviting China's representatives to the inaugural ceremony for the new president. He agreed that it was logical for representatives of China, instead of representatives of Taiwan, to attend the inauguration. But it was difficult for the ANC to persuade the current government not to invite the official representatives of Taiwan.

To indicate our important role in international affairs and expand our influence on South Africa, we decided to participate in the UN Observer Mission in South Africa and dispatched forty-five people to South Africa to observe the general election there.

On March 30, South Africa invited President Zemin to attend the inauguration of the new president on May 10. However, as Lee Teng-hui, the "president" of Taiwan, was also invited, we sent a nongovernmental rather than a governmental delegation.

TALKS WITH FOREIGN MINISTER ALFRED NZO

AFTER THE ANC CAME TO POWER, the new South African government chose not to sever its diplomatic relations with Taiwan immediately. This gave the Taiwanese authorities an opportunity to promote their policies of "dual recognition" and "two Chinas." Taiwan's "foreign minister," Frederick Chien, announced at the "Legislative Yuan" that Taiwan was ready to accept South Africa's "dual recognition" of the two sides of the Taiwan Strait.

Our Ministry of Foreign Affairs lost no time pointing out that Chien's speech revealed another scheme to create "two Chinas" or "one China, one Taiwan," and split China without regard to the cardinal principle of national interest. The Chinese government appreciated Mandela's and the ANC's adherence to the "one China" principle and their commitment to handle South Africa's relations with China according to the UN practice. China believed that its relations with new South Africa would develop, overall, on the basis of the Five Principles of Peaceful Coexistence.

Meanwhile, we increased our communication with the new South African government.

On June 23, Li Zhaoxing, our permanent representative to the UN, met the foreign minister of the new South Africa, Alfred Nzo, in New York. Li offered China's congratulations on South Africa's return to the international family, and expressed China's wish to normalize its relations with South Africa. Nzo first reviewed his visit of 1986 to China, and then said, "I cherish our friendship with the Chinese people, and South Africa attaches great importance to developing its relations with China. But South Africa and Taiwan have after all had longtime relations, involving many agreements and cooperative projects. We wish to have China's understanding that South Africa's adjustment of its relations with Taiwan cannot be accomplished hastily."

In July, I asked Ji Peiding, the newly appointed director of China's Center for South African Studies in South Africa, to send a letter to Nzo. In the letter, I offered my congratulations on the birth of the new South Africa and stressed that its emergence created favorable conditions for the normalization of Sino-South African relations. I said the Chinese government was willing to begin negotiations over the establishment of diplomatic relations between China and South Africa at any time. I also invited Nzo to visit China again. On September 7, Nzo replied to my letter, saying, "South Africa's relations with China go beyond the boundaries of political parties, and draw the attention of South Africa's government of national unity. It is hoped that this issue can be soon settled on the basis of respecting the two countries' interests and international practices."

On September 28, I met Nzo at the UN General Assembly in New York. I said to him, "China has always supported the South African people's just struggle against racism. Now we hope that the normalization of the relations between the two countries can be achieved, as a new South Africa has been born." Nzo acknowledged that the two countries had set up a good relationship when China supported the restoration of all lawful rights of South Africa in the UN. He said, "South Africa understands China's important role in international affairs, and is willing to develop all-around bilateral relations with China. The fact that the racist government of South Africa had relations with Taiwan in the past is a problem facing South Africa's government of national unity. This problem cannot be solved within a short time; patience is needed."

I pointed out, "China has not raised any new requirements for South Africa. We hope only that the new government of South Africa can establish normal diplomatic relations with China as most countries in the world have done." China does not oppose South Africa's having economic relations with Taiwan so long as Pretoria sticks to the 'one China' principle. China is willing to assist South Africa's economic development and welcomes South Africa's participation in international economic cooperation with China. We understand that South Africa's government of national unity has just been set up and that it has to deal with many problems. We will show patience, but we hope that South Africa can assume the same stand as most countries on China-related issues."

GOOD THINGS NEVER COME EASILY

IN THE PROCESS OF DEVELOPING relations between China and South Africa, Nelson Mandela was obviously the key figure, as he enjoyed a high reputation both in South Africa and around the world. His attitude was of vital importance to the establishment of Sino-South African relations, so he became the focal point of our work.

However, Mandela meant to achieve, on the strength of his high reputation, "dual recognition" on the question of Taiwan which none of the big powers of the West, including the United States, Britain, and Japan, had ever accomplished. He had once declared at a press conference that South Africa had no intention to sever its relations with Taiwan, although it hoped to develop diplomatic relations with the People's Republic of China.

In July 1994, a delegation from the Foreign Affairs Committee of the South African parliament visited China at the invitation of the Chinese People's Institute of Foreign Affairs. The delegation, composed of the representatives of major parties in the parliament of South Africa, represented broad sections of the South African people. Before the visit, Mandela gave them special instructions to ascertain the advantages and disadvantages of establishing diplomatic relations with China.

I met the delegation in Beijing and explained our principled stand and our clear position on Sino-South African relations and the Taiwan question. After the visit, members of the delegation had a better understanding of China's refusal to accept "dual recognition." Raymond Suttner, who was the chairman of the Foreign Affairs Committee of the South African parliament and head of the delegation, said that the visit would influence South Africa's adjustment of its policies toward China.

On November 18, Mandela stated, "I have been in contact with Chinese President Jiang Zemin and have a good relationship with Chinese Premier Li Peng. Now we are solving the problem of our diplomatic relations because we still maintain diplomatic relations with Taiwan. I have frequently explained my attitude to the international community: I cannot see any moral obligation for me to sever our relations with Taiwan unless Taiwan does something that proves the relations unworthy. Therefore, I am going to keep our relations with Taiwan. I show my respect for the UN resolution on this issue, but I must act upon the interest of the South African people in this particular situation. I plan to enter into negotiations on this issue."

Mandela's official declaration of his pursuit of a "two Chinas" policy created an obstacle to the establishment of diplomatic relations between China and South Africa, which would be put off again and again if the obstacle was not removed.

On November 30, Jiang Zemin wrote to Mandela: "I appreciate your respect for the UN stand on the Taiwan question and your suggestion for negotiations on the establishment of diplomatic relations with China. I often recall your successful visit to China in 1992, and your commitment that the new South Africa would handle its relations with China according to the international practice remains fresh in my memory. The Chinese people and Chinese leaders, including myself, have always been friendly toward you. In the past, the Chinese people regarded the South African people's struggle for racial equality as our own battle, and shared your joy in the birth of a new South Africa. Both of us realize that a proper settlement of the Taiwan question is the precondition for establishing Sino-South African relations. The Taiwan question is of great importance to China's sovereignty and territorial integrity as well as to the fundamental interests of the Chinese nation and the feelings of the 1.2 billion Chinese people. Therefore, China will never accept 'double recognition.' China has established diplomatic relations with 159 countries, and successfully settled the Taiwan issue with them. I believe you will develop Sino-South African relations in the right direction with your breadth of vision as a statesman. The Chinese government is willing to make an active response to substantial steps toward the development of Sino-South African relations taken by the South African government."

The ANC leadership had a very clear understanding of our stand. Cyril Ramaphosa, chairman of the South African Constitutional Assembly and secretary general of the ANC, once said that Taiwan's attempt to use money to buy South Africa's favor was despicable. South Africa should stop sitting on the fence on this issue, he declared.

At the beginning of December, the ANC assembled its National Executive Committee to discuss South Africa's relations with China. Mandela attended the meeting. The committee proposed that the South African government dispatch a high-level delegation to discuss Sino-South African relations with China in order to initiate the process of normalizing relations. A consensus on South Africa's "one China" stand was achieved at the meeting.

However, Mandela cautioned, "If South Africa severs its relations with Taiwan with only a statement, it will be considered ungrateful, since the ANC has received financial aid from the Taiwan authorities. Someone should be sent to Taiwan to make clear the ANC's stand."

TAIWAN'S INFLUENCE

TAIWAN'S RELATIONS WITH South Africa dated from 1962.

In 1948, when the National Party of South Africa came to power, it intensified racial discrimination measures, known as apartheid. The tyranny of the South African apartheid regime met with fierce condemnation and resistance on the part of the international community.

In 1962, when South Africa was undergoing hard times, Taiwan took advantage of this to establish diplomatic relations at the consular level. This arrangement was upgraded to the ambassadorial level in 1976. In the next decade or so, more than 10,000 Taiwan businesspeople migrated to South Africa to invest in factories, and the number of Taiwan-South African joint-venture companies, banks, etc., exceeded 300. Taiwanese businesspeople also bought vast areas of land. This formed an important economic foundation for the Taiwan authorities to maintain its relations with South Africa. When the international community imposed sanctions on South Africa, economic and trade relations between Taiwan and South Africa developed rapidly, and they signed dozens of "intergovernmental" agreements. The annual bilateral trade volume between Taiwan and South Africa was something between US$1.5 billion and $1.9 billion. South Africa's trade surplus with Taiwan amounted to US$500 million. All together, Taiwan invested US$1.5 billion to $1.6 billion in South Africa's industries: textiles, shoes, plastics, suitcases, metal process-ing, commerce, and service trades. These industries employed some 40,000 people, 85.8 percent of whom were black.

In the early 1990s, as political reform progressed, Taiwan feared that it would lose its position in the new South Africa if black people took power. Therefore, Taiwan showed favor to the black liberation movements of South Africa by attending their national congresses or inviting their leaders to visit Taiwan and accept aid.

After Nelson Mandela became president, Taiwan promised a do-nation of US$40 million for a career-training center for former armed personnel of the ANC. Taiwan gave full support to the Recon-struction and Development Program of the new South Africa by pro-viding four preferential loans to the South African power, telecommunications, and transportation sectors, and a small-scale farming program.

Being extremely nervous about the establishment of diplomatic relations between China and South Africa, the Taiwan authorities in-tensified their activities in South Africa. In 1996, Lee Teng-hui promised annual aid of US$500 million. In late August and early Sep-tember of that year, a delegation led by Xu Lide, "deputy chief of the Executive Yuan of Taiwan," investigated the economic and trade situ-ation in South Africa, and signed several agreements and memoranda on cooperation. Xu Lide even promised US$5 billion to help South Africa build a petrochemicals industry park. This high figure seemed incredible to many South African entrepreneurs and politicians.

Breakthrough

THE BLACK, ASIAN, AND OTHER colored people in South Africa had waged mass movements against apartheid since the 1950s. China had always firmly supported the South African people's struggle against racism, and regarded that struggle as an integral part of the cause of national independence and political liberation on the African conti-nent. China established and maintained friendly relations with the

South African national liberation movements, including the ANC and Pan-Africanist Congress of Azania. In these circumstances, it was naturally impossible for China to establish diplomatic relations with South Africa.

As the new South African government was set up and Mandela came to power, a breakthrough in Sino-South African relations was appropriate.

In late March 1996, South Africa's foreign minister, Nzo, visited China, having received an official invitation. This was the first time since coming to power that Mandela had sent a cabinet minister to China to discuss bilateral relations.

Nzo delivered a letter from Mandela to President Jiang Zemin. The letter said, "Democratic South Africa inherited diplomatic relations with Taiwan from the former regime, and has only nongovernmental relations with the People's Republic of China. We hope to establish diplomatic relations with the People's Republic of China. We agree with your point of view that a proper settlement of the Taiwan question is the precondition for establishing diplomatic relations. Essentially, Taiwan's status is part of the internal affairs of China. We would like to help the People's Republic of China to settle the Taiwan question if required."

Jiang said to Nzo: "President Mandela knows that China has supported the South African people's struggle against racism since Mao Zedong's time. We have always advocated opposing the apartheid system and colonialism. I admire President Mandela for his indomitable spirit during his twenty-seven years of struggle in prison. The Chinese people respect him greatly. We understand that South Africa inherited 'diplomatic relations' with Taiwan from the former regime, and that President Mandela is friendly toward the Chinese people. I just want to tell President Mandela in a direct and frank manner, instead of using diplomatic parlance: Recognition of 'one China' is the paramount precondition for establishing diplomatic relations with China, and we will by no means accept 'dual recognition.' Nor do we hope to see a precedent of 'dual recognition' set by President Mandela."

I had a long talk with Nzo. He told me candidly: "The new South African government inherited this predicament from the former regime. We are in urgent need of a large amount of money to carry out our economic reconstruction and development program, and increase job opportunities. Taiwan promised to aid some projects of the Reconstruction and Development Program, such as building a career-training center and updating weaponry. It is estimated that Taiwan's aid will reach US$300 million, which is badly needed." He continued, "It is abnormal for South Africa to have no diplomatic relations with China. We hope that China can advise South Africa how to handle its relations with China. The most important task of the South African delegation to China is to hear the Chinese government's suggestions for help."

I reviewed the friendship between the Chinese and South African peoples, and the development of the relations between the two countries in recent years. I said, "The former foreign minister, Botha, and I agreed to set up research institutes in each other's territory. The former South African government made some contributions to developing Sino-South African relations. South Africa's Government of National Unity should do more than the former regime. China firmly believes that China and South Africa, as influential powers in their respective regions, have bright prospects for cooperation in politics, the economy, and international affairs. Establishing diplomatic relations as soon as possible will not only serve the fundamental interests of the Chinese and South African peoples but also help to maintain world peace and stability."

I made it clear to Nzo that China would not oppose South Africa's having economic and trade relations with Taiwan after the establishment of diplomatic relations between China and South Africa. On the contrary, China would be glad to see the development of economic and trade relations between South Africa and Taiwan as long as the relations were nongovernmental. Meanwhile, I knew that South Africa had close economic and trade relations with Hong Kong, which was South Africa's second largest investor in Asia. The sea route between South Africa and Hong Kong was of great importance to South

Africa. Therefore, I pointed out that Hong Kong, which had wide economic cooperation with South Africa, would return to China in July 1997, and we hoped that Sino-South African relations could see substantial development conducive to maintaining mutual economic interests between South Africa and Hong Kong.

Nzo said that he had obtained a clearer understanding of these issues, and would report to President Mandela and urge him to make a decision as quickly as possible.

MANDELA'S PAINFUL DECISION

FROM THE END OF APRIL to the beginning of May 1996, the Ninth Session of the UN Conference on Trade and Development in South Africa gave us an opportunity to meet South Africa's leaders. The Chinese government sent an official business and trade delegation, headed by Wu Yi, minister of Foreign Trade and Economic Cooperation, to negotiate with Mandela and Nzo.

At the meeting with Mandela, Wu Yi delivered a letter from Jiang Zemin, in which Jiang reiterated the Chinese government's basic guidelines on the Taiwan question and its principled stand on matters concerning the establishment of diplomatic relations between China and South Africa. He declared that the Chinese people were able to realize reunification independently. Wu Yi explained from an economic and trade perspective the advantages of establishing diplomatic relations. She explained, "In recent years, economic and trade relations between China and South Africa have developed without diplomatic relations or intergovernmental economic and trade agreements. The establishment of diplomatic relations between China and South Africa will lay a stable foundation and provide a good guarantee for developing all-around friendly cooperation between the two countries. Therefore, we hope that you can look into the future of the twenty-first century with your breadth of vision as a statesman and make the decision to establish diplomatic relations with China as soon as possible."

Mandela said, "Most ANC executives are in favor of South

Africa's establishing diplomatic relations with China right now. They are fully aware that China will not approve the establishment of diplomatic relations if South Africa does not sever its 'diplomatic relations' with Taiwan. But this issue requires careful consideration and cautious handling. South Africa will send delegations to Beijing and Taipei to discuss this issue. South Africa is eager to establish diplomatic relations with China as soon as possible, but we also have to give Taiwan an explanation."

On November 26, 1996, Mandela took the initiative to invite Gu Xiner, director of China's Center for South African Studies in South Africa, to lunch. Mandela said that he had decided to sever "diplomatic relations" with Taiwan and recognize the People's Republic of China before the end of 1997 and had informed Lu Yizheng, Taiwan's "ambassador" to South Africa, of his decision earlier that morning.

The next afternoon, Mandela, Nzo, and the vice foreign minister, Aziz Pahad, held a press conference to announce the decision officially. They expressed the hope of beginning negotiations on the establishment of diplomatic relations with China in January 1997.

On November 28, the spokesperson of the Chinese Ministry of Foreign Affairs stated, "We welcome President Mandela's active approach to the normalization of Sino-South African relations. China and South Africa are important countries in Asia and Africa, respectively. To normalize Sino-South African relations as soon as possible according to international practice is in the fundamental interests of the Chinese and South African peoples and will promote friendly cooperation in many fields between the two countries, including consultations and cooperation in international affairs."

Soon afterward, Taiwan's "foreign minister," Chang Hsiao-yen, hurried to Johannesburg in an attempt to retrieve the situation. He asked the South African government to reconsider its decision or defer severing "diplomatic relations" with Taiwan for three years. He also indicated that Taiwan would make a tough response if South Africa acted otherwise.

In a letter to Jiang Zemin on December 5, Mandela stated clearly: "South Africa will put an end to its 'diplomatic recognition' of Taiwan on December 31, 1997. This is an appropriate time for South Africa to abide by international practice and smoothly normalize its relations with the People's Republic of China. South Africa has severed 'diplomatic relations' with Taiwan at a huge cost, but we believe that the rapid development of South Africa's relations with the People's Republic of China will make up for possible losses."

This letter showed that normalizing its relations with China was a difficult decision for South Africa. Therefore, we grasped the opportunity and gave an active response to South Africa.

Jiang sent Mandela a long letter in reply, in which he expressed his appreciation for Mandela's decision and his wish for positive results in the forthcoming negotiations on the establishment of diplomatic relations between China and South Africa. Jiang also said, "At the turn of the century, statesmen of all countries are formulating strategies for development. I would like to discuss with you how to ensure the long-term and stable development of Sino-South African relations with all-around cooperation in the twenty-first century." In conclusion, Jiang invited Mandela to visit China again at a time convenient to him.

In late January 1997, our assistant foreign minister, Ji Peiding, paid a working visit to South Africa. His first round of talks, with South Africa's vice foreign minister, Pahad, concerned the establishment of diplomatic relations between our two countries. Ji delivered a related draft communiqué and memorandum to Pahad. Ji also met Mandela and Nzo and delivered letters to them from Jiang Zemin and myself, respectively. He also explained China's stand and principles to the speaker of the South African parliament and the leaders of all the South African political parties. The South African government reaffirmed the deadline of January 1, 1998, for the establishment of diplomatic relations with China, and basically accepted the stand proposed by China in the related documents.

Great headway was made in the first round of official diplomatic negotiations.

In a letter to Nzo, I spoke highly of South Africa's increasingly important role in African and international affairs since the birth of the new South Africa. I said, "China and South Africa share wide common interests in international affairs. China is willing to promote negotiations and cooperation between China and South Africa. The year 1997 will be crucial for the development of Sino-South African relations. To accomplish the historical mission of setting up normal diplomatic relations between China and South Africa, I invite you to visit China at your convenience in 1997."

The second round of talks started slightly later than the scheduled time. On June 8, 1997, Pahad arrived in Beijing. At the end of his four-day working visit, China and South Africa had reached an agreement on the communiqué and memorandum of understanding concerning the establishment of diplomatic relations between them and had initialed the documents.

South Africa confirmed in the documents that it would establish diplomatic relations with China no later than December 31, 1997, and made a clear commitment to sever "diplomatic relations" and all other official relations with Taiwan, abolish agreements with Taiwan, and close the Taiwanese "embassy" in South Africa. We also made provisional arrangements for South Africa's interests in Hong Kong. Until December 31, 1997, the South African consulate-general in Hong Kong would operate normally, and the civil airline flights and mutual exemption of visas between South Africa and Hong Kong would remain unchanged for the time being. China also allowed South African airlines to fly through China's airspace en route to Japan. The South African government expressed satisfaction with these arrangements.

In September 1997, I attended the UN General Assembly in New York and met Nzo at the UN headquarters. The atmosphere was relaxed and pleasant, since the fundamental matters concerning the establishment of diplomatic relations between China and South Africa had been settled. We discussed some concrete issues, such as the specific arrangements for the normalization of Sino-South African relations, exchanges and cooperation in bilateral relations, and the site of the future embassy of South Africa in China.

Nzo said, "South Africa's decision is irreversible. Specific procedures are now needed to ensure the establishment of diplomatic relations between our two countries by the end of this year. The Chinese and South African foreign ministers will sign the documents. The only problem is finding a convenient time for both countries. If you can come to South Africa to sign the documents, you will receive a warm welcome."

China and South Africa Set Up Full Ties

ON DECEMBER 28, 1997, I began an official visit to South Africa at Nzo's invitation. On December 30, I signed the communiqué and memorandum of understanding on the establishment of diplomatic relations between China and South Africa. According to the documents, diplomatic relations officially began on January 1, 1998.

I arrived in Cape Town when Mandela was on vacation in another city. But he returned home especially to meet me and treated me to a banquet. Mandela said that my first official visit to South Africa was of great significance, and that South Africa hoped to form a "strategic partnership" with China. He recollected the contacts between Chinese and South African leaders in the 1950s and 1960s. Mandela cherished the memory of the Chinese leaders of the older generation, such as Mao Zedong, Zhou Enlai, and Liu Shaoqi, and showed great respect for them.

Referring to the establishment of diplomatic relations between China and South Africa, Mandela said, "All the ANC leaders except me agreed to establish diplomatic relations with China as soon as possible when we discussed this issue. Probably I was more patient than they were, since I was senior in age. As Sino-South African relations have been established, we must let bygones be bygones."

On New Year's Day 1998, Sino-South African relations were officially established, and the opening ceremony for the Chinese embassy in the Republic of South Africa was held. The embassy was a two-story office building situated in the No. 972 courtyard on Pretorius Street, Pretoria. Over 300 people—including Nzo, well-known figures from all walks of life in South Africa, representatives of Chinese

South Africans and overseas Chinese, and the entire staff of the Chinese embassy in South Africa—attended the opening ceremony. Many people spent the first holiday of the new year participating in this historic event.

At nine o'clock that morning, I announced the official opening of the embassy. Then I delivered a speech of congratulations and unveiled the embassy's nameplate. The red five-star flag rose slowly, to the majestic strains of the "March of the Volunteers." People offered congratulations to each other, and the whole courtyard became a scene of jubilation.

Nzo, who had made painstaking efforts to establish diplomatic relations between China and South Africa, was especially happy and offered me warm congratulations on behalf of the South African government.

The establishment of diplomatic relations between China and South Africa received a warm response from people of all circles in South Africa. The ANC took the lead, making a statement that paid tribute to Mandela's decision to sever "diplomatic relations" with Taiwan and establish diplomatic relations with the People's Republic of China; the conservative Democratic Party also considered the establishment of diplomatic relations between South Africa and the People's Republic of China inevitable in view of the international political realities and South Africa's long-term economic interests. The influential newspaper *The Star* published an editorial, "Eventual One-China Policy." This editorial pointed out that the great potential of China's market and the political influence of China as a permanent member of the UN Security Council had long since won the world's recognition of the correctness of the "one China" policy, and South Africa had no other choice but to follow the world trend.

The establishment of diplomatic relations between China and South Africa also earned wide praise from the international community and was acclaimed by many African countries as a significant victory for China's diplomacy. It was of great importance not only for Sino-South African relations but also for Sino-African relations. South Africa had acquired a new and powerful political ally and an indispensable economic partner. Some of the media noted that Taiwan's diplomacy had been dealt another heavy blow, as Taiwan had lost the largest country that had diplomatic relations with it, as well as major diplomatic support in Africa.

During the year from Mandela's announcement of his decision to establish diplomatic relations with China, on November 27, 1996, to the closing of the Taiwanese "embassy" in South Africa, Taiwan's diplomatic organs and their staff had been shrouded in an atmosphere of desolation. The seventy-three-year-old Lu Yizheng, a noted Taiwanese diplomat, had been assigned key posts by all four of Taiwan's leaders thus far—Chiang Kai-shek, Chiang Ching-kuo, Yen Chia-kan, and Lee Teng-hui. His desperate attempt to prevent South Africa from establishing diplomatic relations with China turned out to be a failure.

This is the irreversible trend of the world today.

9 TWO DIPLOMATIC STRUGGLES OVER THE TAIWAN QUESTION

All the big powers in the world promise to pursue the "one China" policy, but the Taiwan question has always been a focus of China's diplomatic struggles. At the instigation of various anti-China forces, some countries break their promises. For example, from 1991 to 1992 France sold armaments to Taiwan; and in 1995 the United States permitted a visit by Lee Teng-hui, head of the Taiwan authorities, which caused diplomatic conflicts.

FRANCE SELLS ARMAMENTS TO TAIWAN

TROUBLE AT A COCKTAIL PARTY

FRANCE WAS THE FIRST WESTERN country to establish diplomatic relations with China, and during the first forty years thereafter the relations between China and France were smooth. However, in the early 1990s France sold armaments to Taiwan on two occasions, making Sino-French relations tense and seriously damaging the long-term friendship.

In April 1991, the French foreign minister, Roland Dumas, visited

China. He was the highest-ranking official of the French government to visit China after the political turmoil in Beijing in 1989, and we gave him a high-level reception. General Secretary Jiang Zemin and Premier Li Peng met with him separately, and I had a long conversation with him. Relations between China and France seemed to be improving.

But, unexpectedly, at a cocktail party held by the French ambassador to China, Claude Martin, Dumas asked me for a private conversation. To my surprise, he said that France intended to sell escort vessels to Taiwan.

In 1989, China had managed, with difficulty, to stop France from selling armaments to Taiwan, and on January 6, 1990, Dumas in person had promised the Chinese ambassador to France, Zhou Jue: "The French president himself has decided that France will never again attempt to sell arms to Taiwan."

Now it was only one year later, and relations between China and France were improving, so why should Dumas break his promise?

As a foreign minister, Dumas knew the sensitivity and seriousness of the issue, and he also knew China's firm position on it. Before Dumas's visit, France had let out no information about this; nor did Dumas mention it in his formal talks with me. The purpose, of course, was to avoid a face-to-face conflict. He obviously thought that the relaxed atmosphere of the cocktail party would be a more suitable environment in which to bring up the issue.

Dumas now said that as the international situation changed, every country was adjusting its policy toward Taiwan. France was preparing to cooperate with Taiwan in environmental protection, sewage disposal, high-speed trains, escort vessels, and other projects. However, France would not sell Taiwan offensive weapons such as fighter planes. But this latter assurance was obviously dubious.

Dumas went on to say that escort vessels were defensive, not offensive, and were an important business for French shipbuilders. In addition, the United States had sold four escort vessels to Taiwan, and France did not see why the United States should get all the advantages of this trade.

Though the cocktail party was not the place for a debate, I still felt it necessary to make clear China's firm stand on this issue. I said that China had a clear and principled stand: we did not oppose France's doing business with Taiwan, but the sale of armaments to Taiwan affected China's sovereignty and security. As for the sales by the United States, it was a historical practice. The United States had troops stationed in Taiwan and had a military treaty with it. When China and the United States established diplomatic relations, they had reached an agreement that the United States should sever its diplomatic relations with Taiwan, abrogate the military treaty, and pull its troops out of Taiwan. After negotiations lasting from 1979 to 1982, China and the United States had agreed that the United States would reduce its sales of armaments to Taiwan year by year, until finally such sales stopped altogether.

Still, Dumas argued that if the United States could continue selling arms to Taiwan after establishing diplomatic relations with China, why couldn't France, which had recognized China much earlier than the United States had?

What Dumas said made me feel that he had intentionally arranged to confront me at the cocktail party—that this was not just an offhand inquiry. The relaxed atmosphere of the party could not disguise the seriousness of the problem. Later, it became known that Dumas had indeed had a thorough discussion with President François Mitterrand about this matter.

I gave instructions to the Chinese embassy in Paris and to the Ministry of Foreign Affairs to start formal negotiations with France. On May 7, 1991, the Chinese ambassador to France, Cai Fangbai, requested an urgent appointment with Jean-Louis Bianco, the secretary general of the official residence of the President of France; Edouard Ripert, the foreign policy adviser to the prime minister; and François Scheer, the secretary general of the Ministry of Foreign Affairs, to set in motion formal negotiations concerning France's bid to sell warships to Taiwan.

On May 9, the director general of the Department of Western European Affairs at the Chinese Ministry of Foreign Affairs, Yang

Guirong, urgently requested an appointment with Gerard Chesnel, minister-counselor of the French embassy in China. On May 17, Jiang Enzhu, assistant Chinese foreign minister, met Claude Martin, the French ambassador to China, to discuss the same topic and request that France keep the promise made by Dumas in 1990 not to sell warships to Taiwan.

The French officials' responses were almost identical. First, they stressed the economic benefits to France of the sale of the warships. Then they claimed that escort vessels were merely defensive, and not a threat to China's mainland. They again argued that if the United States could sell armaments to Taiwan, why should France not do likewise? Finally, they argued that the sale was only proposed, not a final decision.

On June 1, 1991, Premier Li Peng met with and held a banquet for the chairman of the French company GEC Alsthom, Jean-Pierre Degeorges, and Degeorges's party. Li asked Degeorges to inform the French leaders that China attached importance to Sino-French relations but firmly opposed France's selling armaments to Taiwan.

Premier Li also said that China did not object if Western European countries, including France, developed economic and trade relations with Taiwan, but such contacts could only be nongovernmental, and the sale of arms or ammunition to Taiwan infringed on China's sovereignty.

Degeorges recalled afterward that immediately after the banquet he reported the details of his talk with Li to the French government.

However, the situation then took a sudden turn for the worse.

On June 6, 1991, Dumas wrote a letter to me, informing me that the French government had decided not to oppose efforts by French businessmen to sell escort vessels to Taiwan, but such negotiations should be restricted to naval vessels and equipment, excluding armaments. France had made this decision, the letter said, after careful consideration and while taking account of China's reasonable concerns about its security. This was a purely commercial undertaking, and had nothing to do with official relations with the Taiwan authorities. The French government emphasized that this decision would not undermine its consistent policy of recognizing the Beijing government as the sole legal government of China.

The Case of the Lafayette-Class Frigates

WHY HAD THE SAME PRESIDENT, the same foreign minister, and the same socialist government gone back on the promise made just a year before not to sell warships to Taiwan?

Only thirty-six days had elapsed from the time when Dumas mentioned the matter to me to the time when he wrote the letter notifying me of the French government's decision. Clearly, the French government was eager to get these sales for France's shipbuilders. This was an important decision. The French leaders were well aware of China's strong opposition to it and knew that it would jeopardize relations between our two countries. Why on earth should the French government have made the decision so hastily?

To be frank, we were not certain at that time. However, we felt that something was fishy. Much later, we found out that behind the issue was a scandal that concerning French escort vessels of the Lafayette class—a scandal that is not yet entirely clear today.

At the end of 1993, a body was found floating in the sea off Taiwan. It turned out to be that of Yin Qingfeng, a captain in Taiwan's navy. Yin had gone to France in September 1993 to examine Lafayette-class escort vessels, with a view to purchasing some; but he found thirty-four deficiencies in them and therefore opposed the deal. On December 9, 1993, he vanished.

After Yin's death, both Taiwan and France set up special organizations to investigate the case, which evidently involved a large amount of money and many high-ranking Taiwan and French officials. The Taiwan media revealed that in 1991 France had sold six Lafayette-class escort vessels to Taiwan, at a cost of 16 billion francs (about US$2.7 billion)—more than three times as much as Singapore had spent on the same number of vessels. In 2001, Dumas told the French newspaper *Le Figaro* that there had been a secret commission for the sale of the Lafayette-class frigates to Taiwan, amounting to

US$500 million, from which many French politicians benefited. In January 2001, Dumas himself was given a suspended sentence of two years in prison for his involvement in the scandal.

Christine Deviers-Joncour, who was said to have been Dumas's mistress when he was the French foreign minister, had been working as a special public relations adviser to the Elf Oil Company of France in 1991. According to reports in the French media, in order to smooth the way for selling warships to Taiwan, the Thomson Company, the manufacturer of the Lafayette-class vessels, gave Elf US$6 million to get Deviers-Joncour to persuade Dumas to support the deal.

Nobody knows whether it was the woman or the money that finally worked. We do know that that stately-looking Dumas was sued by many people because of the scandal. In January 2003, he was cleared by the Appeals Court in Paris. But Deviers-Joncour was sentenced to two and a half years in prison for her involvement in the case.

Meanwhile, the Taiwan media revealed that, besides Yin Qingfeng, at least seven people who knew the inside story had died in mysterious circumstances, among them information officers, government officials, and bankers.

Hao Baicun, who was then Taiwan's "chief of the general staff," disclosed in his published diary that some high-level figures in Taiwan had been involved in the scandal.

Lee Teng-hui, who was "president" of Taiwan during this period, claimed in November 2001, when questioned about the case, that the purchase of the Lafayette-class frigates had been decided without his knowledge by Hao Baicun and the head of Taiwan's navy, Ye Changtong. Lee also said that if he had refused to approve this deal, Taiwan would "certainly have had a mutiny."

What role did Lee Teng-hui play in this fraud? I believe that time will tell.

Negotiations Between China and France

IN VIEW OF DUMAS'S PROMISES made in his letter to me of June 6 concerning the sale of the Lafayette-class vessels, we proposed to the French government to hold consultations on the matter.

Of course, we knew that consultations would not make France change its decision. But we would be able to present our position again and point out advantages and disadvantages so as to prevent the French government from going too far. We could also discuss some technical measures and try our best to reduce the damage to Sino-French relations.

On June 7, Jiang Engzhu, the assistant foreign minister, met the French ambassador, Martin. Jiang expressed astonishment at the French government's decision and asked France to oppose the sale. He suggested that our two countries begin negotiations on this problem as soon as possible. To ensure that the negotiations would go smoothly, China asked France not to publicize the issue of selling warships to Taiwan during the talks.

On the same day, the Chinese ambassador to France, Cai Fangbai, made the same proposal to Bernard Kessedjian, chief of the Office of the French Ministry of Foreign Affairs.

France at first refused to consult with China, saying that "a decision has been made and there is no need to talk." France was worried that the pressure of negotiations might lose it an arms deal worth over US$2 billion. At the same time, though, it was afraid to confront China. A confrontation would set back relations between the two countries, and such a setback would not accord with France's interests. Therefore, on June 11 France agreed to negotiations on the issue.

On June 25, 1991, China's vice foreign minister, Tian Zengpei, led a Chinese contingent to Paris. In the subsequent negotiations, we tried to persuade France to halt the arms sale to Taiwan, but its attitude was tough and stubborn.

In these circumstances, the consultations focused mainly on how to control and reduce the negative effects caused by France's decision.

China asked the French government to publish a communiqué and restate its policies on Chinese affairs, especially regarding Taiwan, when it announced its authorization of the sale.

France agreed to publish a communiqué stating, "The French government has decided to allow French industrialists to negotiate with Taiwan about selling escort vessels not equipped with armaments. This is a purely commercial trade and does not imply any official relations with the Taiwan authorities. The French government took into consideration China's concern for its security and territorial integrity when making this decision. France reaffirms the Sino-French Joint Statement of January 1964 that the government of the People's Republic of China is the sole legal government of China. France will continue to devote efforts to developing its friendly relations with the PRC government in all fields."

In addition, when Dumas met Tian on July 4, he reconfirmed orally the principles of relations between France and Taiwan: "Taiwan is part of China's territory. France will not change its stand; that is to say, will never have any official relations or official contacts with Taiwan. France has no intention of influencing the security situation of the Taiwan Strait when French firms trade with the island."

Through hard negotiations, we reached a "minimum understanding" with France, and we imposed some restrictions on its sale of armaments to Taiwan. Our purpose was to stabilize Sino-French relations and avoid an overall setback. This was of great importance for improving relations between China and the Western powers and was also an effective way to stop Taiwan's "pragmatic diplomacy." At the same time, through these negotiations, China confirmed its firm opposition to the sale of armaments to Taiwan and left some room for responding appropriately if necessary.

RESELLING MIRAGE FIGHTERS

THE FRENCH GOVERNMENT at that time obviously underestimated China's principled stand and the limits of tolerance, as another incident involving sales of arms to Taiwan soured relations between China and France.

On January 31, 1992, Dumas met me at the UN Security Council. He mentioned that France was thinking of selling Mirage-2000 fighter planes to Taiwan. This was less than half a year after he had made promises in this regard to Tian Zengpei (on July 4, 1991) and the French Ministry of Foreign Affairs had published its communiqué (on August 27, 1991).

When France had sold Taiwan the warships, it had claimed that escort vessels were merely defensive. But by no stretch of the imagination can Mirage-2000 fighter planes be regarded as anything but offensive. This time the French government even ignored its earlier excuse.

China immediately took several measures. First, we approached the French side, pointing out the seriousness of this matter. Second, responding to France's claim that its trade with China was "extremely unbalanced in favor of China," we dispatched an economic and commercial delegation to France, offering to purchase French commodities worth US$2 billion if France gave up the idea of selling Mirage fighters to Taiwan. The delegation also provided a list of fifty cooperative projects in eight categories, with a total value of US$15.4 billion.

However, all these efforts were in vain. On November 18, 1992, Agence France-Presse reported that France and Taiwan had signed a contract for the sale of sixty Mirage 2000-V fighter planes, although neither side had made a formal announcement of the fact.

Not until December 22 did France give the Chinese embassy in France a formal response: although the French government had decided to allow the sale of sixty Mirage 2000-V fighters, the fighters had been modified so that they were purely defensive—they had no in-flight refueling devices and no air-to-surface guided missiles—and would not threaten China's territorial integrity or security.

France also argued that the contract with Taiwan was ordinary commercial practice and that France opposed all market restrictions.

It argued again that if the United States could sell armaments to Taiwan, why couldn't France? Besides, France had a huge trade deficit in China; and the French aviation industry was in difficulties and needed the sale.

At that time, the French government—that of the Socialist Party—was facing a general election, and it had few achievements to show for its term in office. The party would trumpet as an "outstanding achievement" the nearly US$4 billion that the French aircraft industry would earn from the sale of the Mirage fighters to Taiwan. Moreover, China's conciliatory response on French sales of warships was taken as a sign of weakness on the part of China, and the French government thought that China would not protest very strongly.

That turned out to be wishful thinking. China's response was swift and severe.

The Chinese government canceled some of the proposed large-scale cooperative projects with France, such as the Guangzhou subway, the second phase of the Dayawan Nuclear Power Plant Project, and the purchase of French wheat. There would be no further discussions about new important economic or commercial cooperative projects with France. Strict controls were put on contacts between officials of the two countries above the vice-ministerial level, and the French consulate general in Guangzhou was closed immediately. These diplomatic moves shocked the French Socialist Party government.

Making a Fresh Start

IN MARCH 1993, the French right-wing Rally for the Republic was elected, replacing the Socialist Party. The new government immediately began to seek an improvement in France's relations with China.

On May 5, the new French foreign minister, Alain Juppé, wrote to me as follows: "The new French government leaders think it necessary to start considering the status of Sino-French relations immediately. This thinking comes from our friendly consideration for China, which naturally hopes for unity and national development, our full

recognition of the important role that your honored country is playing and will continue to play in the world, and the desire to restore
our two countries' relations on the basis of mutual respect and trust."

The French prime minister, Édouard Balladur, wrote a letter to
Premier Li Peng of China on June 1, expressing the hope that France
would send an envoy to discuss reconciliation.

Among the problems between our two countries, the most important one was how to treat the arms sales to Taiwan allowed by the
former French government and how the new French government
would deal with the matter of selling armaments to Taiwan. If those
two issues were appropriately resolved, there would be good
prospects for the broad development of Sino-French relations.

Balladur sent Jacques Friedman as his envoy in July and December of 1993 to negotiate about these matters with China. Friedman
was not a government official but a director of the French Alliance
Insurance Company at that time. He was a former classmate as well
as a close friend of President Jacques Chirac and also a close friend of
Balladur. When Balladur was the minister of Economy, Finance and
Privatization, Friedman had worked as his commissioner. Friedman
kept a low profile and was a prudent man.

After secret negotiations lasting half a year, the two countries
reached an agreement on normalizing their relations. On December
28, Minister Jiang Enzhu (China's vice foreign minister) and Friedman initialed a Joint Communiqué of the Governments of the People's Republic of China and the Republic of France. The most
important sentence in the communiqué was this: "The French government promises that it will not authorize French enterprises to
participate in arming Taiwan from now on."

The communiqué did not mention the problem of the former
French government's having allowed arms sales to Taiwan and
France promised not to sell armaments to Taiwan in the future. On
this point, the two sides had engaged in very tough negotiations. The
French said that the new government disagreed with the former government's practice of selling weapons to Taiwan. Although the
signed contract had to be implemented, the new French government

would impose restrictions on the sale. For instance, it would not sell fifteen training planes for instructing the pilots of the Mirage fighters. The Chinese side had tried to persuade the new French government to annul the contract for the sale of armaments to Taiwan; but what was more important was halting future sales by France, and preventing other European countries from following France's earlier example.

Exchange of Letters between Foreign Ministers

ON JANUARY 3, 1994, Juppé sent me a letter of confirmation: "The French government promises to stop authorizing the sale of arms to Taiwan." Enclosed was a list of equipment the French government strictly forbade for sale to Taiwan—such as armored vehicles, cannons, submarines, warships, fighter planes, military helicopters, ground-to-air missiles, and air-to-ground missiles—with detailed explanations.

On January 5, I replied to Juppé, confirming the Joint Communiqué that both sides had agreed on.

On January 12, China and France published the Joint Communiqué, and Sino-French relations returned to normal. Officials above the vice-ministerial level resumed contacts, and French enterprises were once more able to compete in the Chinese market, like other foreign companies. Some large-scale cooperative projects that had been suspended could now continue. However, China placed strict sanctions on the four French companies that had directly participated in selling armaments to Taiwan.

From January 22 to 24, 1994, I paid a formal visit to France. Originally, I had no plan to visit France—I was simply to meet the U.S. secretary of state, Warren Christopher, in Paris on my way back from Africa. However as soon as France learned of this, I was invited for a formal visit, including meeting French leaders.

During my stay in Paris, I was met by the French president and prime minister and had talks with the foreign minister.

Mitterrand regarded himself as a defender of human rights and was very arrogant. So far, every time he met me, he had talked about human rights. But this time, he stood at the door waiting for me and was very modest and polite. During the meeting he avoided his favorite topic, instead talking about how he admired the striking speed of Chinese economic development and the ability of the Chinese leaders to govern a large country with a huge population.

When I left Élysée Palace, some reporters asked loudly, "What did you say about the human rights issue to President Mitterrand?" I replied, "We did not mention the issue." The reporters looked surprised.

UNITED STATES PERMITS VISIT BY LEE TENG-HUI

THE UNITED STATES BREAKS ITS PROMISE

ON MAY 22, 1995, the president of the United States, Bill Clinton, gave his permission for Lee Teng-hui, the head of the Taiwan authorities, to pay an "unofficial and personal visit" to the United States during the first week of June of that year, and to attend a graduation ceremony at Cornell University. Only one month earlier, Warren Christopher had assured me that no such visit would be allowed.

Though Li Daoyu, the Chinese ambassador to the United States, had been notified of this decision two days beforehand by the national security adviser, Anthony Lake, and the assistant secretary of state, Peter Tarnoff—this announcement was still shocking. To repeat, Christopher had promised me in person that the United States would not allow Lee Teng-hui to visit.

In mid-April 1995, I went to New York to attend the Review and Extension Conference of the Treaty on the Nonproliferation of Nuclear Weapons. On April 17, at the request of the United States, I conferred with Christopher at the Waldorf Hotel. He had stated clearly that the United States would not allow Lee Teng-hui to visit, because such a visit did not accord with the unofficial relations between the

United States and Taiwan. At the most, he said, the United States would consider extending Lee Teng-hui's transit visa.

Lee Teng-hui's first place of transit in the United States was Hawaii. At that time, the United States permitted him only to stay at the airport. He was very angry about this. He was wearing pajamas and did not get off the plane.

On June 7, Christopher wrote to me, saying that the Senate and House of Representatives had approved a bill by an overwhelming majority to permit Lee Teng-hui to visit the United States. In these circumstances, he said, "the president's consideration is to gain the initiative to prevent the passing of a law which might make U.S.-Taiwan relations seem to be official." However, the so-called solution passed by Congress was only a show of intention. The actual power to issue the visa was still in the hands of the administration. Christopher's comment was, therefore, mere sophistry, meant to conceal the administration's insincerity.

At that time, Lee Teng-hui was promoting his bid to become Taiwan's "directly elected president." He spent a great deal of money, hiring an American public relations firm—Cassidy and Associates—to lobby American senators.

Supporting the Taiwan regime in order to keep China off-balance has been an established policy of every American administration; it only differs in form and degree depending on the different historical backgrounds. After the cold war ended, some people in Western academic circles thought that because the Soviet Union and the eastern European bloc had fallen apart, the strategic bond between China and the United States no longer existed. Some of them even thought that China would become a rival of the United States, replacing the Soviet Union. Therefore, they advocated a "strategic containment" of China. In particular, Gerald Segal, at the International Institute for Strategic Studies in London, became notorious for concocting the "China Threat." When he first published an article on this, in early 1995, he proposed "constraining China by using Taiwan." He said that the problems of human rights and most-favored-nation treatment could not hold China back, and that only Taiwan could get on China's nerves. Also, at this time, under pressure from the international anti-China forces, the American government wanted to test China's tolerance regarding Taiwan.

According to U.S. newspapers and magazines, every year Taiwan spends millions of dollars trying to boost its image with the American public. In 1994, it signed a three-year, $4.5 million contract with Cassidy and Associates just to have them canvass for Lee Teng-hui's visit to the United States. Moreover, Taiwan spares no expense to invite American government officials at all levels to visit; and it offers substantial funds to American think tanks, universities, and research institutes to influence public opinion and official decision making. In 1994, Taiwan donated $4.5 million to Cornell University in the name of Lee Teng-hui. Apparently, Lee Teng-hui thought that money could buy anything. He even claimed publicly, on his way back to Taiwan from the United States, that he could buy Taiwan's membership in the UN for US$1 billion.

CHINA FIGHTS BACK

BY ALLOWING LEE TENG-HUI to visit the United States, ending a seventeen-year ban, Clinton damaged the political base of Sino-American relations; encouraged the Taiwan authorities to pursue their policy of "two Chinas" and "one China, one Taiwan"; and reinforced the arrogance of the Taiwan authorities and the international anti-China movement.

Facing this diplomatic challenge from the United States, the Chinese government had to counterattack.

On May 23, as vice premier of the State Council and foreign minister, I summoned the U.S. ambassador, Stapleton Roy, and lodged a strong protest against Lee Teng-hui's proposed visit. On the same day, the Ministry of Foreign Affairs, the Committee of Foreign Affairs of the National People's Congress, and the Committee of Foreign Affairs of the Chinese People's Political Consultative Conference all issued statements condemning and protesting the United States' action.

On May 26, the Ministry of Foreign Affairs announced that the Chinese government had decided to delay a visit by Chi Haotian, State Councillor and minister of national defense, to the United States, originally scheduled for June. At the same time, Li Guixian, State Councillor, and Yu Zhenwu, commander of the People's Liberation Army (PLA) Air Force, also canceled their visits to the United States.

On May 28, the Chinese government decided to suspend consultations between Chinese and American experts on the Missile Technology Control Regime (MTCR) and nuclear cooperation. Also, delays were requested for the visits to China of the director of the U.S. Arms Control and Disarmament Agency and the deputy assistant secretary of state for political and military affairs, scheduled for June and July, respectively. All meetings of high-ranking officials at the vice-ministerial level or above and some important bilateral consultations were canceled.

On June 16, the Chinese ambassador to the United States, Li Daoyu, informed the U.S. government that he had been summoned to return to China for consultations because of Lee Teng-hui's visit.

In July 1995, China carried out two large-scale missile tests; in March 1996 it delayed the second round of talks between Wang Daohan, head of its Association for Relations Across the Taiwan Straits, and Koo Chenfu, president of the Strait Exchange Foundation in Taiwan.

The measures brought the debate on the United States' policy toward China to a climax. The result was that the two major U.S. political parties reached a common understanding: China's rise and development could not be held up. To "isolate" and "contain" China was not the best policy. Only keeping in contact with China corresponded with the United States' long-term interests.

Repair Efforts

on june 7, 1995, the day Lee Teng-hui began his visit to the United States, Warren Christopher sent me a letter stating that Lee's visit was "purely personal." No officials of the administration would meet him, and Lee would not be allowed to engage in any official activity. I did not reply to his letter.

From June 7 to 11, Lee stopped in Los Angeles, Syracuse, New York (about one hour's drive from Cornell University), and in Anchorage, Alaska. On June 9 at Cornell University, Lee made a highly political speech, "The People's Wishes Are Always in My Mind," publicizing the "Taiwan experience" and declaring that Taiwan was "breaking out of its diplomatic isolation" and strengthening its relations with the United States.

Still, the U.S. government did take some measures to keep Lee's visit "unofficial." Lee was met only by local officials on his stopovers; no U.S. state officials or governors met him. In addition, Lee was not allowed to stop in New York, the flag of Taiwan was not allowed to be flown, and its anthem was not allowed to be played. Furthermore, a news conference Lee had been scheduled to give at Cornell University was canceled, and his wife was not allowed to visit the White House.

As Lee was arriving at Cornell University, on the afternoon of June 8, President Clinton met Ambassador Li Daoyu at the White House. In their meeting, Clinton reaffirmed the United States' "one China" policy, which precluded "two Chinas" and "one China, one Taiwan." Clinton also said that no matter how Taiwan publicized it, Lee's visit to the United States was unofficial and personal, and in no way signified that the U.S. government recognized Taiwan. He stressed that the United States would continue to seek a constructive relationship with China and would maintain its current policy on China.

Departing from the usual custom, Clinton arranged for the media to photograph the meeting to highlight the conciliatory atmosphere.

However, these steps were not enough to dispel the cloud of suspicion that had settled over Sino-American relations. Nor did they give China a clear answer as to how the U.S. government would deal with such issues in the future. Ambassador Li Daoyu told Clinton on the spot that China could not accept his explanations.

Christopher Casts Bait

IN EARLY AUGUST 1995, the Twenty-eighth ASEAN Ministerial Conference and the ASEAN Regional Forum were held in Bandar Seri Begawan, the capital of Brunei. As "dialogue members" of these two conferences, China and the United States were in attendance. Warren Christopher asked to meet me during the conferences and said that he carried an important letter from President Clinton for President Jiang Zemin.

On July 28, before going to Brunei, Christopher gave a speech at the American Press Club. He talked about the situation in Asia, concentrating on China's importance. He said that the United States would stick to its "one China" policy, recognizing the People's Republic of China as the sole legal government. He reiterated that the United States did not support the concept of "two Chinas" or Taiwan's admission into the UN, etc.

At that time, contact between high-level officials of China and the United States had not been restored and the sanctions against China were still in place, yet in pursuance of our principle of practicing diplomacy on just grounds, to our advantage and with restraint, I agreed to meet Christopher. On the afternoon of August 1, at the International Conference Center in Bandar Seri Begawan, I met him for about one hour. He first handed me President Clinton's letter to President Jiang Zemin. The letter mentioned that the United States continued to pursue its "one China" policy, observe the three Joint Communiqués, and oppose the concepts of "two Chinas" and "one China, one Taiwan," as well as Taiwan's independence and its admission to the UN. But it did not mention how to deal with the problem of visits to the United States by official figures from Taiwan.

Stressing that the United States hoped to establish an equal partnership with China, Christopher said that Clinton wanted to invite Jiang to visit Washington in the near future. He gave no details of the time and form of the visit. Apparently, Christopher wanted to use this bait to persuade me to agree to resume dialogues, consultations, and high-level contacts between China and the United States.

China was most concerned about how the United States would deal with the problem of visits to the United States by Taiwan officials. As I have just mentioned, Christopher made no clear comment on this, so I myself gave no positive response to his suggestions. However, I agreed that the United States could dispatch its deputy secretary of state, Peter Tarnoff, to Beijing to negotiate with the vice foreign minister, Li Zhaoxing.

Tarnoff visited Beijing from August 24 to 27 and talked with Li Zhaoxing about improving Sino-American relations. Tarnoff reported several restrictions that the United States had imposed on future visits by Taiwan officials. First, such visits must be personal and unofficial and must have no political purpose. Second, the visits must be devoid of protocol and of any symbols that might be seen as having political connotations. Third, such visits should be few, should be allowed only in special circumstances, and should be approved case by case.

As these criteria basically met the Chinese government's serious concerns, the central leadership decided to restore gradually high-level contacts between China and the United States.

In October 1995, after attending the ceremonies for the fiftieth anniversary of the UN, President Jiang Zemin had a formal meeting with Clinton in New York. The U.S. side intended to invite Jiang to Washington. But it claimed that it was difficult to arrange a "formal state visit" for Jiang, so it proposed a "formal working visit." The main difference between a working visit and a state visit is that for the former, there is no welcoming ceremony; nor is there a twenty-one-gun salute on the South Lawn at the White House. Generally, there are two reasons for a working visit. One is that both sides need to talk about some important and urgent topics, but there is no time to arrange a formal state visit. If the content of the visit is simple and the visit is to be short, the ceremony can be simplified. The second reason is that the relations between the two sides are not good enough for top-level protocol, but they need to maintain working relations. The form of the visit demonstrates this relationship. Jiang's visit was the first for a top Chinese leader since 1985, and it had great significance for the reconciliation between China and the United States. It should, therefore, have been a formal state visit in content and form. When the United States refused to arrange a formal state visit, this meant that its government lacked the political will to move forward on improving and developing relations with China. To break this deadlock, we proposed that the two leaders hold a meeting in New York.

The New York Summit

ON OCTOBER 24, 1995, the leaders of China and the United States held a conference at Lincoln Center in New York and reached a strategic consensus on developing Sino-American relations. This conference paved the way for the future restoration and development of those relations.

At the conference, Clinton agreed with Jiang's suggestion that in the new century, the two countries should improve their relations at the level of overall strategy. They agreed that between such large countries, isolation, containment, and confrontation were out of the question; the only correct choice was to keep up constructive contacts.

Regarding the Taiwan question, Clinton said that the United States strictly observed the three Joint Communiqués, recognized that there was only one China, that Taiwan was part of China, and that the government of the People's Republic of China was the sole legal government of China. The United States hoped that the question of Taiwan would not become a source of division between the two countries.

Warren Christopher, who was present, explained that visits by leaders of Taiwan would be "private, unofficial, and rare, and would be dealt with on a case-by-case basis." But at the same time, he hinted that the United States could not completely rule out the possibility of such visits in the future.

Addressing the United States' proposal to resume consultations on nonproliferation of missiles, on cooperation in the peaceful utilization of nuclear power, and on arms and export control, I suggested that such consultations should include China's most serious concern: the problem of the United States' selling arms to Taiwan.

The Chinese ambassador to the United States, Li Daoyu, who had been recalled, accompanied President Jiang to the New York summit and returned to his post afterward. This signified an improvement in relations between China and the United States.

Thereafter, high-level visits and political consultations between China and the United States were gradually resumed. The Chinese minister of national defense and minister of justice visited the United States in 1996. The political disturbance caused by Lee Teng-hui's visit was almost over.

CLINTON'S "THREE NOS"

THROUGH THIS STRUGGLE, the Clinton administration clearly realized that Taiwan was a sensitive issue, and that Sino-American relations were important. Consequently, those relations began to develop comparatively smoothly and were even upgraded in Clinton's second term.

In 1997, President Jiang Zemin paid a state visit to the United States.

In 1998, Clinton paid a formal visit to China, and publicly elaborated the United States' "three nos" policy regarding Taiwan. That was on the morning of June 30, when Clinton and his wife were holding a roundtable conference with the people's representatives in the Shanghai Library. The "three nos" policy consisted of no support for Taiwan's independence; no support for "two Chinas" or "one China, one Taiwan"; and no support for Taiwan's entry into any international organization joined by sovereign states. This was the first time a president of the United States had made the three promises publicly.

10 THE RETURN OF HONG KONG AND MACAO

The return of Hong Kong and Macao to China was an important component of national reunification, a cause for which several generations of Chinese people had struggled bravely. The course of the return was a long one. I felt honored to witness it, and even more honored to be involved in the process. In my tenure as foreign minister, which was in the later part of the transitional period, I participated in the diplomatic negotiations and presided over the preparations for establishing the special administrative regions of Hong Kong and Macao. In my diplomatic career, that was a very rare and unique experience.

THE CONTEST BETWEEN CHINA AND THE UK IN THE RETURN OF HONG KONG

THE TRANSITIONAL PERIOD

THE RETURN OF HONG KONG to China was first and foremost a diplomatic question. The recovery of part of the motherland's territory from foreign occupiers through peaceful means necessitated diplomatic negotiations.

There was a very long transitional period from the agreement on the principles of the return to the transfer of government. During that period, the UK needed to ensure that Hong Kong's daily administration would be conducted properly and that local stability and prosperity would be maintained. China had to formulate a series of specific practical policies for a special administrative region after the handover in accordance with the agreement between the two sides so as to put into effect the policy of "one country, two systems" and ensure Hong Kong's long-term stability and prosperity.

In the long transitional period, diplomatic negotiations covering various fields were needed to implement the agreements and to fulfill the promises of both sides. China's policy was to cooperate but not interfere with the daily administration of Hong Kong in the transitional period; China had the right to discuss and even participate in affairs related to the return of Hong Kong and to the rights and interests of the future special administrative region.

Deng Xiaoping sagaciously perceived that a smooth handover depended on whether stability could be maintained in the transitional period so that the question of Hong Kong could be resolved according to the concept of "one country, two systems."

At that time, we had a great deal of confidence in the prospects for Hong Kong but we also had concerns about whether the territory could be kept stable during the long transitional period. We hoped that there would be no twists and turns that might harm the long-term stability and prosperity of Hong Kong.

TROUBLED COOPERATION

DURING THE DIPLOMATIC consultations on the return of Hong Kong to China, there was a "honeymoon period" between China and the UK, when both sides cooperated very smoothly. In 1988, when I started to participate directly in the consultations, this honeymoon period was not yet over.

At that time, the two countries had signed the Sino-British Joint

Declaration on the Question of Hong Kong, and the transitional period had begun. The atmosphere at our conferences was good. When there was a disagreement, both sides considered each other's stand, exchanged ideas, and finally reached a common understanding.

My first British counterpart in the negotiations was Foreign Secretary Geoffrey Howe, who had participated in the whole process thus far. He was very familiar with China and the question of Hong Kong and very cooperative.

In the years 1988 and 1989, I conferred with Howe three times. The first two times were at the Special Session on Disarmament of the UN General Assembly held in New York in June 1988; and the UN General Assembly Session held in September. The third time was at the funeral of the Japanese emperor Hirohito in Tokyo. I remember that the main topics then were the Basic Law of the Hong Kong Special Administrative Region, which was being drafted by China; and the question of the confidence of the people of Hong Kong. Both sides had a full exchange of opinions in a pleasant atmosphere.

But after the turmoil in Beijing in June 1989, Sino-British relations suddenly deteriorated. As the UK and other Western countries imposed sanctions on China, relations between China and the UK were severely hampered. The UK seemed to be having second thoughts about the Sino-British Joint Declaration on the Question of Hong Kong formally signed in December 1984.

On June 19, Howe wrote to me, and unilaterally proposed to delay the Thirteenth Session of the Sino-British Joint Liaison Group, which had originally been scheduled for July. This was unusual: there had been no unilateral move to delay negotiations since the Joint Liaison Group was established in 1985.

Soon afterward, Howe wrote to Vice-Premier Wu Xueqian, claiming that Hong Kong's confidence had been badly dented by the disturbances in Beijing. Howe wondered if Chinese troops should be stationed in Hong Kong after the handover. He said that the UK was planning to reconsider the arrangements for the direct elections of

1991 in Hong Kong, and at the same time asked China to postpone promulgation of the Basic Law.

The stationing of Chinese troops in the Hong Kong Special Administrative Region had been included in the Sino-British Joint Declaration much earlier, and the two sides had reached a consensus on the arrangements for the 1991 elections. Obviously, the UK was raising these issues because it wanted to try to reverse the agreements.

Two weeks later, I replied to Howe's letter, emphatically opposing his argument about Hong Kong's confidence and pointing out what had undermined this confidence was a series of unfriendly actions on the part of the UK. Moreover, China would not agree to any one-sided change concerning Hong Kong's political system.

Before long, Geoffrey Howe was replaced as Britain's foreign secretary by John Major. Major was from an ordinary family and had risen quickly in the Conservative Party through his own efforts; such a rise is rare in Britain, where tradition is emphasized. His tenure as foreign secretary was short, and soon he became prime minister, succeeding Margaret Thatcher.

I met Major only twice. The first time was at the end of July 1989 in Paris, at the International Conference on Cambodia. Major was modest in behavior. When I said he was a "rising star" with a bright future, he replied that he was still a "green hand." In our meeting, he tried to influence our draft work on the Basic Law. For example, he wanted to revise the articles about the stationing of troops. I pointed out that drafting the Basic Law was China's own affair. If Britain had any good suggestions, we would consider them. However, it was impossible to force China to change the provisions agreed on by both sides. I stressed that the stationing of Chinese troops had been included in the Joint Declaration, with the agreement of both sides, and should not be brought up again. Also at this meeting, Major agreed to resume the work of the Joint Liaison Group.

The second time I met Major was at the UN Assembly in New York that autumn. He reiterated that Britain was planning to speed up the reform of Hong Kong's political system and increase the quota of directly elected members of the Hong Kong Legislative Council. I stated that political reform must accord with the Basic Law to be issued in the future, and China insisted that democracy should be implemented step by step in Hong Kong.

A diplomatic row was looming between China and the UK.

A SECRET BRITISH ENVOY VISITS CHINA

THE DISAGREEMENT OVER reforming Hong Kong's political system soon became an open dispute at the diplomatic conference table.

At the end of 1989, with the return of stability to our national situation and sustainable economic development, the Western countries began to relax their sanctions against China. First, the United States sent a special secret envoy to China, seeking to improve Sino-American relations. The British prime minister, Thatcher, sent an adviser to the foreign office, Percy Craddock, as a special secret envoy to China on December 4, 1989. Craddock handed a formal letter from Thatcher to General Secretary Jiang Zemin, and discussed the possibility of improving bilateral relations. This was an important contact between China and the UK, as it was the prelude to a confrontation on the question of Hong Kong's political system which lasted for several years.

Craddock had served as British ambassador to China, and was considered a "China expert." He had participated directly in the negotiations on Hong Kong's future. He was well versed in Chinese affairs, and at the same time he knew how to safeguard the basic interests of Britain. On the question of Hong Kong, he held a different view from the mainstream of the ruling British Conservative Party. After he resigned from his post, he often criticized the British government's policies on Hong Kong. He insisted on maintaining cooperation with China instead of allowing confrontations. However, this time, as a secret envoy to China, his purpose was to implement Thatcher's policy faithfully.

Thatcher's letter to Jiang was fairly long. In it, she said that she hoped to reverse the trend of deterioration of the two countries' relations and restore the good communications of the past. She reiterated that the stand of the UK was to follow strictly the Joint Declaration, and especially to pledge "to have no intention to use Hong Kong as a base of subversion" and no intention to "internationalize" the question of Hong Kong. Then, Thatcher suddenly changed the subject, saying that the UK was facing huge pressure to "increase substantially" the quota of the directly elected members of the Hong Kong Legislative Council in 1991—pressure that she could not ignore. She hoped that China would keep in step with the UK's arrangement when drafting the Basic Law.

After Craddock arrived in Beijing, he talked with the Chinese vice foreign minister, Zhou Nan, for a whole day about Sino-British bilateral relations and the Hong Kong question. Craddock suggested increasing trade between the two countries and restoring high-level official contacts. He also informed Zhou Nan that the UK was planning to increase the quota of directly elected seats on the Hong Kong Legislative Council from ten to twenty.

The following day, Jiang met Craddock for nearly two hours. Craddock revealed the UK's real intention, saying that Sino-British relations should be treated as a whole and if there were any difficulties in any aspect, progress could hardly be achieved in the overall relationship between Britain and China. If the two sides could reach an understanding on the issue of the Basic Law and the quota of directly elected seats on the Legislative Council, the door to restoring good relations was open. Obviously, the issue of the election in Hong Kong became a precondition for normalizing our relations. Jiang rejected this idea of exerting pressure. Later, the British ambassador to China explained to our side that Craddock had been conveying the instructions of his superiors in London.

About two weeks later, Jiang formally replied to Thatcher. While praising the UK's positive attitude toward China, Jiang's letter stated that the final version of the Basic Law would not differ much from the current draft. If the number of seats to be elected directly on the Legislative Council in 1991 was greatly exceeded, it would be difficult to accord with the Basic Law in the future. This meant that China would not accept the UK's proposal, but there was still a possibility of revising the draft. Both sides could discuss it further, and the door was not completely closed.

On the last day of Craddock's visit, his last formal meeting was with me. He was disappointed that he had made no headway, and he was eager to grasp a final chance to make even some small achievement.

Craddock told me that there was a large gap in the stands of the two sides, and he feared that it might affect their relations. He asked me if I would allow him to give a verbal message to Thatcher before Jiang wrote back to her. I asked him in principle to pass the following message to his prime minister: the governments of China and the UK should strictly abide by the principles of the Joint Declaration, and that in the interest of Hong Kong's stability and prosperity matters already discussed and decided on should not be lightly altered.

When our meeting began, Craddock handed me a letter from the new British foreign secretary, Douglas Hurd. In his letter, Hurd formally and comprehensively stated the specific positions of the UK on the Basic Law draft. It was a detailed list. And so my exchange with the third British negotiator started from an exchange of mail.

In my tenure as foreign minister, I dealt with five British foreign secretaries. Besides the three I have already mentioned, there were Malcolm Rifkind and Robin Cook. The first four all belonged to the Conservative Party; Cook belonged to the Labour Party. Not until the handover ceremony for Hong Kong's return did I meet Cook the first time. Among the five, Hurd was the one with whom I had the most frequent dealings. From the end of 1989 to 1995, we were in touch for nearly six years, in the period of greatest tension between China and the UK over Hong Kong's political system. Complicated and numerous issues that the two sides could not agree on, and the pressing timetable, prompted us to make contact frequently and to negotiate repeatedly by letters, formal visits, and international meetings. This was a rare situation in my dealings with foreign ministers.

Hurd's first letter showed that the British government had changed its stand on Hong Kong following the turmoil of 1989. There had been smooth cooperation between the two countries in drafting the Basic Law and the British side had had no objections to the published draft. But Hurd's letter raised considerable disagreements about the draft law, especially the development of Hong Kong's political system, and added more requirements, such as increasing drastically the proportion of directly elected members in the Hong Kong Legislative Council.

I did not reply directly to this letter. I simply said that experts on both sides should further exchange opinions.

SEVEN DIPLOMATIC DOCUMENTS

IN EARLY 1990, THE SITUATION was even more tense. The Basic Law of Hong Kong was to be finalized in February. It was also time for the UK to decide how to manage the election of 1991. However, despite Craddock's visit and other negotiations, there was no agreement on the direct election. The two sides had reached a deadlock.

The UK was anxious to reach a compromise with China before the Basic Law was finalized. Hurd and I exchanged letters frequently, and our embassies kept in close touch with each other to pass on information from the foreign ministers. This information was not in the form of letters with a personal signature, but it was contained in written documents rather than oral messages; we call such material "written information." This was a convenient format and was often used in the consultations and negotiations between China and the UK over Hong Kong.

In less than one month—from January 18, 1990, when Hurd first wrote to me, to February 12, when Hurd wrote to me to confirm our common understanding—the two sides exchanged written information seven times. At that time, such liaisons were considered internal consultation and had to be kept secret. Later, with the intensification of the dispute over Hong Kong's future political system, each side published the seven documents.

The focus of that round of exchanges was the arrangement for the election of the Hong Kong Legislative Council. People might wonder why the two countries made such a fuss over a few directly elected seats more or less in the Legislative Council. In fact, what China and the UK were arguing about was not only the quota of directly elected seats but the overall political system after the return of Hong Kong to China. To understand this point, it is necessary to know the background of the development of Hong Kong's political system and the basic considerations of the UK adopting its policy of "political reform" during the transitional period.

In its century of colonial rule in Hong Kong, the UK had practiced a system of autocracy, through a governor appointed by London. Under the governor, there were the executive and legislative councils, which served as consultative bodies. The governor appointed all the council members. It was an executive-led system.

In the 1980s, after China and the UK signed the Joint Declaration on the Question of Hong Kong, China began to draw up a draft for the Basic Law for the future Hong Kong Special Administrative Region and to design a brand-new political system embodying the concept of "one country, two systems."

At this time, the UK intended to use the transitional period to carry out the reform for a so-called "representative government," so that it would become a fact before the Basic Law was finalized, thus influencing the Basic Law arrangements for the future political system. The goal of the "representative government" was actually to change the executive-led setup into a legislative-led one, to restrain the executive body by enhancing the power and status of the legislative body, and finally to transform the returned Hong Kong into an "independent entity" separated from the motherland for the benefit of the UK's long-term political and economic interests there.

Even before the Joint Declaration was signed, the British government had begun to make preparations for this. After it was signed, the UK immediately started to deploy its political reform. First, in 1985, some legislators were chosen by indirect election from functional constituencies (representing different sectors or professions). Then, in 1991, when the election was held, a new system of directly electing some legislators from regional constituencies was introduced. The UK planned to abolish totally the appointment system in

1995 and have the Legislative Council chosen by functional constituency election, indirect election by the election committee, and
direct regional elections.

When China was soliciting the UK's opinions about the Basic
Law, the UK strongly recommended the maintenance of the executive-led system of Hong Kong. China also thought that this system
was appropriate for Hong Kong, and that it would be conducive to a
highly efficient administration, and to stability and prosperity. In the
meantime, China was also in favor of a gradual application of democracy to Hong Kong, and the ultimate total popular election of the
Legislative Council. At that time, the UK agreed. The relevant contents of the Basic Law were therefore drafted according to the principles of an executive-led system and gradual approach.

But after 1989, the UK changed its mind and asked that political
reform be speeded up drastically. The most controversial issue was
that the UK wanted to increase the proportion of directly elected
members of the Legislative Council quickly and dramatically.

Before Hurd wrote to me on January 18, the UK had proposed to
increase the number of directly elected legislators from ten to twenty
in 1991, and then to twenty-four in 1995. That number was much
more than the eighteen directly elected legislators in 1997 planned
by China in the draft Basic Law. If we had accepted the UK's arrangement, there would have been problems in the coordination of Hong
Kong's political systems before and after its return to China in 1997.

In the interest of the stable transition of Hong Kong, China made
a considerable compromise. On January 15, we suggested fifteen seats
in 1991 and twenty in 1997. The UK expressed its appreciation for
China's "positive spirit" and said it would discuss the "possibility of
fewer than twenty in 1991."

The flurry of letters between Hurd and myself during this period
can be summed up as follows. The UK responded to China's plan of
January 15 and proposed eighteen seats in 1991 and twenty-four in
1997. China offered eighteen seats in 1991 and twenty in 1997. The
UK refused this offer and threatened that if China did not revise the
number of seats in the draft Basic Law, the members of Hong Kong's

Executive and Legislative councils would resign. The UK also pro-posed sending high-ranking officials to discuss this matter face-to-face in Beijing. China responded that its important compromise had not received a positive response from the UK, and that therefore there was no need for the UK to send anyone to Beijing. If the UK re-fused to accept China's suggestion, the Basic Law Drafting Commit-tee would have to make a decision according to the original plan. The UK asked China to clarify several questions, such as the arrangement of the election committee and the election method. In clarifying those questions, China accepted some of the UK's suggestions. Ulti-mately, the UK accepted (in written form) China's suggestion of eighteen seats in 1991 and twenty in 1997, and promised to sustain the "continuity" of Hong Kong before and after 1997.

Then there was an interlude. Several days before the UK accepted our suggestion, Hurd wrote me a letter saying that his side was un-able to give a final answer before the meeting of the Basic Law Draft-ing Committee and asked the Drafting Committee to leave a blank for the number of directly elected seats in 1997 to be filled in later. We expected that the two sides might reach an agreement before the meeting, and they did. Since this letter was not related to the sub-stance of the negotiations, it was not published with the seven docu-ments.

The seven diplomatic documents show that when the two sides agreed on the draft version of the Basic Law, they had reached an agreement and understanding on the pace of development of Hong Kong's political system. And the UK had to observe the principle of discussing matters with China until a consensus, and coordination with the Basic Law, had been reached.

Before I met Hurd, I had made an important agreement with him by letter, which was the only written agreement I made with the UK in my tenure as foreign minister. Unexpectedly, this agreement was revoked by the UK. A debate ensued, involving China, the UK, and the mass media, on whether the seven diplomatic documents consti-tuted in form and content agreement and understanding of both sides and whether they were binding on both sides. Actually, anyone with diplomatic common sense can easily come to a correct conclusion, to say nothing of those who are familiar with the history of the negotiations between China and the UK on Hong Kong.

VISITS BETWEEN THE CHINESE AND BRITISH FOREIGN MINISTERS

IN APRIL 1990, after China and Britain had reached an agreement and understanding on the election, the Basic Law of the Hong Kong Special Administrative Region was formally promulgated. It seemed that the dispute over the development of Hong Kong's political system was over, but in fact it was not. As the election of 1991 for the Hong Kong Legislative Council approached, Britain increased the pace of the reform for a "representative government."

At that time, the foreign ministers of the two countries exchanged their first visits since 1989, and Sino-British bilateral relations became better. Hurd visited China in the spring of 1991, and I had a formal meeting with him. The Chinese leaders met with him and gave him a high-level courteous reception. Hurd had once worked in the British embassy in Beijing, and he was very familiar with Chinese affairs. In 1974, he had visited China with Prime Minister Edward Heath and had met Chairman Mao Zedong. During Hurd's visit this time, both sides decided that in the future they should increase contacts and that the foreign ministers of our two countries should meet twice a year to discuss topics which cropped up during the transitional period.

From 1990 to 1991, the consultations on the construction of the new Hong Kong airport were in full swing, so other problems faded from view for a while. Hurd came to Beijing mainly to talk about the new airport. The problems of building the Hong Kong airport and the development of the political system were two different things, but they both went beyond the handover date of 1997, affecting the rights and interests of the government of the special administrative region, and therefore needed to be discussed and approved by both sides. The discussion about the new airport lasted several years and is another complicated story; but I will not give a detailed account of it here.

About one year later, in the spring of 1992, I paid a formal return visit to the UK for the first time. This was just before the twentieth anniversary of the upgrading of Sino-British diplomatic relations, and the leaders of our two countries had recently signed a memorandum of understanding about the new airport. Therefore, my visit was conducted in a pleasant atmosphere.

However, at the same time Britain was plotting to promote a new structure called a "standing committee" in the Hong Kong legislature to strengthen the power of the legislature to restrain the executive sector of the government.

I specifically raised this matter with Hurd in our talks, pointing out that the Basic Law had designed the executive-led system for the future special administrative region, and it had been working very well for the past few years. If we changed it into a legislative-led system, this would contradict the Basic Law, and China hoped that this would not happen. At that time, Hurd was still saying that the UK had no intention of changing the executive-led system into a legislative-led system.

Concerning the last Legislative Council elections in 1995, I warned Britain that the electoral method should conform to the Basic Law, or else there could be no direct transition to the system after the handover. Hurd said that the UK would consult with China before making any decision in 1993. However, shortly after I visited the UK, the British government—in April 1992—appointed a former chairman of the Conservative Party, Chris Patten, known to have a "strong backbone," as the last governor of Hong Kong, succeeding David Clive Wilson, who was considered too "submissive" to China. Patten changed the UK's policies regarding Hong Kong even more drastically. The dispute over the direction of the development of Hong Kong's political system soon became a serious public confrontation between the UK and China.

The UK's Scheme of Political Reform: "Three Violations"

NORMALLY, THE TASK of the last British governor would be to ensure cooperation with China in the final phase of Hong Kong's transitional period to guarantee a smooth transition. If Patten had done this, it would have been an excellent achievement, and he would have gone down in history as a wise governor. However, he acted in the opposite way, seeming to fear that Hong Kong's return to the motherland might be too smooth.

Shortly after taking office in July 1992, Patten started to implement a new plan for political reform in Hong Kong that brought him into confrontation with China, and he made completely different arrangements for the District Board elections in 1994 and the Legislative Council elections in 1995. Superficially, this plan would still maintain the executive-led system, but in fact it would drastically change the political system and rapidly enhance the status and power of the legislative body. The main measures included changing the functional constituency of the Legislative Council and the indirect election of the election committee into a direct election in disguised form; immediately canceling the appointment system for the district organizations; and changing the nongovernmental characteristics and functions of the district organizations.

Patten announced his plan for political reform when he delivered his first policy speech on October 7, 1992, soon after taking office. Before this, on September 25, when I met with Hurd at the UN General Assembly in New York, Hurd informed me of the contents of the political reform plan. At the same time, Britain also presented an official document to Beijing through diplomatic channels. I made my position known on the spot, emphasizing that the arrangements for the elections in 1995 should be discussed and agreed upon by both sides and should conform to the provisions of the Basic Law. Several days later, China decided to send Lu Ping, Minister of the Hong Kong and Macao Affairs Office of the State Council, to meet Robin McLaren, the British ambassador to China, to make a preliminary comment on Patten's plan. Lu specifically explained that some aspects of the plan went against the Basic Law, pointing out the possibility that the legislative body produced by the scheme would not be able to survive the transition in 1997, and particularly warning the UK not to stir up a public debate.

However, it seemed that Britain had decided to start trouble, regardless of China's opposition and warnings. The UK published this plan for political reform unilaterally, without any consultation. That violated the provisions of the Joint Declaration and was an intentional challenge. The UK tried to utilize public opinion to put pressure on China. As soon as the plan was published, the British prime minister and foreign secretary openly showed their support.

China also stated its position openly and immediately, expressing its deep concern over the UK's move and pointing out that China would not take the responsibility for the discontinuity of Hong Kong's political system before and after the takeover. The relevant bodies of the special administrative region would be established in accordance with the Basic Law and the decision made by the National People's Congress.

After publishing his plan, Patten visited Beijing on October 22. He wanted to blackmail China by doing this as a fait accompli. He asked the Chinese government to make counterproposals on the basis of his political plan.

We insisted on solving this problem in accordance with the provisions of the Joint Declaration, holding that the arrangements for the elections of 1994–1995 would directly affect the smooth transition of Hong Kong. Therefore, they must be discussed and agreed upon by both sides. The UK should not have taken any step unilaterally and without any consultation. Therefore, China asked Patten to withdraw publicly his plan for political reform in Hong Kong.

During the meeting, China repeatedly and specifically analyzed how the political reform plan violated the Joint Declaration, how it violated the principle of conformity with the Basic Law, and how it violated the relevant agreements and understandings the two sides had reached in the past. We called these the "three violations."

At that time, our impression was that Patten was unaware of the agreement and understanding reached by the Chinese and British foreign ministers in 1990. When I met Patten, I sternly pointed out that his plan presented a challenge to Sino-British cooperation. We had to decide whether we should continue to cooperate or "go our separate ways" and "make a fresh start." I had never used such harsh words in any previous contacts or negotiations in the transitional period. Unfortunately, Patten disregarded China's sincere advice and warning. Thus, Patten's visit to Beijing was fruitless, and resulted in an open confrontation.

However, we analyzed the situation calmly, and concluded that the UK's "three violations" had a complex background and were not just a coincidence. There was no doubt that the plan seriously threatened Hong Kong's smooth transition, and that such a threat was totally unacceptable.

To cope with the possible crisis, we made two preparations: on the one hand, to take a firm stand and launch the struggle that seemed necessary to maintain the base of bilateral cooperation; on the other hand, to be well prepared for a fresh start in case of an eventual discontinuity between the political systems.

In March 1993, after Patten published his plan for political reform in the Hong Kong government's official gazette, China took its first countermeasure, and the establishment of the Preparatory Committee of the Organizing Committee of the Hong Kong Special Administrative Region was approved by the Eighth National People's Congress.

Seventeen Rounds of Diplomatic Negotiations

When the UK saw that China resolutely opposed Patten's scheme, and that the scheme was coming under strong criticism from different circles, it suggested solving the dispute through formal diplomatic negotiations.

On February 6, 1993, Hurd wrote to me, proposing that both

sides negotiate "without preconditions." At that time, we still hoped that Britain could change its mind, come back to the road of the "three conformities," and continue to cooperate with China, so we agreed to the British proposal for negotiations.

I replied to Hurd on February 11, proposing that the negotiations should be carried out on the basis of the "three conformities," as a response to the UK's "no preconditions." I also pointed out that if the UK presented its plan of political reform to Hong Kong's Legislative Council for discussion, it would harm the negotiations.

Over the next two months, we held repeated consultations on many issues, such as the publication of details of the negotiations and the composition of the delegations. Finally, a decision was made that on April 22, 1993, negotiations between the delegates of the two governments would start in Beijing. The Chinese delegate was the vice foreign minister, Jiang Enzhu; the British delegate was the ambassador to China, Robin McLaren.

This confrontation between China and the UK lasted half a year. All together, seventeen rounds of negotiations were held, and the process was both complicated and tough. China put forward many reasonable suggestions to solve the impasse, and made necessary compromises to safeguard cooperation between the two sides. Unfortunately, the UK refused to abandon its "three violations." The worst part of the negotiations was the last phase, when the two sides had almost reached an agreement on most of the problems. Suddenly, the UK broke off the negotiations unilaterally. Later, Patten presented his plan for political reform to the Legislative Council for approval. That marked a complete break with China on the part of the UK, and ushered in a period of confrontation and no return.

Later, China and Britain published the details of their negotiations separately.

Originally, China and the UK had already reached a common understanding on the continuity of the political systems before and after Hong Kong's return to China in 1997. The seven diplomatic documents formed the basis of the agreement on the arrangements for the members of the last term of the Hong Kong Legislative Council in office before the handover to become the ones of the first term in office after the handover. This was in accord with a decision of the National People's Congress in April 1990 and was called the "through-train" arrangement.

The seventeen rounds of negotiations in Beijing in 1993 focused on the arrangements for Hong Kong's elections of 1994–1995. The general goal was to try to save the "through-train" arrangement under the threat of Britain's "three violations," so as to ensure the continuity of the political systems before and after 1997.

While the negotiations were going on, I had two long meetings with Hurd to discuss and solve the problems we were encountering. The "through-train" arrangement was one of the toughest time-consuming topics.

In July 1993, Hurd visited China again. At that time, the negotiations in Beijing were still in their initial stage. Discussions focused on matters of principle only. Not much was achieved, and the prospect ahead was not clear. I suggested that the two sides prepare a written outline of the principles discussed during this period. But Hurd said that it was better to go into details first, and the outline could be done when the gap between the two sides narrowed. So no results were achieved on this issue.

Given the state of the negotiations at that time, I stressed the importance of the "through-train" arrangement and asked the UK to treasure this result achieved after years of negotiation. The "through-train" arrangement meant that during the transfer of government between two different regimes, one side would use certain procedures to allow the legislators of the former regime to continue as legislators of the new regime. I pointed out to Hurd that in the UK when the Conservative Party or the Labour Party came into power, one supplanting the other, it was possible to change all the previous policies and arrangements, but it was not possible for the two parties to discuss any "through-train" arrangement for members of the former cabinet to enter the new cabinet. However, in the case of the return of Hong Kong to China, a "through-train" arrangement was possible. This was, in fact, completely unprecedented creative work.

Hurd, however, simply reiterated the UK's position, adding only that there should be a clear and objective criterion when the Organizing Committee for the Special Administrative Region confirmed the "through train" arrangement.

After these negotiations, the outside world saw clearly where the crux of the problem lay. A newspaper in Hong Kong reported that progress in the negotiations depended on how much compromise each side could make on the "through-train" issue.

In early October 1993, when Hurd and I met again in New York, the negotiations in Beijing were still deadlocked. Both sides expressed disappointment about this and were not optimistic about the prospects. The UK side even began to spread the view that the negotiations might fail.

At that time, relations between the two countries were frigid. Hurd himself went so far as to oppose publicly China's bid to host the 2000 Olympic Games, arousing indignation in China.

In late September, China published Deng Xiaoping's three important talks from 1982 to 1984 about Hong Kong (one with Margaret Thatcher on September 24, 1982; one with Geoffrey Howe on July 31, 1984; and one at the Third Plenary Session of the Central Advisory Commission of the Communist Party of China on October 22, 1984).

Though these talks had taken place in the 1980s, when China and the UK had just started negotiating about Hong Kong, they were realistic and had great significance when they were published in 1993; and they aroused a strong response from the media. The general view was that the publication was a stern warning to the UK to abandon its confrontation with China.

Deng said that if serious trouble arose in Hong Kong during the transitional period, the Chinese government would have to reconsider the time and way of recovering Hong Kong. We were very concerned over the transitional period. It was our hope that no trouble would occur during the transitional period, but we must be prepared against contingencies that we could not control.

In fact, at the First Plenary Session of the Preparatory Committee of the Organizing Committee of the Hong Kong Special Administrative Region in July 1993, I had made public Deng's talk with Thatcher. His talk had become common knowledge in Hong Kong; it just had not been published formally. Actually, this talk had become China's main declaration of countermeasures against the UK's plan of political reform.

The meeting between Hurd and me in New York was held in this atmosphere. A sharp confrontation, it was our longest meeting—two and a half hours.

GOING SEPARATE WAYS

THE ONLY THING HURD AND I agreed on was that there were two possibilities for the negotiations: to reach or not to reach an agreement.

I stressed that to reach an agreement would surely be beneficial to all sides, but even if no agreement could be reached, China still had the confidence and ability to realize a smooth handover and maintain Hong Kong's stability and prosperity.

Hurd made it appear that he did not mind whether there would be an agreement or not. He said if no agreement could be reached, then there would only be a second-best choice, which would adversely affect Hong Kong's confidence and prosperity.

Having heard this, I had to point out our perspective of "making a fresh start." I said that if we did not reach an agreement, the tenure of the members of the Legislative Council elected in 1995 would expire on June 30, 1997, the date of the handover; and the Organizing Committee for the Special Administrative Region would institute measures to form the first Legislative Council of the Hong Kong Special Administrative Region in 1996.

Both sides understood that we were preparing for the failure of the negotiations.

Regarding the specific arrangements for the method of electing the members of the Legislative Council, each side restated its own stand, and no progress could be made. During the negotiations in Beijing, the two sides had almost clarified the specific arrangements for the various elections and their respective viewpoints. The UK had explicitly proposed holding parallel talks on the criterion for certifying the "through train" and the election arrangements. Ten days before the meeting in New York, Hurd transmitted a message to me, emphasizing that the criterion for certifying the "through train" was a "fundamental" issue for the UK, and it was "extremely important" to discuss this problem in the next round of negotiations (the twelfth round, to be held on September 26). It would help the UK to consider comprehensively the negotiation prospects at the meeting in New York. If such a discussion were to be delayed, it would be impossible to achieve anything concerning the elections.

I did not agree with his opinion. I only restated China's position.

The "criterion for certifying" the "through train" was an idea raised by the UK during the initial stage of the negotiations held in Beijing. The UK thought that the legislators in office at the time of the handover could become the members of the first Legislative Council of the Special Administrative Region as long as they swore an oath of allegiance in accordance with Article 104 of the Basic Law. China, however, held that this matter had to be handled in accordance with the decision made by the National People's Congress and the relevant provisions of the Basic Law, and that there must be no infringement on the certifying power of the Organizing Committee of the Special Administrative Region bestowed by the National People's Congress. China also held that we should first solve the problem of arranging the elections of 1994–1995. Only when this problem had been solved could we talk about certifying the membership of the Legislative Council—provided that the composition of the last Legislative Council conformed to the decision made by the National People's Congress and the relevant provisions of the Basic Law. In other words, there must be "through train" before we could discuss the "certifying criterion."

During the meeting in New York, Hurd urged China to discuss the "certifying criterion" in detail and considered it to be the key to the progress of the negotiations. It was obvious that the UK was most concerned over the regulation made by the National People's Congress: that after the return of Hong Kong to the motherland, Hong Kong's legislators must "uphold" the Basic Law and "pledge loyalty" to the Special Administrative Region. At that time, I stated that the legislators' "transition" would not be a problem if the elections could be arranged satisfactorily and in compliance with the Basic Law. We were in no position to determine the criterion for the Organizing Committee of the Special Administrative Region. We could only state our personal view. If any legislator was unwilling to pledge loyalty to the Special Administrative Region, was unwilling to uphold the Basic Law, or opposed the Basic Law and "one country, two systems" by word and by deed, he or she would be ineligible for office after the transition.

To speed up the talks, I suggested to Hurd that we first solve the comparatively simple problem of arranging Hong Kong's district organizational elections of 1994; that would give us time to solve the more complicated problem of arranging the Legislative Council elections of 1995. But Hurd did not agree. He kept insisting that the major problems should be tackled simultaneously, and that there should be a package solution to all those issues.

Later, during the negotiations in Beijing, the UK agreed to discuss the arrangements for the district organizational elections first, but raised some preconditions. China compromised, and the two sides reached a basic consensus on the arrangements for the district organizational elections. To our chagrin, at the final moment the UK demanded that the problem of the Legislative Council election of 1995 should be solved at the same time. Thereupon, the seventeen rounds of negotiations came to a halt on November 27, when the UK declared unilaterally that they were over. That was also the end of the negotiations in Beijing.

On November 30, Hurd wrote to me to explain why the UK had insisted on solving the problem of the 1995 Legislative Council elections. He also said that the UK had decided to present the plan of political reform to the Hong Kong Legislative Council for discussion in mid-December.

In fact, this was a declaration of a showdown with China.

The following day, I replied to Hurd, saying that China would never accept the UK's presentation of the political reform plan to the Hong Kong Legislative Council, and that the opinions of the Legislative Council could not supersede the discussion between the two governments. This was a matter of principle to China, I stressed. I restated China's declaration at the beginning of the negotiations in April that if the UK presented the political reform plan to the Legislative Council, it would mean a breakdown in the bilateral negotiations. But the UK did not heed China's warning; it presented the political reform plan to the Hong Kong Legislative Council for approval in February and June 1994.

China's response was immediate. We published a formal statement to the effect that, in accordance with the provisions of the Sino-UK Joint Declaration, the UK's administration of Hong Kong would end on June 30, 1997, and the Chinese government would resume the exercise of sovereignty over Hong Kong on July 1, 1997. As components of the political structure of Hong Kong under British administration, the last Hong Kong District Council, two Urban Councils, and the Legislative Council must be terminated with the expiration of the UK's administration. From July 1, 1997, on, the political structure of the Hong Kong Special Administrative Region would be formed in accordance with the decisions made by the National People's Congress and the relevant provisions of the Basic Law.

Thus the "through train" ceased to be "through" because of the UK's sabotage, and China had to make a fresh start. The confrontation concerning the future of Hong Kong's political system between China and the UK was over. The two sides "went separate ways" over this issue, and were further alienated.

ENDLESS REPERCUSSIONS

IN MARCH 1996, the Organizing Committee of the Hong Kong Special Administrative Region formally decided to establish the Interim Legislative Council.

As there was no "through train," and there was a great deal of preparatory work to do for establishing the Special Administrative Region on July 1, 1997, the legislative work in particular had to be done well ahead of time. But as the first Legislative Council could not be formed before the establishment of the Special Administrative Region, an interim legislative body had to be formed to complete the necessary legislative work. This Interim Legislative Council would begin to function formally as the legislative body of the Special Administrative Region on the day of the handover. Its life was scheduled for one year—that is, until the establishment of the first Legislative Council.

Strictly speaking, this arrangement was a matter exclusively for China, and the UK had no right to interfere in it. Of course, we still hoped that the UK would cooperate with us in the preparation for the Special Administrative Region by providing certain facilities, but we were not optimistic, recalling the uncooperative attitude of the UK toward the work of the Organizing Committee for the Special Administrative Region two years ago.

As we expected, the UK strongly opposed the setting up of the Interim Legislative Council. For instance, it refused to allow the Interim Legislative Council to hold a meeting in Hong Kong, so the council had to begin its work in Shenzhen. Not until Hong Kong was returned to China did the council move to Hong Kong. During this period, the UK constantly included the Interim Legislative Council as a problem on the agenda of the two countries' foreign ministers.

At this time, the British negotiator I worked with was the foreign secretary, Malcolm Rifkind. I met him when I visited Britain again in October 1995. Later, he visited China, and he also contacted me by mail. Once, he objected to a suggestion by the Law Team of the Preparatory Committee that certain articles of the Hong Kong Bill of Human Rights be abolished. He said that this would seriously undermine the confidence of the people of Hong Kong, and he urged China to reconsider the matter. I replied that all of Hong Kong's laws should follow the Basic Law, not defy it. In early April 1996, shortly after China decided to establish the Interim Legislative Council, Rifkind wrote to me, complaining that some Chinese officials had requested that any Hong Kong civil servant who wanted to participate in the new government after the Special Administrative Region was inaugurated must declare his or her support for the Interim Legislative Council. This, he said, would cause a conflict of loyalty among Hong Kong's civil servants, undermine public confidence, and so on. I did not reply to this letter.

On April 20 of that year, I had the chance to meet Rifkind for the first time, at the Chinese ambassador's official residence in The Hague, Netherlands. At the meeting, he harped on the issue of the Interim Legislative Council, saying that the establishment of the council before the handover of Hong Kong did not accord with the Joint Declaration, which stipulated that the UK was responsible for Hong Kong's administration until then. Moreover, the coexistence of two legislative bodies would cause confusion in Hong Kong. This was a clear reversal of right and wrong and cause and effect in the debate on the "through train."

I explained that it was precisely because there was no "through train" and because elections for the Legislative Council could not be held before July 1, 1997, that it was necessary to establish an Interim Legislative Council. The preparation done by the Interim Legislative Council would come into effect on July 1. Therefore, there was no such problem as the coexistence of two legislative bodies. I said that I hoped that the UK would face this fact. I also emphasized that, in the remaining 400 days before the return of Hong Kong, both sides should concentrate on practical matters rather than quarrel, and achieve cooperation instead of trouble.

Rifkind sent me more letters, raising complaints. I did not answer them all. Nevertheless, the cooperation between the two sides did make some satisfying progress. For example, at the New York meeting in the autumn of 1996, we confirmed the proposals for the handover ceremony agreed on by the Sino-British Joint Liaison Group, thus settling one important matter concerning Hong Kong's return to China.

THE UK'S MISCALCULATION OF THE SITUATION

IN RETROSPECT, THE DISPUTE between China and the UK over Hong
Kong's political system derailed the "through train," and finally led
to a complete lack of cooperation. It was undoubtedly the greatest
disturbance in the whole process of handover. China had tried to
avoid this, but had failed. Why?

The mass media came up with various explanations. The com-
monest explanation emphasized the personal influence of Chris Patten. Although at the time we also had the impression that the
government in London was responding to Patten's advice, I thought
we should view this matter from a wider perspective.

After 1989, the UK proposed speeding up the pace of Hong
Kong's "democratization." But it had to do this in consultation with
China, so as to conform to the Basic Law. Then in 1992, the UK put
forward the political reform plan characterized by the "three violations"—unilaterally, regardless of the agreements and understandings of the two sides. The UK provoked a public debate and proceeded
to get the plan approved by the Legislative Council, thus destroying
the possibility of a continuity of the political systems before and after the changeover.

It is difficult to conclude that the UK changed completely its policy of cooperation with China on the question of Hong Kong just because of one person's influence. There must have been a deeper
international background.

The international background was the violent change in Eastern
Europe and the disintegration of the Soviet Union in the early 1990s.
The government of the UK, in this context, miscalculated China's future prospects for development. The UK considered that it had made
excessive concessions over Hong Kong, and it wanted to take this opportunity to regain lost ground. I think this was the basic reason why
the UK provoked a disturbance over Hong Kong's political system.

On July 1, 1997, as a member of the delegation of the Chinese
government, I attended the handover ceremony and saw the five-star
national flag slowly raised over Hong Kong. Realizing that this was

the end of foreign rule of a part of China's territory, I could not contain my excitement. Days and nights, rains and storms in the long transitional period all condensed into this one historic moment. It was raining the whole day of the handover ceremony, but I am sure that all Chinese in the world felt that this was a refreshing shower, washing away China's humiliation—which had lasted over 100 years—and presaging a new future for Hong Kong.

THE PEACEFUL RETURN OF MACAO

CALM AND TRANQUILLITY

IF HONG KONG'S RETURN to China was stormy and turbulent, Macao's return could be described as calm and tranquil.

The negotiations between China and Portugal on Macao's return were very smooth. This success was attributable to a revolution in Portugal in the 1970s.

On April 25, 1974, the Portuguese dictatorship, which had lasted for almost half a century, was overthrown by a "Salvation Committee" formed by a group of young officers. The coup was known as the "April 25 Revolution." The new government abandoned Portugal's traditional policy of colonialism. First it granted independence to Portugal's African colonies. Then, from the end of 1975 on, it began to withdraw troops from Macao, and it recognized Macao as a Chinese territory administered by Portugal in the Macao Articles of Association promulgated later. In 1979, when China and Portugal established diplomatic relations, Portugal again acknowledged to China that Macao was Chinese territory.

In the 1980s, when China and Portugal began negotiations to solve the question of Macao, the issue of sovereignty and ownership of the territory, unlike the question of Hong Kong, had already been resolved. Therefore, the negotiations had a sound basis. In drafting a Joint Declaration, the two sides soon reached agreement on the wording about territorial sovereignty. In the Joint Declaration, both sides declared that Macao was China's territory and China would resume the exercise of sovereignty over Macao. In contrast, the UK was not willing to say in the Sino-British Joint Declaration that Hong Kong was China's territory. Therefore, the two sides could not reach a common statement, and the governments of the two countries had to make separate declarations: the Chinese side declared that the recovery of Hong Kong was the common aspiration of the entire Chinese people, and China had decided to resume the exercise of sovereignty over Hong Kong; the UK side declared that it would restore Hong Kong to China.

The next question regarding Macao was the specific time when China would recover it. Portugal wanted to delay the handover until well into the twenty-first century. Considering the overall cause of reunification, China thought it must be returned by the end of the twentieth century. But the handover did not have to coincide with Hong Kong's return. China and Portugal spent much time and effort on this issue, and finally the decision was made that the handover of Macao would be completed ten days before the end of the twentieth century—on December 20, 1999.

As relations between the two countries had always been friendly, China, taking into full consideration the characteristics and actual situation of Macao, gave as much special consideration as possible to the reasonable requirements and opinions raised by Portugal when formulating specific policies toward Macao in accordance with the principle of "one country, two systems." There were Portuguese who had been living in Macao for generations, known as "Macaenses"— locally born Portuguese. They had a special social status and their own interests. China promised in the Joint Declaration that the interests of these residents would be protected, and their habits and cultural traditions would be respected in accordance with the law. Moreover, China agreed to add "to protect cultural relics in Macao in accordance with the law" to the Declaration, and concurred that the Portuguese language could still be used as a teaching language as well as an official language. Also, clauses concerning culture, education, and language were given more prominence in the Declaration.

Since Portugal had long since withdrawn its troops from Macao, there was no problem of a military handover like the one in Hong Kong. Therefore, a unit of the Chinese People's Liberation Army was sent to be stationed in Macao under the bright sun on the day of the return—rather than at midnight, as had happened when Hong Kong was being handed over.

A SMOOTH TRANSITION

MACAO'S TRANSITIONAL PERIOD was almost as long as Hong Kong's, but the problems involved were different. To ensure a smooth transition, "three major issues"—language, personnel, and law—had to be solved during the transitional period. Those three issues had been the major topics throughout the diplomatic consultations between Portugal and China. China actively promoted and helped Portugal settle these difficult issues at various levels. During the process of the handover of Macao, there were some differences of opinion, but the debates were not made public, and we successfully completed the work through consultations.

During this period, the leaders of China and Macao visited each other many times and discussed the question of Macao. Their good cooperation in this regard improved their bilateral relations.

In February 1991, I visited Portugal for the first time. I received a friendly welcome, and we reached a formal agreement on the official status of the Chinese and Portuguese languages in Macao, which constituted an important step in the solution of the "three major issues."

Actually, it was no coincidence that Portugal became the first Western country to receive an official visit from a Chinese foreign minister after 1989. Because of the smooth cooperation on the question of Macao, both sides could see a bright future for Sino-Portuguese cooperation. Therefore, a common understanding was gradually formed in the contacts between the high-ranking officials of the two countries, which promoted not only Sino-Portuguese relations but also Sino-EU relations.

During the transitional period, I met with the Portuguese foreign minister many times. I also visited Portugal many times in my capacity as foreign minister or as a delegation member with our state leaders.

My first visit to Macao left me with a deep impression. In March 1999, I attended the opening ceremony of the Macao Cultural Center in the capacity of vice-premier at the invitation of the governor of Macao, and I met President Jorge Sampaio of Portugal. That was my first visit to Macao. (By contrast, before the return of Hong Kong, I never paid a formal visit there in an official capacity.)

Macao is unique for its blend of traditional Chinese, Portuguese, and indigenous culture. There is a long patriotic tradition in Macao. The precursor of China's democratic revolution, Dr. Sun Yat-sen, lived and practiced medicine in Macao in his early years. The composer of the *Yellow River Cantata*, Xian Xinghai, was a native of Macao.

At my meeting with Sampaio, he expressed concern about whether Macao would keep its special characteristics after it was returned to China, and said that he hoped the end of Macao's transitional period would introduce new, positive elements into Sino-Portuguese relations. He also informed me that he would attend Macao's handover ceremony. We exchanged opinions on mutual cooperation and on all the outstanding issues in the last 270 or so days of Macao's transitional period, and we made some progress. We had a very pleasant talk.

On December 20, 1999, China and Portugal completed the handover of Macao smoothly. As a member of the delegation of the Chinese government, I attended the handover ceremony and witnessed that exciting historic moment.

Following the return of Hong Kong and Macao to the motherland, the Chinese people had reason to anticipate the early return of Taiwan to the motherland, so that the great cause of reunification would finally be fulfilled.

When both sides of the Taiwan Strait are unified, my final wish in my old age will also be fulfilled.

APPENDIXES

Five Speeches at the School of International Studies, Peking University

APPENDIX I

Economic Globalization and Other Issues
(JANUARY 1, 2000)

TODAY IS A GOOD DAY to visit Peking University, as the Chinese capital has seen a heavy fall of snow. Snow foretells bumper crops. At the beginning of the new year, the new century, and the new millennium, I take this occasion to send New Year greetings to the teachers, other staff members, and students of the School of International Studies, Peking University. At the same time, I extend my apologies for being unable to make contributions to the school as honorary dean. After I arrived here today, I visited the school's office. I found that the teachers and students are full of vitality and are making many contributions to the school, despite the fact that the working conditions at institutions of higher learning are quite poor. The Ministry of Foreign Affairs built a grand office block after Hong Kong returned to China in 1997. Before then, our working conditions had been poor for the forty years since the founding of the People's Republic of China. One room would have seven or eight desks, making it look like a classroom. Nevertheless, we made remarkable achievements in our diplomacy. And now, since working conditions have been improved a great deal, we hope to do even better than before. But no matter what kind of conditions we have to work in, a revolutionary and enterprising spirit, and unremitting efforts are the decisive factors for success. I believe that all the teachers and students of Peking University have this kind of spirit which is the foundation for doing things well. Of course, conditions should also be improved so that we can develop science and education, which are necessary for the rejuvenation of our country. However, this strategy cannot be carried out without the spirit of dedication to work. I have benefited greatly from today's visit to Peking University.

Now, I would like to give my opinions on the present world situation, rather than give a lecture.

Last year, 1999, should be called the unforgettable year. There was a Soviet film called *The Unforgettable Year of 1919*, about the October Revolution. Now we have a film called *Unforgettable 1919*, about Gu Weijun, who refused to sign the peace treaty at the Versailles Peace Conference.* The year 1999 was indeed unforgettable for us, because we went through several battles. We won victories in all these battles by rallying closely around the Party Central Committee with Comrade Jiang Zemin at the core. Many important events took place last year, such as the celebration of the fiftieth anniversary of the founding of the People's Republic of China, the successful launching of the spacecraft *Shenzhou*, and the return of Macao. Although Macao is not large, it is of great significance. Portugal occupied Macao for 442 years, nearly half a millennium, which is quite a long time. The return of Macao marked the end of European colonialism in China, and indeed in Asia.

Our economy was rather poor in the past. We had an economy of shortage most of the time. Now we are short of demand rather than supply. We used to advocate taking grain production as the guiding principle for agriculture. Now, the amount of stored grain equals the total grain output for a whole year, which is a large amount. We used to take steel production as the guiding principle for industry. Now, China is the biggest steel producer in the world, surpassing the United States and Japan. We need to cut steel production and restructure our industry this year. Will the economy be perfect after we achieve this objective and shake off the last vestiges of the shortage economy? No. From an epistemological perspective, we cannot understand certain things until we reach a certain stage. When we develop to a new stage, new problems crop up. The new

---

* The conference allowed Japan to take over Germany's holdings in China (note by translator).

problem in our present economy is how to restructure industry and increase the content of science and new and high technology, to catch up with the new trend of world economic development. This is a problem for science and technology, the information industry, and the knowledge economy, as well as for grain and steel production and general needs. Anyway, despite many difficulties, we scored great achievements last year, and, looking into the new year, we are full of hope.

Next I would like to talk about international relations.

Since you are experts in and scholars of international studies, you know that "international relations" refer mainly to political and economic relations. I have read some of your work. It is all of a high standard. Today, I would like to discuss several issues with you.

First of all, there is economic globalization. Economic globalization is a hot topic these days, and a major trend in world economic development. It is an objective reality, but how did it come about? After the cold war, the confrontation between the two world blocs ended; free trade and free investment increased; political and economic barriers are being removed gradually. Moreover, science and technology, especially information technology, have been developing rapidly. In addition, the multinational corporation is becoming a common pattern for business operations: that is, each multinational corporation rather than each country runs a business. In the global market, large and small multinational corporations are the real operators. Under certain conditions, corporations within nations will soon turn into operational entities beyond national boundaries. As you all know, Finland is a very small country, with only a few million people. Nokia was once a small company in Finland, engaged in the timber industry and the wood pulp business. Later, it entered the information industry and patented many inventions. Gradually, it developed into a large multinational corporation. Such examples are numerous. The elimination of various barriers and the development of science and technology after the cold war enlarged the entire market. With multinational corporations as the carriers, economic globalization is inevitable.

But economic globalization will not bring about global harmony. Despite economic globalization, conflicts are sharpening. Consider the recent WTO conference in Seattle, for example. The theme of this conference was to further develop economic globalization. It turned out that the conference could not even hold its opening ceremony, because some of the delegations were kept away from the venue by protesters. No agreement was achieved, owing to a divergence of views. Therefore, it was a conference without an opening ceremony or final documents. There were many conflicts at the conference, and agreement was difficult to reach, while demonstrations were in full swing outside the conference hall the whole time. Both inside and outside, chaos reigned. The authorities in Seattle had to use tear gas and pepper fog to maintain public order. So economic globalization, involving many conflicts of interest, is not that easy to achieve. At the conference in Seattle, the topics concerning agriculture brought up by the United States clashed with the interests of Europe, Japan, and the developing countries. The developing countries thought that no new topics should be raised, since the agreements that had resulted from the long-running Uruguay Round had brought no benefits to them at all. Various conflicts prevented the discussions from reaching agreement. Outside the conference venues there were demonstrations by protectionists, environmentalists, and labor unions, demanding better environmental protection standards, higher pay for workers, and steps to avoid losses in U.S. agriculture. They formed pressure groups, demanding that the U.S. government solve these problems. The government, in turn, was more than willing to use its support to implement the U.S. proposals. But things did not turn out the way the government wished, and the protesters effectively ruined the conference.

Let's take a look at the east Asian financial crisis of two years ago. Hong Kong returned to China on July 1, 1997. The following day, a financial storm broke out, spreading from Thailand, with the depreciation of the Thai currency, and to other ASEAN countries, South Korea, and Japan. The situation was particularly serious in Malaysia and Indonesia. The financial storm came all of a sudden, without any warning, like a natural disaster, sweeping away every tree and destroying every building. Now the storm has died away, and the economies of the east Asian countries are gradually recovering. Leaving aside the weaknesses in the economic and financial policies adopted by the stricken countries, if such a storm spreads worldwide, it will stir up enormous trouble with an invisible hand. This is another manifestation of globalization.

Economic globalization does not mean a worldwide economy or an Americanized economy, because national functions still exist and will continue to exist all over the world. The nation state remains a major factor in economic development. The state's role in regulating the market is irreplaceable. Although multinational corporations are active worldwide, they are regulated by the laws of each particular country. In addition, conflicts of interest between countries are endemic. For instance, Britain and France had a fierce quarrel over the issue of beef, and went to an international court over it. France refused to recognize the arbitration decision, and was penalized. Then France appealed to some higher court. How could beef cause so much trouble in a globalized economy? Agricultural and textile products cause the same kind of conflicts. In short, the particular interests of each country still exist, and so conflicts are inevitable. Economic globalization by no means equals universal harmony or the integration of the whole world. People who hold this view are armchair strategists. Many problems can be solved in theory, but not in practice. Therefore, economic globalization is no more than a trend; conflicts remain, and the world has not yet become a global village. It is wrong to think that all countries have common interests, and that everyone can benefit. On the contrary, economic globalization cannot lead to the political integration of all countries.

During the eighteenth and nineteenth centuries, developed countries like Britain did everything they could to open the world market, a goal that was then much more difficult than now. Navies and cannons were used to open markets in those days. If you did not have trade relations, the developed countries would force you to accept trade relations, through war if necessary. This was called gunboat diplomacy. Nowadays, in this era of globalization, it is not that complicated to open world markets. There is no need for gunboats, armed force, or war. Colonialism, in a sense, can be established through finance and trade. This kind of colonialism relies on the invisible hand, not necessarily on military force. The means of conquering a country have undergone changes from military expansion to commodity export to capital export and then to the dominance of financial markets and the invisible hand. For example, during the Asian financial crisis of 1997, "hedge funds" and "tiger funds" exerted a devastating effect.

Many issues related to economic globalization, such as the relationship between the market economy and administrative intervention, deserve study. The market economy takes different patterns in different parts of the world. For instance, the United States practices a largely free market economy; Germany has adopted a social market economy centered on social welfare; and Japan has a social market economy guided by the government. In fact, an absolutely free market economy does not exist anywhere, and one could say that such a phenomenon is impossible; there is always government intervention to varying degrees. The market economy is unavoidably connected with government intervention and macro-control of a certain scope. The problem is to what degree a government should intervene in the market, and whether such intervention should be strengthened or weakened after a financial crisis.

Some development has taken place in capitalist economic laws. It was believed that periodic economic crises were inevitable in the development of a free economy, marking a cycle of prosperity and depression. Changes have happened to such economic laws. John Maynard Keynes introduced his theory that a certain amount of government intervention was necessary in the later stage of market economy. Idle funds totaling several trillion dollars are flowing around the world all the time. No one knows where they go, but they will get somewhere spontaneously, and may stir up trouble. We all hope that the trouble will be small and controllable. How to control the trouble—that is, how to establish an appropriate relationship between the market economy and government intervention—is a question remaining to be answered.

The second issue concerns Euro-American and east Asian patterns of economic development. The east Asian pattern, in which the economy developed very rapidly, once produced the miracle called the "four Asian dragons" and "four Asian tigers." But the weaknesses in this pattern became manifest following the financial crisis: too much government intervention and "crony capitalism." The economy develops rapidly in one period, but problems soon emerge. Then a question is raised: Is the east Asian pattern still useful? In fact, the east Asian pattern, which played an important role during a certain period, is a combination of export-oriented development strategy and governmental promotion efforts. Experience has shown us that economically poor countries have to rely on government involvement in and organization of economic activities to create favorable conditions for economic development and to realize economic modernization. A certain degree of government intervention is necessary for these poor countries to catch up and compete with other countries in the global market. Therefore the east Asian pattern was successful for quite a long period of time. An absolutely free economy without any government intervention has been found to be impossible. Without government protection, developing countries will be vulnerable to external impacts.

The third issue is free trade and protectionism. Free trade requires the lowering of tariffs. In order to participate in the world economy, every country grants preferential treatment to attract foreign investment. The present average tariff accounts for only about ten percent of the amount when GATT was in effect. Does this mean that protectionism has disappeared? No. Protectionism actually still coexists with opening-up; only the means have changed. The most common method of trade protection is antidumping laws. For instance, the production cost and prices of commodities of developing countries are relatively low. Theoretically, low-price commodities should be imported in a system of free trade. However, many countries enact antidumping laws to protect the interests of home producers. Although tariffs are lowered, antidumping duties are added. In this regard, consider the price of Japanese rice, for instance. It is about seven times that of U.S. rice. If Japan did not protect its farmers' interests, its rice production or even its agriculture would soon be diminished to nothing.

So, a certain degree of protection is necessary. There are many pretexts for protection, such as environmental protection and opposition to genetic engineering, on the assumption that genetically modified crops are harmful to health. This shows that protectionism is still prevalent in the world. The prices of Chinese products are relatively low, but this fact is said to be violating the antidumping laws in foreign markets. We actually do not dump any products. Our prices are low only because our labor force is cheap. The Seattle Conference intended to stipulate a unified price for labor all over the world, to make production costs more or less equal. But this is not easy. The world is not uniform, and it is impossible to make it uniform. Although barriers are undesirable in theory, they exist in reality. Both free trade measures and trade barrier measures can be discussed at the WTO forum. The former supports globalization and intellectual copyright protection and opposes subsidies, while the latter advocates protectionism and firmly opposes bringing labor and environmental protection into WTO agreements. This conflict will continue for the foreseeable future.

The fourth issue is free finance and the regulation of capital. An unprecedentedly large global capital market has taken shape. The gross amount of money of all the capital markets adds up to US$35 trillion, surpassing the total output value of the whole world. The everyday trading volume on foreign exchange markets is US$1.5 trillion, as much as the total world trading volume for four months. Only about five percent of such a huge amount is related to commodity transactions and services. That is, only five percent of US$1.5 trillion is based on real goods, and the other 95 percent, consisting of stocks and currencies, is fictitious capital. This involves a huge risk. Profit is made through the interest rate differential of the mock capital. Therefore, there is a general request for regulation of the idle capital that does not go into production and is only for speculation. But this is very difficult. During the financial crisis, Malaysia took measures to prevent liquidity of foreign currencies. A country may do this in a short period, but this measure cannot be adopted worldwide. In fact, this problem is more serious than free trade, which takes the form of commodities and services. Capital flow is a purely financial concept, which no country has found an effective way of regulating.

The next topic is international political relations. The Kosovo War cannot be ignored when political issues are mentioned. It happened in Europe, and more than ten NATO countries became involved in Kosovo. The war reflected the great turbulence in international relations, but it did not change the overall international trend. Some issues arising from this war deserve study. One is humanitarian intervention. In recent years, more than forty books and more than 100 articles have been devoted to this subject. One major argument is that human rights should take priority over the traditional reverence for sovereignty. Another is that the international community has a responsibility to intervene wherever bad government or tyranny appears. A third is that wars should be fought for values that uphold justice, as well as for territory and sovereignty. Once there were such wars, such as the eastern expeditions of the Crusades and the "holy wars" waged by some Muslim countries. It was not accidental that these arguments emerged after the end of the cold war. During the cold war, the struggle between the two opposing superpowers took center stage. Some countries followed one or other of the two superpowers, while others remained unaligned. Who is the present enemy? For instance, NATO's former enemy was the Warsaw Treaty Organization, which has disintegrated. Indeed, many of its member countries have become members of NATO. Since no enemy can be found, morality and values are sought to justify more wars.

Another argument holds that we should heighten our vigilance against terrorism, and that some countries harbor terrorism. Nowadays some Western scholars are confused about who the enemy is, but they will go to any lengths to set a goal to fight for, such as human rights. This needs to be justified by a theory that human rights are more important than sovereignty and that the concept of national states has become obsolete and should be discarded. In fact, this principle is hard to apply in practice. It is easy for a dozen countries to attack Kosovo, which occupies only some 10,000 square kilometers. But it is not likely that other countries will form an alliance and fight a large country for a principle. If fighting for a principle depends on the size of the target country, then is attacking small countries the principle? That is no different from the law of the jungle, which was the backbone of imperialist and colonialist theory.

The next issue is unipolarity and multipolarity. The worldwide polarized confrontation has ended. Will the world head for unipolarity or multipolarity? NATO's expansion consists of three steps. The first is expansion to the east; the second is NATO's new strategy; the third is taking action. This is actually a trend toward unipolarity, enabling NATO to intervene in affairs all over the world. As a result, the Kosovo War was not brought to the UN Security Council for a vote. Why? Because it was not likely to get approval from the Security Council, which was composed of fifteen countries—ten nonpermanent members and five permanent members. The Security Council, responsible for maintaining world peace and security, has the sole authority over the use of peacekeeping forces. All five permanent members have veto power. NATO intended to bypass the Security Council, but finally it had to turn to the UN again after it failed to replace the Security Council with the Group of Seven and the Group of Eight. It is not easy to carry out unipolarity, but it will also take a long time to realize multipolarity. Generally speaking, pure unipolarity can get nowhere in the present world.

The so-called unipolarity means that one country has such enormous power that it can decide all the world's affairs, and will use force against anybody who disagrees. In a multipolarized world, it should be the UN Security Council and not just one country that makes decisions on the world's problems. In this case, many issues are more complicated than in a unipolarized world, and cannot be decided arbitrarily by one country. NATO, which is led by the United States, agrees with almost every U.S. decision. But the UN cannot be led by one country, because it represents all the countries in the world.

Disarmament also becomes a problem in the new situation. Over the years, some progress has been made in solving this problem. In the past, disarmament chiefly concerned the two superpowers—the United States and the Soviet Union. Their bilateral talks were the nucleus of the international disarmament issue, because disarmament mainly concerned missiles and nuclear weapons, which were mostly possessed by them. After the disintegration of the Soviet Union, who should be disarmed and what the purpose of disarmament should be came into question. Recently, there was a dispute about whether to amend the Anti-Ballistic Missile Treaty. It turned out at the conference that France, Russia, and China did not approve and only a few insisted on amending the treaty.

Now the United States wants to build a national missile defense system. Many countries are against this plan, considering it the start of a new arms race. Then why does the United States want to build this system? Where does the menace come from? The Soviet Union has disintegrated and is no longer a menace to the United States. The United States claims that there are some irresponsible countries and terrorists around. We will surely wonder how a small country can be a menace to such a great power as the United States. These small countries do not possess nuclear weapons. Even if they have intercontinental missiles, the power of such missiles would not be much different from that of ordinary bombs when they reached U.S. territory. Then what is the purpose of building a national missile defense system? This method of defense against intercontinental missiles is not necessary to cope with terrorism. In fact, terrorism has many ways of hitting its targets far less costly than intercontinental missiles. Therefore, this national defense system has no logical basis, and in UN discussions the majority of countries consider it unnecessary.

The next issue is whether the strategic emphasis of the United States is on Europe or on Asia. Traditionally, U.S. strategy has emphasized Europe. However, the new guideline of the security treaty between the United States and Japan directs more attention by the United States to Asia than ever before. Nevertheless, generally speaking, the emphasis remains on Europe. After the Kosovo War, many countries woke up from their complacency, and began to reflect on what had happened. They came to the conclusion that they had better be cautious. So the Kosovo War is regarded as a special case but not a precedent. The situation in Europe is entirely different from that in Asia. Two world wars broke out in Europe. Europe is a small place, where countries are close to each other. Throughout history, several large countries have fought to dominate Europe. Asia has an area several times the size of Europe. Nearly the whole of Asia was colonized by European powers in the recent past. But now it is not as easy to gain hegemony in Asia as it was in those days. Times have changed completely, and the United States' strategic emphasis, in the spheres of the economy, politics, history, and so forth, is still on Europe.

Next, we come to the issue of relations between the major powers. I think that both Sino-American relations and American-Russian relations sagged to their lowest point in 1999 and began to recover in the latter half of last year. After the attack on Kosovo, internal differences began to emerge in the EU. Over eighty percent of the military operations were performed by the United States in the Kosovo War. That is to say, Europe could not fight any battle without U.S. support. Britain, Germany, and France then saw the necessity of building a large all-European army that could operate within a certain scope. We can see from the situation in the latter half of 1999 that all the large powers hope to maintain relaxed relations, and this may be the situation for some time.

The preceding analysis shows that the international situation is full of uncertainties. We should take stock of ourselves in the global context, and realize that although China's economy has developed greatly and achievements have been made in all aspects, we must have a clear judgment of ourselves.

China's GNP ranks seventh in the world, but we lag behind in terms of per capita GNP. In 1999, our GNP was over US$ 1 trillion, or US$800 per person. But, to put this in perspective, China's GNP accounts for only about 3 percent of the world GNP. It is tiny. China ranks eleventh in the world in trade volume, but in fact accounts for only about 3 percent of total world trade volume. Therefore, we should not be complacent or conceited. China is a peace-loving nation, concerned with construction, not expansion. We have the patience to achieve the goal of "peaceful reunification, one country, two systems." In the final analysis, it is up to us alone to solve our problems by managing our own affairs well. To do this, we must be fully aware of China's position in the world.

I believe that in international studies several spheres of activity need to be coordinated. Take diplomacy, for example. Diplomatic activities are in the front line; research institutes are in the second line; and academic institutes and institutions of higher learning are in the third line. All three are very important, and each should perform its own special functions and coordinate with the others. For instance, the Chinese Ministry of Foreign Affairs has to cope with daily matters. It must be well informed of everyday events, in order to make correct judgments and then take action. It also studies world developments. Research institutes concentrate on medium- and long-term strategies. Institutions of higher learning study academic matters of an even longer term and from an overall historical perspective. Huntington, an American professor, wrote a book called *The Clash of Civilizations*, in which he devised future scenarios. Whether his argument can be proved or not and how the world will develop in the future are other matters. Professor Ezra Vogel of Harvard University wrote a book called *Japan as Number 1*, which also deals with conjectures about the future. Research that discusses long-term strategies instead of concentrating on current affairs or serving short-term policies is needed. We have only a small amount of such research, compared with the numerous works of this kind published in the rest of the world. We cannot boast great works on world affairs like Zbigniew Brzezinski's *The Grand Chessboard*. Our diplomatic, research, and academic work at the institutions of higher learning should be coordinated, and the personnel concerned should participate in each other's work. I hope that the research work of the School of International Studies of Peking University can make continuous progress in turning out talented people and producing first-class writing, and thus make important contributions to our country.

APPENDIX II

Some Thoughts on International Studies
(MAY 26, 2000)

I AM VERY GLAD TO VISIT Peking University again. Today, I have come here to participate in the celebration of the fifth anniversary of the founding of the university's School of International Studies, as well as for the fortieth anniversary of the founding of its predecessor, the Department of International Politics. As the saying goes, "At thirty, one should

be well established in life; when one reaches forty one is no longer perplexed by the complexities of the world." Not being perplexed is very important in research work, especially in international studies. But it is not
an easy state of mind to reach.

I will not give a detailed introduction to international relations, since
you are all very familiar with this subject. I just want to bring up some issues, and give my opinions on them for your reference. The world is undergoing rapid and daily changes. It is certainly not easy to keep up with
these changes, come to a deep understanding, and make correct judgments. But these changes must be taken into consideration in both diplomacy work and international studies.

The following points deserve particular attention from researchers:

1. We are now in the era of the information society. With the development of information technology, knowledge spreads much more rapidly
and widely, and in larger quantities, than ever before. The ancients said,
"A scholar knows all the world's affairs without stepping outside his
gate." These words were, of course, unrealistic and exaggerated even in
ancient times. We can be well informed of the latest world affairs and situations as long as we keep our eyes and ears open. The problems involve
information overload rather than any shortage of information. There are
various kinds of information: true information, misinformation, misleading information, rumors. In a certain sense, information overload causes
more difficulties for international studies than information shortage.

The new situation requires immediate understanding of events, swift
research, correct judgment, and quick response in our international studies. In an information society, the public can acquire a large amount of
relevant information right after any event takes place. Therefore, if comrades engaged in research and diplomatic work are slow to react, they will
probably find themselves in an awkward position. Furthermore, the scope
of foreign affairs has been extended, since all information is open nowadays. Objectively speaking, everyone can participate in diplomacy in the
information age. When we make judgments and responses, we should take
domestic opinion as well as international opinion into consideration, since
foreign affairs and internal affairs are interrelated. In other words, our
diplomatic activities should win the support of the internal pubic as well
as the international community. Diplomacy is of course a state activity,
and many internal matters must be kept confidential for the time being.
But the rest must be open to the public. We reply with "No comment" to
some questions, but such a reply cannot solve problems.

The standard of international studies should be greatly raised. There
was a dearth of such studies in the past because of a shortage of informa-

tion. Now, the "information explosion" requires our researchers to have a really high standard of expertise in order to discard the unimportant and the false, retain the essential and true, and analyze the issues from the outside to the inside and get to the key problems. In particular, they should be able to identify at a glance false and misleading news and information, which are circulated to spread rumors. Some newspapers and information sources specialize in fabricating rumors. People often said in the past that rumors could kill. Although rumors cannot kill directly, they can have an equally devastating effect if they become widespread. Goebbels, Nazi Germany's minister for propaganda, said, "If a lie is repeated a thousand times, then it becomes a truth."

In fact, a monopoly of information does exist. On the surface there is free publicity and free choice. But the more money one possesses, the greater the power one has to publicize one's information, the more one can make oneself heard by more people. Whoever controls the network of publicity has the major say and the widest influence. The U.S. government has accused Bill Gates of having a monopoly of information technology. This issue is partly about technology. But why is the monopoly of the content of information ignored? Preconceived notions with wide coverage have monstrous power. Doubts gradually turn into echoes of others' views without thinking, under the subtle influence exerted by the domination of the media and the ability to shape public opinion through penetration, influence, and seizing a critical opportunity. Therefore, I think that an understanding of the nature of the information society is a vital element for international studies and diplomacy.

2. Economic globalization. Economic globalization is having a strong impact on the global economy and political structure. This can be perceived in the following examples. First, multinational corporations and enterprises operate beyond national boundaries. The proportion of total output, overseas investment, and volume of internal and external trade of multinational corporations is 40 percent, 90 percent and 60 percent, respectively, of the totals for the whole world. This new situation shows that the operations of multinational corporations have gone beyond national boundaries. Second, the capacity and scale of the world market have undergone unprecedented expansion. The world's daily volume of foreign exchange twenty years ago was ten billion dollars, but now it is US$1.5 trillion. Worldwide exports accounted for about 14 percent of world's GNP in 1970, but now it accounts for 24 percent. Thus, the worldwide import and export market, foreign exchange market, and investment market have all been greatly expanded. This is partly because the development of information technology, especially the promotion of economic information resources by the Internet,

has created favorable conditions for the global circulation of capital and goods. In addition, economic rules, such as the WTO regulations, are moving toward global unification.

The trend of economic globalization brings new changes to the world situation. As the pioneer of the new economy, the United States is obviously in a leading and dominant position. The United States has had about ten years of economic prosperity. And Europe and Japan are speeding up internal adjustment and the development of overseas markets to win bigger shares of the emerging markets; some developing countries opening to the outside world are grasping the opportunity to hasten their development. However, many developing countries fear they are in danger of being marginalized by economic globalization and lag far behind in this process. Economic globalization leads to imbalanced economic development as well as the promotion of economic development. The imbalance in the international economy will result in imbalanced political development, and will have an ominous impact on the world political structure.

3. The influence of religion on international relations. Many hot issues are closely related to religious and racial problems, which have a long history and came into focus following the end of the cold war.

We can say that the influence of religion on international relations reached two climaxes in the past. The first was in the Middle Ages, when the rise of Islam led to "holy wars" to spread that faith and the Christian West responded with the Crusades. Muslims and Crusaders fought all the way from Europe to West Asia. This climax lasted a long time, resulting in great turbulence in international relations. The second climax was in modern times and is marked by the Afro-Asian struggle, with the aid of state religions, against missionary colonialism. Now we are in the midst of the third climax. The conflict in Bosnia-Herzegovina was, to a certain extent, a clash between the Orthodox church and Islam, as was the Kosovo crisis. The conflicts in Chechnya, East Timor, and Sri Lanka; the Israeli-Palestinian conflict, and problems in Northern Ireland also have religious roots. Huntington, an American scholar, predicts that a "clash of civilizations" between Christianity, Islam, and Buddhism is bound to occur. Of course, we can hardly agree with him, as it is clear that religions and civilizations can live in harmony if their differences are properly handled. Nevertheless, this issue deserves our attention, because it has the following characteristics. (1) Religion is often connected with racial issues. (2) Religious freedom is often interrelated with human rights. (3) Religion often has links to fundamentalism and terrorism. (4) Religion is often connected with politics, racial division, and resistance to unity. (5) Religious identity goes beyond national and racial boundaries and sometimes has great influence. Religion can penetrate every aspect of life, as when Hindus opposed the setting up of McDonald's restaurants in India.

From a historical perspective on international relations, we can see that religious and racial conflicts often reignite problems that were thought to have been brought under control or even solved after a great change in the international situation. Religion is a Pandora's box, which is easy to open and hard to close without long-term efforts. Moreover, some countries' interference in the internal affairs of other countries in the name of protecting religious freedom and human rights sharpens the conflicts. In addition, poverty and instability may become the seedbed of religious conflict.

Religion is an inevitable phenomenon in human society. It is a religious concept that the year 2000 marked the start of the third millennium worldwide. The history of human society is certainly much longer than 2,000 years. For the whole of human society, everything undergoes changes and the process of birth, growth, development, and death. But the history of religion is much longer than the history of any country. Therefore, religious issues deserve our attention.

Recently, the pope did penance for the sins committed by the Roman Catholic church in the past 2,000 years, and prayed to God for mercy. He listed seven sins of the Roman Catholic Church: (1) forcing Catholics to do penance; (2) launching the Crusades and establishing the Inquisition; (3) participating in a split in Christianity; (4) being hostile to Judaism; (5) propagating the Catholic faith by force; (6) discriminating against women; and (7) being indifferent to social problems. It was unprecedented for a pope to admit these seven sins. But he did not mention the role of religion in the imperialists' invasions of China. Nor did he mention that we took the initiative in setting up churches after the founding of the People's Republic of China and applied for the Vatican's approval of the ministers and bishops we had chosen. But the Vatican not only refused to give approval; it severed relations with us. The sins of the Roman Catholic church are certainly far more than the seven listed above.

4. Sovereignty and its relationship with human rights in international relations. State sovereignty comes into being with the creation of a state. Mutual respect for sovereignty and equality is the basic principle of international relations, as enshrined in the constitution of the UN at its founding after World War II. It is a dangerous tendency to think that attaching importance to human rights means the principle of sovereignty has become obsolete and there is no need to adhere to it. At the UN Millennium Summit, some people argued that human rights should take priority over state sovereignty. But if all countries and the UN gave priority to human

rights over state sovereignty, the whole world would be thrown into disorder. The equality of more than 180 sovereign states constitutes the foundation of the UN. The UN has its charter and must formulate rules concerning the relations between different countries. This is very natural. Of course, you may talk about human rights, security, or any other issue. But the tenets, charter, and principles of the UN were intended to draw a lesson from World War II. The half century of peace after World War II would have been impossible without these.

Let's look at some examples, to examine the view which purports to give the highest priority to human rights.

First, the Kosovo War, in which force was used in the name of humanitarianism, turned out to be a humanitarian catastrophe that is still ongoing. Some countries have reflected on this.

Second, international trade. It is natural for countries to trade with each other under WTO regulations. As a founder member of GATT, China is making great efforts to become a member of the WTO. An act just passed by the U.S. House of Representatives has removed its restrictions on normal trade relations between the United States and China. This issue is not about China's joining the WTO, because that does not need approval of the U.S. Congress. What are normal trade relations? They are what used to be known as most-favored-nation treatment, which is actually not a favor at all. Trade rules and the import duty rates of a country should apply to all other countries without any discrimination. Where did refusal of most-favored-nation treatment originate? It arose from an act known as the Jackson-Vanik Amendment, passed by the U.S. Congress in the 1970s. The Soviet Union was the first target of this act, which demanded that the Soviet Union allow free emigration of its Jewish citizens; otherwise, the United States would adopt measures that discriminate against Soviet trade.

How was such a measure imposed on China, which has no Jewish citizens? This is a so-called extension of that act. If the United States does not want to give a country normal trade treatment, it would say that the act applies to such a country. When China and the United States established diplomatic relations in 1979, they were on good terms, and the volume of trade was small. But as the trade volume grew, frictions developed and the U.S. government started to submit to Congress for discussion annual applications for extension of most-favored-nation treatment to China. In fact, the application is approved every year, but a hot debate is inevitable, since opinions in Congress are divided. The policy and debate have continued since Clinton became president. So every year, there is a quarrel in Congress. China has two divergent views in establishing permanent normal trade relations with the U.S. First, most-favored-nation treatment—the name itself. China neither considers this most-favored-nation treatment nor wants to be the most favored nation; we demand only normal treatment. Sino-American trade relations should have been normalized when the two countries signed a trade agreement. But it took seven or eight years to change the term "most-favored-nation treatment" (MFN) to "normal trade relations" (NTR). Second, China advocates that annual extension runs counter to NTR. The fair decision of granting China permanent normal trade relations (PNTR) has finally come after years of efforts. In my view, it is a most reasonable demand, yet it took years to be met. On the one hand, we must admit that President Clinton had indeed made efforts toward achieving this top diplomatic goal before leaving his post. On the other hand, the United States was inviting trouble for itself. It created something unreasonable and then took enormous trouble to cancel it.

I take this example to show that it is dangerous to connect everything with human rights. If you have Jews, you must allow them to emigrate; if you have no Jews, other aspects of human rights will be examined. Faults can always be found here and there that can be used as an excuse to hamper trade relations. But no profit can be gained without trade. So the United States wanted to carry on the trade. Then, annual extensions were added, and every year, the United States created some trouble, but it was actually inviting trouble. The PNTR was finally adopted after all those efforts. Now the United States is to set up a committee to examine China's human rights conditions, which will not affect trade relations. The United States is inviting more trouble. There will be similar problems in the future, and surely the United States will lose more popularity.

Next, the question of Taiwan. It was two whole months from the election of the Democratic Progressive Party's candidate Chen Shui-bian to the "presidency" of Taiwan on March 18, 2000, to his inaugural speech on May 20, 2000. What is the present situation in Taiwan? The ascent to power of the Democratic Progressive Party has caused sudden changes in the political situation and is adding new uncertainties to relations across the Taiwan Strait. A poll found that only 39 percent of the Taiwanese electorate voted for Chen Shui-bian; the other 60 percent fell into two categories: supporters of the Kuomintang's candidate and supporters of the candidate from a new party, which had split from the Kuomintang. It turned out that a candidate with less than half the votes was elected "president." Moreover, the Democratic Progressive Party states clearly in its program that it would push for independence for Taiwan, a policy which won the support of probably less than half of the 39 percent who voted for Chen Shui-bian. Another half voted for Chen Shui-bian because they opposed the

Kuomintang's "black gold politics" (political corruption). Within the two months from March 18 to May 20, most countries restated their support for the "one China" principle. People from all walks of life in Taiwan also hope to break the stalemate and improve relations across the Taiwan Strait. In particular, business circles in Taiwan are more than willing to develop economic and trade relations between the mainland and Taiwan. In the mainland, we are consistent and unanimous in our attitude toward Taiwan. In these circumstances, Taiwan's elected "president" is actually ill prepared. So he has moved from an overt independence policy to a covert one in order to relieve pressures from both inside and outside. Chen Shui-bian has been using stalling tactics in dealing with relations across the Taiwan Strait to gain a breathing spell to stabilize the inside and consolidate his political power. He appeared to take a down-to-earth attitude of compromise and goodwill, and to have committed himself to the "four nos"—not declaring Taiwan independent, not writing the doctrine of state-to-state relations into Taiwan's "constitution," not holding a referendum on unification or independence, and not changing Taiwan's "national title." In addition, Chen pledged not to abolish the National Unification Council or the National Unification guidelines. But he refuses to accept the "one China" principle. He has assumed a posture of nonrecognition and evasiveness regarding the key principle of Taiwan's being part of China.

We must persist in the "one China" principle and not make any compromise on it. We should combine persistence with flexibility in our policies. If he continues to reject the "one China" principle, we will make efforts to present a positive image to win favorable world opinion and the support of the people of Taiwan, while keeping pressure on Chen Shui-bian. That is our basic stand on the Taiwan issue. We will reveal Chen Shui-bian's real intention of dodging the "one China" principle and his empty promise to improve relations across the Taiwan Strait, and force him to fulfill his commitment to the "four nos." At the same time, we should take the initiative in demanding dialogue and the "three direct links" (in mail, transportation, and trade) across the Taiwan Strait.

The question of Taiwan involves many difficulties and requires many-sided efforts. Comrade Deng Xiaoping once said that the question of Taiwan could be solved only with "both hands." The right hand, which is stronger, seeks a peaceful solution, but the left will resort to military force in case of failure by the right one. No flexibility is allowed, except patience. We respect the reality of Taiwan. Taiwan can keep its existing social system, its policies, and its own armed forces of a certain scale, and continue its trade, commercial, and individual contacts with foreign countries. The Taiwan people's lifestyle will be preserved. The income of the Taiwan people will not decrease; on the contrary, it will increase. All these things can be realized only within the "one China" framework, which is our basic requirement. Comrade Deng once commented that there are no preconditions for the "three direct links," which are a means to promote understanding and negotiation between the peoples and governments on both sides of the Strait. All foreign friends are welcome to make sincere efforts to promote China's reunification. But decisions on China's reunification should be made by the leaders and peoples of the mainland and Taiwan. If the leaders on both sides of the Taiwan Strait can accomplish China's reunification, their splendid achievement will go down in Chinese history. We hope that Taiwan's leaders will broaden their minds and be farsighted. Comrade Deng also said that this kind of problem could not be solved within one month, and a long time was needed. We by no means want to take Taiwan captive and put it in a position of subjugation. Our stand is expressed clearly in Comrade Deng's words.

From our point of view, Taiwan is the most important and sensitive topic in Sino-American relations. The three Sino-American Joint Communiqués focus on this question. We believe that the Taiwan question is an internal affair of China's. Sales of weapons to Taiwan by the United States are an interference in China's internal affairs, and impede a peaceful resolution of the Taiwan question. If the U.S. Congress continues to interfere in China's internal affairs, turbulence will occur in Sino-American relations. All in all, we are consistent in our stand on the question of Taiwan, and the basic policy of "peaceful reunification and one country, two systems" remains unchanged.

APPENDIX III

Some Aspects of the Current World Situation
(SEPTEMBER 10, 2001)

IT IS A GREAT PLEASURE to come to Peking University again. First of all, let me congratulate you on the beginning of the new academic year and welcome the newcomers to the School of International Studies. Today is Teachers' Day. I would like to extend warm greetings to all the teachers! Today I will deal with some questions.

First, is the global economy favorable to China or not? In one sense, the fact that colonial and semicolonial countries became independent does not mean that the large Western powers have entirely given up controlling and looting small, weak nations. But they have changed their ways to adapt to public opinion, culture, ideology, values, and economic and cultural influences. So the global economy brings advantages as well as disadvantages to China, where challenges and opportunities coexist. As the global economy is a double-edged sword, the problem is how to control it. Managed well, it will bring advantages. Otherwise, it will bring disadvantages. In short, the global economy will not automatically give birth to a new international economic order. On the contrary, it will probably widen the gap between developed and developing countries. Furthermore, one phenomenon deserves attention. In recent years, many political and economic international meetings held in the West—for instance, the Seattle World Trade Organization Ministerial Conference in 1999, the Genoa Group of Seven Summit in July 2001, and the World Economic Forum in Davos—were all confronted with street demonstrations, some of which even led to violence and injuries. Those demonstrators mostly came from developed countries and included members of environmental groups, industrial and agricultural trade unionists, and the Green Party. Left-wing communists and people on the far right took part, too. They shouted all sorts of slogans, which had one thing in common: discontent with the global economy. At present, there is an upsurge of amalgamations between multinational corporations to improve their competitive strength, followed by the widespread adoption of new technology and layoffs of large numbers of workers. No doubt this sharpens the competitive edge, but it adds tension to employee-employer relations and causes new social conflict. Therefore, the global economy has enhanced the interdependence between countries and, at the same time, widened the gap between rich and poor. However, Western countries have become aware of this. More than half of the discussions at the Genoa Summit were about how to help developing countries; that is quite unusual. The summit also formulated the Genoa Plan for Africa to set up a close new partnership with African countries. However, action and not words will be needed to put it into effect.

Every country should participate on equal terms in the economic globalization. We adhere to a social system, pattern of development, and traditional culture that conform to the reality of China. By so doing, we are contributing to economic globalization instead of opposing it. In fact, we cannot benefit from the global economy without contributing to it. So, in the new century, China's security will rely not entirely on military force but more important, on comprehensive national strength. Deng Xiaoping said that development is the top priority. The role that China plays in international affairs depends on its achievements in building its economy.

Our key task is still building the economy, which is the material base for solving domestic and international problems.

In the global economy, the mobility of commodities, capital, technology, and labor has been enhanced, as has interdependence between countries. There are more and more overlapping areas where our country and others all benefit. With both common interests and differences, we will reach a win-win situation as long as we cooperate more. For example, during the Asian financial crisis, China committed itself in the face of enormous pressure not to devalue the renminbi, thus helping ease the crisis and benefiting us. In fact, China cannot keep its integrity if Asia is in a state of chaos. However, if we help to maintain stability and solve any difficulties, both China and other countries will benefit. In addition, environmental protection and also the fight against drug trafficking, terrorism, and multinational crime are in our common security interests, so international cooperation is necessary. At present, China's reform and opening-up and its efforts to join the WTO are all strategic moves to take the initiative in joining the global economy, aimed at speeding up its own development by extending its contacts and cooperation with the international community. Of course, we have to pay a price to join the current international order. But it is worthwhile and not detrimental to our basic interests. What China has achieved in its more than twenty years of reform and opening-up have proved the success of its policy of playing an active role in the global economy. As the world's largest developing country, China is one of the five permanent members of the UN Security Council. As well as going deep into the globalization process, we will have a say in the current order and rules of the game. Taking part in these, we can seek advantages, avoid disadvantages, act in good time, and gradually improve matters. We do not consider the current order and rules of the game to be flawless. However, unless we have a hand in them, we cannot seek advantages, avoid disadvantages, and change whatever is irrational. Actually, no country can be divorced from the international situation or isolated from the international community. Whether you like it or not, you have to face the challenge.

The current economic situation in the world is very disappointing. After ten years of developing at top speed, the U.S. economy started to decline last year. Seven times, the Federal Reserve Bank has announced a reduction in the interest rate. The interest rate has dropped to about 3.5 percent, which is still not working. The European economy has slowed down, too. The Japanese economy has been stagnant and has been declining for about ten years. That is to say, the three locomotives of the Western economy—the United States, Europe, and Japan—all have declining economies. For the United States, it is estimated that, in 2001, the rate of growth of the GDP will be 3.15 percent (for the first quarter of this year the growth rate was 1.2 percent and for the second quarter it was only 0.2 percent); in Japan it could be 0.2 percent and in Germany 0.9 percent. Comparatively, the situation in Asia is better. It is estimated that China's economy will grow by 7.5 percent this year. Under such circumstances, China, with its considerable national strength, will develop more quickly by taking advantage of the global economy as long as it implements the correct policies and measures. With the absolute superiority of the large domestic market, we maintained a high growth rate even during the Asian financial crisis, and we helped Asia remain stable.

Second, will a booming economy lead to external expansion? Historically, some countries expanded externally as their economies grew quickly, including Spain, Portugal, the Netherlands, Britain, France, Japan, Germany, and the United States. When the United States was established in 1776, there were only thirteen states. After the economy boomed, another thirty-two states and five territories were incorporated into the United States by means of war, purchase, and annexation. There are fifty states altogether. But can we conclude that every country expands externally when its economy is growing quickly? I don't think so.

A booming economy does not automatically entail expansion. For one thing, not every external expansion was caused by a booming economy. In modern French history, the Napoleonic wars resulted in an upsurge of expansion for the domination of Europe. However, during the French Revolution before the wars and during the period of multinational interference by a European coalition against France, French economic growth and industrial development were not always rapid. In modern history, productivity in czarist Russia was very backward compared with that of other European countries. Russia still had a system of serfdom in the nineteenth century. However, its ambition to expand at the cost of war did not weaken accordingly. Although the economy was growing slowly, Russia burned with a wild ambition to expand. So there is no inevitable link between economic growth and external expansion.

Furthermore, a booming economy does not necessarily cause external expansion. After World War II, it took Germany and Japan about thirty years to rise from the ruins of war to become the most developed countries. During that time, their economies developed quickly but the two countries did not expand externally. Lenin said that countries in economic crisis are more likely to follow the road of imperialist expansion. We are quite familiar with the examples of Nazi Germany and Japanese militarism in the 1930s. Then, they expanded although their economies were not booming. This shows that setting out a causal relationship between a booming economy and external expansion will probably lead to a unilateral and extreme conclusion.

Noting China's rapid economic growth, some people spread the theory of the "China threat" and say that China is becoming an expansionist country and that the world will be thrown into disorder as China becomes powerful. That idea is utterly baseless. During more than twenty years of reform and opening-up, China's economy has continued to develop quickly. At the same time, the four Asian "dragons" (Hong Kong, Singapore, South Korea, and Taiwan) and the four Asian "tigers" (Indonesia, Malaysia, the Philippines, and Thailand) are also experiencing a period of economic growth. Since the Asian financial crisis broke out in 1997, China has maintained steady economic growth and committed itself to refrain from devaluing the renminbi, thus contributing to the recovery of the Asian economy. All this shows that China's booming economy has not obstructed the development of neighboring countries but brought them new opportunities. China's thriving economy has not snatched away the neighboring countries' market but expanded it.

Some people also claim that a rising China will surely demand more territory from neighboring countries once it becomes powerful. This is not true, either. In the dispute regarding the South China Sea, China has offered the principle of "putting aside disputes and engaging in joint exploitation" and has actively consulted the countries in the Association of Southeast Asian Nations (ASEAN) about setting up rules of conduct for the South China Sea region. In the past few years, China has solved border questions through friendly consultations with Kazakhstan and Kyrgyzstan, signed a border agreement with Tajikistan, demarcated most of its border with Russia, and signed the Treaty on the Sino-Vietnamese Land Border and Agreement on the Demarcation of Beibu Bay with Vietnam. Obviously, China, with its thriving economy, neither expanded externally nor sought external expansion but engaged in peaceful and harmonious coexistence with neighboring countries.

Confucius said, "Now the man of perfect virtue, wishing to be established himself, seeks also to establish others; wishing to be enlarged himself, he seeks also to enlarge others." * This means that in their social conduct, people should consider the legitimate interests of others and share benefits with others. Confucius's words suggest that China is rational and open-minded when dealing with relations between countries. For China, the priority is concentrating on economic development. Its eco-

---

* See *Analects*, chapter 6, Legge's translation (note by translator).

nomic growth requires stable international and domestic markets, as well as a good environment with its neighbors and internationally. Only by having friendly relations with neighboring countries and by cooperating with other countries in a spirit of mutual benefit can we maintain the external conditions necessary for building our own country. China must rise peacefully. This is in our country's fundamental interests and is its unshakable basic long-term policy. As for the questions of Taiwan and Tibet, both are matters of safeguarding national unity, sovereignty, and territorial integrity, rather than any kind of external expansion.

Our country's comprehensive national strength has increased remarkably. But we should be fully aware of the nature of our strength. In some fields, we still lag behind. Our total economic output—that is, our gross domestic product (GDP)—has exceeded US$1 trillion, ranking seventh in the world. However, our per capita GDP—that is, the total economic output divided by the number of people in our country—was not even the hundredth on the list. This shows that the overall level of modernization is comparatively low. In our country, millions upon millions of people still have problems feeding and clothing themselves, and the national educational level is relatively low, far behind that in the developed countries. In China, among the population above twenty-five years of age, only 590 in every 10,000 people have been educated to junior college level or above. Here are three examples of elsewhere: 4,650 in the United States; 2,070 in Japan; and 730 in India. So we have nothing on which to capitalize for expansion. The essence of socialism determines that China will not expand externally. Moreover, China does not need to expand. There are more and more overlapping areas in every country's interests. One has to pay a higher and higher price to expand. The loss outweighs the gain. We seek equal and mutually beneficial cooperation with other countries, and we develop together. That is in line with current trends and safeguards the nation's fundamental interests. Clearly, the conclusion that China will surely expand and threaten the security of neighboring countries once it grows strong, taken from a comparison between China and Western imperialist countries of the eighteenth, nineteenth, and twentieth centuries, is completely groundless.

Third, will the contradiction between China and the United States lead to any conflict or war? It has been said, on the basis of the theory of the West's realist school, that if the overall strength of a rising large power approaches or exceeds that of the hegemonic countries, the possibility of conflict and war between them will increase enormously. A few years ago, two U.S. journalists based in Beijing wrote the book *The Coming Conflict with China*, which said that war was inevitable between China and the

United States. We disagree with them. A basic rule of study is to evaluate how rational a particular school's theory is before using it. Although the realist school is highly influential among academics in international relations, its flaw is obvious—that is, it emphasizes the international balance of power, while ignoring the impact of complex domestic factors on a country's external behavior. Many people believe that it is very useful to apply this theory to an analysis of international issues. But in fact it is one-sided. We should put theory into practice, and take care to avoid applying certain theories blindly and mechanically. As for the overall strengths of China and the United States, they are not on the same level. China's GDP is only one-ninth that of the United States, while the population of China is five times as big as that of the United States. Although it is rising at great speed, China still has a long way to go to catch up with and surpass the United States. We aim to reach the level of a medium-developed country when the three-step development strategy is fulfilled by the mid-twenty-first century. That is to say, China will not catch up with the United States in fifty years.

China and the United States do have differences and conflicts, but they have common interests as well. In fact, China does not pose any threat to the United States. The theory of a "China threat" is spread by some Westerners and members of the U.S. Congress and in newspaper and media reports, but the United States does not regard China as a real rival. Now the world is becoming more multipolar, and relations between the large powers are complicated. The United States is facing challenges in many respects. It is remaining on the lookout in case Russia reestablishes power; it is afraid that a rising China might challenge its status; it is concerned about a united Europe's fight for freedom; it feels anxious about Japan's development. In addition, it fears that some countries might possess weapons of mass destruction, thus posing a threat to it. So, the contradiction between China and the United States is only one of numerous contradictions. The United States wants to take charge of things all over the world, but matters often run counter to its wishes. It is difficult for the United States to concentrate on dealing with China, and also unnecessary. Confrontation is not in keeping with the basic interests of the two countries.

Currently, China's economic relations and trade with the United States are continuing to grow well. Last year, the total volume of bilateral Sino-American trade came to US$74.07 billion, according to our statistics. According to U.S. statistics, it exceeded US$100 billion. The United States is China's second largest trading partner, and China is the United States' fourth largest trading partner and largest export market. As of the end of

May of this year, U.S. investment ranked first among all foreign investment in China. More than half of the 500 largest enterprises in the United
States have invested in China.

The foregoing comments have been about economic and trade relations. Next, China and the United States need to work together on many
regional and global issues, including those of the Korean peninsula and environmental protection. Therefore, the Sino-American relationship is
based on intertwined interests, unlike the American-Russian relationship
during the cold war. Although some people in the United States spread the
theory of the "China threat," aiming to create confrontations between
China and the United States, this is not a mainstream opinion. The U.S.
government pursues a policy of both containment and engagement toward
China, instead of complete confrontation. Not long ago, the Sino-American relationship suffered twists and turns, especially the plane crash in
April. We struggled from a just position, to our advantage and with restraint, and eventually the United States softened its stand and wanted to
establish a constructive relationship with China. Recently, there have been
more people in the U.S. government in favor of contact with China; this is
a positive indicator. In fact, most Americans advocate developing the relationship with China.

The question of Taiwan is a very sensitive issue and the most likely to
cause confrontation between China and the United States. Starting this
year, there has been a drastic increase in the quality and quantity of
weapons sold to Taiwan by the United States. The United States also claims
that it will do all it can to help defend Taiwan, thus encouraging attempts
by the Taiwanese independence movement to separate Taiwan from China.
Instead of lightly giving up Taiwan as a card in its hand, the United States
will use this issue to contain China over the long term. But, owing to its
own interests, the United States will not openly support Taiwanese independence, and neither will it fight a war with China over Taiwan.

Some scholars maintain that the strategic priority of the United States
has been moved eastward. Since the disintegration of the former Soviet
Union, the United States' strategic priority has shifted from Europe to the
Asia-Pacific region. But strategically, Europe is still of vital importance to
the United States. It is not true that the United States has shifted its
strategic priority to Asia. Zbigniew Brzezinski put forward a new strategic
line of thinking, whereby Eurasia is like a chessboard that cannot be divided. The United States has only a chain made up of peninsulas and is-
lands at the edge of the Asian continent, not as widespread as its military
presence in Europe. During the cold war, although its strategic priority was
Europe, the United States still fought the Korean War and the Vietnam

War in Asia. The United States ended up with failure in both wars, which were the largest in scale since World War II. Therefore, strategic priorities are one thing, while military operations are quite another.

The issue of a strategic shift is currently being discussed in the United States. The United States has proposed the National Missile Defense and Theater Missile Defense programs, collectively known as the missile defense programs. It is attempting to develop a land-based, sea-based, and air-based missile defense system, active in offense and defense. As a weapons system for land, sea, air, and space, it obviously covers both the internal and the external, both Europe and Asia. During the Kosovo War, as the area of conflict was in Kosovo in Yugoslavia, the U.S. planes flew from the United States to Yugoslavia to drop bombs and then flew back. Today—unlike the time of the attack on Pearl Harbor—regional differences are no longer great. So we cannot say that the United States will not start a war in Asia if its strategic priority is not in Asia—or that if its priority is in Asia, it will certainly unleash a war there. History is advancing, times are changing, and the situation is complicated. Thus, never apply any theory mechanically when studying international relations. Otherwise, your conclusions will be biased.

Fourth, Sino-Japanese relations. Recently, the Japanese government has engineered a continuous series of incidents regarding historical issues and Taiwan, causing considerable trouble to Sino-Japanese relations. Lee Teng-hui's visit to Japan for medical treatment, the issue of Japanese history textbooks, and the recent visit of the Japanese prime minister, Junichiro Koizumi, to the Yasukuni Shrine have all done great damage to Sino-Japanese relations. Showing their fervent patriotism, Beijing's undergraduates fiercely opposed the Japanese government's actions, as was natural and understandable. Why did the Japanese government engineer these incidents? It was for both domestic and international reasons. Internally, there have been frequent governmental reshuffles in recent years. With a turbulent political situation and a declining economy, Japan's international standing has fallen. The entire Japanese public is very disappointed. It has been said that the 1990s were Japan's lost decade. In sharp contrast with Japan, China has a stable political situation, its economy is developing, and its international status is rising. Japan has lost its prolonged psychological superiority over China. Narrow-minded nationalist sentiments are high in Japan, where there is a big market for the "China threat" theory. Historically, the United States has propped up Japan ever since Tokyo's surrender. In Japan, unlike Germany, the remnants of its militaristic forces have been protected and fostered. In the 1980s, with the economy thriving, Japan was so arrogant that it wanted to buy many buildings in the United States and every famous foreign painting. At that time, a book called *The Japan That Can Say No* was very popular. Since the late 1980s and early 1990s, the bubble of Japan's economy has burst and Japan has been unable to regain its old vitality. Japan experienced economic stagnation for a decade. The Japanese people were significantly influenced, as was Japan's policy toward China. Our policy toward Japan is explicit: it is based on the Five Principles of Peaceful Coexistence; is aimed at developing political, economic, and cultural relations with Japan; is in the spirit of "using history as a mirror and looking forward to the future"; and is strongly against the perverse actions of the right wing on the question of Taiwan and on historical issues.

Fifth, cross-Strait relations. What needs to be done regarding relations between the two sides can be summarized in three points. Point one is adherence to the "one China" policy; point two is cross-Strait negotiations; and point three is realizing the "three direct links"* as soon as possible. That there is one China is an indisputable fact. There is only one China in the world. There are neither "two Chinas" nor "one China and one Taiwan." We maintain that there should be no preconditions for realizing the "three direct links," which would help strengthen understanding between people on both sides. We will continue to demonstrate through our actions our hope for a peaceful settlement of the Taiwan question, and gain the support of Taiwan's people as well as the international community. Now people on the two sides have a close relationship, especially economically. Last year, 3 million Taiwanese compatriots came to the Chinese mainland to visit relatives, do some sightseeing, trade, invest, and engage in technological, cultural, and athletic exchanges. Since Taiwanese compatriots were allowed to visit their relatives on the mainland in 1987, 20 million "person-times" in total have been to the mainland. Furthermore, the annual number has increased by a large margin. It was 500,000 in 1997, and is 3 million now. Last year, the total volume of indirect trade between the two sides of the Strait came to US$30.5 billion, the highest in recent years. With a balance of trade of more than US$20 billion in its favor, Taiwan benefits from cross-Strait trade. There being no direct trade, the volume of indirect trade alone between the two sides has come to US$204.9 billion. There has been a dramatic reduction in Taiwan's economic growth lately. Taiwanese compatriots complain about the declining economy, the turbulent political situation, and widespread anxiety. It has been said that in the past Taiwan was engaged in building its economy while the mainland was

---

* Direct trade, transport, and postal links with Taiwan (note by translator).

engaged in the "cultural revolution." Nowadays, the mainland is engaged in building its economy while Taiwan is in internal conflict. Chen Shui-bian took power with only 39 percent of the votes and wields state power in a minority administration. A minority is also in power in the Legislative Yuan. So the political situation is volatile and in disorder. This year, Taiwan's economy is expected to grow by 1.2 percent, imports to drop by 22 percent and exports by 17 percent, and manufacturing output to decrease by 7.2 percent, which would be the sharpest decrease in twenty-six years. The exchange rate has also dropped dramatically, and the stock market has fallen to its lowest point in eight years. The stagnant economy, as well as the turbulent political situation, has created discontent among the public. Since April, according to a public opinion poll, there has been an obvious increase in the rate of support for "one country, two systems." The Gallup poll found that the rate of support for "one country, two systems" has reached 47.5 percent, whereas it was only 10 percent in the past. Obviously, public opinion in Taiwan is changing. When Juan Antonio Samaranch, the president of the International Olympic Committee, announced on July 13 that Beijing had succeeded in its bid to host the 2008 Olympic Games, Wu Ching-kuo, the Taiwanese member of the International Olympic Committee, walked to the platform and told us that he had wished for that for a long time and it was the common desire of all Chinese people, as well as something glorious for the Chinese nation. All circles in Taiwan responded enthusiastically to Beijing's successful bid for the 2008 Olympic Games. They believed that the successful Olympic bid, welcomed by both sides, would benefit cross-Strait relations and peaceful reunification. They also hoped that they could jointly host the Olympics with the mainland and that the torch would be carried via Taiwan. All this shows that blood is thicker than water and that over the years our policies and work regarding Taiwan have been effective. In short, Taiwan's return to its motherland and the realization of national reunification depend on our own growing strength. Our basic policy on Taiwan is still peaceful reunification and "one country, two systems." China will do its best to achieve peaceful unification. However, we cannot simply wait for it. We will need to work hard. China will not promise to rule out the use of force, which would be directed only against schemes to create an independent Taiwan and against foreign interventionist forces. The "one China" policy means that there is only one China in the world and that both the Chinese mainland and Taiwan are part of it. State sovereignty and territorial integrity are inseparable. As for "one country, two systems," Taiwan will benefit from a more relaxed policy than has been applied to Hong Kong and Macao. The Taiwan dollar will still be able to circulate. The army, tariff area, and political structure will remain intact. The Chinese mainland will not impose any tax on Taiwan or appropriate any funds from Taiwan. Taiwanese people will retain their lifestyles, and Taiwanese entrepreneurs will keep the property they own. Taiwan will enjoy the freedom to use its own personnel. The mainland will not send any officials to Taiwan; and so on. We are fully confident and capable of resolving the question of Taiwan once and for all. No attempt to separate Taiwan from the mainland will succeed. National unification and rejuvenation are certain to be achieved. To repeat: China will not promise to rule out the use of force. Otherwise, Taiwanese independence would be encouraged and it would be difficult to settle the issue peacefully. We will work hard with our Taiwanese compatriots and the various parties. Now, the situation is good. Since the person who advocates Taiwan's independence took office as "President," Taiwan's economy has gone into the doldrums. So, fierce debates are going on in Taiwan and many people believe that Taiwan's economy will find no outlet until the issue of reunification is resolved.

Sixth and finally, the relationship between sovereignty and human rights. There have been many debates about sovereignty since the cold war. One of the key issues is the relationship between sovereignty and human rights. National sovereignty and human rights are two related, not opposing, concepts. They have both taken shape in the course of the development of human society. Human rights are people's common ideals, formed as human society developed. However, historically, human rights existed only among white societies for quite a long period in the West. Black slaves were openly traded. Colored people were considered uncivilized. So, human rights at that time referred to the human rights of white people. In the colonies of large European powers, black people had no right to establish their own independent countries. The concept of national sovereignty, formed in the process of international contact, is the foundation of international relations. Today, it is still widely accepted by the international community. National sovereignty is a significant premise for realizing and safeguarding human rights. It is similar to the old Chinese saying "With the skin gone, to what can the hair attach itself?" Many countries in Africa, Asia, and Latin America were colonies, semicolonies, or dependencies for quite a long time. They had no national sovereignty, so human rights were out of the question. At present, the world has no international government. If a country surrenders its sovereign rights, the lives, freedom, and dignity of its people will have no effective lawful guarantee. Under foreign rule, there are no human rights to speak of. At the end of the Qing dynasty, China's sovereignty ceased to exist in all but name. When the eight-power allied forces* (all of them but the Austro-Hungarian Empire still exist) occupied Beijing in 1900, did the Chinese people enjoy any human rights? As for the issue of Kosovo, the West intervened in Yugoslavia under the banner of humanitarianism, only to produce humanitarian tragedies. Today, this issue has not yet been resolved, so endless trouble is in store. Therefore, it is impossible to improve human rights until national sovereignty has been guaranteed and safeguarded. As Comrade Deng Xiaoping pointed out, "Actually, national sovereignty is far more important than human rights."

Human rights are universal, not the preserve of Western countries, because every nation stresses the protection of an individual's life and dignity. At the same time, human rights are implemented in different ways. It is impossible for all countries, which differ in their politics, economies, social conditions, religions, traditions, histories, and cultures, to have the same ideas and to conceive of human rights in the same way. The urge to achieve a single identity is not realistic. Humankind as a whole is progressing in world history. The content and scope of human rights are expanding. Western countries always denounce developing countries for denying individual rights and political rights on the pretext of the right to exist and collective rights. In fact, developing countries, ruled under colonialism for a long time, are poverty-stricken, so why should they not give priority to national sovereignty, the right to exist, and the right to develop? For example, in Africa, every country except Ethiopia was a colony in the past—even Ethiopia was occupied by Italy and eventually became its colony. So, when you talk about the issue of human rights, the whole of Africa is excluded. Many independent states in Asia used to be colonies of large Western powers. India, Malaysia, and Singapore were British colonies; Indochina was a French colony; the Philippines were a colony of the United States; Indonesia was a Dutch colony. Only China was a semicolony because it was too large for the eight-power allied forces to divide up. However, Japan occupied Taiwan and the three northeastern provinces† one after another and then invaded the whole country, trying to make China its colony. Therefore, on the whole, every Asian country except Japan was a colony or semicolony in the past. Japan turned into a militaristic country that invaded others. In Latin America, countries were carved up by Spain and Portugal, with the permission of the pope, who delimited the borders.

Since the Second World War, humankind has made considerable

---

* Austria-Hungary, Britain, France, Germany, Italy, Japan, Russia, the United States (note by translator).

† Heilongjiang, Jilin, and Liaoning provinces (note by translator).

progress, the greatest aspect of which is the independence of colonial and semicolonial countries. However, these countries face many problems, the problem of food being the most basic. The other day, I met a U.S. senator, who agreed that the three most important human rights are the right to food, the right to shelter, and the right to education. He also said that education had not been spread widely enough in the United States. Moreover, social welfare, including medical treatment and unemployment insurance, was unsatisfactory. So, no resolution can be achieved through a single effort, and the international community should be fully aware of this. But Western countries adopted human-rights diplomacy and went to war in Yugoslavia, not to safeguard human rights there, but really for the purpose of interfering in other countries' internal affairs.

Many Westerners like to discuss the issue of human rights in China. However, false reports in the Western media usually lead to prejudice and misunderstanding. No wonder that, when foreigners come to China, they often say, "It's very different from what we have heard." In March of this year, during a visit to the United States, I gave a speech on the development and history of Sino-American relations. I said that the earliest Americans, as well as other Westerners, who came to China consisted of two kinds of people—traders and missionaries. Traders came to China to develop new markets for their products. Missionaries wanted to preach the Gospel and civilize the "barbarians" through a spirit of devotion. What are missionaries? While traders pursued markets and material gain, aiming at profit, missionaries were engaged in ideology and cultural infiltration. Of course, missionaries later ran hospitals and schools and implemented Western education—all to our advantage. But their original intention was nothing more than carrying out heaven's mandate and civilizing the pagans and "barbarians." Not long ago, there were celebrations of the 500th anniversary of a "discovery"—that is, when Portuguese navigators found India and China. In fact, many countries, including India and China, have ancient cultures, much older than Portugal. The Portuguese were not even the earliest navigators. It is soon going to be the 600th anniversary of Zheng He's voyages to the Western Seas.

The issue of "most-favored-nation" (MFN) status has persisted between China and the United States for a long time. The United States examines China's trade and human-rights situation every year. As long as the United States is dissatisfied, it will withhold MFN treatment from China. We have constantly said that it should be called not "most-favored-nation" status but "normal trade relations." It took many years of twists and turns to change the wording to "normal trade relations" during the administration of President Bill Clinton. MFN status is based on a piece of

U.S. legislation stipulating that trade with the Soviet Union would not be permitted unless Jews were allowed to leave freely. There are no Jews in China, and the West opposes immigration from China, so MFN status for China has nothing at all to do with this piece of legislation. Now, the U.S. Congress has granted permanent normal trade relations to China. However, so-called free trade is not free. Even when we were bidding for the Olympic Games, the United States connected that bid with the issue of human rights. The United States has put forward ten anti-China proposals at the United Nations Commission on Human Rights, all of which have ended in failure. According to my calculation, there were 10 occasions in twelve years. The only two exceptions were during the Gulf War and during President Clinton's visit to China. Obviously, the United States acts according to circumstances. With ten failures, it should have reflected on its behavior. But those "human-rights guardians," with their rigid thinking, never admit defeat. With the devoted spirit of a missionary, they are like the knight Don Quixote, who fought windmills. In fact, the West has used the issue of human rights to exert political pressure on China, only to destroy international cooperation on this issue.

China has worked hard in international cooperation on the issue of human rights. Since 1980, we have signed eighteen international agreements on human rights, including the International Covenant on Economic, Social and Cultural Rights. We advocate exchange in the field of human rights, being in dialogue with the European Union, Australia, the United States, and others. But we allow no intervention in China's internal affairs. Whatever happens, we will be clearheaded and stick to our own path.

APPENDIX IV

The United States After September 11
(SEPTEMBER 10, 2002)

TODAY IS TEACHERS' DAY. I was here on the same day last year, giving a speech on the world situation. However, the earthshaking "September 11" event happened the next day. I remember that it was a little after eight o'clock in the morning New York time when the incident was broadcast on television. We held a meeting that very night, watching the live broadcast while discussing developments. Led by President Jiang Zemin, we soon came up with appropriate measures. Nobody had predicted the disaster. Now, September 11 has become a symbol and an indication that the biggest threat to the United States is terrorism. This had not been realized before. After taking office, the Bush administration advocated strengthening National Missile Defense—until September 11. The United States has become aware of the limits of its powerful weapons. Terrorists with no high-tech equipment can easily cause disaster at the financial center, while National Missile Defense is useless.

Since the end of the cold war, the U.S. government has been discussing who on earth the main postwar "enemy" is. The answer had eluded it until September 11: the enemy was at home, not abroad. The terrorists of September 11 had lived in the United States for a long time and obtained green cards. They had even learned how to fly at U.S. schools. Without new-style weapons, missiles, long-distance delivery methods, or powerful explosives, they hijacked U.S. civilian airliners in the United States by using fruit knives. Those airliners, filled with enough aviation fuel for long-distance flights, took off from New York and Boston. So, when they crashed into the buildings, the explosion of hundreds of tons of gasoline caused raging flames. The steel structures melted in the great heat and the buildings collapsed. The world was shocked. The attack taught the Americans a lesson.

For this reason, relations between the large powers have obviously been eased this year. Changes have taken place in American-Russian relations and in relations between Russia and NATO. Sino-American relations have also improved. Most of them have agreed on the need to avoid a world war and to safeguard peace. Cooperation between them should be strengthened to face the challenge of terrorism.

Since the events of September 11, the Americans have dramatically adjusted their external policies and strategies. The fight against terrorism and domestic defense have become the priorities. The Bush administration set out the new concepts of "preemptive strikes" and "offensive" defense. That is, on the basis of its own judgment, the United States would decide which countries were involved in terrorism and whether to attack them suddenly. As for the struggle against terrorism, the United States will continue to control the proliferation of weapons of mass destruction and their means of delivery. However, the events of September 11 have proved that weapons of mass destruction do not always need means of delivery. Relying solely on National Missile Defense may not work in the fight against terrorism.

The United States has been the only superpower since the end of the cold war; the "new economy" has grown steadily for ten years, gathering plenty of wealth and a fiscal surplus; and, with victories in the Gulf War and Kosovo War, the U.S. Army has become extraordinarily strong. However, the events of September 11 have destroyed the myth that the United States is absolutely safe. The U.S. mainland was believed to be very safe, with the Atlantic Ocean and Pacific Ocean on two of its coasts. Now, however, domestic safety has been placed at the top of the United States' national security agenda. In June of this year, President Bush proposed setting up a Department of Homeland Security, aimed at guarding against terrorist attacks through the efforts of the entire nation. Homeland security was formally incorporated into the general framework of national security strategy in the reports on a homeland security strategy submitted to Congress by President Bush in July. At the same time, there is ever more heated discussion about the United States and the future world order. The liberals believe that, strong as the United States is, it cannot take on everything; the conservatives have put forward the "new empire" theory. The U.S. government has started to stress the relationship between the big powers, which should avoid conflict through peaceful competition in order to fight against terrorism together. The Americans have realized that only cooperation with the international community, including the other big powers, can ensure their own safety.

Two recent articles merit attention. One is "American Primacy in Perspective,"* published in *Foreign Affairs*. It says that the United States will not meet any real challenger in the foreseeable future, owing to its overwhelming superiority in economics, the military, technology, and other fields. The other article is "The Eagle Has Crash-Landed,"† published almost at the same time in the magazine *Foreign Policy*. The author points out that the United States is becoming powerless in international affairs, as a result of the same political, economic, and military factors that once gave it hegemony. The "hawks" believe that the United States should act like an imperial power because it is the strongest and invincible; otherwise, it will be discriminated against in the international community. However, the author of "The Eagle Has Crash-Landed" holds the opposite opinion, saying that this unilateral policy will hasten the decline of the United States. The two articles mentioned have strikingly different viewpoints. These are all ideas for you to consider, and I hope everyone will discuss them.

Let's focus on the U.S. economic situation. Recently, many economic scandals have been continually exposed to the public in the United States.

---

* By Stephen G. Brooks and William C. Wohlforth, July–August 2002 (note by translator).

† By Immanuel Wallerstein, July–August 2002 (note by translator).

Some big companies fudged their accounts only to have their stocks fall to a five-year low and the customers' confidence drop dramatically. Since President Bush assumed office, unemployment has risen by 2 million, while foreign investment has fallen by 60 percent. This is now widely discussed in the United States. The optimists think that the U.S. economy is basically in good shape, that the macroeconomic policy is conducive to the upturn of the economy, that the stock-market bubble has almost collapsed, and that recovery is just around the corner for the information-technology industry. However, the pessimists believe that the United States has bleak economic prospects, that the important economic indexes have not improved, that financial deficits have increased, and that the scandals of fudged accounts have resulted in serious consequences. These two viewpoints are also completely different from each other. Further observation is needed.

In short, the United States is still number one as far as strength is concerned. But it cannot do whatever it likes. Today, the tide of globalization is surging. The high-speed circulation of capital, technology, and information has intensified the interdependence between countries. Only when there is a division of labor as well as cooperation among countries can sustainable development be realized. This has been proved by the changes in the world situation after the events of September 11.

Therefore, relations between major powers are comparatively stable despite local tensions and turbulence. There is no foundation for a world war. With more and more extensive diplomatic space, our diplomatic resources are becoming more and more abundant. Economic globalization is an opportunity, as are stable relations between major powers. Our own country can anticipate plenty of opportunities in the next ten to twenty years.

Now let's discuss Sino-American relations. It has been thirty years since President Nixon's visit to China, which opened the gate for bilateral relations. In the last thirty years, we have been through countless hardships and many matters worth considering and summing up. All of us are concerned about Sino-American relations. I suppose you must have discussed this often. We can, in fact, discover an intrinsic law no matter how complicated Sino-American relations look. Using dialectics to analyze these relations, we can stand up high and see far ahead, free from any deviation caused by one single event or by a situation at one moment in time.

Sino-American relations have advanced over the past thirty years, although there have been ups and downs. Since 1989 in particular, Western countries, headed by the United States, have imposed so-called sanctions against China. Relations were shrouded in darkness for some time. Fortunately, we withstood the pressure. Soon afterward, the Gulf War broke out, making the United States realize the importance of China. Then relations improved with the increasing number of high-level exchanges between the two countries. Bilateral trade agreements were signed. The United States supported China's accession to the WTO. Besides these positive aspects, there were a few negative aspects—for example, Li Teng-hui's visit to the United States, the bombing of the Chinese embassy in Yugoslavia, the air collision above the South China Sea, and so on. Sino-American relations have continued to change, dazzling many people. Has anything remained unchanged? I believe so.

First, the basis of cooperation between the two countries has not changed. China and the United States are two world powers. Out of economic and security considerations, the United States relies on China's market, with its great potential and internationally important strategic position. The United States has to face up to the rise of China. A U.S. official once said that the United States did not want to obstruct the rise of China and did not have the power to do so even if it wanted to. I think he was quite right. China's rise is irresistible. The people of the United States think so too. They do not want a confrontation between our two countries. We can see the two countries cooperating in more and more fields: trade, science, technology, the campaign against terrorism, nuclear nonproliferation, the safety of the Asia-Pacific region, and so on. China and the United States have common interests regarding many bilateral and international issues. The basis for cooperation has not changed.

Second, the basic systems in the two countries have not changed. The United States always regards its own values and social and economic systems as universally applicable truths and tries to impose them on others. We do not force anything on others, but we permit no intervention in China's internal affairs. We are open to anything that is advanced, including advanced ideology, culture, and technology. Students are sent abroad, and foreigners are invited to teach in China. However, we strongly oppose any intervention or infiltration. In this aspect, contradictions do arise. This has not changed either.

Third, the dual character of U.S. policy toward China has not changed. There is not only cooperation but also conflict between China and the United States, so all past administrations since President Nixon's, regardless of party affiliations, have carried out a policy of "cooperation and scrutiny, engagement and containment." This dual character is determined by the nature of the United States' monopolistic capitalist class and U.S. national interests. Therefore, as you can see, although Sino-American relations have suffered twists and turns, they have never been irreparably broken, and new problems often crop up when relations have made headway.

The three preceding points are the basic rules of Sino-American relations. As objective conditions change, the relationship may have different manifestations, such as that of the cold war, or that of the twenty-first century. For example, the United States has put forward anti-China proposals at the United Nations Commission on Human Rights almost every year since 1989. But it has not done so this year. Why not? On the one hand, it is giving priority to the campaign against terrorism, for which it needs China's cooperation. On the other hand, the United States has put forward ten anti-China proposals, all of which have ended in failure. To prevent another failure, it has not put forward a proposal this year.

China has been in contact with the United States for more than 100 years, since the Treaty of Wangxia (Wanghia) was signed in 1844. We can say that every adjustment of Sino-American relations during those hundred years is a reflection of changes in the strength of the two sides. At the time of the Treaty of Wangxia, China was being trodden underfoot by other countries, and it was extremely weak in the late nineteenth century and early twentieth century. Then, U.S. missionaries and traders came to China to preach the Gospel and develop new markets. Arriving quite late, the United States foisted an "open door" policy on China to secure the same privileges as the other imperialist powers. In the twentieth century, the Chinese people roused themselves from a deep sleep as the new democratic revolution proceeded. Particularly after the establishment of the People's Republic of China in 1949, China was getting stronger and stronger, and its strength affected Sino-American relations. The Chinese people became the masters of their own country. Unable to stand this, the U.S. government imposed a blockade and sanctions against China, causing twenty years of isolation and hostility between the two countries. Confronted with China's rising international status, the Americans eventually admitted that they had lifted a rock only to drop it on their own feet in an attempt to isolate China. Thus President Nixon crossed the Pacific Ocean, opening the gates to bilateral relations.

The theory of the "China threat" has run rampant in recent years. In July of this year, the U.S. Department of Defense released its "Annual Report on the Military Power of the People's Republic of China," which was closely followed by "National Security Implications of the Economic Relationship between the United States and China" (released by Congress and the U.S.-China Security Review Commission). These two reports share the same fundamental view that a rising China threatens U.S. interests, as well as the security of the Asia-Pacific region and the whole world. In addition to the "China threat" theory, there is the "China collapse" theory. In July of last year, a Chinese-American published the book *The Coming Collapse of China*, using this sensational title to attract attention and spread his "theory." Actually, the "China threat" theory and the "China collapse" theory are two sides of the same coin, around which there is such a clamor by the anti-China forces, which are in the minority. The fallacies cooked up by these forces are not worth disproving. But why did they become active at this time? In my analysis, the emergence of the "China threat" theory shows that China is becoming stronger and has a growing international influence. Those clinging to the cold war mentality felt unhappy and thus made up this bizarre story. If our overall national strength had remained at the level it was decades ago, the "China threat" theory would not have attracted such attention. If our overall national strength develops steadily for another several decades, there will be no market for the "China threat" theory. More and more people will recognize China's stability and prosperity and the opportunities China brings to the world.

Therefore, I believe that, as long as our overall national strength continues to grow, Sino-American relations will change in our favor. Furthermore, there will be a multipolar world structure and democratic international relations. All countries should handle their internal affairs independently, and their international affairs should be settled through consultations. Of course, some Americans disagree. They put forward a theory of the "clash of civilizations," imagining various confrontations between China and the United States. But they are not the mainstream and are opposed by insightful Americans. The U.S. Secretary of State Colin Powell once said that they were not afraid of a modernized China, and called for more military exchanges between the two countries.

Changes in the world's structure depend on the balance of power. It is quite possible that international relations will become more peaceful and steady. Last year, President Bush came to China twice in only four months, first to Shanghai and then to Beijing. When he was running for the presidency, he called China a "strategic competitor" of the United States. Now he advocates developing constructive and cooperative relations with China. This is a positive change. However, we notice that the Bush administration aims to contain China more while improving bilateral relations. Regarding Taiwan, for example, the United States increased military supplies to Taiwan, and Taiwan's "minister of defense" was allowed to attend summit meetings on defense in the United States. So we must be on the alert.

The people of the United States are friendly toward the Chinese people. But some Americans lack an understanding of China, having been misled by the Western media, and they have all kinds of prejudice against China. We should improve the mutual understanding between the people of the two countries through various channels, including nongovernmental exchanges.

Sino-American relations have encountered many problems. Over the past ten years, there have been four major conflicts between our two countries: first, the sanctions against China applied by the United States beginning in 1989; second, Li Teng-hui's visit to the United States; third, the bombing of the Chinese embassy in Yugoslavia; fourth, the air collision above the South China Sea. Fortunately, the Party Central Committee made wise decisions. We struggled on just ground, to our advantage, with restraint, to safeguard national sovereignty and dignity and the Chinese people's fundamental interests. However, we should address ourselves to struggle as well as development and cooperation. These two tactics are equally significant.

We encourage Sino-American cooperation, which restrains the anti-China forces.

Through thirty years of Sino-American relations, there have been more and more common interests, as well as tighter and tighter links between the two countries. Exchanges in trade, culture, and personnel have expanded from zero to numerous and large-scale. Last year, the total volume of Sino-American trade reached US$80.4 billion, which is thirty-three times the amount for 1979, the year in which diplomatic relations were established. Today, the United States is China's biggest export market and second largest trading partner. China is the United States' fourth largest trading partner. The Chinese mainland has overtaken Taiwan, which is the United States' eighth largest export market. Direct U.S. investment in China has reached US$35 billion, the largest amount of foreign investment. Thirty-one Chinese provinces and major cities and thirty-one American states and 110 sister cities in each country have established ties. Every year, more than 900,000 U.S. visitors come to China and more than 200,000 Chinese go as students to the United States. In general, the enhancement of Sino-American cooperation conforms to modern trends and follows the wishes of the people of the two countries. The United States certainly will not stop plotting to disintegrate and "westernize" China, but it cannot pay the price of a rupture of its friendly relations with China. As Sino-American cooperation develops, anti-China forces in the United States will become more isolated and attempts to sabotage bilateral relations will have less and less support. While struggling against the United States' anti-China forces, we will work to win over and mobilize those Americans who are in favor of developing Sino-American relations, enhance cooperation between our two countries, and guide our relations to a better situation.

Since President Bush assumed office, President Jiang has had two important meetings with him. Next month, Jiang is going to visit the United States, by invitation, and meet President Bush at his private ranch in Texas. Vice President Hu Jintao also visited the United States in the first half of this year. All these are significant measures that we have adopted to improve Sino-American relations. With more U.S. policies of containment against China, summit meetings are very important for the stability and development of our relations.

In the last week of August, the United States finally declared the East Turkestan Islamic Movement (ETIM) in China's Xinjiang region an international terrorist organization. During the war against Afghanistan, the United States arrested a few terrorists who had escaped from Xinjiang in China. Some of them were important ringleaders and were kept at the U.S. military base in Cuba. Later, Chen Shui-bian put forward his referendum proposal and his theory of "one country on each side of the Taiwan Strait," which were strongly condemned by all Chinese patriots in China and abroad. Most countries, including the United States, announced that they would adhere to the "one China" policy and oppose Taiwan independence. Obviously, Taiwan independence lacks support not only in Taiwan but also in the international community. Whenever cross-Strait relations or Sino-American relations make headway, Taiwan secessionist forces always come out into the open to create trouble. This shows how frightened and weak they are. China's unification is irresistible. No matter what measures are taken, no one can hold back that trend.

In conclusion, when handling Sino-American relations, we should pay attention to both the advantages and the disadvantages. We should be clearheaded and vigilant when our relations have made progress. When bilateral relations suffer a setback, we should take the initiative on the basis of the state's basic interests. We should contend with the adversary in terms not merely of strength but also resourcefulness. However, we should avoid becoming angry easily, seeking momentary satisfaction, or competing with the United States for temporary advantage. As Su Shi said in his *Liu Hou Lun*: "When abused, an ordinary man draws his sword and rises to fight, which is not true bravery. A man of great courage keeps his presence of mind in the face of sudden disaster, free from anger, because he cherishes high ideals and has lofty aspirations." That is to say, do not get too angry over a small insult and "rise to fight"; that is "not true bravery." A truly brave man observes things calmly and thinks them over. Because we "cherish high ideals," we have lofty aspirations. Su Shi was singing the praises of Zhang Liang, a politician of the Western Han dynasty 2,000 years ago. We should certainly have more wisdom than Zhang Liang.

APPENDIX V

The Iraq War and the United States
(SEPTEMBER 10, 2003)

It is a great pleasure to be here at the School of International Studies of Peking University again, especially as today is Teachers' Day. And so, first of all, I'd like to extend warm greetings to all the teachers. Then, let me welcome the newcomers in the new academic year, and congratulate you on the beginning of a new stage in life. Next, I want to thank all the teaching and administrative staff as well as the students for your contribution to the fight against SARS in the past few months. May all of you make progress in all fields in the new academic year.

Last Teachers' Day, I gave a speech about the United States after the "September 11" incident and about Sino-American relations. Complex changes have taken place in the world situation in the past year, the most eye-catching of which has been the Iraq War.

This war lasted from March 20 until May 1, when President Bush declared that combat operations had finished. It was not a long war—all together only six weeks, including three weeks of fighting. Since we all know this well, I will add no more. Today, I am going to focus on how to view this war against the overall international background and its influences upon U.S. strategy.

I will begin with how the "September 11" incident affected U.S. global strategy. After "September 11," the United States held that the world had entered a new era—the "post-post–cold war period." The United States regards the disintegration of the former Soviet Union as the main symbol of the "post–cold war period," in which the United States was free from the Soviet threat. The "post-post–cold war period" is characterized by the threat of global terrorism. The United States has changed the order of primary targets of its global strategy.

The elimination of the threat of terrorism against the homeland has become the priority of U.S. security strategy. In retrospect, U.S. security strategy adjustment has undergone roughly three stages in the past two years:

The first stage, the reaction stage, began at about the time of the "September 11" incident, and ended in early 2002. Suffering its most serious attack in the last 200 years, the United States responded rapidly and fiercely. The United States vigorously strengthened domestic defense, prepared for the establishment of the Department of Homeland Security, and reconstructed the Federal Bureau of Investigation (FBI) and the Central

Intelligence Agency (CIA). At the same time, it mobilized all its diplomatic resources to promote the establishment of an international counterterrorism alliance, launched a war against Afghanistan, and speedily destroyed the Taliban regime and the headquarters of the Al-Qaeda terrorist network. At this stage, the United States entered the central Asian region, which it had found difficult to enter in the past, on the excuse of counter-terrorism, but what it did was primarily responding to terrorism and strengthening its defense.

The second stage—the preparatory stage—lasted from January 29, 2002, when President Bush issued his "state of the union" message, until the publication of the Counterterrorism Strategy in February 2003. In this stage, the United States underwent the most profound reflection since the end of the cold war. It released a series of documents, including the National Drug Control Strategy; National Strategy for Homeland Security; National Security Strategy; National Strategy to Combat Weapons of Mass Destruction; National Strategy for Network Security; National Strategy to Protect Major Infrastructure Facilities, and Assets; and Counterterrorism Strategy. In his state of the union message in January 2002, President Bush set forth his concept of the "axis of evil." On June 1 of the same year, when he delivered a speech at the West Point military academy, he put forward the concept of "preemptive strikes."

Three changes in this period deserve our attention.

First, regarding terrorist attacks as acts of war, the United States focused on military force instead of traditional means of administration and law to deal with terrorist acts. The trend of militarism in U.S. external policies kept rising, and the U.S. Department of Defense exerted more influence on diplomatic decision making.

Second, the United States had changed its target of attack in the war against terrorism. The Al-Qaeda terrorist network had been hit so badly that it reorganized itself into small units. The United States then concentrated on preventing terrorist organizations from gaining weapons of mass destruction (WMD). The United States declared in the National Security Strategy document that "rogue states and terrorists are sworn allies" and that it would stop such states from conveying "the most lethal weapons" to "the most dangerous enemy." In this way, the United States linked its antiterrorism campaign and enforcement of nonproliferation to the punishment of "rogue states." Moreover, it proposed to reshape the Middle East. Following Afghanistan and Iraq, North Korea, Iran, and Syria had become America's new targets.

Third, the United States believed that "weakened and failed states" could easily be used by terrorist organizations. The "unstable arc" stretching through the Middle East, central Asia, southeast Asia, and northeast Asia was the weak link in counterterrorism. In order to strengthen its control and response capability in these regions, the United States announced that it would review the structure of its military forces and draft programs for the redeployment of U.S. troops overseas. Thus, the United States could tighten its control of important strategic points under the name of "antiterror."

The third stage is the stage of implementation. The Iraq War shows that the United States has started to fully implement its new global strategy of military security.

Since the Gulf War of 1991, the issue of Iraq had not been thoroughly solved. For years, the United States had pursued a policy of containing Iraq and toppling Saddam Hussein, and refused to lift the sanctions against it. However, Iraq from time to time suspended its cooperation with the United Nations as regards weapons inspection, thus providing the United States with an excuse to step up its own hostility toward Baghdad. A solution to the issue was important for the United States so that it could tighten its control of the Middle East, pursue hegemonism and power politics, and ensure its supremacy in the world. According to an article published in the French newspaper Le Figaro on April 18 of this year, before President Bush assumed office, "neoconservatives," represented by Vice President Cheney, Secretary of Defense Rumsfeld, and Deputy Secretary of Defense Paul Wolfowitz, had put forward a plan to invade Iraq and overthrow Saddam Hussein, in "Project for the New American Century" published in September 2000, as the first step toward safeguarding world peace under U.S. hegemony.

The United States aimed to overthrow Saddam and dominate the Middle East and its resources by taking advantage of the international climate of fear following the "September 11" incident. Since the beginning of the inspection crisis, troops from the United States and Britain had been assembled around Iraq, despite the UN Resolution 1441, which announced the resumption of weapons inspection in Iraq. Actually, the United States had already made up its mind to attack Iraq with or without the authorization of the UN Security Council. The United States and Britain proposed a new draft resolution only because they wanted to fight under the cloak of UN legality, "for a just cause."

The other big powers and the international community were fully aware of that, so there was a heated debate in the Security Council. After amending and postponing the new draft resolution, the United States had to give it up, because there was no chance of getting it passed. Then after a forty-eight-hour ultimatum to Saddam, it hurriedly launched the war.

This indicates that under the present circumstances when the world is un-balanced in terms of strength, the other large countries were neither will-ing to compromise with the United States nor ready to confront it. The international community does not accept a unipolar world, or allow the United States to do whatever it likes.

Perhaps you noticed that when President Bush declared war against Iraq on March 20, in the background there were two photographs—one showing his two daughters and the other his wife and pet dog. He wanted to show his care for his family and his respect for humanity, intimating that his purpose was to liberate the people of Iraq. On May 1, he flew to the carrier *Lincoln*, which had just returned from the Gulf, and announced the end of the major military operations. The background of the carrier in-dicated the mentality of the U.S. administration.

Viewed from a military angle, the war was quite successful. In 1991, the United States had bombed the Gulf region for nearly forty days, and 550,000 American soldiers had been involved. The ground operation had lasted less than 100 hours. But this time, the force involved was only one-third as large, and as soon as the war broke out, the American troops started ground operations. Baghdad was captured within twenty-one days. But this was not a victory for the United States in a true sense.

The international community has raised lingering doubts about the reasons for the invasion. Until now, the United States has not found WMD in Iraq or evidence that Saddam had links with the Al-Qaeda terrorist net-work. In the United States itself, some anthrax spores that led to five deaths and caused nationwide terror were found. Reportedly, the anthrax had been stolen by a biochemical weapon expert from a laboratory of the American army. It is widely suspected that the U.S. and British govern-ments falsified intelligence reports on the question of Iraq's possession of WMD. The British Parliament's Foreign Affairs Committee reported that the government of the UK had exaggerated the threat from Iraq. A British weapons scientist, David Kelly, who had offered the BBC related informa-tion, committed suicide, causing a great uproar in Britain.

The intelligence committees of the U.S. Senate and House of Repre-sentatives held secret hearings. Senator John Kerry, the Democratic candi-date for the presidency in 2004, and the former governor of Vermont Howard Dean openly accused the Bush administration of misleading the public. In his state of the union message in January, President Bush had ac-cused Iraq of trying to buy nuclear materials from Niger and this accusa-tion was said to be false. The director of the CIA, George Tenet, confessed to neglect of duty, and President Bush had to indicate that he would accept responsibility, too.

In the face of doubts from all sides, Secretary of Defense Rumsfeld put forward a new kind of statement: In fact, he said, the U.S. administration had no new intelligence about Iraq's possessing WMD; rather the "September 11" incident had made Americans examine past intelligence in a new way. He had made a similar odd remark last June: "The absence of evidence is not evidence of absence." The *Washington Post* commented on June 33: "So far, the United States hasn't found any WMD in Iraq, casting a slur on its military victory, because Iraq's possession of WMD was the reason for the United States to start the war. Now, the 'preemptive strike' strategy—the core of the Bush administration's foreign policies—is at risk." The British newspaper *The Independent* listed twenty lies that the United States and Britain had fabricated to launch the war.

Now, four months have passed since President Bush declared that the war had ended, but victory on the battlefield has not brought peace or stability to Iraq. When the war started, Beijing had just begun to suffer the SARS epidemic. Now, the war against SARS is over, but the United States is still facing many problems in Iraq: the whereabouts of Saddam are unknown; demonstrations against the United States are ceaseless, calling for the immediate withdrawal of U.S. troops; the U.S. troops are being attacked constantly, suffering more casualties than during the military operations. The total number of men killed in action from the beginning of the war till now is much higher than in the Gulf War in 1991. Even Rumsfeld has to admit that instability in Iraq could last at least several months. So the United States asked for cooperation in peacekeeping from other countries, and has launched many elimination actions. And yet the United States cannot free itself from the predicament of suffering at least a death a day. Obviously, it is easy to take military action but difficult to gain public support, and even more difficult to reform a society. According to a recent U.S. poll, owing to the predicament in Iraq and the slowness of the work of reconstruction, the support rate for the occupation of Iraq has dropped from 73 percent in April to 50 percent now.

Recently, President Bush gave a special talk on the issue of Iraq, aiming to gain more internal support for the coming election and seeking international cooperation in the face of external pressure.

Let us make a comparison between the Iraq War and the Afghanistan War.

They have many things in common. For example: both were local wars launched after the United States had adjusted its security strategy and given priority to counterterrorism; the goal was to eradicate dictatorship, fight terrorism, introduce democracy, and liberate the local people; both helped U.S. troops enter important strategic areas and continue to carry out the United States' unipolar strategy. The U.S. troops overthrew both regimes quickly, suffering few casualties. But they cannot find either Osama Bin Laden or Saddam Hussein, and they face the challenge of endless resistance.

However, there are also significant differences between the two wars.

First, they drew different international responses. The U.S. attack on Afghanistan's Taliban regime and the Al-Qaeda terrorist network, soon after "September 11," received much international sympathy and support. Many countries sent troops to participate in the multinational force and aided in the reconstruction of Afghanistan. As to Iraq, however, ignoring the strong opposition of most countries and antiwar forces throughout the world, and ignoring the progress the UN had made in weapons inspection for many years, the United States launched a "preemptive strike" without any evidence that Iraq possessed WMD and without authorization by the UN Security Council. This is what we call an "action without justification." Generally speaking, the international community's response is passive.

Second, the aims were different. The aim of the U.S. military action against Afghanistan was relatively clear and limited: to eradicate Bin Laden and Al-Qaeda. It was precisely for this aim, not for reforming Afghanistan, that the U.S. troops toppled the Taliban regime. Therefore, the United States not only made use of the forces of the Northern Alliance but also considered the interests of the Pashto people, who account for the majority of the country's population. Even the former king, Zahir, was taken care of. So a balance was maintained. The overthrow of the Taliban theocratic regime helped Afghanistan revive its traditional values and social structure. So nearly all the anti-Taliban forces attended the Bonn Conference, elected Karzai president, and established a balance of forces in Kabul, where foreign embassies are back to normal. The U.S. forces there can now focus on suppressing Al-Qaeda.

But the United States is much more ambitious in Iraq. It aims not only to destroy the Saddam regime, but also to establish a democratic state, cast off the yoke of Islamic tradition, and set a democratic example for the Arab and other Middle Eastern countries. Such an aim was unlikely to attract opposition factions in Iraq. Actually, the Saddam regime was a secular power. Many opposition factions, especially the influential ones, have a tribal or religious background, and are against both Saddam and the United States. It is very difficult for the United States to find an ideal person to replace Saddam. The interim administration confronts many problems, and foreign embassies are far from operating normally.

During their advance, the U.S. troops focused on striking the party,

government, army, and police of the Saddam regime, and basically destroyed the original power system. The power vacuum brought two problems in its aftermath: first, social chaos, robbery, and revenge, with U.S.
troops forced to maintain law and order, thus hardening their role as an
army of occupation and stiffening the resistance of the local people; second, an increase in the influence of Islamic organizations. Nicholas
Kristof, a columnist for the *New York Times* (and a former resident corre-
spondent in Beijing), sent a report from Basra on June 24, saying that the
chief beneficiaries of the collapse of the Saddam regime were Islamic fundamentalists. In Basra, shopkeepers who sold alcohol were shot dead, cinema managers were in constant fear, and signs were posted saying,
"Sisters, wear your veils." During the reign of Saddam, females made up
eighty percent of the students in the Basra University Science Department. Now, however, women are increasingly afraid to be seen unveiled.
The title of Kristof's report was in fact "Wear Your Veils." The report also
mentioned that while the exiled opposition factions were living comfort-
ably in London, Islamic fundamentalists were engaged in underground
work at the risk of their lives, winning the support of the local people. The
report warned that an Islamic fundamentalist iron curtain would probably
fall over Iraq.

After the end of the war in Iraq, media throughout the world presented a great deal of discussion on the U.S. antiterrorism strategy. According to the *International Herald Tribune,* President Bush believes that
the United States has a mission to bring peace to the world. The mission
will be accomplished as soon as the United States wins the war against terrorism. But, "multipolar" and balanced international relations constitute
obstacles to it. The national security adviser, Condoleezza Rice, gave an ex-
haustive explanation of this during a speech at the International Institute
of Strategic Studies in London on June 26. She said that it was necessary to
break the destructive international system of confrontation between the
powers, which took shape after the rise of nation-states in the seventeenth
century. European countries must reject the concept of multipolarity, because it brought big-power confrontation and competition over values, instead of peace.

In my opinion, what Rice said implied that there should be a new system, replacing the United Nations under multipolarity and going beyond
the authority of NATO. Now, the United States is no longer satisfied with
NATO, because it is moving toward multipolarity internally. Its internal
equality constitutes an obstacle to the United States.

Rice's speech was a response to the appeal of American and European
leaders to rebuild the Atlantic partnership. On May 14, eighteen formerly

important U.S. political figures, including Madeleine Albright and Zbigniew Brzezinski, issued a joint statement on the improvement of relations between the United States and the European Union. On June 14, formerly important European political figures, including Helmut Kohl and Valéry Giscard d'Estaing, responded actively. They agreed that U.S.-EU solidarity should be stressed to face the challenge of globalization; that in their existence and development the United States and Europe have been closely related; they have a common destiny; and that the two sides should enhance their cooperation on tense international issues and share the responsibility of upholding international security.

Let us compare the views of the two sides. The United States opposes multipolarity, regarding it as the cause of confrontation between the powers, as well as an obstacle to the United States' new mission in the world. The European countries, however, stress cooperation and the need to share the responsibility for international security. Without European help, the United States cannot cope with its challenges by itself.

All through its 200 years of history, the United States has pursued a policy of "neutrality" toward Europe. This was a trend of isolationism, aimed at preventing the young America from being engulfed in European wars. The United States did not enter World War I (1914–1918) until April 1917, and it did not enter World War II (1939–1945) until after Pearl Harbor was attacked in December 1941.

Since the end of World War II, the United States has been a superpower, both economically and militarily, and since the end of the cold war, it has been the only superpower. If anyone thinks that unipolar theory is applicable by relying on military and economic superiority, it would inevitably lead him to seek unipolar freedom of action, and even contravene international law, undermine the United Nations, and embark on the road of pursuing the policy of force.

Some American scholars have already started thinking deeply about this. For example, in May 2003, the American magazine *Foreign Policy* published "The Paradoxes of American Nationalism," by Minxin Pei, a scholar at the Carnegie Endowment for International Peace. It begins, "Nearly two years after the horrific terrorist attacks on the United States, international public opinion has shifted from heartfelt sympathy for Americans and their country to undisguised antipathy. The immediate catalyst for this shift is the United States' hard-line policy toward and subsequent war with Iraq. . . . The growing unease with the United States should be seen as a powerful global backlash against the spirit of American nationalism that shapes and animates U.S. foreign policy."

The article says that Americans are extremely patriotic. Researchers at the University of Michigan reported that more than 70 percent of those surveyed declared themselves "very proud" to be Americans. By comparison, the same survey revealed that less than half of the people in other Western countries felt "very proud" of their nationality. But "nationalism" is a dirty word in the United States, because American nationalism differs from other nationalisms in many ways. First, the United States sees itself as a cultural and ethnic melting pot, believing that "there is no American race; there is only an American creed." American nationalism is based on values regarded as universally applicable, not those of cultural or ethnic superiority. Second, American nationalism is triumphant and forward-looking, because its short and glorious historical memory makes it believe that the future would be better. Hence the United States has little understanding and empathy for the whining of aggrieved nations whose formative experience consisted of a succession of national humiliations and setbacks.

Therefore, as an amalgam of political idealism, national pride, and relative insularity, American nationalism has an inborn arrogance and a missionary spirit. The paradox is that although the United States is highly nationalistic, it does not see itself as such. Consequently, it inevitably clashes with nationalism abroad. There are three immediate consequences. The first is the high level of resentment that the United States generates, both among foreign governments and among their people. The second is that United States' attempts to undermine hostile regimes abroad tend to backfire. Third, the United States' behavior abroad for the sake of its state interests inevitably appears hypocritical to others. Over time, such behavior can erode the international credibility and legitimacy of the United States.

In fact, what this article discusses is not new. As we look back on the past, we find that the same paradox of nationalism appeared when the Western powers were engaged in aggression and expansion. Western countries hold that Christian values, a market economy, and democracy are the three pillars of the success of capitalism. These three are regarded as universally applicable, and as surpassing the cultural and religious traditions of "uncivilized nations." Therefore, capitalism starts its global expansion with missionaries in the lead to civilize the local people. They are followed by businessmen seeking profits, and when the time comes, backed by military force, capitalism would remold the "uncivilized barbarians" completely, regarding their attempts to protect their own cultures and religious traditions as "narrow," and even "evil," nationalism.

Recently, there has been a debate on the issue of the "American Empire." This discussion focuses on whether the United States is an "empire," and whether it plays the role of an "empire." "Neoconservatives" argue that the United States is an empire. They insist that the United States should impose its political values on the world, launch "preemptive strikes" by relying on its overwhelming advantage, and remold the world in its own image. A British historian at Oxford University has suggested that the United States should learn from the British Empire, which made "contributions" to the world by giving it "prosperity and progress" in the nineteenth and twentieth centuries. However, "paleoconservatives" oppose the wording "American empire," regarding it as quite dangerous. They argue that the United States should reflect on the decline of the Roman Empire. Some have initiated a "Committee for Safeguarding the Republic," preparing to open a seminar on the "American empire" in New York. "Liberals" are also against the building of an empire, advocating flexible ways for the United States to play the leading role in international affairs.

President Bush has emphasized many times that the United States is not an "empire," as it differs essentially from past "empires" in action. But in his administration, many people do advocate popularizing American values by force, and establishing an "American empire."

In brief, the groups involved in the debate have the same goal of safeguarding, strengthening, and extending the dominant position of the United States, but differ on the best ways to realize it. This debate will exert a far-reaching influence on future American foreign policies.

Joseph S. Nye, Jr., dean of Harvard University's Kennedy School of Government, in his "The Strength and Strategy of the United States after the Iraq War," pointed out the differences within the Bush administration on how to implement the new strategy. Some members of Bush's team want to get rid of the framework of international rules established by the UN after World War II; others believe that it would be easier to realize the goal within the present framework. In Nye's opinion, it is better for the United States to make use of the UN to carry out the new strategy, cooperating with the other powers that have a veto, than to ignore or try to reform it. There are many affairs beyond the control of even the strongest country in the twenty-first century. Expansion cannot overstep public tolerance. According to a poll taken after the Iraq War, the American public is not interested in an "American empire" and opposes any invasion of Syria or Iran. On the contrary, Americans continue to support multilateralism and the role of the UN.

On August 3, the *Los Angeles Times* reported that the United States might pursue a milder foreign policy—shifting from winning wars at a high cost to withdrawing from hot spots; and shifting from high-cost intervention to low-cost diplomatic mediation. The factors involved are the coming election, the attitude of the American public, the lesson drawn from the intelligence event, and the difficulties in the postwar reconstruction of Iraq.

All these are reflections of public opinion. How might the situation develop? We may continue to study this.

Next, let us talk about the current situation in the Middle East.

The Iraq War has had an obvious impact on this region. Now, the United States has turned its attention to Iraq's neighbors and the Middle East region in general. On April 30, the United States, Russia, the European Union, and the UN formally presented a "road map" plan for peace in the Middle East to Israel and Palestine. The United States started promoting the peace process again in order to ease external pressure, pacify the Arab world, and strengthen its leading position in the progress toward peace, using the momentum of its successful overthrow of the Saddam regime. This can be called the United States' second step toward remolding politics in the Middle East. In the face of internal and external pressure, Israel's military operations, and "targeted elimination," radical organizations including Hamas agreed to a cease-fire that has lasted several months. But the peace process still faces multiple obstructions. Recently, the Palestinian president, Abbas, resigned; Israel attacked Hamas; and the "road map" seems to be at a standstill.

The United States thought that the overthrow of the Saddam regime and the boycotting of Arafat would restrain the Palestinians' anti-Israel activities and bring Palestine and Israel to a compromise. But actually, radical organizations such as Hamas are becoming more and more influential among the Palestinian people. In the latest elections to the UN Committee for Welfare and Employment in Gaza, members of Hamas, which the United States calls a terrorist organization, got 80 percent of the votes. Analysts say that Hamas is popular with the Palestinians because it perseveres in the resistance against Israel and provides a great deal of aid to the people of Gaza through its charity network. Compared with the Palestinian cabinet members, who are well dressed and live in villas, the frugal leadership of Hamas is gaining more and more influence among the Palestinians. So, if the United States cannot be fair in dealing with the conflict between Palestine and Israel, and continues in its partiality toward Israel, it will bring about new conflicts and a more complicated situation. The progress toward peace in the Middle East will again be in danger of stalling.

Before transforming the Middle East, the United States has to solve two other key issues: Syria and Iran. At present, U.S. policy is comparatively mild toward Syria, but more hostile toward Iran. On the one hand, Iran is stronger and has influence among radical organizations in the Middle East. In Iraq, the Shiite majority opposes both Saddam and the United

States. In Iran, the Shiites are the overwhelming majority in power. On the other hand, the United States and Iran have a historical grudge against each other. Iran, though inimical to the Arabs in history, is also a Muslim country. It used to be under the influence of the Soviet Union. Stalin chose to meet Roosevelt in Tehran during World War II. After that war, Shah Pahlavi of Iran was pro-United States, and the United States intended to transform Iran into an anti-Soviet base, sparing no effort to help Pahlavi westernize his country. As a result, Iran split into an American-influenced upper class and a Muslim lower class. There was a serious social polarization, and the public was extremely hostile to the United States. After the overthrow of the shah by the Khomeini revolution, relations between the United States and Iran became worse and worse. At one point, the staff of the American embassy in Tehran were held hostage. President Carter's failure to rescue the hostages spelled the end of his political career. This is one example of the United States' failure in dealing with foreign nationalism.

During the Iraq-Iran war, the Western countries were unanimous in their support of Saddam. The United States especially provided him with a large amount of weapons and war equipment. Because of this support, Saddam believed that the Western countries would not oppose his invasion of Kuwait. But the invasion of Kuwait threatened the United States' strategic interests in the Middle East, and so the United States launched the Gulf War, and after twelve years of sanctions, invaded Iraq.

Given the present situation in the Gulf and Middle East region and inside the United States, the latter is unlikely to start a war before the election. However, the Iraq War has posed a new problem for us. I have mentioned before that the United States has adopted a "preemptive strike" strategy. The United States will attack countries which it disapproves of, or which it suspects of involvement in terrorism or own WMD or threaten world peace. This is a significant change in international relations. Will it affect our estimates of the important period of strategic opportunities?

Well, first, and above all, China is a big country. As long as we keep developing in good order, and make more friends and fewer enemies internationally, no one will dare to provoke us. Second, since the "September 11" incident, the United States has realized that it needs other powers' cooperation in its antiterrorism campaign and nonproliferation efforts. Thus, it has eased its pressure on China. It no longer trumpets the missile defense as it used to do. Recent failures of the missile interception experiment may have something to do with inadequate input. Third, the United States' battle fronts are overextended. For example, the United States has sent troops to the Philippines to help it with its antiterrorism efforts. Problems have cropped up in Liberia, involving many American descendants. The United States is considering whether it should send troops there. Also, U.S. troops are bogged down in both Afghanistan and Iraq. There are so many countries in the world that the United States cannot transform all of them into states of American-style freedom. Above all, religious traditions cannot be simply uprooted. There are too many variables in the world for the United States to tackle alone.

We have talked about the eastward shift in U.S. strategic priorities. In recent years, the United States has increased its input into the Asia-Pacific region, especially since the "September 11" incident. However, we cannot conclude from this that U.S. strategic priorities have moved eastward.

First, Europe is still the top priority of U.S. global strategy. Recently, changes have taken place in U.S.-EU relations. Among all the differences between the United States and Europe, those regarding Iraq are the most serious. Although the coalition remains, there is a crack in it. The United States claimed that it would forgive Russia and take no action against Germany, but would not let France off. It talked about the "new Europe" and "old Europe." Some countries in the "new Europe" follow the United States, for example, Poland, which was assigned an area of occupation in Iraq by the United States. But France and Germany are the main forces of Europe. If the differences keep growing, the United States' traditional influence in Europe will shrink, and U.S.-EU relations will become unstable.

Second, from the military angle, it is not necessary for the United States to deploy troops on a large scale in the Asia-Pacific region. It can fight through remote operation, with aircraft carriers as bases. Bombers can take off from the mainland, drop accurately guided bombs far from the battlefield, and then fly back. It is all programmed. The U.S. troops are facing the problem of being too close to the battlefield, especially in South Korea, where they have to withdraw 200 kilometers from the DMZ. In every war, however, the United States has to spend much time on troop movements and much energy handling relations with many countries and persuading its own people.

Third, the United States is pursuing an antiterrorism campaign, trying to stop the proliferation of WMD, and seeking more cooperation with China at present and for the future. The United States has no need to besiege China and no ability to do so, because other Asian countries would not go against their own interests by joining an anti-China alliance.

So, as long as we work hard, there is a good chance for long-term stability in Sino-American relations and a twenty-year period of strategic opportunity.

This is the fifth time that I have come here to talk to you. Over the past five years, groups of professionals have been trained at the School of International Studies. I want to thank all the teaching and administrative staff for their hard work. I have retired from my position of leadership, and I will ask leaders of Peking University to relieve me of my duties as Dean of the School of International Studies. I hope that you young people will grow up quickly, and make contributions to our country's future.

INDEX

Afghanistan
  Geneva Agreement, 37–38, 39
  Soviet war in, 1, 2, 4, 5–6, 9, 18, 22, 23,
    37–38
Africa
  economic aid from China, 203–4
  Qian Qichen in, 45, 47, 122, 191–204,
    207–9
  Sino-African relations, 155–56,
    191–204
  Soviet pressure on, 202
  support of China during sanctions pe-
    riod, 155–56, 200–201
  Western political pressure on, 201–3
  See also South Africa; Qian Qichen;
    specific countries
Akihito, Emperor of Japan, 84–85, 152
Alatas, Ali, 33, 91, 97–98, 99–103
Algeria, 191, 192, 202
Andropov, Yuri, 13, 14, 15, 17
Angola, 197–99, 201
APEC (Asia-Pacific Economic Coopera-
    tion), 105–10, 111, 112, 119, 148
Arafat, Yasir, 72
Arbatov, George A., 167, 173
Arhipov, Ivan, 15–17

Armacost, Michael, 41
Armenia, 175, 177
ASEAN (Association of Southeast Asian
    Nations), 25, 35, 38, 39, 45, 49, 50, 89,
    96
  agreements with China, 104
  China-ASEAN free-trade region, 104
  member nations and diplomatic rela-
    tions with China, 89–90, 96, 98–99,
    103–4, 156
Asian Games, 111, 116, 117
Australia, 107
Azerbaijan, 175, 177
Aziz, Tareq, 69, 71, 80, 82

Badawi, 33
Baker, James, 34, 46–50, 61–65, 67, 68, 69,
    74–77, 78, 79–81, 132, 145–49
Balladur, Édouard, 241
Bangladesh, 96
Beavogui, Edouard, 197
Bianco, Jean-Louis, 233
Biya, Paul, 203
Bolkiah, Mohamed, 33
border issues
  Amur (Heilongjiang) River, 18, 19, 20

border issues (*cont.*)
   "Shanghai Five" mechanism, 182
   Sino-Russian and CIS, 178–79, 180–82
   Sino-Soviet, viii, 5, 11, 18, 19, 20,
     21–22, 26
Botha, P. J., 205
Botha, Pik, 205–9, 222
Botswana, 201
Bo Yibo, 16
Brezhnev, Leonid, 2, 3, 13, 14, 17
Britain
   deterioration in Sino-British relations,
     254–79
   Hong Kong handover ceremony,
     278–79
   Hong Kong issues, visits between Chi-
     nese and British foreign ministers,
     264–77
   Hong Kong return, "honeymoon pe-
     riod," 254
   Hong Kong return, transitional period,
     253–54
   Qian Qichen visits to, 265
   sanctions on China, 255, 257
   secret British envoy visits China, 1989,
     257–60
   seven diplomatic documents on Hong
     Kong, 260–64
   See also Hong Kong
Brunei, 98–99, 103, 156, 248
Bush, George H. W., 48, 75, 168
   beginning of lifting of sanctions against
     China, 146–49
   China visit, 1989, 41, 76
   Gulf crisis of 1990, 57, 62, 74, 77, 79–80
   letters, open, to Deng Xiaoping, 139,
     145
   letters, secret, to Deng Xiaoping,
     131–32, 137–38
   Qian Qichen and, 76, 77, 80–82
   secret envoy sent to China, 131–37
Byelorussia, 166, 170, 171, 175, 176
Cabral, Amilcar, 195

Cabral, Luis, 194, 195
Cai Fangbai, 233, 237
Cambodia
   China and negotiations for peace,
     35–37, 41–46, 100–101
   Democratic Kampuchea party, 35, 36,
     39, 47, 49
   Khmer Rouge, 39, 39n, 40–41, 45,
     46–49, 53
   Paris Conference, 46–50, 62, 90, 97, 256
   Paris Conference Proposal, 40–41
   Peace Agreement, 33–35, 34n, 50–53
   political factions, 35, 36, 39, 45, 47–49,
     50, 51, 52
   Prince Sihanouk, 25, 33, 34–35, 36, 38,
     39, 40, 41, 42, 44, 47–48, 50, 51, 52,
     53, 100
   Vietnam's invasion of, 1, 4, 5, 8, 9–12,
     17–18, 19, 20, 21, 22–23, 24–28,
     35–44, 49, 90
   Supreme National Council, 33, 51, 52
   See also Soviet Union
Cameroon, 203
Cape Verde, 195, 196
Castro, Fidel, 130–31
Ceau_escu, Nicolae, 17, 20, 143–44
Chang Hsiao-yen, 224
Chen Chu, 16, 162
Cheney, Dick, 157
Chen Yun, 4–5, 16
Chernenko, Konstantin, 12, 13, 14, 17
Chernyaev, Anatoly, 168, 173, 174
Chesnel, Gerard, 234
Chiang Ching-kuo, 229
Chiang Kai-shek, 229
Chien Frederick, 215
Chi Haotian, 246
China (People's Republic of China)
   cultural revolution, 163
   five-year plan, 16
   founding of, 162
   market economy created in, 183–84
   modernization efforts, viii, 19

population, 92, 96
socialism of, 161–62, 177–78, 187
See also China's foreign policy; *specific
individuals; specific issues*
China's foreign policy (and Ministry of
Foreign Affairs)
APEC membership, 105, 106, 107–10,
111, 112, 119
Arab countries and, 65–69
Arab envoys to China, 57
ASEAN member countries and, 89–90,
98–99, 103–4, 155–56
athletics, international participation,
111, 113, 116, 117, 271
August 17 Communiqué, 2
Cambodian issue, statement on, 1988,
38–39
Cambodian peace negotiations, 34, 37,
41, 44–50, 52, 100–101
economic sanctions, 1989, issue of,
viii–ix, 44–45, 47, 97, 127, 131, 134,
135, 138, 139–43, 145–55, 201, 248,
255, 257
Gulf crisis and Iraq invasion of Kuwait
positions, 56, 58, 60, 63–64, 69–70,
74–79
Hong Kong's return, 253–79
international pressure following
Tiananmen incident, 127–57, *see also*
economic sanctions, 1989
Macao's return, 279–82
meeting of ministers with Deng and
Sino-Soviet relations, 1982, 4–5
Middle East policy, 59–60
non-paper, 61, 61n
"one China" policy, 101, 103, 108, 200,
206, 214, 215, 216, 218, 228, 245–51
nuclear proliferation, position on, 152,
243, 246, 250
"paper" visas, 113–14, 113n
press conference, first ever given, 2–3
press conferences, practice of, 4
Sino-African relations, 191–204

Sino-American relations, 2, 13, 46, 48,
59, 61, 61–65, 74–77, 80–82, 89, 117,
131–49, 156–57, 233, 242–50
Sino-British relations and the return of
Hong Kong, 253–79
Sino-Cuban relations, 129–31
Sino-DPRK relations, 114–19, 122–25
Sino-European Community relations,
152–55, 281
Sino-French relations, 193, 231–43
Sino-Guinean relations, 196–99
Sino-Indonesian relations, 88–103, 108,
156
Sino-Indonesian relations, press confer-
ence, 95–96
Sino-Italian relations, 153–54, 155, 193
Sino-Japanese relations, 85–87, 89, 117,
146, 149–52
Sino-Japanese War, position on, 85
Sino-Portuguese relations, 279–82
Sino-ROK relations, normalization of,
105–7, 110–14, 116–17, 119–22,
125–26
Sino-Russian (and CIS) relations, 174–89
Sino-South African relations, 204–29
Sino-Soviet "cold war," 163
Sino-Soviet relations, 2, 14–15, 19–20,
23–28, 41–44, 130, 144, 161
Taiwan positions, 2, 231–51, *see also*
"one China policy"
Vietnamese representatives sent to,
1989, 1990, 42–44, 50–51
world peace, aim of diplomacy, 60
"written information," 260
See also Qian Qichen; *specific individu-
als; specific issues*
Chirac, Jacques, 241
Christopher, Warren, 242, 243–44,
246–47, 248, 249, 250
Clark, Charles, 47
Clinton, Bill, 157, 243–51
"three nos" and visit to China, 1998,
157, 251

Collins, Gerard, 153
Commonwealth of Independent States
    (CIS), 171, 176
    Sino-Russian (and CIS) relations,
        174–89
Cook, Robin, 259
Cornell University, 243, 245, 247
Côte d'Ivoire, 202, 203
Craddock, Percy, 257–59
Cuba, 79, 129–31
cultural exchanges
    Russia and, 187
    South Africa and, 207
    Soviet Union and China, 8, 15
    student exchange, 15, 162–63

Dai Bingguo, 24, 187
Degeorges, Jean-Pierre, 234
de Klerk, Fredrik Wilhelm, 212
De Michelis, Gianni, 153–54
Deng Xiaoping, viii, 123, 124, 208
    Ceau_escu meeting with, 17, 20
    on Chinese socialism, 177–78, 187
    George H. W. Bush letters, open, to,
        139, 145
    George H. W. Bush letters, secret, to,
        131–32, 137–38
    George W. W. Bush meeting with, 41
    Hong Kong's return and, 254, 271–72
    Hosni Mubarak and message to Bush, 144
    Kissinger and message to Bush, 139–40
    Mike Wallace interview with, 1986, 20
    modernization of China and, viii
    normalization of Sino-Soviet relations
        and, 2, 4, 5, 7, 14, 16, 17, 20, 26–31,
        36–37
    "package solution" for sanctions im-
        passe, 140–43
    secret American envoy sent to, 131–37
    Sino-ROK relations and, 116–17
    summit meeting with Gorbachev, 26–31
    trade reform, 16
    visit to ASEAN member countries, 89

Deviers-Joncour, Christine, 236
Dinh Nho Liem, 43–44
Do Muoi, 50
Dumas, Roland, 33, 44, 45–46, 48, 59,
        231–39

Eagleburger, Lawrence, 132–37, 140–41,
        142
EC (European Community)
    lifting of sanctions on China, 152–55
    normalization of relations with China,
        152–55
    trade and China, 146, 154
economy and trade
    Africa and China, 196, 203–4
    agreements between China and former
        Soviet countries, 176–77
    ANC and China, 210
    Britain and China, 258
    China-ASEAN free-trade region, 104
    China and ASEAN members, 90, 155
    China International Chamber of Com-
        merce, 118
    Chinese reforms, 16, 115, 183–84
    European Community and China, 146,
        152–55
    French projects canceled, 240
    General Agreement on Tariffs and
        Trade (GATT) and China, 148
    Guinea and China, 196
    Japan and China, 150, 152
    ROK and China, 112–13, 117–18, 126
    Russia and China, 179–80, 183–84, 186,
        187
    sanctions on China, viii–ix, 44–45, 47,
        97, 127, 131, 134, 135, 138, 139–43,
        145–55, 248, 255, 257
    South Africa and China, 212
    Soviet Union and China, 8, 15, 16, 17,
        21
    Taiwan and France, 231–42
    Taiwan and South Africa, 219–20, 222
    U.S. and China, 140, 146, 148

EEC (European Economic Community), 97, 281. *See also* EU (European Union)

Egypt, 60–61, 64
  Qian Qichen in, 59, 191, 192, 202

ESCAP (UN Economic and Social Commission for Asia and the Pacific), 120

Estonia, 165, 170, 174

Ethiopia, 202

EU (European Union), 47

Evans, Gareth, 33

Evans, Leo Henry, 205

Exceeding Time and Space (Troyanovsky), 30

Eyadema, Gnassingbe, 203

Fahd, King of Saudi Arabia, 65, 72, 73

Faisal, Prince of Saudi Arabia, 55–56, 68–69, 72–73

Fang Lizhi, 140, 142

Fedotov, Vladimir P., 19

Five Principles of Peaceful Coexistence, 30–31, 88, 90, 91, 92–93, 95, 96, 136, 175, 178, 215

France
  Gulf Crisis, 1990, and, 59
  Indochina and, 40
  Paris Conference on Cambodia, 46–50, 62, 90, 97, 256
  Paris Conference Proposal, 40–41
  resolution of Taiwan-China issue, 240–43
  sale of Mirage fighters to Taiwan, 238–40
  sale of warships to Taiwan, 231–35, 237–38
  scandal over the Lafayette-class frigates, 235–36
  Sino-French relations, 193, 231–43
  Tiananmen incident and anti-China sanctions, 1989, 44–46

Friedman, Jacques, 241

G-7 group (Seven-Nation Economic Summit), 47, 97, 127, 134, 149–50

Gan Ying, 65

Gao Shumao, 129

Georgia, 165, 166–67, 175, 177

Ghana, 192, 202, 207

Gide, André, 172–73

Gorbachev, Mikhail, 17–22, 24, 37, 128, 130
  Cambodia negotiations and, 42
  collapse of the Soviet Union and, 166–71, 173
  "new thinking," 24, 37
  summit meeting in China, 1989, 26–31
  Vladivostok speech, 18, 19, 20, 21, 22, 37

Gromyko, Andrey, 12–13, 15

Guangzhou Trade Fair, 1977, 90

Guinea and Guinea-Bissau, 191, 192–93, 202
  Angolan issue and, 197–99
  Qian Qichen as Ambassador, 194–99

Gu Xiner, 224

Han Nianlong, 7

Han Sung Joo, 126

Han Xu, 48

Hao Baicun, 236

Hashimoto, Ryutaro, 150

Hawke, Robert, 107

Heath, Edward, 264

Heng Samrin, 35

Hirohito, Emperor of Japan, 83–86, 91, 255

Hiroshi, Mitsuzuka, 47

Hong Kong, ix, 70, 71, 117, 131, 207, 222–23, 253–79
  airport built, 264–65
  APEC and, 106, 107, 108, 109, 110
  Basic Law issues, 255, 256, 257, 258, 259–60, 261, 262, 263, 264, 265, 266, 267, 273, 274, 276, 278
  Bill of Human Rights, 276

Hong Kong *(cont.)*
  Britain's "three violations," 266–68,
    270, 278
  Chinese troops in, issue of, 255–56, 281
  Chris Patten as last governor, 265,
    266–68, 269, 278
  colonial rule of, 261
  deterioration of China-British relations
    following Tiananmen incident,
    255–56, 259
  failure of China-British negotiations,
    272–75
  "honeymoon period" between China
    and Britain, 254–57
  Interim Legislative Council, 275–77
  Legislative Council, 256–57, 260–61,
    265, 266, 269–70, 272, 274, 275, 276,
    277, 278
  "one country, two systems," 254
  political system and elections issue,
    256, 258–68, 269, 274
  Qian Qichen's analysis of Soviet col-
    lapse and Britain's behavior, 278
  return to China (handover), 223, 259,
    275, 277, 278–79
  secret British envoy visits China, 1989,
    257–60
  "seven diplomatic documents," 260–64
  "seventeen rounds of diplomatic nego-
    tiations," 268–72
  Sino-British Joint Declaration, 254–55,
    256, 261, 267, 275, 280
  "three conformities," 269
  "through train" arrangement, 270–71,
    273, 275, 276, 277, 278
  transitional period between China and
    Britain, 253–54, 281
Houphouët-Boigny, Felix, 203
Howe, Geoffrey, 255, 256, 271
Huang Hua, 14–15
Hungary, 110
Hun Sen, 45, 49, 50
Hu Qiaomu, 14
Hurd, Douglas, 34, 259, 260, 262–64, 265,
  266, 268–69, 270–72, 273–75

Hu Sha, 191
Hussein, Saddam, 62, 65, 66, 67, 69–74, 80, 82
Hussein Ibn Talal, King of Jordan, 59,
  68–69

Ilyichev, Leonid, 5–6, 7, 8–9, 10–12, 23
India, 96
Indonesia
  Bandung conference, 1955, 88, 90, 95
  Cambodia issue and, 51, 90
  "cocktail party" on Vietnam's with-
    drawal from Cambodia, 39, 40
  diplomatic breach with China, 89
  "five basics," 93
  Madiun incident, 93, 93n
  normalization of Chinese relations
    with, ix, 89–103, 108, 156
  population, 92, 96
  September 30 incident, 88–89, 91, 93,
    93n, 94
  Treaty on Dual Nationality, 88
Iran, 56, 73, 74
Iraq
  China's position on settlement of Gulf
    crisis, 56, 58, 60, 63–64, 69–70, 74–79
  Iran-Iraq war, 56, 73
  history of Kuwait dispute, 56
  Kuwait invasion, 55–82, 144–46
  Qian Qichen in, 59, 69–74
  sanctions on, 57, 58, 61, 64, 71
  U.S. military response, 1990, 57, 58–59,
    69, 70
Ireland, 153
Israel, 62
Italy, 153–54, 155, 193
Ito, Masayoshi, 87
Ivashchenko, Vladimir, 169

Japan
  Emperor Akihito visit to China, 150,
    151, 152
  funeral for Emperor Hirohito, 83–85,
    84n, 91, 255
  Japan and lifting of sanctions against
    China, 149–52

Korean War and, 114–15
loans to China, 150, 152
North Korea and, 112
population, 96
Shinjuku Imperial Park, Tokyo, 83–84
Sino-Japanese Joint Declaration, 85, 86, 87
Sino-Japanese Peace and Friendship Treaty, 85, 87
Sino-Japanese relations, 85–87, 89, 127
Sino-Japanese War, 85–87, 114, 152
Jiang Enzhu, 234, 237, 241, 269
Jiang Zemin
    Bush letter to, regarding Gulf military intervention, 77
    Cambodian peace negotiations, 51
    Hong Kong return and, 257–59
    Japan visit, 1992, 152
    Nelson Mandela and, 210, 213, 214, 217, 218, 221, 223, 224–25
    Russian visit, 1994, 188
    Russian visit, 2001, 189
    Sino-African relations and, 202
    Sino-American relations and, 140, 141, 142, 157
    Sino-French relations, 232
    Sino-Indonesian relations and, 99
    Sino-ROK relations and, 118, 122–23, 125
    Sino-Russian relations and, 183, 186–89
    Soviet Union visit, 1991, 167
    Taiwan issue and, 214, 217, 218, 221, 223, 224–25
    U.S. visit, 1995, 248–50
    U.S. visit, 1997, 157
    U.S. visit, 2002, 81
Ji Peiding, 215, 225
Ji Xianlin, 191
Jordan, 57, 59, 60–61, 68
    Qian Qichen in, 59, 68
Juppé, Alain, 240, 242

Kaifu, Toshiki, 151–52
Kanmi, Muranaoru, 85

Kapitsa, Mikhail, 5, 6
Kazakhstan, 166, 171, 174, 175, 176, 181, 182, 182n
Keite, Modibo, 192
Kenya, 202
Kessedjian, Bernard, 237
Khieu Samphan, 100
Khrushchev, Nikita, 6, 12, 22, 163, 164
Kim Dae Jung, 126
Kim Il Sung, 114, 118, 119, 122–25
Kim Yong Nam, 117–18, 123, 125
Kim Yong Sam, 126
Kissinger, Henry, 132, 133, 134, 139–40
Koo Chenfu, 246
Korea, Democratic People's Republic of (DPRK or North Korea)
    diplomatic relations of, 112
    UN admission, 112, 118–19, 120
    Sino-DPRK relations, 114–19, 122–25
Korea, Republic of (ROK or South Korea, ix
    APEC and, 105, 108, 109–10
    Asian Games, 111, 117
    diplomatic recognition of by Soviet and Eastern European countries, 110–11
    Olympic Games, 110, 111, 117
    "paper" visas, 113–14, 113n
    Sino-ROK relations, normalization of, 105–7, 110–17, 119–22, 125–26
    trade with China, 112–13, 117–18, 126
    Taiwan issue, 121–22, 125
    UN admission, 112, 118–19, 120
KOTRA (Korea Trade and Investment Promotion Agency), 118
Kozyrev, Andrei, 175, 178, 179–80, 184, 187
Kravchuk, Leonid, 170
Kryuchkov, Vladimir, 168
Kunaze, Georgi, 175, 181
Kuwait
    border disputes with Iraq, 56
    China's position on Iraqi invasion, 56
    Chinese workers in, 56–57
    diplomatic relations with China, 57
    Iraqi invasion and Gulf crisis, 55–82, 144–46

Kuwait (*cont.*)
  request for liberation, 64
Kwon Byong Hyon, 121
Kyrgyzstan, 175, 176, 181, 182, 182n

Lake, Anthony, 243
Lamos, Domingo, 196
Latvia, 165, 170
Le Duan, 39
Lee Jong Ock, 117
Lee Sang Ock, 106, 111, 112, 120, 125–26
Lee See Young, 108–9
Lee Teng-hui, 214, 220, 229, 236, 243–47
Lesotho, 201
Liang Zhaoli, 204
Li Daoyu, 243, 246, 247, 251
Ligachev, Yegor, 173–74
Li Guixian, 246
Li Lanqing, 105, 175, 176
Lilley, James Roderick, 62, 132, 142
Li Luye, 91
Li Peng
  Bush letters to, regarding Gulf crisis, 77
  Cambodia peace negotiations, 51
  DPRK visit, 1991, 118
  France and Taiwan armament sales, 232,
    234, 241
  Indonesian visit, 1990, 99–100, 101
  Nelson Mandela and, 210, 217
  Sino-American relations, sanctions, and
    Baker meetings, 147–48
  Sino-American relations, sanctions, and
    Scowcroft meetings, 133–34, 136–37,
    141
  Sino-Russian relations, 175, 178
Li Tao, 162
Lithuania, 165, 170
Liu Danian, 85
Liu Shaoqi, 227
Liu Shuqing, 43, 47
Liu Xiao, 162
Liu Xinquan, 164
Li Xiannian, 4

Li Zhaoxing, 3, 24, 215, 249
Loncar, Budimir, 34
Louhanapessy, Johan, 98
Lukyanov, Anatoly, 169
Lumumba, Patrice, 198
Lu Ping, 266–67
Luxembourg, 153, 154
Lu Yizheng, 224, 229
Lu You, 16

Macao, 207, 279–82
  Chinese troops in, 281
  handover, date, 280
  Joint Declaration, 279–80
  Macaenses of, 280
  "one country, two systems," 280
  "three major issues," 281
  transitional period, 281
Major, John, 47, 256
Malaysia, 89, 90, 104
Malcev, 6–7
Mali, 191, 192, 193, 202
Ma Lie, 164
Mandela, Nelson, 209–11, 213, 215,
    216–21, 223–29
Manglapus, Paul, 33
Mao Zedong, 164, 185, 194, 227, 264
Martin, Claude, 232, 234, 237
Matlock, Jack, 168
Ma Xusheng, 6–7
Mbeki, Thabo, 211, 213–14
McDougall, Barbara, 33
McLaren, Robin, 266–67, 269
Mendes, Francisco, 195
Mexico, 129
Mitsuzuka, Hiroshi, 150
Mitterrand, François, 40, 233
Miyun Reservoir, 11
Mobutu Sese Seko, 198
Moldova, 175, 177
Mongolia (People's Republic of Mongo-
    lia), 1, 5, 9, 11, 18, 26
Morocco, 64, 202

Moseneke, Dikgang, 209
Mozambique, 201
Mubarak, Hosni, 65, 144
Mugabe, Robert, 201
Murdiono, 91–94, 96, 101

Nakajima, Toshijiro, 86
Nakao, Eiichi, 150
Nakayama, Taro, 150, 151
Namibia, 202, 207
Nazarbayev, Nursultan, 174
Nguyen Co Thach, 42–43
Nguyen Dy Nieu, 51–52
Nguyen Manh Cam, 34, 52
Nguyen Van Linh, 39, 50
Nixon, Richard, 89, 132, 134
non-paper, 61, 61n
nuclear proliferation, disarmament, and
    treaties, 152, 243, 246, 250, 255
Nzo, Alfred, 214–16, 221, 222, 223, 224,
    225–28

Olympic Games, 110, 111, 116, 117, 271
Oman, 59
Ordonez, Francisco F., 154

Pahad, Aziz, 224, 225, 226
Pakistan, 96
Palestine, 59, 68, 71
Pankin, Boris D., 34, 53
"paper" visas, 113–14, 113n
Park Chul Un, 113–14
Pascoe, B. Lynn, 76–77
Patten, Chris, ix, 265, 266–68, 269, 278
Peking University, School of Interna-
    tional Studies, ix
Peng Zhen, 16
Pereira, Aristides, 195
Perez de Cuéllar, Xavier, 33, 58–59, 82
Pham Van Dong, 50
Philippines, 89, 90, 103
PLO (Palestine Liberation Organization), 72
Politics of Diplomacy, The (Baker), 132

Pol Pot, 47
Poos, Jacques, 153
Popov, Gavriil, 168
Portugal, 279–82
    "April 25 Revolution," 279
    See also Macao
Primakov, Yevgeny, 59
Pugo, Boris, 168
Putin, Vladimir, 188–89

Qasem, Marwan, 68
Qian Qi'ao, 113
Qian Qichen
    in Africa, 45, 47, 122, 191–204, 207–9
    as Ambassador in Africa, 194–99
    Boris Yeltsin and, 182–88
    Brent Scowcroft and, xi, 80, 81–82,
        141–42
    Britain, the return of Hong Kong and,
        254–56, 259–60, 262–79
    Britain, visits to, 1992 and 1995, 265,
        276
    British foreign secretaries and, 259,
        260, 262–77
    Cambodian peace negotiations, 34, 37,
        41, 44–50, 52
    developing countries, meetings with
        during sanctions period, 155–56
    DPRK and, 117–19
    as envoy to Hirohito's funeral, 86–87,
        255
    Fidel Castro and, 130–31
    George H. W. Bush and, 76, 77, 80–82
    Gulf crisis and, 55–56, 59–82
    Hosni Mubarak and, 65
    Indonesian officials and, 91–101
    Indonesian press conference, 101–3
    James Baker and, 46–50, 61–65, 67, 68,
        69, 74–77, 78, 79–81, 145–46, 147,
        148
    Japanese lifting of sanctions and,
        150–51
    Johannesburg, South Africa visit, 207–9

Qian Qichen (*cont.*)
Kim Il Sung and, 118, 119, 122–25
King Fahd and, 72, 73
King Hussein and, 68–69
Kuwaiti Emir and Crown Prince and,
56, 64, 66
Latin American visit, 1989, 128–31
Macao visit, 282
Middle East journey, 1990, 65–69
Pik Botha and, 205–9
Portuguese visits, 281–82
press conference on Tiananmen Square
Incident, 128–29
Prince Faisal and, 55–56, 68, 72–73
retirement, xiii–xiv
Roh Tae Woo and, 110–14, 125–26
ROK (South Korea) and, 105, 110–14,
120–22, 125–26
Russian visit, 2001, 189
Saddam Hussein and, 69–74
Saudi Arabia visits, 55–56, 59, 66–69
Sino-French relations and, 232–35, 239,
242–43
Sino-Russian relations and, 28, 174–75,
179–80, 187, 189
Sino–South African relations and,
205–9, 211–12, 214–16, 222–23,
225–26, 227–28
Sino-Soviet relations and, 1–4, 23–28,
37–38, 41–42, 128, 130, 164
Sino-Soviet relations and Gorbachev,
23–28, 42, 128, 130, 164
Sino-Soviet relations and Shevard-
nadze, 24–28, 37–38, 41–42
in the Soviet Union, 1954–1974,
159–65, 193
Soviet Union collapse and, 169–70
Soviet Union visit, 1988, 23–26
Spain visit and Ordonez meetings,
1990, 154–55
Suharto and, 88, 94–95
UN representation by, 37, 41, 48, 58, 59,
60, 77–79, 128, 155, 180, 216, 226,
239, 256, 266

as vice minister, 1, 3, 4
Warren Christopher and issue of Tai-
wan-U.S. relations, 242, 243–51
Yasir Arafat and, 72
Qiao Guanhua, 7
Qin Huasun, 77, 109

Ramaphosa, Cyril, 218
Reagan, Ronald, 13
Rice, Condoleezza, 157
Rifkind, Malcolm, 259, 276–77
Rio Group, 155
Ripert, Edouard, 233
Roberto, Holden, 197
Roe Ching Hee, 121
Rogachev, Igor, 21–23, 28, 38, 180
Roh Moo Hyun, 126
Roh Tae Woo, 110–14, 125–26
Rolland, Romain, 172
Romania, 143–44
Roy, Stapleton, 245
Rumsfeld, Donald, 157
Russia
border issues and China, 178–79,
180–82
collapse of Soviet Union and, 166, 168,
170–71, 174–75
Jiang Zemin visits, 188, 189
Sino-Russian (and CIS) relations,
174–89
trade with China, 179–80, 183, 184,
186, 187
treaties with China, 182n, 186, 187, 189
See also Putin, Vladimir; Yeltsin, Boris
Ryzhkov, Nikolai, 174

Sabah, Emir Jaber al-Ahmed al-, 64,
66–67
Sabah, Prince Saad Al-Abdulla al-Salem,
al-, 56, 67
Sampaio, Jorge, 282
Sarasin, Arsa, 34
Saudi Arabia, 64
China, diplomatic relations with, 55, 57, 60

Kuwaiti government in exile in, 66
Qian Qichen in, 55–56, 59, 66–69
Savimbi, Jonas, 197–98
Scheer, François, 233
science and technology
  Sino-Russian exchanges, 187
  Sino-Soviet exchanges, 8, 15, 16, 21
Scowcroft, Brent, xi, 80, 81–82, 132–37,
  140–43
Segal, Gerald, 244
Senegal, 202
"Shanghai Five" mechanism and Shang-
  hai Cooperative Organization (SCO),
  181–82, 182n
Shenzhen Special Economic Zone, 16
Shevardnadze, Eduard, 23–24, 26–28,
  37–38, 42, 49, 53, 59
Shokhin, Aleksandr, 175, 187
Shushkevich, Stanislav, 170
Sihanouk, Prince Norodom, 25, 33,
  34–35, 36, 38, 39, 40, 41, 42, 44,
  47–48, 50, 51, 52, 53, 100
Silayev, Ivan, 169
Singapore, 89, 98–99, 102, 103, 107, 156,
  235
Sipraseuth, Phoune, 33
Sissoko, Fily, 198
Sisulu, Walter, 209, 210
Solanki, Madhavsinh, 33
Solomon, Richard, 62
Solovyev, Nikolai, 169
Son Sann, 35, 50, 100
South Africa, ix, 204–29
  ANC and China, 209–29
  Chinese economic aid to, 212
  Chinese embassy established, 227–28
  general election, 1994, 214
  Qian Qichen meeting in Johannesburg,
    1992, 207–9
  relations with China during apartheid,
    204–9
  Taiwan aid to and trade with, 219–20,
    222
  Taiwan issue and normalization of

Sino-South African relations, 204–9,
  210–29
South Korea. See Korea, Republic of
  (ROK, South Korea)
Soviet Union
  Afghanistan war, 1, 2, 4, 5–6, 9, 18, 22,
    23, 37–38, 39
  alcohol ban, 14
  "August 19 Incident," 165–70
  border disputes with China, 5, 11, 18,
    19, 20, 21–22, 26
  Chinese delegation in Moscow, 1988,
    24–26
  Chinese representation at Brezhnev's
    funeral, 14–15
  collapse and dissolution of, 31, 165–74
  economic and trade, scientific, techno-
    logical, and cultural exchanges with
    China, 8, 15, 16, 17, 21
  "8.19 incident," 53
  Five Principles of Peaceful Coexistence,
    30–31, 88, 90, 91, 92–93, 95, 96, 136,
    176, 178, 215
  flaws of socialist economy in, 163–65,
    172–73
  Gulf crisis of 1990 and, 57, 59
  historical feud with China, 1
  Korean War, 114–15
  meeting of Wu Xueqian and Vladimir P.
    Fedotov, 1985, 19–20
  Mongolia and, 1, 4, 5, 9, 11, 18, 26
  Qian Qichen in the Soviet Union,
    1954–1974, 159–65
  ROK and, 110, 111
  Sino-Soviet "cold war," 163
  Sino-Soviet conflict at Zhenbaodao, 19
  Sino-Soviet relations, 161
  Sino-Soviet relations, normalization of,
    ix, 1–31, 36–37, 38, 41–44, 130, 144,
    165
  student exchange with China, 15,
    162–63
  summit meeting with China, 1989,
    26–31

Soviet Union (*cont.*)
  "three major barriers" to Sino-Soviet
    relations, 4, 5–6, 7, 8, 12, 13, 15, 17,
    18, 19, 20, 35, 37
  trade agreements with China, 16, 17
  Treaty on Dual Nationality, 88
  Twelfth National Conference of the
    Communist Party, 7
  U.S. and, viii, 13, 139, 141
  Vietnam in Cambodia and, 1, 4, 5, 8,
    9–12, 17–18, 19, 20, 21, 22–23, 24–28,
    35–44, 49
Spain, 154
Suharto, President of Indonesia, 88, 90,
    91–92, 94–95, 99
Sun Yat-sen, 282
Suttner, Raymond, 217

Taiwan (Chinese Taipei), ix, 2, 46, 56–57,
    103, 117, 282
  APEC and, 106–7, 108, 109–10, 148
  China and ROK, 121–22, 125
  GATT and, 148
  Lee Teng-hui visit to U.S., 1995, 243–47
  normalization of Sino-South African
    relations and issue of, 204–9, 210–29
  "one China" policy and, 101, 103, 108,
    200, 206, 214, 215, 216, 218, 228,
    245–51, 282
  sale of French Mirage fighters, 238–40
  sale of French warships to, 231–35,
    237–38
  scandal over the Lafayette-class
    frigates, 235–36
  Sino-French relations and, 231–42
  South Africa and, 204–9, 210–29
  UN and, 200
  U.S. and, 2, 233, 243–51
Tajikistan, 175, 176, 181, 182, 182n
Takeshita, Noboru, 84–85, 86, 87, 96
Talyzin, Nikolay V., 21
Tanzania, 193, 202
Tarnoff, Peter, 243, 249

Taro, Nakayama, 33
Ten Thousand Whys, 131n
Thailand, 41, 47, 89, 90, 103
Thatcher, Margaret, 256, 257–58, 259, 271
Tiananmen incident, 1989 ("turmoil in
    Beijing"), 128–31
  Deng's "package solution" to impasse
    with U.S. over, 139–43
  developing countries support of China
    during sanctions period, 155–56,
    200–201
  EC and lifting of sanctions on China,
    152–55
  G-7 imposition of sanctions on China,
    149–50
  Japan and lifting of sanctions, 149–52
  sanctions imposed on China, viii–ix,
    44–45, 47, 97, 127, 131, 134, 135, 138,
    139–43, 145–55, 201, 248, 255, 257
  secret American envoy sent to China,
    131–37
  secret letters from George H. W. Bush
    to Deng Xiaoping and reply, 131–32,
    137–39
  Sino-American relations and, 131–49,
    156–57, 248
  Sino-British relations and, 255, 259
Tian Zengpei, 22, 23, 38, 170, 175, 212,
    213, 237–38, 239
Tikhonov, 17
Togo, 203
Toure, Sekou, 193, 194, 196–99
trade issues. *See* economy and trade
Transcaucasian republics, 166
Turkmenistan, 175, 176

Uganda, 202, 210
Ukraine, 166, 169, 170, 171, 175
United Kingdom (UK). *See* Britain
United Nations, 249
  admission of DPRK and ROK (North
    and South Korea), 112, 118–19, 120
  African support for China, 200

Article 51, 62
Cambodia, peace agreement and, 33, 36, 40, 41, 48, 50–53
Forty-fifth General Assembly, 58, 62
Forty-fourth General Assembly, 62
Millennium Summit, 189
normalization of Sino-Soviet relations and, 23
Qian Qichen at, 37, 41, 48, 58, 59, 60, 77–79, 128, 155, 180, 216, 226, 239, 256, 266
Resolution 678 on authorization of military force in Iraq, 78–79, 81–82
Resolution 660 on Iraq's invasion of Kuwait, 57, 78–79
Russian Federation assumes Soviet seat, 171
Security Council air embargo on Iraq (Resolution 670), 57, 58, 61, 71
Security Council and China, 57, 58, 59, 60, 61, 67, 69–70, 74–79, 88, 89, 145–46
Security Council military action on Iraq, 59, 61–65, 69, 70, 74–79, 145–46
Security Council and Russia seated, 178, 180
Sino-Indonesian relations and, 97–98
661 Committee, 57
Taiwan issue, 200, 245, 248
Third Special Session on Disarmament, 37, 41
United States
August 17 Communiqué, 2
Cambodian issue and, 35, 46–50
"China Threat" and strategic containment policy, 244–46
Clinton administration and China, 157, 243–51
communiqués with China, 1982, 2
destruction of Chinese embassy in Yugoslavia, 157
George H. W. Bush administration and

China, 41, 48, 57, 62, 74, 76, 77, 79–82, 131–39, 145–49
George W. Bush administration and China, 157
Gulf crisis of 1990, 57, 58–59, 61–65, 69, 70, 73–79, 144–46
Korean War, 114–15
Middle East peace process and, 64
North Korea and, 112
"one China policy" and, 245–51
sanctions on China, 97, 127, 131, 134, 135, 138, 139–43, 146–49, 248
Sino-American relations, 2, 13, 46, 48, 59, 61, 61–65, 74–77, 80–82, 89, 131–49, 156–57, 233, 242
Soviet Union and, viii, 13, 139, 141, 174
Taiwan and, 2, 233, 243–51
Tianamen incident, official and unofficial reactions to, 131–43, see also sanctions on China
Vietnam War, 89
Yinhe incident, 157
Uno, Sosuke, 86–87
Uzbekistan, 175, 176, 182, 182n
Tashkent, 2, 3

van Dunem, Pedro de Castro, 201
Vietnam
Cambodia invasion, 1, 4, 5, 8, 9–12, 17–18, 19, 20, 21, 22–23, 24–28, 35–44, 49, 90
China, negotiations with, 42–44, 50–51
"cocktail party" on Cambodia, 39, 40
Paris Treaty on Peace, 89
withdrawal of troops from Cambodia, 39
Viljoen, Gerrit, 212

Wallace, Mike, 20
Wang Changyi, 77–78
Wang Daohan, 246
Wang Jinqing, 164, 175, 176, 177
Wang Youping, 7

Wilson, David Clive, 265
Wong Kan Sheng, 34
World Transformed, A (Scowcroft), 133, 143–44
"written information," 260
Wuhan Iron and Steel Works, 16
Wu Xueqian, 19–20, 90, 255
Wu Yi, 223

Xian Xinghai, 282
Xu Dunxin, 51–52, 98, 121
Xu Jingwu, 159
Xu Lide, 220

Yanayev, Gennadi, 168–69
Yang Fuchang, 56
Yang Guirong, 233–34
Yang Shangkun, 62, 77, 122, 125, 133, 152, 175, 185–86, 187, 210
Yangtze River Bridge, 16
Yang Xiufeng, 191, 193
Yani, Ahmad, 88
Yanshan Petrochemicals Company, 16
Yao Yilin, 15, 16, 17
Yazov, Dmitriy, 168
Ye Changtong, 236

Yeltsin, Boris, 170, 175, 178, 182–83
  China visits, 180, 182–88
Yemen, 68, 79
Yen Chia-ken, 229
Yinhe incident, 157
Yin Qingfeng, 235, 236
Yugoslavia, U.S. destruction of Chinese embassy, 157
Yu Hongliang, 5, 6, 7
Yu Zhan, 7
Yu Zhenwu, 246

Zambia, 201, 210
Zanzibar, 193
Zhang Dequn, 162
Zhang Ruijie, 121
Zhang Wentian, 162
Zhang Xueshu, 159
Zhang Yijun, 77
Zheng Dayong, 82
Zhou Enlai, vii–viii, 88, 180, 192, 194, 227
Zhou Jue, 232
Zhou Nan, 128, 258
Zhu Qizhen, 80, 146–47
Zimbabwe, 201